O Brother, What Might Have Been

O Brother, What Might Have Been

Three Lost Screenplays

Preston Sturges

Sticking Place Books
New York

ISBN 979-8-89976-017-4

Contents

Foreword by Tom Sturges

This book of my father's three unproduced and undirected screenplays is beyond a dream come true. It is a promise kept and one of the final steps in my lifetime journey of ensuring that Preston Sturges' story is told and that his legacy has every chance to survive and possibly even thrive.

He died when I was three. The last time I saw him I was one. So much for explaining the closeness of our father/son relationship. I was enthralled by someone I never actually met. My whole life I've been chasing a ghost. My mom would show his films on a sheet hanging from the living room ceiling and I came to love his work, film by film, laugh by laugh, line by line. This started when I was maybe six or seven years old. And as I listened to the crowded room react with their laughter or tears, bucking forward in their seats and slapping their knees, or reveling in his genius afterward, I got it. Though just a kid, I understood what was going on. Whatever it was that one needed to make a great film, he had it.

Although the scripts you are about to read are "finished," his scripts were never finished. At least not until the final edit was approved and the celluloid was in a big can being sent off to some distant theatre. This because throughout the productions he would make changes. Changes to motivations or reasons why, to lines or replies to lines, even to a character's shrugged shoulders or raised eyebrows. Change was a constant upon which anyone who worked with him could rely.

Eddie Bracken told me that my father had a standing rule on the set. If you thought of something that was funnier than what he had written, he would reach into his pocket and pull out the cash and pay you right there. $5 for a laugh, $1 for a chuckle. Can you imagine telling Preston Sturges you had an improvement to his script? I imagine that took a lot of courage, or what the Irish like to call chutzpah.

The example Eddie gave me you can see yourself. It's in *The Miracle of Morgan's Creek*. Bill Demarest, as Sgt. Kockenlocker, and Eddie Bracken as Norval Jones, have just had a discussion about how to win over a girl who doesn't want to be won over. During their chat, the sergeant's gun accidentally goes off, and Norval looks as though he may have just suffered an embarrassing personal accident. Eddie told the set master to remove several of the tacks that were holding the screen to the screen door. So right after the gun goes off, he literally walks through the screen door without even opening it. My father was sitting on the dolly with the camera on a jib, unaware of what had been planned, and laughed so hard you can see the camera shake, still today. Eddie was very proud of himself, fifty years later when he told me the story. He had the five dollar bill signed, in a frame, up on a wall.

All that to say that these scripts would have undergone another draft or two or three in the writing process, and another polish or two or three in the filming of the script that survived. So, you will just have to imagine there was more to be done. And since he never got to do that or direct them or see what might have resulted had he just had the chance, this book represents his work in progress, his art in process, sketches he drew before the final renderings of the portraits he envisioned.

For all those who count such things, this is the 28th book having to do with my father, his life's work, his writings. I think he might have been pleased.

My thanks first to Nat Segaloff for the introduction to the founder, owner and editor of the film book publishing house Sticking Place Books, Paul Cronin. My thanks then to Paul for believing in the idea of this work and for having the vision and faith to see it through to its publication. Lastly, of course, thanks to film aficionado Jay Rozgonyi for his insightful and thorough introductions, which bring a historical and passionate appreciation to these nearly forgotten works.

I hope you all enjoy what might have been.

Tom Sturges
Los Angeles, California
June 2025

Prelude to Genius: An Introduction to the Screenplay for *Song of Joy*

Jay Rozgonyi

It's always seemed ironic that Preston Sturges, one of the best comedy stylists in Hollywood history, spent years in the industry before ever penning an original comic script. Prior to heading out west from New York he'd had great success with comedy on Broadway, most notably with 1929's *Strictly Dishonorable*, but like most East Coast playwrights imported by the studios in the waning years of silents, he was immediately put to work writing dialogue—that is, punching up and improving the spoken words that the industry's established writers had no experience crafting. For more than five years Sturges toiled in this way, as one writer among many on nearly every genre of film. He produced one original script, 1933's *The Power and the Glory*, a dramatic meditation on business and power, but otherwise performed his assigned writing tasks with an increasing sense of frustration.

By 1935, although Sturges' name was commonly seen in the credits of dramas, his true talent as a contributor to comic screenplays was starting to become known. The first film that has any of the feel of a Preston Sturges comedy is his 1935 adaptation of the Ferenc Molnar play *The Good Fairy*, directed by his good friend William Wyler. Although the script largely sticks to the play's plot, Sturges slipped in a number of elements that were to become familiar in his original screenplays: the odd character names such as Luisa Ginglebusher (the lead character, simply named "Lu" in Molnar's play) and Maurice Schlapkohl; the clever use of physical comedy both in a new opening sequence at an orphanage and in our glimpse of Luisa at work as a movie usherette; and the transformation of a key role—the head waiter—from a suitor in the play into an eccentric supporting character. Though offering hints of what was to come, *The Good Fairy* lacks the distinctiveness of a full-fledged Preston Sturges screenplay.

Just two years later, however, following a handful of dramas and a by-the-book assignment for George Burns and Gracie Allen, *Easy Living* burst onto movie screens as a fully formed version of the unique world of

Preston Sturges. Everything—from the abundance of quirky characters spouting comic gems, to the madcap opening, to the pointed satire of the wealthy and powerful—is in place, as if Sturges had suddenly found the pot of golden ideas that would sustain him for the rest of his career. It was a huge leap from *The Good Fairy*, as enjoyable as that film is, to *Easy Living*, and looking at the films that came in between provides little clue as to how he got there.

That clue has finally become available to us now, though, with the publication of the unproduced script Sturges wrote in between the two: *Song of Joy*. Written in 1936 and 1937 as a vehicle for European opera star Marta Eggerth, the screenplay was an original commission from *Good Fairy* producer Henry Henigson, who gave Sturges little more to go on than the title and the idea that opera singing would be involved. Sturges had written original screenplays before, but this would the first time he could write a comedy with virtually no restrictions on its content. Given such freedom, especially after having had a successful experience writing *The Good Fairy*, must have seemed like an immense opportunity for the increasingly self-assured writer. And Sturges took great advantage of it, for *Song of Joy*—as Diane Jacob's enthusiastically noted in her biography *Christmas in July: The Life and Art of Preston Sturges* (1992)—is the first of his screenplays to display all the originality and exuberance he would later become famous for.

Sturges ended up concocting the story of a famous European opera singer named Lilli who has been signed by a big Hollywood studio to make a movie. But when she arrives in California, the studio boss has no idea why she's there and is forced to come up with a script and a shooting schedule with ridiculous speed, since the singer's contract is costing him $19,000 per week. He, his director, and his scriptwriter stumble along while the opera singer falls for a lowly music department assistant from whom she keeps her true identity. It's a madcap Sturgean tale that also includes the mistaken-/hidden-identity theme that will surface again in *Easy Living*, *Remember the Night*, *Christmas in July*, *The Palm Beach Story*, *Hail the Conquering Hero*, and other Sturges screenplays.

In *Song of Joy*, Sturges creates the type (and number) of characters that he would become so adept at dropping into his later films. Off-beat and distinctive, they often appear in only one or two scenes on the margins of the main action, but they invariably supply laughs and—in many cases—a sophisticated commentary on the characters or the action. These signature roles are truly integrated into the action in *Song of Joy*, popping up throughout the story. As you read the pages ahead, look for the following examples.

- Vladimir Von Stark, the European film director whose fractured English continually infuriates Mr. Apex, and who provides a template for any number of future Sturges characters who comically mangle the language.
- Lawrence Langsome, the dance director, and Ernie, his pianist partner, who make a charmingly off-kilter duo, playing off one another beautifully. (The stout Lawrence's dance demonstration is a physical comedy highlight, even in its written form. One can only imagine where Sturges would have taken it with the proper casting and direction.)
- J. P. Smiley, the deadpan mortician, who can't comprehend why someone thinks there's anyone *living* in his funeral parlor.
- The chauffeur, a cleverly conceived and fully wordless creation who offers the opportunity for great visual humor—and who tantalizes our imaginations with ideas of who Sturges might have cast in the role.

We also get some typical Sturges-style names along the way, too: Lilli's maid, Sophie Schnortz; two of the characters in the screenplay written for Lilli, Trudel Edelweiss and Julius Overholtzer; Lilli's manager, Mr. Magnolius; and of course, Vladimir Von Stark.

If the script's notable features were only great supporting characters and bits of well-placed physical comedy, however, *Song of Joy* wouldn't represent that much of an advance over *The Good Fairy*. But this time around Sturges displays more creativity in his scenes and, more important, an understanding of film construction that makes clear just how much he had learned about moviemaking—and how well-positioned he already was in 1936 to become a director.

An early example of this can be seen when studio head Mr. Apex, screenwriter Jasper Balcom, and director Vladimir Von Stark first try to devise a story for their film (pp. 27-33). Their endless round of brainstorming is full of quick dialogue and comic wordplay ("irritation is the mother of invention"), and—a Sturges favorite—there's a European character whose heavily accented pronunciations only add to the chaos (isn't it obvious that "a goil sinkink" means "a girl singing"?). In future films Sturges will frequently return to this type of scene, from Mr. Wagglebury's frustrated interactions with the slogan jury in *Christmas in July* to Mayor Noble's attempt at speechwriting in *Hail the Conquering Hero* among others. Sturges presents the same situation each time—an agitated (and usually dull-witted) authority figure tries to solve a problem and get his way, only to be thwarted by a collection of underlings who won't (or can't) see things as he does. These scenes, which originate in *Song of Joy*, are full of the witty comic dialogue that highlight so many of Sturges' scripts, and they take the best advantage of the distinctive character actors he so wonderfully cast. Sturges even incorporates his sly humor into the script's character notes, as when we first encounter "Jasper Balcom, the harassed writer," who is described with the parenthetical sentence, "His face, with one single expression, reflects all the grievances of the Writers' Guild."

In another memorable sequence, Sturges creates an ingenious running gag that plays out in the background as Lilli and the studio songwriter she's falling for (referred to in the script only as The Boy) spend an evening on the town (pp. 52-59). Because the Boy doesn't realize who Lilli really is, her chauffeur/studio-provided protector is forced to slink along after the pair to keep an eye on the star while not revealing his presence. In a series of scenes Lilli and the Boy wander the city on a "date," browsing shop windows, while the chauffeur follows behind surreptitiously, trying to kill time with a variety of solitary activities. In the coming years Sturges would perfect similar small comic sequences, enlivening the actions of the protagonists with touches of clever humor from the minor characters.

The script is overflowing with examples of the comic wordplay that Sturges later became known for. He loved to use characters who spoke with accents, which could lend themselves to mispronunciations, misunderstandings, and verbal miscues. In *Song of Joy*, much of this humor comes from the character of Vladimir, whose pronunciations Sturges spells out in the script (like "goil sinkink" above). In the previously mentioned sequence, when Apex and his staff are developing the story, Vladimir tells his collaborators, "I've got a great title! The Song… of Yoy!" then responds to their confusion by adding, "Not Yoy, Yoy!" Later, when Lilli meets the Boy, he tells her that he's a music copyist and aspiring songwriter, to which she responds that someday he'll be a great "compositor" (pp. 49). In addition, Sturges uses Madame Schnortz, Mrs. Edelweiss in the film scenes, and Lilli herself to score laughs from their tangled English.

Perhaps the script element that most significantly foreshadows the artist Sturges was to become, however, is the satire that animates so much of the film. Many small touches are found throughout, such as in the window-browsing sequence with Lilli and the Boy. Sturges' script pointedly calls out what the couple are looking at in each of the shop windows, and taken together, the items on display represent a satiric view of mid-1930s America. We see a home furnishings display ("Everything for the bride: $129.66. You furnish the girl, we furnish the rest"); a make-your-own-records store ("Four-inch record – 25¢; Eight-inch record – 50¢; Ten-inch record – 75¢. Hear yourself as others hear you"); and a store with tool chests, lathes, rifles, cameras, shoes, tennis rackets, a cat, and much, much more in the window ("A drug store," the Boy explains) (pp. 52-59).

Sturges focuses his most sustained and sophisticated satire on the movie business itself, and in so doing anticipates his brilliant Hollywood comedy to come, *Sullivan's Travels*. At the time he wrote *Song of Joy*, he'd already taken a poke at the movie industry in *The Good Fairy*. There the lead character of Luisa Ginglebusher, an orphan who's plucked from her institution and given the chance to work as a theater usher, is transfixed by a portion of a film on her first night of work. The sequence is a comic send-up of romances and their often-overwrought dialogue, as a middle-aged woman pleads with her lover that they remain together—and he simply replies, again and again, "Go!" As a Broadway scribe imported to Hollywood with the birth of the talkies, Sturges must have cherished this opportunity to ridicule bad dialogue (and bad acting), with the only possible retort to it being a single repeated word.

He brings this same spirit to *Song of Joy*, in which he mocks any number of Hollywood conventions, beginning with the studios' pretentiousness. As we watch the first completed sequence of the Lilli Pogany movie, we're presented with the Apex Studios logo (pp. 34-35). As it's described in the script:

> To the sound of martial music, the base of the mountain descends like an elevator and brings into view its snow-capped peak. On this sits a lion holding on one raised paw the world. We hear the sound of a motor and around the world comes an airplane. As its noise grows loud the lion roars, radio signals, radio waves flash from the peak of the mountain and on top of the world appear the glowing letters: 'APEX.'

Sturges manages, in this brief sequence, to make references to the logos of Paramount (the snow-capped mountain), MGM (the lion), Universal (the airplane coming around the world), and RKO (the radio waves). Finally, the martial music that's called for undoubtedly refers to the still-recognizable 20th-Century Fox theme music. On its own each logo might scarcely be noticed by moviegoers, but Sturges' combination of all of them calls attention to the pomposity of studios that invoke such magisterial images and emblems.

In a later scene, during Lilli and the Boy's window-shopping excursion, they stop by a movie theater where Sturges takes the opportunity to skewer the studios' predictable recycling of film titles (pp. 69-70). The theater is festooned with advertising banners, which he carefully describes in the script:

> "Three features. One Night of Love. One Heavenly Night. It Happened One Night. Admission 10 cents. Children free." Second, smaller sign: "Next week: The Night Was Made for Love. Night After Night. What a Night! Also Newsreel. Timely Events. Suitable Shorts and Color Cartoon. Ladies Free on Saturday Night. Watch the Newspapers for 104-Piece Free Crockery Competition."

Movie titles would always serve as a favorite target of Sturges' mockery. In *Sullivan's Travels*, for example, Sully's successful movie titles are called out by the studio heads as they try to convince him not to make a serious film. There's *So Long, Sarong*; *Hey, Hey in the Hayloft*; *Ants in Your Plants of 1939*; and *Thanks for Yesterday*. Sturges the iconoclast, who would spend many future years fighting with studio brass, then has an executive offer up the most odious suggestion for Sully's consideration: to forego *O Brother, Where Art Thou?* and instead make *Ants in Your Plants of 1941*.

The connection with *Sullivan's Travels* is much deeper than movie titles, however, reaching to the business of movie making itself. By 1936, Sturges, who had been working in Hollywood for about seven years, had formed a distinct impression of how the film studios operated. Their conveyor-belt approach to movie production would of course rankle anyone who saw him- or herself as a creative artist, but Sturges was also especially frustrated by the foolishness of the people who made the filmmaking decisions and the way in which they did so. And in response to that frustration Sturges turned his razor-sharp wit on the structure that he found himself a mere cog within.

In some of the most biting scenes in *Sullivan's Travels*, the studio chiefs work as a team first to dissuade their headstrong director from making a social drama, then to take over his plan to experience life on the road by making the whole endeavor into an over-the-top promotional stunt. All they can conceive of is to confine Sully's serious creative project into their narrow definition of a successful (i.e., remunerative) movie, and they stumble over themselves and each other to push the plan to increasingly outrageous extremes.

Song of Joy contains a similar set of scenes that represent a first shot across the bow for Sturges in his caricaturing of Hollywood. The jumping-off point for the entire story—the fact that Mr. Apex has signed Lilli to a one-picture deal but has no memory of it until she shows up to start filming—hardly portrays the studio owner as exceptionally intelligent.

Shortly thereafter, we're introduced to the self-important European director and the acerbic screenwriter whom Apex corrals into developing a movie for Lilli (pp. 27-33). As the lengthy brainstorming session plays out, we get a mass of crosstalk and small jibes as well as rudimentary ideas that somehow wind up being tossed together to create an opening scene. As a first-rate example of how a movie should not be devised, the scene contrasts strongly to Sturges' own preferred method of crafting original scripts: from a singular vision delivered with cohesiveness, nuance, and wit.

Recognizing that he has a good target in his sights, Sturges returns to his trio of bumbling movie creators numerous times as they argue their way through the development of further scenes. They're seen in the studio projection room after viewing some scenes (all of which are, of course, full of Hollywood cliches), in a Rolls Royce driving along the streets of Hollywood, and in Apex's office, continuously arguing over their haphazard construction of the movie plot. Since Lilli, an opera star, will certainly sing in the film, Apex thinks it logical that there should also be dancing. The "song" he asks to be choreographed is The Blue Danube — and neither the director, the writer, the music director, or his accompanist find this idea absurd. As they later admit, they've just been shooting "anything at all" because they've had no idea as to what to do. Any movie produced in such a way would have to be horrible — or perhaps, Sturges is saying, it would simply be a typical Hollywood feature.

Song of Joy is a delight to read in light of the work Preston Sturges had ahead of him. The originality of its characters, the sharp, fast-paced dialogue, the moments of physical comedy, and the deft satire are all harbingers of the films yet to come. The script even contains a surprise story twist that brings all the characters happily together in an inventive and satisfying finale. Although the script doesn't display the intricacy of structure that was to become a hallmark of Sturges' Paramount films, or the brilliant interweaving of story and characters and humor, the elements are all in place.

Additionally, the screenplay traces the beginnings of Sturges' evolution from being a contract writer who could pen dramas or comedies to one who could blend aspects of both in a single movie. Most noteworthy is a brief sequence, after Lilli and the Boy have a fight and part ways, in which the script calls for crosscuts between the Boy playing his song on the piano and Lilli singing it in her bedroom, culminating in a double-printing that shows them both on the screen at the same time (pp. 92-93). This touching moment reminds us of the way Sturges inserted serious-ness — and a touch of sadness — into comedies like *The Great McGinty* (when McGinty has to say goodbye to his stepkids), *Remember the Night* (when Lee receives a Christmas gift), and *The Miracle of Morgan's Creek* (when the pregnant Trudy and her family have been banished to a rural farmhouse on Christmas Eve). And it also shows how he was already conceiving of the ways his scripts should be directed, specifying the details of cross cutting that make the sequence especially effective.

For all of these reasons — but especially for the sheer inventiveness that Preston Sturges brings to this script — discovering *Song of Joy* is a bit like finding a diamond in the rough. This is not the work of a man who had already been on top and was trying and get back there again; it's the work of an artist still finding himself, testing out new ideas and seeing many of them succeeding. Sturges' filmography as a writer in the 1930s has always felt a bit inexplicable to me. I had often wondered how he went from the very-good-but-not-extraordinary comic screenplay of *The Good Fairy* in 1935 to the brilliant *Easy Living*, his next original comedy in 1937. But now I know: *Song of Joy* is the joyful missing link.

SONG OF JOY

***
An original screenplay

by Preston Sturges

While the Main Titles
are showing, the overture
music changes to the final
of "Faust". We hear the
orchestra and the opera singers.

FADE IN: OPERA HOUSE — PARIS

A-1--A-21
          THE FINALE OF FAUST

          It has the standard set-
          ting and it is beautifully
          sung. Our interest is
          centered on Lilli Pogany
          who sings Marguerite. As
          Marguerite starts for heaven.

          CUT TO:

A-22   A DRESSING ROOM IN THE
          PARIS OPERA HOUSE

          It is stuffed with trunks
          and flowers and costumes
          and suitcases. Porters in
          blouses hurry in and out
          and a large, middle-aged
          maid directs operations
          forcefully and in French.
          A middle-aged gentleman
          secretary hurries in with
          a handful of tickets. He
          is horrified to find the
          luggage still here. He
          points to it with an operatic
          gesture.

                         MR. MAGNOLIUS (in Italian)
                              How come?

                         SOPHIE   (indignantly and in
                                      Italian)
                              What do you mean 'how come'?
                              Who do you think you are
                              to ask me how come?

                         MR. MAGNOLIUS (in Russian)
                              Now, Sophie...

                         SOPHIE   (in Russian)
                              Sophie yourself! They're
                              here because they haven't
                              been taken out yet. If
                              they'd been taken out they
                              wouldn't be here. And be-
                              sides, it's none of your
          (CONTINUED)   business and besides, you
                              always sang flat anyway.

9

                                        MR. MAGNOLIUS   (furiously in
                                                          French)
                                            Me?

He points his finger
at her.

                                            You mean you!

                                        SOPHIE   (horrified in Hungar-
                                                     ian)
                                            I sang flat? Let me tell
                                            you in a few words what I
                                            think of you.

She draws a long breath.
The manager of the Opera
House hurries in in a
beard, waving his arms.

                                        MOUSIEUR DUBONNET   (in French)
                                            What's going on a round
                                            here? It has not penetrat-
                                            ed to you perhaps that we
                                            are singing an opera here
                                            just outside and the cus-
                                            tomers would rather hear
                                            that than you. Silence!

        CUT TO:

A-23   CLOSE SHOT..MARGUERITE
        PRACTICALLY IN HEAVEN

        There is a great deal of
        singing going on around
        her.

        CUT TO:

A-24   PART OF THE ORCHESTRA
        PATRONS OVER THE CON-
        DUCTOR

        They are applauding en-
        thusiastically.

        CUT TO:

A-25   FULL SHOT OF THE STAGE
        WITH THE CURTAIN FALLING

        CUT TO:

A-26   A HIGH PARALLEL BACKSTAGE

        Ag ainst this leans a ladder
        with a strong hand-rail.
        Lilli appears, flanked by
        a couple of angels. As she   SOUND: Finale music
        prepares to climb down the   and applause.
        ladder, she frowns and looks
        down at something.

        CUT TO:

A-27   HIGH CAMERA SHOT DOWN
ON THE STAGE

In the crowd of singers,
supers and hurrying stage-
hands we see Mr. Magnolius,
Sophie and Mr. Dubonnet.
They teeter with excitement,
motion her to hurry down,
and point to their watches.

CUT TO:

A-28   CLOSE SHOT..LILLI

She is undecided for a
moment, then she lifts her
dress to her knees, puts
her leg over the hand-rail
and slides down it. THE CAMERA
FOLLOWS her down.

CUT TO:

A-29   MR. MAGNOLIUS, MR. DUBONNET
AND SOPHIE

Sophie holds her head and
squeals. Mr. Dubonnet and
Mr. Magnolius catch Lilli
as she slides into their
midst.

                SOPHIE   (in Hungarian)
                    What are you trying to do,
                    break your neck?

                MR. MAGNOLIUS (in Russian)
                    Leave her alone. If she
                    broke anything it wouldn't
                    be her neck.

                M. DUBONNET
                    Madame! Mademoiselle! Mon
                    Dieu'.

Lilli laughs.

                SOPHIE   (in Hungarian)
                    The train! The boat! The
                    contract!

                MR. MAGNOLIUS (in French)
                    Jump into a coach! Jump
                    into a anything! But
                    hurry!

                M. DUBONNET
                    Vous allez rater le train,
                    nom de Dieu!

He pulls out his watch.
They run to the dressing
room.

CUT TO:

11

A-30   A WHITE MERCEDES-BENZ
AT THE STAGE DOOR OF THE
PARIS OPERA HOUSE.

      A crowd, some poor, some rich,
      is gathered to see the singers
      come out. A sergent-de-ville
      keeps a passageway clear. A
      group of porters hurries out
      with baggage which they throw
      into the front seat of the
      Mercedes. M. Dubonnet follows
      with flowers. Lilli appears
      next with more flowers and a
      fur coat thrown over her cos-
      tume. Sophie and Mr. Magnolius
      bring up the rear with flowers,
      suitcases and jewel-cases. They
      dive into the Mercedes which
      pulls away as the crowd cheers.

      DISSOLVE TO:

A-31   CLOSE SHOT..A FRENCH STATION
MASTER

      He blows on a small ox-horn
      complacently. Suddenly he
      frowns, raises his hand to
      countermand the order and blows
      six staccato blasts.

      CUT TO:

A-32   MOVING SHOT AHEAD OF A RUNNING
GROUP

      The group comprises porters,
      Lilli's chauffeur, M. Dubonnet,
      two American reporters, Mr. Mag-
      nolius, Lilli and Sophie. M. Du-
      bonnet yells at the top of his
      lungs:

                      M. DUBONNET (at the top of his
                                    lungs)
                      Attendez! Mais attendez-
                      donc, nom de Dieu!

      The first American reporter
      pulls out a note-book as he
      runs:

                      FIRST AMERICAN REPORTER (to Lilli)
                      I'm from The Herald, Miss
                      Pogany. What are you going
                      to America for?

                      LILLI   (breathlessly)
                      To make a picture talking.

                      SECOND REPORTER
                      What company, Miss Pogany?

                      LILLI
                      I forget... If I don't catch
                      this I don't make no picture
                      talking.

    (CONTINUED)

12

A-32   (CONTINUED)

                                    M. DUBONNET
                                        Mais depechez-vous, nom de
                                        Dieu!

                                    SOPHIE   (furiously)(in french)
                                        What do you think we're do-
                                        ing, nom de Dieu?

                                    M. DUBONNET
                                        Est-ce que je vous a i de-
                                        mandez quelque chose, a
                                        vous?

                                    SOPHIE   (in Russian)
                                        I hope you fall down and
                                        break your nose.

            CUT TO:

A-33   CLOSE SHOT..A FRENCH
        COMPARTMENT CAR
        ─────────────────────────
            The group rushes into the
            picture and throws the
            luggage inside . As Lilli
            climbs up the steps.

            CUT TO:

A-34   THE FRENCH STATION MASTER
        ─────────────────────────
            He blows happily on his ox-
            horn.

            CUT TO:

A-35   CLOSE SHOT..FRENCH LOCOMOTIVE
        ─────────────────────────
            It begins to move and we see
            a cloud of escaping steam.

            CUT TO:

A-36   LILLI'S COMPARTMENT
        ─────────────────────────
            M. Dubonnet, the porters
            and the reporters are push-
            ing Sophie into the compartment.
            They walk along the platform
            as the car moves.
                                    M. DUBONNET
                                        Aurevoir! Aurevoir!

                                    THE TWO REPORTERS
                                        Good luck!

                                    THE PORTERS
                                        Bon Voyage!

            Lilli, Mr. Magnolius and
            Sophie stick their heads
            through the window.

                                    LILLI
                                        Aurevoir, merci, Goodbye,
                                        goodbye

        (CONTINUED)

A-36   (CONTINUED)

LILLI   (she laughs and sings
               Tosti's Goodbye)
           Goodbye forever....

MR. MAGNOLIUS (chiming in in a
                  bass voice)
           Goodbye forever.....

SOPHIE   (chiming in, alto)
           Goodbye....

ALL THREE
           Goodbye, goodbye, good by-
           hi-hi.

FADE   OUT

END   OF SEQUENCE   "A"

SEQUENCE "B"

FADE IN:

SHOT FROM THE AIR
ON THE ROOF OF A SOUND
STAGE

On this we read: "APEX
FILM COMPANY. SOUND STAGE".

CUT TO:

B-2   INTERIOR..AIRPLANE

Here we see Lilli, Sophie,
Mr. Magnolius and the
chauffeur. All except the
chauffeur are very nervous.
We hear the roar of the
plane. Suddenly Mr. Magnolius
lets go the side of the plane
long enough to point down to
something.   SOUND: Roar of airplane.

CUT TO:

B-3   THE ROOF OF THE APEX FILM
       COMPANY SOUND STAGE

Over this drifts the shadow
of the airplane.

CUT TO:

B-4   FULL SHOT OF COMPANY SHOOTING
       IN THE OPEN

In the foreground we see the
sound man. The airplane noise   SOUND: Roar of plane.
becomes very loud. The sound
man removes his ear-phones and
speaks:
                    SOUND MAN
                         (disgustedly)
                    Airplane.

He looks up at the sky and
mutters uncomplimentary things.

DISSOLVE TO:

AN ORNATE MAHOGANY DOOR
LETTERED: "APEX FILM COMPANY,
ADOLPH APEX, PRESIDENT"

DISSOLVE TO:

B-6   FULL SHOT..MR. APEX'S OFFICE

In the foreground we see a
conference table with ten or
twelve gentlemen waiting. In

                                        (CONTINUED)

15

B-6   (CONTINUED)

the background sits Mr.
Apex at his desk. He is in
a fever of activity. Secretaries run in and out with
things to read and papers to
be signed. Behind him an
agent sits on a radiator.

CUT TO:

B-7   MR. APEX, THE AGENT AND
DISAPPEARING SECRETARIES

MR. APEX (into first telephone)
All right. At that price
tell him no.

He puts up the telephone.

(into second phone)
No, tell him yes...No, no,
no: yes is my answer.

(three phone bells ring)

(into first telephone)
What?...And what did I say?
... Well, if I said that,
that's it. I'm a man of my
word and that's better than
any contract.
(into third telephone)
Oh he won't, won't he? Well,
you tell him to sign it and
sign it quick. How can you
do business that way

A secretary puts a batch
of papers in front of him.
He signs them rapidly and
automatically as he speaks
into the fourth telophone
very gently.

(into fourth tele-
phone, very gently)
Yes, Louie...Well, if they
did, it was entirely without my knowledge. Well
naturally, Louie. Why
certainly, Louie. Any time,
Louie. Positively on Tuesday, then, but I'll only
have time for nine holes.
Goodbye, Louie.

He pushes a button and speaks
into a dictaphone.

(into dictaphone)
Who's been trying to get
L. away from M.C.N.?...
Any luck?...Good.

He hangs up. The secretary
takes the papers away and
another secretary puts a
cable in front of him. Mr.
Apex reads it, then holds
his head in thought.

(CONTINUED)

16

B-7   (CONTINUED)

                                 MR. APEX
                                 If I did, I don't remember
         it.
                  (he yells across
                  the room)
        Can anybody use an animal
        act?

      CUT TO:

B-8   A SUPERVISOR

                             THE SUPERVISOR
                           I could use some snakes.

      CUT TO:

B-9   MR. APEX

He hands the cable book
to the secretary.

                          MR. APEX
                        Give this to Mr. Jonas.

He swings on the agent.

                          (severely)
                  Now there's no use fooling
                  around, Sam, I'm a busy man.
                  I'll buy your leading man
                  but I won't pay any twelve-
                  fifty.

                     THE AGENT (mildly)
                  I didn't ask for twelve-
                  fifty. I said three hundred.

                    MR. APEX (happily)
                  Now you're talking.

                    THE AGENT (mildly)
                  And it wasn't a leading man,
                  it was a character woman.

                    MR. APEX (slapping his desk)
                  Three hundred dollars for a
                  character woman!

                    THE AGENT
                  She plays mothers.

                    MR. APEX (gently)
                  Oh, mothers. Well, why
                  didn't you say so? Bring
                  her in in the morning.

He picks up the telephone.

                        (into telephone)
                  No, no and no. I'm in con-
                  ference. I'm not to be
                  disturbed.

He rises briskly.

                    Now, gentlemen.

THE CAMERA PANS WITH HIM
a little way.

CUT TO:

B-14   CLOSE SHOT...MR. APEX

He frowns in perplexity.

CUT TO:

B-15   THE DOORWAY

Mr. Magnolius comes through, smiling and bowing from right to left.

CUT TO:

B-16   MR. APEX

His forehead becomes more corrugated than ever.

CUT TO:

B-17   LILLI COMING THROUGH THE DOORWAY

She smiles charmingly and looks very pretty.

CUT TO:

B-18   MR. APEX

He is smiling also. Suddenly, however, he frowns as he realizes it isn't the person he expected. He leans to the gentleman next to him.

                    MR. APEX
                      Who's this?

                    GENTLEMAN NEXT TO HIM
                      Search me.

CUT TO:

B-19   PUBLICITY MAN, LILLI AND MR. APEX.

                    PUBLICITY MAN
                      ...and this is our president, Mr. Apex himself.

Lilli smiles graciously and takes his hand.

                    LILLI
                      How do you do.

Mr. Apex bows from the waist.

                    MR. APEX
                      How do you do, how do you do.
                        (to the publicity man)
                      I didn't quite catch the little lady's name.

                    PUBLICITY MAN (in astonishment)
                      This is Miss Lilli Pogany, the famous opera star.

                              (CONTINUED)

18

B-19   (CONTINUED)

>   MR. APEX (confused)
>   Oh, Miss Pogany! Well, for
>   heaven's sake. Welcome to
>   California and uh...thank
>   you for the honor of visit-
>   ing our studio. Ha ha ha.
>   (to the publicity man)
>   Get a picture, get a picture.
>
>   PUBLICITY MAN
>   (to somebody outside)
>   Pst, psst!

The still man comes in.

>   MR. APEX
>   Well, well, well, well!
>   And how do you like
>   California?
>
>   LILLI
>   Beautiful. This is
>   Mr. Magnolius.

Mr. Magnolius bows and
shakes hands.

>   MR. MAGNOLIUS
>   (bowing)
>   Magnolius.
>
>   MR. APEX
>   Apex.
>
>   LILLI   (indicating Sophie)
>   And this is Madame Schnortz,
>   my duenna.
>
>   SOPHIE   (shaking hands)
>   Schnortz.
>
>   MR. APEX
>   Apex.
>
>   THE STILL CAMERA MAN
>   Look this way, please.

The bulbs flash as the
picture is taken.

>   MR. APEX (after the picture)
>   How long are you going to
>   be in Hollywood, Miss Pogany?
>
>   LILLI
>   Only four weeks. Then I
>   sing at La Scala in Milan.
>
>   MR. APEX
>   Well, well, well, that
>   certainly is too bad. We
>   might have been able to make
>   a little picture together,
>   ha, ha, ha.
>
>   LILLI   (sadly)
>   Then we don't make the
>   picture?
>   (CONTINUED)

19

B-19   (CONTINUED)-2

                                  MR. APEX (with a trace of
                                              anxiety)
                                     What picture is that?

                                  LILLI
                                     The picture I come here
                                     to make.

                                  MR. APEX (woofling a little)
                                     The...the...p-picture you
                                     came here to m--make?

                                  THE STILL MAN
                                     Hold it please, and with a
                                     smile.

Mr. Apex turns a toothy
countenance. The lights
flash.

                                  MR. APEX (immediately after
                                              the flash)
                                     Just w-why did you c-come
                                     here to make a p-picture?

                                  LILLI
                                     Because I have a contract.

                                  MR. APEX (with false joviality)
                                     Oh...well, then we're all
                                     prepared for you. For a
                                     moment there you had me a
                                     little nervous...I thought
                                     there'd been a slip-up. One
                                     of these other gentlemen
                                     must have put the deal
                                     through. But for a moment
                                     there...

He mops his head, then
turns to the producers.

                                     Who made the deal with
                                     Miss Pogany?...
                                          (he adds a little
                                           more sharply)
                                     And who forgot to tell me
                                     about it?

He smiles wolfishly.

CUT TO:

B-20   POINT OF VIEW SHOT
       FROM MR. APEX'S POSITION

       THE CAMERA PANS from one
       producer to another so
       that we see them as Mr.
       Apex would see them.

                                  MR. APEX'S VOICE
                                     Come on now...who was it?...
                                     This is no time for kidding.

The producers all look
blank. AS THE CAMERA
completes its circle, it
ends on Mr. Apex, Lilli,
Sophie and Mr. Magnolius.

                                              (CONTINUED)

B-20 (CONTINUED)

MR. APEX (mopping his forehead)
Well, there seems to be
some little uh...

He forces a smile.

...some kind of a little uh
...discrepancy at that, ha
ha ha...just a slip-up.

LILLI
Oh, up-slip.

MR. APEX
That's a good...name for
it, ha ha ha.

He smiles confidentially.

And how much was our little
contract for?

LILLI   (innocently)
Oh, just my usual salaree...
nineteen thousand dollars
a week.

MR. APEX (swallowing hard)
Just the...usual.

LILLI
For four weeks.

MR. APEX
For four weeks. Yes, yes,
ha ha ha.

He glares around at his
producers, then smiles
like a tiger.

Just a little up-slip.

He turns to Lilli.

Well, Miss Pogany, we're
very happy to see you here
and uh...we'll uh...find
you a dressing room in the
style to which you are uh...
no doubt accustomed, and
uh...I'll just take the
matter up with my uh...
business associates here.

He turns around and gives
them a fulminating look.

LILLI   (sweetly)
Do we start the picture
right away or only tomorrow?

MR. APEX (weakly)
I think only tomorrow would
be about the soonest. Yes,
I think we'll need at least
that much time, Miss
Pogany, although, ha ha ha,
with the brilliant assistance I have around here...

He gives them a look.

...almost anything is
possible.

(CONTINUED)

B-20   (CONTINUED)-2

He yells at somebody.

                              MR. APEX
                              I want some tests of Miss
                              Pogany right away; voice
                              tests, makeup tests, light
                              tests, wig tests and
                              costume tests.

                              THE MAN ADDRESSED
                              What kind of costumes?

                              MR. APEX
                              How do I know...am I a mind-
                              reader? Just...see what
                              she looks good in.
                                    (then to Lilli)
                              Goodbye, Miss Pogany, good-
                              bye. Mr. Johnson will take
                              care of you. Goodbye,
                              Mister uh...

He waves at Mr. Magnolius.
                              And you, Mrs. uh...

                              SOPHIE
                              Schnortz.

                              MR. APEX
                              Apex.

                              LILLI   (leaving)
                              We make a good picture, hunh?

                              MR. APEX
                              With a start like this, how
                              can we fail? Goodbye, good-
                              bye.

He closes the door gently
after her, then turns on
his producers like an
infuriated lion.

                                    (furiously)
                              Now! Somebody gets it
                              somewhere.

He strides across the room
to his desk, unhooks two
telephones, then pushes the
buzzer on the dictaphone.

                                    (into dictaphone)
                              If we have a contract with
                              Lilli Pogany...

He holds up crossed fingers.
                              ...bring it to me and bring
                              it quick.

He rubs his hands together,
then clenches his fists,
places them on the desk and
leans forward.

                              Enough is a sufficiency...
                              and a sufficiency is too
                              much.

He raises an index finger
to the ceiling.

                                          (CONTINUED)

22

B-20   (CONTINUED)-3   MR. APEX (cont.)
                                        This is the end and that's
                                        only the beginning: For
                                        ten years you've been kick-
                                        ing my money around and did
                                        I say anything? Nothing!
                                        You threw it away by the
                                        handful. Did I complain?
                                        Never. You wasted it by the
                                        shovelful and what did you
                                        hear from me? Silence...I
                                        am calloused. But, gentle-
                                        men, when you drive in with
                                        a horse and haul it away by
                                        the wagonload like this
                                        Pogany business, then,
                                        gentlemen, the time has come
                                        to say whoa and I say halt!
                                             (he mumbles)
                                        Who do you think we are...
                                        the government?

He looks around at his
producers.

                                        Who did this?
There is no answer from
the producers.

He glares at them.   You can't take it, hunh?

                                        Nineteen thousand a week
                                        and no story!

       CUT TO:

B-21   THE DOORWAY

       A gentleman in an eye-shade
       and sleeve-protectors hurries
       in with a contract in his hand.

       CUT TO:

B-22   MR. APEX

       He holds his hand out for
       the contract.
                                   MR. APEX
                                        Aha! Now! Somebody had
                                        better reach for his hat.
       He grabs the contract and
       starts going through the
       pages.   Whoever signed this...

       His mouth drops open and his
       eyes protrude slightly. He
       looks around the room with a
       sickly grin, then scowls at
       the contract again.
                                        What a business!
       CUT TO:

B-23   THE LAST PAGE OF THE
       CONTRACT

       Among other signatures we
       see boldly written:
       "Adolph Apex, President."

                                             FADE OUT.

23

FADE IN:

B-24   MED. CLOSE...LILLI AS
BRUNNEHILDE:

With mock seriousness she
sings a Wagnerian strain.
The costume woman comes
into the picture, squints
at the CAMERA, then re-
arranges the mail skirt a
little. Lilli smiles and
strikes a pose. The wig
man steps into the picture.

> THE WIG MAN
> Just a moment, please.

Lilli does not stop singing
as he removes her steel
helmet complete with wig
and puts in its place an
even funnier one with cow-
horns sticking out the
sides of it. Lilli gives
him a look and rolls her
eyes up to try to see it.

> THE COSTUME WOMAN
> I like the other one better.

> THE WIG MAN
> (waspishly)
> When I want your advice,
> Sarah, I'll ask for it.

> THE COSTUME WOMAN
> (belligerently)
> You could use some advice.

> THE WIG MAN
> So could you, dear. That
> skirt looks like an ashcan,
> and as for this hardware
> up here...
> (he points to the
> breastplate)

CUT TO:

B-25   THE CAMERA CREW

The cameraman is looking
through a black eyeglass.

> THE CAMERAMAN
> Kill that Baby and gimme a
> Mama Dietz in there.

CUT TO:

B-26   THE SOUND MAN AT HIS PANEL
AND HIS ASSISTANT ON THE
TRIPOD

> THE SOUND MAN
> Come in lower with that
> mike.

His assistant starts turning a crank and lowering
the weighted arm.

CUT TO:

B-27 MED. CLOSE...THE WIG MAN

> THE WIG MAN (belligerently)
> ...and if anybody should ask
> you, dear, she looked like
> Frankenstein.

The microphone comes in
from the top and bangs
him on the head. The wig
man rubs his head and
turns furiously.

> Why don't you look where
> you're going with that
> thing?

CUT TO:

B-28 LOW CAMERA SHOT UP AT
      THE MAN ON THE TRIPOD

> THE MAN ON THE TRIPOD
> Why don't you keep your
> puss outa the picture?

CUT TO:

B-29 CLOSE SHOT...MR. MAGNOLIUS
      AND MADAME SCHNORTZ

They put their heads on one
side and cluck with pleasure.

CUT TO:

B-30 LILLI WALKING INTO A SHOT

She is dressed as Thais
and sings appropriately.

CUT TO:

B-31 THE COSTUME WOMAN

She smiles with pleasure.

CUT TO:

B-32 THE WIG MAN AT HIS
      WIG TABLE

He looks sour for a moment,
then picks up a large
powdered wig of the Louis
XVI period and walks out
of the SHOT.

CUT TO:

B-33 LILLI SINGING

The wig man walks in with
the white wig.

> THE WIG MAN
> Just let me have a gander
> at this one, dear.

Lilli turns in bewilderment.

> THE COSTUME WOMAN
> (coming into the pic-
> ture)
> What's that got to do with
> this?
> (CONTINUED)

25

B-33   (CONTINUED)

The wig man indicates
Lilli's dress, then puts
the wig on her.

>THE WIG MAN
>What's this got to do with
>that? I'll take care of
>the hair, Minnie.

He puts the wig on Lilli
and moves between her and
the camera as he moistens
a beauty spot and sticks
it on her cheek.

>THE CAMERAMAN'S VOICE
>Hey; Will you get your
>back out from in front of
>the camera?

The wig man turns and
gives him a look as we

DISSOLVE TO:

B-34   LILLI AS CARMEN

She sings a few strains.

DISSOLVE TO:

B-35   LILLI IN RIGOLETTO

DISSOLVE TO:

B-36   LILLI IN THE GIRL OF THE
        GOLDEN WEST

DISSOLVE TO:

B-37   LILLI AS SALOME WITH
        JOHN'S HEAD ON THE PLATTER

DISSOLVE TO:

B-38   LILLI AS MADAME BUTTERFLY

As she sings

CUT TO:

B-39   THE WIG MAN

He is oblivious to her
singing. In his left hand
he holds up a long-haired
golden wig which he combs
admiringly.

CUT TO:

B-40   SHOT FROM THE LIGHT
        PLATFORM ABOVE THE
        LITTLE SET

As Lilli sings we see a man
handling a sun arc, focus it
carefully and train it at
the rear of the wig man's
trousers.

CUT TO:

B-41   CLOSE SHOT...LILLI SINGING

       She sees what is happening
       to the wig man. She giggles
       once, then continues her
       song with an effort.

       CUT TO;

B-42   THE WIG MAN FROM THE REAR...
       CLOSE SHOT

       As he finishes combing the
       wig, a wisp of smoke comes
       between him and THE CAMERA.
       Satisfied now, he starts
       forward.

                      THE WIG MAN
                        Just a moment, dear.

       Suddenly he stops and
       looks thunderstruck.

                      Ha! Ho! Help!

       He drops the wig and
       reaches for his trousers.
       The rest of his remarks are
       drowned in laughter. He
       runs out of the picture.

       CUT TO:

B-43   LILLI LAUGHING VERY HARD

       DISSOLVE TO: OFFICE OF MR APEX

B-44   CLOSE SHOT...MR. APEX
       NOT LAUGHING AT ALL

                      MR. APEX (desperately)
                      You know I never ask favors,
                      Jasper...it goes against my
                      ego. You've taken years on
                      my scripts and did I say
                      anything? Very little, if
                      anything. But here now with
                      this dame getting nineteen
                      thousand a week and this
                      unfortunate...oversight, if
                      you could just come through
                      with something...anything.

       CUT TO:

B-45   JASPER BALCOM,
       THE HARASSED WRITER

       His face, with one single
       expression, reflects all
       the grievances of the
       Writers' Guild.

                      JASPER
                      How soon do you need this
                      epic?

       CUT TO:

B-46   MR. APEX

                      MR. APEX (vehemently)
                      Yesterday, if not sooner.

       CUT TO:

B-47   VLADIMIR VON STARK

    Mr. von Stark is tho
    supreme director of the
    industry, and looks it.

                    VLADIMIR (raising a hand)
                      Mr. Apex, I don't shoot no
                      quickies.
    CUT TO:

B-48   SHOT OF THE THREE GENTLEMEN

                MR. APEX
                  Mr. von Stark, you shoot
                  what you get.

                VLADIMIR
                  I don't shoot no quickies.

                MR. APEX
                  I'll say you don't. You
                  were fourteen months on the
                  last one. Fourteen months
                  of my life's blood. And
                  what did I say?

                JASPER
                  Plenty.

                MR. APEX
                  That is neither here nor
                  there. Apex is cornered and
                  we've got to get out from
                  under.

                JASPER
                  Or over.

                VLADIMIR
                  Or t'rough...wit courage
                  and conviction.

                MR. APEX
                  Never mind that stuff.

                VLADIMIR
                  But no quickies.

                MR. APEX
                  Vladimir, will you shut up
                  and give Jasper a chance to
                  think?

                JASPER
                  Don't stop him. He
                  stimulates me.

                VLADIMIR
                  Vot?

                JASPER
                  Irritation is the mother of
                  invention.

                MR. APEX (soothingly)
                  Go on, Jasper, go on.

                          (CONTINUED)

B-48   (CONTINUED)-2

                          JASPER
                              Does she speak any English
                              at all?

                          MR. APEX
                              Only a very slight accent.

                          VLADIMIR
                              I don't make no pictures
                              vit' eccents.

                          JASPER
                              That's what you think.

                          MR. APEX
                              Gentlemen, please!

                          JASPER
                              Well, boys, as I analyze
                              the situation, it's very
                              simple: All we need is a
                              story that gives her a
                              chance to sing, that
                              explains a slight accent
                              and that is exceptionally
                              good.

He spreads his hands.   MR. APEX
                              Exactly.

                          JASPER
                              Precisely.

                          MR. APEX
                              And we need it yesterday.
                              Now: What's it about?

                          JASPER
                              I was afraid you were
                              going to ask that.

                          VLADIMIR (inspired)
                              Don't move! I've got a
                              great title: The Song...
                              of Yoy.

                          JASPER   (considering)
                              The Song of Yoy.

                          VLADIMIR (furiously)
                              Not Yoy, Yoy!

                          JASPER
                              Yoy...I should say that
                              fitted the story about as
                              well as anything else
                              right now.

                          VLADIMIR
                              Yoy.

                          JASPER
                              I get you.

                          VLADIMIR
                              Maybe: "One Day of Love."

                                      (CONTINUED)

29

B-48   (CONTINUED)-3

JASPER   (coldly)
          Or Rhapsody in Red.

VLADIMIR (shaking his head)
          Too familiar.

MR. APEX
          We'll fight the title later.
          Where does it begin and why?

JASPER
          That is the question.

VLADIMIR
          How about: "It Happened
          One Morning."

MR. APEX
          Nothing happens in the
          morning. Ssh!

JASPER
          The story begins in a
          Mennonite village.

VLADIMIR (immediately)
          I don't make no pictures
          about Russia.

JASPER   (ignoring him)
          Which is, of course, in
          Pennsylvania...where the
          Pennsylvania Dutch come
          from.

MR. APEX
          Aha! The accent.

VLADIMIR
          I don't make no pictures...

MR. APEX (menacingly)
          Vladimir...

Mr. von Stark gives him
a look and subsides.

Mr. Apex and von Stark
move in closer.

JASPER   (in a slight trance)
          I see a lazy...hazy Sunday
          morning.

          I see a simple...white
          Colonial church.

MR. APEX (moved)
          Beautiful!

JASPER
          Inside the church ...

VLADIMIR
          ...comes down a slenting
          ray of sunshine...

JASPER
          That's it.

                        (CONTINUED)

> VLADIMIR
>> A single ray.

> JASPER
>> Right.   And at the end of
>> it stands...

> VLADIMIR
>> A goil sinkink.

> MR. APEX
>> What is she thinking about?

> VLADIMIR
>> No, sinkink.

> JASPER   (touching his neck)
>> Wit de troat.

> MR. APEX
>> Oh...beautiful!

> JASPER
>> And she is singing...

> VLADIMIR
>> ...Ave Maria...

> MR. APEX (happily)
>> Of course.

> JASPER
>> Which one

> VLADIMIR (surprised)
>> How many are there?

> JASPER
>> Thirty-two...if you count
>> the medieval ones with the
>> square notes.

> MR. APEX (decisively)
>> She sings the latest one.

> JASPER
>> Right. As she sings we cut
>> to a beautiful limousine.
>> Just as it passes the church
>> there is a loud explosion...

> VLADIMIR
>> Boom!

> JASPER
>> ...and the car comes to a
>> stop...

> VLADIMIR (happily)
>> Wit a flat tire.

> JASPER
>> You guessed it.

> VLADIMIR
>> The door opens and comes
>> out...
>>   (CONTINUED)

31

B-48   (CONTINUED)-5

JASPER
...the mysterious stranger
in the fur collar.

MR. APEX (happily)
Aha! He hears the singing..

VLADIMIR
...goes into the chorch...

JASPER
...and is knocked right on
his flannagan.

MR. APEX
The Hays office will cut
that out.

JASPER
All right. He falls into
a pew.

VLADIMIR
A what?

MR. APEX (impatiently)
A bench.

VLADIMIR
Wit carvings.

JASPER
With or without. Immediately after the performance...
uh...

MR. APEX
Ceremony.

JASPER
Ceremony...they gather in
the family farmyard...

VLADIMIR
...wit pigs...

JASPER
...or without, and the
mysterious stranger tells
the family she's wasting
her time.

MR. APEX
The girl's family.

VLADIMIR (crossly)
Who else?

JASPER   (spreading his
            arms happily)
So it is decided she will
go to the city and take
singing lessons.

MR. APEX
Marvelous.

(CONTINUED)

32

B-48   (CONTINUED)-6

                                JASPER
                                    Naturally, she has a boy
                                    friend she hates to leave...

                                VLADIMIR (as if it were obvious)
                                    And the rich farmer who
                                    holds the tittles to her
                                    father's farm.

Mr. Apex looks inquir-
ingly at Mr. von Stark.
                                JASPER
                                    The mortgage.

                                VLADIMIR
                                    Sure.

                                JASPER
                                    There is a beautiful scene
                                    in the apple orchard where
                                    she says goodbye...

                                VLADIMIR
                                    Peaches!

                                JASPER   (shrugging his
                                              shoulders)
                                    Prunes! And there we see
                                    the little girl full of
                                    hope, full of ambition,
                                    full of maidenly dreams
                                    and...

                                MR. APEX (rising)
                                    It's beautiful! Jasper,
                                    I'll never forget this
                                    moment. If ever a man came
                                    through, it's you. We'll
                                    shoot it first thing in the
                                    morning...

                                VLADIMIR
                                    I don't start no pictures
                                    on Friday.

                                MR. APEX (at the top of
                                              his lungs)
                                    You started yesterday!

                                VLADIMIR (with force)
                                    Good!

                                JASPER   (quietly)
                                    That remains to be seen.

                                            FADE OUT.

            END OF SEQUENCE "B"

                                33

SEQUENCE "C"

With a fanfare of trumpets we

FADE IN:

C-1   ON THE BASE OF A PAINTED
       MOUNTAIN

       To the sound of martial
       music, the base of the
       mountain descends like
       an elevator and brings
       into view its snow-capped
       peak. On this sits a lion
       holding on one raised paw
       the world. We hear the
       sound of a motor and
       around the world comes an
       airplane. As its noise
       grows loud the lion roars,
       radio signals, radio waves
       flash from the peak of the
       mountain and on top of the
       world appear the glowing
       letters: "APEX".

       CUT TO:

C-2   A PLACARD READING:
       "SONG OF JOY (TEMPORARY
       TITLE)"Underneath:
       "CREDITS MISSING"

       CUT TO:

C-3   ANOTHER PLACARD

       "OVERTURE MUSIC (missing)"

       CUT TO:

C-4   ANOTHER PLACARD

       "FADE-IN (Missing)".

       CUT TO:

C-5   A SLEEPY VILLAGE STREET

       It is deserted but for a
       dog in the foreground which
       is scratching itself. We
       hear a male choir which
       sounds like an organ. A
       magnificent limousine appears
       and comes toward us. As it
       gets quite close, we hear the
       sound of an exploding tire.
       The car pulls over to the curb,
       the chauffeur descends, examines
       the tire and removes his coat.

       CUT TO:

34

C-6   THE SIDE OF THE LIMOUSINE..
      CLOSE SHOT

      A magnificent gentleman
in a fur collar sticks his
head out and frowns. The
**music of the male choir
drifts to his ear. He
raises his eyebrows, then**
ignores it and looks at
his tire again. Comes now
a beautiful soprano voice
singing Ave Maria. He
twists his head slowly,   SOUND: Lilli singing
squints his eyes, raises   Ave Maria.
his eyebrows at an excep-
tional note, then slowly
opens the door of his
limousine and goes past
THE CAMERA.

      CUT TO:

C-7   THE MAGNIFICENT GENTLEMAN
      FROM THE REAR

      He is walking on tiptoe
toward a little white church.

      CUT TO:

C-8   A PLACARD

      It reads "DISSOLVE MISSING".

      CUT TO:

C-9   INTERIOR...CHURCH

      LOW CAMERA SHOT up at a
small rose window. Through
this slants a powerful ray
of sunshine. THE CAMERA
FOLLOWS this ray of sunshine
down onto Trudel Edelweiss
(Lilli Pogany) singing Ave   SOUND: Male choir and
Maria. The male choir,   Lilli singing
dressed in black suits,   Ave Maria.
sounds like an organ. Trudel
is full of freshness and
beauty. Her hair is in
plaits. She sings beautifully.

      CUT TO:

C-10 MR. AND MRS. EDELWEISS

      They smile proudly. Mrs.
Edelweiss exchanges a look
with a neighbor, then
returns her gaze to Trudel.
Mr. Edelweiss beams happily
at Trudel, then gives a dirty
look to the person next to
him. THE CAMERA PANS to Mr.   SOUND: Lilli singing.
Julius Overholtzer, a rich
but oafish-looking gentleman
of forty. He is also looking
very proud. He beats time
with the music gently.

      CUT TO:

C-11   TRUDEL SINGING

As she sings she steals
a look at someone in the
back of the church.

SOUND: Lilli singing
        Ave Maria.

CUT TO:

C-12   A HANDSOME BOY OF TWENTY

His poor clothes and the
cowlick on his forehead
suggest that he is a
farmhand. His expression
is palpitating. He sways
with love and with the
beauty of the music. As
the boy watches, the
magnificent gentleman in
the fur collar appears
behind him looking very
tense. He removes his
derby hat and, the better
to hear and see, steps
forward and onto the corn
of a local rustic. He
apologizes in whispers,
drops his derby, then
slips into a pew. A
second later he feels
under him and most
apologetically lifts out
and returns to its owner
the remains of a Sunday
hat. He leans forward
now and sticks his head
between the heads of two
women in front of him.

SOUND: Lilli singing
        Ave Maria.

CUT TO:

C-13   TWO SPINSTERS WITH THE FUR
        COLLAR BETWEEN THEM

The fur collar leans further
and further forward, then
puts a pincenez on his nose.
The spinsters become aware
of him, give him a dirty
look, then one of them flips
her feather boa around her
neck and hits him in the eye.
He smiles apologetically.

SOUND: Lilli singing.

CUT TO:

C-14   TRUDEL SINGING

We stay with her now for
about a minute as, with
fervor and matchless
purity, she finishes the
song. As the last note
dies out there is a burst
of applause. Everybody
turns in horror.

SOUND: Lilli singing.

CUT TO:

36

C-15   CLOSE SHOT...THE FUR COLLAR

He notices the looks and
quickly stops applauding.
He smiles lamely from left
to right, then with gestures
and shoulder-shrugging, indicates that it was a slip,
a spontaneous gesture arising
from his emotional enthrall-
ment.

CUT TO:

C-16   MR. AND MRS. EDELWEISS
AND MR. OVERHOLTZER LOOKING
BACK OVER THEIR SHOULDERS

Mr. and Mrs. Edelweiss look
surprised, but Mr. Over-
holtzer looks very severe.

CUT TO:

C-17   A VERY MILD-LOOKING OLD
CLERGYMAN

He removes his pince-nez,
the better to see and then
clears his throat gently.
He lifts a graceful hand
and waves it at the male
choir. A psalm begins
and Trudel joins her parents
in the pew. She takes her
place between her father and   SOUND: Male choir
Mr. Overholtzer. Mr. Over-   singing psalm.
holtzer looks very possessive.
Trudel looks at him with distaste and moves away an inch.

CUT TO:

C-18   CLOSE SHOT...THE BOY
WITH THE COWLICK

His eyes are full of
longing as he tries to
see the back of Trudel's head.

CUT TO:

C-19   THE GENTLEMAN IN
THE FUR COLLAR

Contrite, he has pulled
himself in to half his
width and half his height.
He looks quite small as he
glances around anxiously.

CUT TO:

C-20   A PLACARD

It reads: "FADE-OUT MISSING"

CUT TO:

C-21 A PLACARD

It reads: "FADE-IN MISSING".

CUT TO:

C-22 A PLACARD

It reads:
"INSERT OF PIGS MISSING".

CUT TO:

C-23 FULL SHOT...
THE EDELWEISS BARNYARD

This is more of a court-
yard contained within the
four walls of the house.
Here amongst dogs, cats,
chickens, ducks, geese,
cows, ploughs, pigeons,
rabbits, pigs and a
horse, we see a group
comprised of Mr. and Mrs.
Edelweiss, Mr. Overholtzer,
Trudel and the gentleman in
the fur collar.

CUT TO:

C-24 CLOSE SHOT ON THE GROUP

THE FUR COLLAR (perplexed)
What did she say?

TRUDEL
She said in der whole world
she didn't gewusst drei
hundred dollars gives.

MRS. EDELWEISS (clucking to
herself)
Drei hundred dollars for
nur ein jahr!

THE FUR COLLAR
What?

TRUDEL
She says for only one year
only so much it gives.

THE FUR COLLAR (laughingly)
You tell your mamma I wasn't
by the year getalking...
you've got me doing it now...
I meant you might get that
much a week.

TRUDEL
Oh, you are jokes gemaking.

MRS. EDELWEISS
Vas sagt him?

THE FUR COLLAR
No I am not jokes gemaking.
I am seriously gespeaking.

(CONTINUED)

Mr. Edelweiss laughs
uproariously.

Mr. Edelweiss roars again.

Trudel puts her hands over
her face and giggles also.

TRUDEL
    Er sagt es ist für nur eine
    woche.

MRS. EDELWEISS
    Er ist in der head verückt.

THE FUR COLLAR (crossly)
    Who's in the head gewhat?

       (indignantly)
    What's the matter with you
    people? I'm giving you a
    tip that's worth a fortune
    and you stand around and
    giggle like a bunch of...
    gehalf-wits.

TRUDEL (seriously)
    You mean honest a week?

THE FUR COLLAR
    Certainly I do.

TRUDEL (to her mother)
    He is de vahrheit getelling.

MRS. EDELWEISS (thunderstruck)
    Nein!

TRUDEL
    Ja!

MRS. EDELWEISS
    Nein!

TRUDEL (joyously)
    Aber ja!

Mrs. Edelweiss throws
her arms around Trudel
and they dance up and
down.

      (to the fur collar)
    When do I go?

THE FUR COLLAR
    That's up to you.

Mr. Overholtzer pushes
into the picture.

MR. OVERHOLTZER (disgruntled)
    Excuse.
      (he indicates Trudel
      with his thumb)
    If to the city she goes,
    vare do I come out?

THE FUR COLLAR (coldly)
    Where did you come in?

MR. OVERHOLTZER
    You don't versteh me. If
    she goes, who am I?

THE FUR COLLAR
    I'll bite, who are you?

             (CONTINUED)

C-24   (CONTINUED)-2

MR. OVERHOLTZER (indignantly)
Who! Who are you to ask me
who are you? Did I ask you
who are you, no?

THE FUR COLLAR
No.

MR. OVERHOLTZER
Yes!

THE FUR COLLAR
No.

Mr. Overholtzer throws
his arms to heaven.

MR. OVERHOLTZER
Vot gives?
(he turns on her parents)
Trudel is by mir gepromised
und ven sie beim city geht,
vo ist der promise?

THE FUR COLLAR (to Trudel)
Who is this gink?

Mr. Overholtzer turns
furiously.

MR. OVERHOLTZER
Gink! She is by mir in
marriage gepromised, so ven
you say gink, just...be
careful how...und vy don't
you keep your nose from my
business out?

THE FUR COLLAR
What business are you in?

MR. OVERHOLTZER
Vot?

MR. EDELWEISS
Money lender.

Mr. Overholtzer turns
on him furiously.

MR. OVERHOLTZER
Ja...und you vuz glad
enough my money to lend,
you crook you.

Mr. Edelweiss clenches
his fists and steps
forward.

Und now if beim city Trudel
gesended gets, then off the
land you go und into the
house a stranger comes und
sits with his feet on the
stove and the stranger ha'ha
it's me ha ha. You'll see!

He flourishes his stick at
them all, turns furiously
and falls over a pig. They
all laugh as he picks himself up and hurries away,
brandishing the stick.

TRUDEL   (on the verge of tears)
Now what gives?

MRS. EDELWEISS
Go.

(CONTINUED)

40

C-24 (CONTINUED)-3

                    MR. EDELWEISS (bravely)
                         Ja.

                    TRUDEL (shaking her head nobly)
                         Nein.

                    MRS. EDELWEISS
                         Ja.

                    MR. EDELWEISS
                         Ja ja.

                    TRUDEL
                         Nein.

                    MRS. EDELWEISS
                         Ja.

                    MR. EDELWEISS
                         Ja.

                    TRUDEL
                         Nein.

                    THE FUR COLLAR (raising a hand)
                         You can finish after I've
                         gone. All I want to say is,
                         here's my card and if you come
                         to Hollywood, look me up.

Mrs. Edelweiss clasps her
hands in a gesture of
thanks.

                              (raising a hand)
                         Don't thank me; it's nothing.
                         I heard a voice in the wil-
                         derness...I tried to do my
                         duty.

He raises his derby with
a noble gesture, turns
and falls over the same
pig. The Edelweiss
family picks him up and
scrapes some of the mud
off him. The Fur Collar
takes it in good heart.

                         It's nothing, folks, it's
                         just my duty.

He raises his derby again,
turns rapidly and, just in
time, sees the pig and
walks around it. He turns,
gives it a dirty laugh and
falls over a sheep.

        CUT TO:

C-25 A PLACARD

        It reads:
        "DISSOLVE MISSING".

        CUT TO:

C-26 A VERY CUTE PENNSYLVANIA
        DUTCH BEDROOM ON THE
        GROUND FLOOR

        Trudel is arranging her
        things on the bed. Her
        father enters with an

                                        (CONTINUED)

41

C-26 (CONTINUED)

old-fashioned round-
backed trunk. He puts
it down sadly, wipes his
nose on his finger as he
snuffles, then hugs Trudel
to his breast. After a
moment he cups her face in
his hands and kisses her
on the forehead, then turns
and exits, closing the door
after him. Trudel's lips
tremble, then she begins to
pack her thick underclothes
fringed with heavy home-
made lace into the old-
fashioned wall-paper lined
trunk. We hear a whistle.
Trudel stops and turns.
The whistle is repeated.
Trudel gives a frightened
look toward the door, then
goes on tiptoe to the
window and opens it in.
She whistles in return.

CUT TO:

C-27 SHOT AT AN APPLE TREE
IN BLOSSOM

Among the blossoms we see
the head of the boy with
the cowlick. He smiles
and beckons to us.

CUT TO:

C-28 EXTERIOR...TRUDEL'S WINDOW

She climbs out the window
and her home-made dress
catches on a nail. We see
her legs in thick white
stockings and some of the
home-made underwear above.
She frees herself of the
nail and comes forward.

CUT TO:

C-29 THE TRUNK OF THE APPLE TREE

The boy's legs come in
from above as Trudel walks
into the picture. The boy
drops to the ground and
seizes both of her hands.

                    THE BOY
                      Trudel.

                    TRUDEL
                      Yonny!

He kisses her on both
cheeks. She looks away
nervously, then says:

                      Yonny, I'm going to the
                      big city away.

                         (CONTINUED)

42

C-29   (CONTINUED)

                         YONNY   (anxiously)
                              Von do you viodor hoim come?

                         TRUDEL
                              I don't know, yonny...
                              I take singing lessons.

                         YONNY
                              Singing lessons!

                         TRUDEL
                              Ja, singing lessons to
                              learn singing.

                         YONNY
                              Then you won't hoim gocome
                              for a long...long time.

                         TRUDEL
                              Maybe yes, Yonny.

He looks away a long
moment, then puts his
hands on her shoulders.

                         YONNY
                              I'm glad...terrible glad...
                              for you.

                         TRUDEL   (gently)
                              Yonny.

                         YONNY
                              For me doesn't matter...
                              every day in my heart I'll
                              see you...and every night
                              ...in my dreams.

                         TRUDEL
                              Me too, Yonny.

Very softly she sings
something like this:

                              "Each night
                              Each day
                              When we are far apart
                              You'll be in my heart.

                              Each night
                              Each day
                              When you are far away
                              You'll be in my heart.

                              Each second of the hour
                                  I'll pine
                              Sentimentally
                              No second love will
                                  ever be mine
                              Through eternity.

                              Until the day
                              When I am old and gray
                              You'll BE...in my heart."

          CUT TO:

C-30   A PLACARD

It reads: "SLOW FADE-OUT
WITH MUSIC (MISSING)".
Against this rises Mr.
Apex's silhouette. He
blows his nose musically.

           MR. APEX (strangled with tears)
                Okay, boys, let's have some
                light.

The projection room
lights go on and we
see a CLOSE SHOT OF
Mr. Apex.

           Vladimir, that's beautiful.
           What I like is it's got a
           real heart -throb...a tug.

CUT TO:

C-31   GROUP IN THE PROJECTION ROOM

We see Mr. Apex, Jasper,
Lilli and Vladimir.

          VLADIMIR (rising sourly)
           For me dot's only poofle wit
           de eyes closed...I vant to do
           someting wordy...something
           immense.

          LILLI   (rising)
           When do I sing the Blue
           Danube?

          MR. APEX (perplexed)
           Oh...The Blue Danube ha,ha.

He bends a look at Jasper.

          When does that come in, Jasper?

          JASPER
           We uh...sort of work that in
           later.

          MR. APEX
           Aha. Good.

He smiles at Lilli.

          LILLI
           I wait in my dressing room.

          MR. APEX
           Yes, my dear, just take it
           easy for a few minutes.

          LILLI
           Thank you.

She exits.

          MR. APEX (closing the door after
               her)
           Oh, Jasper. One thing I
           didn't understand: why did
           that fellow in the fur collar
           say: "If you come to Hollywood
           look me up"? Why Hollywood?
           Why not Brooklyn or Cincinnati
           or Chicago even?

CONTINUED

44

                                    JASPER   (on the defensive)
                                        Because he's in the moving
                                        picture business and they
                                        make moving pictures in
                                        Hollywood.

                                    MR. APEX (blankly but with dis-
                                                taste)
                                        He in the moving picture
                                        business?..I thought he was
                                        a singing teacher.

He scowls.
                                    JASPER
                                        No, no, he's a moving picture
                                        producer.

                                    MR. APEX (furiously)
                                        A picture producer! That guy
                                        who falls over pigs is a
                                        picture producer? What are
                                        you trying to get away with?

                                    JASPER   (acidly)
                                        Couldn't a picture producer
                                        fall over a pig?

                                    MR. APEX (at the top of his lungs)
                                        Not with my money he couldn't.
                                        Jasper, what's the matter with
                                        you? Why does he have to be
                                        a picture producer, anyway?

                                    JASPER
                                        How are you going to make a
                                        Hollywood story without a
                                        picture producer. You tell
                                        me and I'll do it.

                                    MR. APEX (horrified)
                                        A Hollywood story! Who asked
                                        you for a Hollywood story?
                                        What's Hollywood got to do
                                        with it?

                                    JASPER
                                        It's all about Hollywood.

                                    MR. APEX
                                        Not with my money it isn't.
                                        I wouldn't put a dime in a
                                        Hollywood story. They're sick
                                        and tired of Hollywood stories.
                                        Who cares about Hollywood
                                        stories? I don't.What does
                                        this guy do when he gets her to
                                        Hollywood?

                                    JASPER
                                        Well you see, he's a phoney
                                        producer who only...

                                    MR. APEX (leaping off the ground)
                                        A phoney producer! All I've
                                        got to do yet is put my money
                                        into a phoney producer who
                                        swandangles little girls to
                                        Hollywood and....

CONTINUED

JASPER
He doesn't do anything to her.

MR. APEX (at the top of his lungs)
It looks like he's going to.
That's enough. It's too much.
It's out! What are you trying
to do...give the industry a
black eye?

He strikes a pose
and speaks nobly.

Gentlemen...let us not foul
our own nest.

VLADIMIR (resentfully)
I don't make no pictures dot
foul nothing!

JASPER   (sourly)
Then what do we do with this
turkey?

MR. APEX
We change it or...
        (he
...we scrap it. The littl
girl who goes
that's all right.
singing lessons, that's okay.
Maybe she could get to be an
understudy to some opera singer...

JASPER   (sourly)
That's new.

MR. APEX
Good. Then work it out in
that way, Jasper. Something
clean, something fine...

VLADIMIR
Something big!

MR. APEX (with distaste)
Not necessarily. Just the
right size. Think of the
families that go to the movies,
Jasper. Think of the little
tots who don't understand
anything yet. That's who you're
    writing for. Bear them in
mind and forget about moving
picture producers who fall over
pigs and stuff like that. I
take full responsibility and if
it lays an egg...it lays an egg.

JASPER
It's going to lay an egg all
right. All I hope is it's a
fresh one.

He smiles sourly at Mr.
Apex.

DISSOLVE TO:

C-32   LILLI'S DRESSING ROOM

She reclines on a chaise
longue and looks very pretty.
The chaise longue is next to
the window. Mme. Schnortz
sits on a straight chair near
her. Each of them holds an
English conversation book.

> MME. SCHNORTZ (reading in very
> bad English)
> Does your grandmo-ter possess
> an ow-tomobile?
>
> LILLI (reading from her book)
> No, but my oonole has a
> fountane pen.
>
> MME SCHNORTZ
> Vot does he do vit dis instru-
> ment?
>
> LILLI
> He vrites checks for my ah-oont.
>
> MME SCHNORTZ
> Good. Vare does he vrite de
> checks?
>
> LILLI
> In his hooss.
>
> MME. SCHNORTZ (laughing)
> No, no, no. In his ho-ooze.
>
> LILLI (pointing to her book)
> No, hooss.
> (in Hungarian she spells;
> h-o-u-s-e, and adds as if
> it were obvious)
> Hooss.
>
> MME. SCHNORTZ (pointing to her book)
> Ho-ooze!
>
> LILLI (crossly)
> Hooss.
>
> MME. SCHNORTZ (with mounting anger)
> HO-OOZE!
>
> LILLI   (shaking her head)
> Hooss.
>
> MME. SCHNORTZ (In Hungarian)
> I'm going to tell you once
> more and that's all. Ho..ooze.
>
> LILLI   (mildly)
> Hooss.

Mme. Schnortz rises
majestically, bangs the
the book together, stalks
out the door and slams it
after her. Lillis gives
her a look

CONTINUED

47

then returns to her book.
After a moment she looks
up puzzled. Her gaze wanders
to the window. She stretches
her neck to see a little
better and goes to the window
and opens it.

                              LILLI
                         How do you say: Hooss or
                         ho-ooze?
        CUT TO:

C-33   MED.CLOSE..THE BOY

We see him from the
exterior of his window
which is open. He sits
in a cubbyhole office
copying music. Behind
him are framed diplomas.
He has an intellectual
and kindly face.

                         THE BOY   (smiling)
                         I beg your pardon?
        CUT TO:

C-34   LILLI FRAMED IN HER
        WINDOW...

                              LILLI
                         How do you say it: Hooss or
                         ho-ooze?
        CUT TO:

C-35   THE BOY...

He looks perplexed.
                         THE BOY
                         Hooss or ho-ooze...Hooss?
        CUT TO:

C-36   LILLI IN HER WINDOW..
        OVER THE BOY'S SHOULDER..
                         LILLI   (lifting up her book)
                         It says:
                              (she reads)
                         "He writes checks for my
                         ah-cont. Where does he
                         write the checks? In his
                         hooss."
        CUT TO:

C-37   CLOSE SHOT...THE BOY

                         THE BOY   (smiling)
                         House.
        CUT TO:

kb C-38   LILLI...CLOSE SHOT

LILLI   (smiling and frowning
          at the same time)
      House?
          (she points to the book)
      Hooss?

THE BOY'S VOICE
      No, house.

LILLI   (dubiously)
      All right....but to me it
      look like hooss.

CUT TO:

C-39   THE BOY OVER LILLI'S
        SHOULDER..

THE BOY
      Are you in the Pogany
      picture?

LILLI
      Oh yes.
          (she laughs)

      I am in it. How do you
      know?

THE BOY
      I'm working on the music so
      I thought you might be in
      it...with that costume...I
      know there were a lot of
      girls in the church scene.

LILLI
      Oh yes. Are you a composi-
      tor?

THE BOY
      Well...yes I am. I uh...I
      studied quite a lot.

He points to his diplomas.
      But here I'm a...a copyist.
CUT TO:

C-40   LILLI OVER THE BOY'S
        SHOULDER...

LILLI   (shaking her head sadly)
      Oh.
          (then she smiles)
      Well, some day you be a big
      compositor and write an
      opera for...Lilli Pogany.

The boy chuckles.
THE BOY
      What's she like anyway?

LILLI
      You never see her?

THE BOY
      No...I don't get around much.

LILLI
      What you think she's like?

(CONTINUED)

49

kb C-40 (<u>CONTINUED</u>)

THE BOY
I don't know. I suppose
she's like most opera singers...big and...and...

He makes a gesture of
the arms indicating a
chest of large capacity.

LILLI   (nodding her head)
That is exactly right;
(she laughs)
She is very big...

She stretches her arms
around.

....like a hippo-popo-papa...

THE BOY
Like an elephant;

LILLI   (emphatically)
Yes...just like a elephant;

The boy shakes his head.

THE BOY
That's the way it goes..and
pretty girls like you have
to play extra. Can she sing?

LILLI
Who?

THE BOY
Pogany.

LILLI
Oh, Pogany. No, no. She
sing like a <u>gwat</u>;

THE BOY
A gwat?

LILLI
You know...a gwat?

She puts her hand to
her chin and waggles
her fingers.

THE BOY
Ohhh...a gwat...of course.
I didn't understand for a
minute.
(he chuckles)
A mountain gwat or a plain
gwat?

LILLI
Just...a gwat.

She laughs at him then
prepares to close her
window;

Thank you very much for the
hooss...house;

THE BOY
That's all right...any time;
I'm glad to have met you. I
get sort of lonely here;

(CONTINUED)

kb   C-40   (CONTINUED)

                  LILLI
                      I'm sorry...it is bad for a
                      compositor to be lonely...
                      He should have inspiration.

                  THE BOY   (nervously)
                      You...well...I mean I...You
                      wouldn't care to..to sort of
                      ... You've got to eat some
                      place and so do I and maybe
                      ...we could have dinner
                      together? Or am I being
                      too....I don't want you to
                      think that I'm the sort of
                      person...,

                  LILLI   (laughing at him)
                      I think it is very expensive
                      for a young man to take me to
                      dinner...no?

                  THE BOY   (seriously)
                      Well not...where..I was
                      going to take you.

Lilli roars and he
laughs too.

                  LILLI
                      All right. I meet you where?

                  THE BOY
                      I'll wait for you at the
                      extra gate.

                  LILLI   (puzzled)
                      Where is that?

                  THE BOY
                      Where you came in.

                  LILLI
                      I find it...I be there...
                      six-thirty?

                  THE BOY   (happily)
                      Six-thirty.

                  LILLI   (smiling)
                      Then...gwat.

She puts her hand to
her chin and waggles
it.

                  THE BOY   (laughing)
                      Gwat.

                  LILLI
                      Gwat.

She closes her window.
The boy sighs heavily
and returns to his work.

DISSOLVE TO:

kb C-41 THE FEET AND LEGS OF
LOADS OF EXTRA GIRLS..

We hear the clippity-clop
of their high heels.

CUT TO:

C-42 THE LEDGE OUTSIDE THE
CASHIER'S DESK..

Girls' hands come in with
pay checks and the
cashier's hand passes out
the money. Presently
Lilli's hand comes into
the picture minus the
pay check.

CUT TO:

CLOSEUP..... SEVERE-
LOOKING CASHIER...

                          THE CASHIER
                             What am I supposed to do?
                             Where's your check?

CUT TO:

LILLI SMILING AMIABLY
OUTSIDE THE CASHIER'S
WINDOW...

She is dressed in a
very simple suit.

                          LILLI   (Blankly)
                             Check?

                          THE CASHIER (through the window)
                             No tickee no washee, sister.
                             NEXT!

Lilli looks around at
the girl behind her,
giggles, then moves on.

CUT TO:

C-45 EXT. OF THE EXTRA GATE

The boy stands on the
sidewalk in front of a
large, white Isotta Fraschini.
The uniformed chauffeur smokes
a cigarette and looks around
disdainfully.

CUT TO:

C-46 HIGH CAMERA SHOT AT LILLI
IN THE CROWD OF EXTRA GIRLS

She is pushed hither and
yon and eventually through
a turnstile. As she passes,

CUT TO:

kb C-47   THE BOY IN FRONT OF
THE ISOTTA FRASCHINI

He sees Lilli, smiles
and steps forward.
Almost simultaneously
the chauffeur throws
away his cigarette, throws
a robe over his arm;
leaps out of the car and
stands at attention at
the door:

CUT TO:

C-48   CLOSE SHOT...LILLI AMONGST
THE EXTRA GIRLS...

She smiles at the boy as
he comes into the picture.

               THE BOY   (removing his hat)
                 This is very nice.

               LILLI   (enjoying herself)
                 I think so too.

CUT TO:

C-49   CLOSE SHOT...THE CHAUFFEUR
AT ATTENTION...

His head twists three
degrees and his expression
becomes slightly more stupid
than before.

CUT TO:

C-50   LILLI AND THE BOY

The boy has his back to
the Isotta Fraschini.
Lilli looks past him and
shakes her head faintly
to the chauffeur.

CUT TO:

C-51   CLOSE SHOT..THE CHAUFFEUR

He blinks and looks
completely vapid.

CUT TO:

C-52   MOVING SHOT DOWN THE
SIDEWALK AHEAD OF LILLI
AND THE BOY...

               THE BOY
               You know...in my excitement
               about your having dinner
               with me and..and..I forgot
(CONTINUED)   to ask you your name.

kb   C-52   (CONTINUED)

                                    LILLI
                                         Oh...Lilli.

                                    THE BOY   (smiling)
                                         Lilli! That's a pretty name.

                                    LILLI
                                         Thank you.

                                    THE BOY
                                         Lilli what?

                                    LILLI
                                         Oh.

            She frowns for a
            moment.   My father's name is Bush-
                                         miller.

                                    THE BOY   (nodding pleasantly)
                                         Bushmiller! That's a very
                                         pretty name too.

                                    LILLI   (surprised)
                                         You think so?

                                    THE BOY
                                         Yes, certainly. I see a bush
                                         and a mill behind it and
                                         there stands the miller
                                         smoking his pipe in the
                                         twilight.

                                    LILLI
                                         I never saw all that in it.
                                         If I had a name like
                                         Bushmiller I would have
                                         changed it...unless I
                                         decided not to.
            She looks at him uneasily.
                                    THE BOY
                                         I can see what you mean..
                                         My name is........ Maybe I
                                         should have changed it.
                                    LILLI
                                         No. I like it.
            CUT TO:

    C-53   THE CHAUFFEUR BESIDE
            THE ISOTTA FRASCHINI..

            He is looking terribly
            puzzled. He removes his
            cap and scratches his
            head, but looks just as
            puzzled. He gets into
            the front seat of the car
            and starts his engine.

            CUT TO:

                                    54

kb   C-54   A STREET CAR SAFETY ZONE

A lot of people are waiting
for the street car. The
street car appears and stops.
Lilli and the boy hurry into
the picture and climb on just
as it starts away. As it
starts THE CAMERA MOVES with
it and, from an automobile,
follows it for a few seconds.
We see the boy take Lilli's
arm and pilot her inside.
The street car goes faster
but the CAMERA CAR continues
at the same speed. As the
street car draws ahead, the
bonnet of the Isotta Fraschini
comes into view right behind
it. The chauffeur is looking
as astonished as ever. The
Isotta Fraschini passes out
of the picture and it is replaced by a magnificent black
Rolls Royce. As it comes
abreast of us we see Vladimir
von Stark waving his arms.

CUT TO:

C-55   INTERIOR OF THE ROLLS ROYCE

It contains Jasper, Vladimir
and Mr. Apex.

                    VLADIMIR (at the top of his
                                lungs)
                        Dot's vy!

                    MR. APEX (at the top of his lungs)
                        All right. But why does
                        she have to sing The Blue
                        Danube?

                    VLADIMIR
                        She don't have to!

                    MR. APEX
                        I don't mean that.

                    JASPER   (at the end of his
                                patience)
                        Because she's an opera star!
                        You wanted her to be an
                        opera star...all right.
                        She sings The Blue Danube.

                    MR. APEX (furiously)
                        Don't tell me what I know.
                        What I'm asking you is: How
                        did she get to be an opera
                        star?

                    JASPER   (as loud as he can)
                        She took lessons.

          (CONTINUED)

kb C-54   (CONTINUED)

Ho throws his arms
wide and noarly pokos
Vladimir in tho oyo.

                              MR. APEX (nearly in tears)
                                  But wo havon't shown that;

                              VLADIMIR (coldly)
                                  Dot's only a tochnality. Wo
                                  show it lator.

Ho now bocomos oxcited.

                                  Wot wu got to do is wo got to
                                  got startod on tho musical
                                  numbors.Thoy got to havo..
Ho strotchos his arms and   havo...
noarly pokos Mr.Apox in tho
oyo.   I want costumos..I want spaco
                                  ...I want SYMBOLS.

                              MR. APEX (doggodly)
                                  But whoro did sho got tho
                                  music lossons?

                    (JASPER
                    (Paris
         SIMULTANEOUSLY (VLADIMIR
                    (Rome

                              MR. APEX
                                  What

                    (JASPER
                    (All right, Rome.
         SIMULTANEOUSLY (VLADIMIR
                    (All right, Paris.

                              MR APEX   (holding his hoad)
                                  But WHEN? That's what I
                                  want to know: whon did sho
                                  got tho music lossons?

                              VLADIMIR (at top of his lungs)
                                  Boforo sho got to bo an
                                  opora star!

                              MR. APEX (stupofied)
                                  Before.

                              JASPER
                                  Naturally.

                              MR. APEX (weakly)
                                  Thon wo're right back whoro
                                  we startod from.

                    (JASPER
                    (No.
         SIMULTANEOUSLY (VLADIMIR
                    (Yos.

          (CONTINUED)

D-6   LILLI AND THE BOY

Sho roalizos sho has mado
a slight mistako and looks
at him shoopishly. Sho smilos
to hido hor ombarrassmont.

CUT TO:

D-7   REVERSE SHOT..LILLI, THE
BOY ..ND THE CASHIER

Tho cashior counts out tho
chango and looks vory dis-
ploasod. Tho chango is mostly
in ono-dollar bills and makos
a largo pilo.

                              THE CASHIER (with falso swootness)
                                   Shall I wrap it up?

                              LILLI
                                   No, thank you.

Sho jams tho change in
hor bag and sho and the
boy leave hurriedly.

                              THE CASHIER (to tho man from behind)
                                   Wiso guys.

CUT TO:

D-8   TRUCKING SHOT...A LITTLE
AHEAD OF LILLI AND THE BOY

Sho holds his arm and looks
a little contrito. Thoy go
by lightod storo windows.

                              THE BOY   (forgivingly)
                                   That's all right...but you
                                   shouldn't carry fifty-dollar
                                   bills around that way.

                              LILLI   (contrite)
                                   I know.

Suddonly she has an
inspiration.

                                   I tako it for my rent.

Sho smiles at him.

                              THE BOY   (astoundod)
                                   You pay that much rent?

Hastily Lilli raisos
two fingers.

                              LILLI   (watching him anxiously)
                                   Two weeks.

                              THE BOY   (thunderstruck)
                                   Two wooks!

CONTINUED

D-8   CONTINUED

                                    LILLI   (hastily)
                                       Two months.
                                          (she laughs)
                                       Two months.

                                    THE BOY (relaxing)
                                       Oh...that's better.

                                    LILLI
                                       Yes.

They smile at each other
and walk along.

CUT TO:

D-9   CLOSE SHOT FROM THE
      SIDEWALK ONTO THE STREET

The Isotta Fraschini passes
slowly near the curb. The
chauffeur is frowning and
eating a sandwich.

CUT TO:

D-10 LILLI AND THE BOY WALKING
      TOWARD US

The Isotta Fraschini creeps
along behind. She stops and
looks into a store window.
The boy looks also.

CUT TO:

D-11 LILLI AND THE BOY IN FRONT
      OF A WINDOW WHICH CONTAINS
      A LOT OF VILE-LOOKING FURNITURE
      AND CROCKERY

In the middle, a sign reads:
"Everything but the bride: $129.66.
You furnish the girl, we furnish
the rest. No down-payment. Five
years to pay."

                                    LILLI   (amused)
                                       It make everything very easy.

                                    THE BOY (embarrassed)
                                       Yes.
                                          (he laughs)

Their eyes meet and they
look away. He takes her
arm and they walk by.

CUT TO:

D-12 THE CHAUFFEUR...CLOSE SHOT

He looks past us with a face
full of curiosity, then takes
a swig of beer from a bottle.

CUT TO:

D-13   LILLI AND THE BOY WALKING
        TOWARD US

        She stops in perploxity and
        looks into a window. She
        frowns.

        CUT TO:

D-14   LILLI AND THE BCY IN FRONT
        OF THE WINDOW

        This contains tool-chests,
        a small lathe, flat irons,
        a lawn-mower, shoes, tennis
        rackets, hot water bottles,
        stockings, duck trousers,
        rifles, cameras, thermos bot-
        tles, dolls, several musical
        instruments and a cat. On a
        counter which makes the back
        of the window a fat man in
        white is slicing a ham.

                        LILLI   (in perploxity)
                          What kind of store?

                        THE BOY
                          A drug store.

                         LILLI   (in surprise)
                           Pharmacy?

                        THE BOY
                          Yes.

                        LILLI   (laughing)
                          Nice.

        They walk on.

        CUT TO:

D-15   THE ISOTTA FRASCHINI

        The chauffeur raises an
          ice cream cone to his
        lips.

        CUT TO:

D-16   SHOT FROM INTERIOR OF
        MAKE- YOUR-OWN-RECORDS STORE

        The noise is deafening as many
        people sing and play at once.
        In the foreground we see a sign
        reading: "Four-inch record..25¢
                   Eight-inch record.50¢
                   Ten-inch record...75¢
                Hear yourself as Others
                hear you."
        Lilli and the boy stops outside and
        we see them through the glass window.
        Apparently she asks him what it is and
        when he explains, she seems delighted.
        She tells him she will make him a record.

D-16   CONTINUED

and they come into the shop.
At this moment the Isotta
Fraschini comes slowly into
view. The chauffeur cranes
his neck to see where they've
gone, then bumps gently into
a taxi cab, stopped in front
of him.

CUT TO:

D-17   MOVING SHOT...
EXTERIOR OF BOOTHS

The noise of singing is quite
loud. The manager leads Lilli
and the boy past several booths
as he looks for an empty one.
Through the glass partitions we
see various types singing: A
large colored lady, a long-
haired tenor singing soulfully,
a Japanese student sending a
record to his parents, and a
quartet singing in very close
harmony.

CUT TO:

D-18   INTERIOR OF A BOOTH

The manager precedes Lilli
and the boy into this. It
contains a special sort of
phonograph, a microphone
and a piano.

                              THE MANAGER
                         There you are, folks. Just
                         sing into this....
                              (he indicates a microphone)
                         ...and watch those lights.
                         If this one goes on, it's too
                         loud. If that one don't go
                         on, it ain't loud enough.
                         Push this to start and ring
                         this bell if you want another
                         record. Go to it. You might
                         be another Bing Crosby, who
                         knows.

He exits.

                              LILLI
                         What shall we sing?

                              THE BOY
                         What do you know?

                              LILLI   (after chuckling)
                         What can you play?

                              THE BOY
                         Almost anything.

                              LILLI
                         Can you play "Romeo and Juliet"?

    THE BOY
     I guess so...but that's
     pretty hard, isn't it?

    LILLI
     For *you?*

    THE BOY   (laughing)
     No, for you.

    LILLI
     Oh...yes. Very difficult...
     but I try.

    THE BOY   (striking a chord)
     You must have taken lessons.

    LILLI
     A little bit one time.

She smiles at him.

    THE BOY
     Do you want a rehearsal?

    LILLI
     Oh, no...why? If I sing bad,
     I sing bad.

He looks at her in some
surprise and plays some
chords. She walks over
to the machine, pushes
the button, looks at it
curiously, then waves
the beat to him. She sings   SOUND: Lilli singing
beautifully and the boy
watches her, first in astonishment, then in delight.
Presently we --

CUT TO:

D-19   THE MANAGER'S DESK IN THE
    OUTSIDE ROOM

The noise is deafening but
over it all we hear Lilli's
high notes. He looks up and
squints his eyes, then claps
a pair of ear-phones on his
head and sticks the plug into
several sockets. listening the
while. Suddenly he finds the
right one and his expression
changes. He takes it big.
After a moment he yells past
the CAMERA.

    THE MANAGER
     Hey, Dave.

CUT TO:

D-20   A DISAPPOINTED LOOKING
        GENTLEMAN IN A HARD HAT

        Nearsightedly he is reading
        a newspaper folded into its
        smallest or subway-dimensions.

                            DAVE   (without looking up)
                            What do you want?

        CUT TO:

D-21   CLOSE SHOT...THE MANAGER
        IN EAR-PHONES

                        THE MANAGER
                        Got a load of this.

        CUT TO:

D-22   DAVE

                        DAVE   (sourly)
                        I had all the laughs I can
                        stand for one day.

        CUT TO:

D-23   THE MANAGER

                        THE MANAGER
                        This ain't to laugh at.

        CUT TO:

D-24   DAVE

                      DAVE
                        I suppose I'm going to break
                        down or something?

        Newspaper in hand he
        crosses the room and
        THE CAMERA PANS with
        him. As he reaches
        the desk he says:

                        Let's have it.

        Sourly he takes the ear-
        phones from the manager
        and holds one of them to
        his ear. One second later
        he claps the other one to
        the other ear and the con-
        necting band almost knocks
        his hat off.

                        Holy smoke!

        He removes his hat.

                      THE MANAGER(looking at him)
                        I don't know nothing, hunh?

                      DAVE
                        Shut up.

        CUT TO:

D-25   CLOSE SHOT..LILLI
        AGAINST THE GLASS
        PARTITION
        _____

        She is singing beautifully   SOUND: Lilli singing.

        CUT TO:

D-26   CLOSE SHOT..THE BOY AT
        THE PIANO
        _____

        He tries to play and listen
        at the same time.

        CUT TO:

D-27   LILLI AGAINST THE GLASS
        PARTITION
        _____

        As she sings Dave appears
        beyond the partition. He
        looks very mysterious. Sud-
        denly we hear a buzzer. Lilli
        frowns, then stops singing,
        then she laughs as she under-
        stands.

                                LILLI
                                    Oh...
        She points to the machine.
                                    All finished.

        The boy walks into the
        picture.
                            THE BOY (happily)
                                That's great....You ought to
                                do something with that voice.

                            LILLI   (shrugging her shoulders)
                                Just because the room is
                                small. In the bathtub it
                                is even better.

                            THE BOY
                                Oh no, that's beautiful.

                            LILLI   (in mock surprise)
                                Really? You think I should try
                              to do something with it?

                            THE BOY
                                Of course you should.

                            LILLI
                                But I don't like to sing.
                                It..how you say..it boores me..

        There is a sharp
        knock on the glass
        door. They turn in
        surprise.

        CUT TO:

D-28   DAVE COMING INTO THE
       ROOM.

He shuts the door behind
him.

              'Evening, folks...pardon my
              intrusion.. I'm from the
              Apex Film Company.

CUT TO:

D-29   LILLI AND THE BOY

She looks very nervous.

              LILLI   (frowning)
              What you want?

Dave comes into the picture.

              DAVE
              I want to give you the
              chance of a lifetime, young
              lady.

              LILLI   (imperiously)
              Who are you?

              DAVE   (benignly)
              I'm old Dave Horner, the
              talent scout.

              THE BOY   (pleased)
              Oh, yes, I've seen you
              around.

              I've been around a long time,
              young man. I discovered
              Beery. I discovered Gable.
              I discovered Karloff, I
              won't tell you where, and
              though I don't get credit
              for it, I discovered Garbo
              and some people say Chaplin!
              (he smiles) Now if you'll
              just let me have that record
              ...I'll gladly pay...

There is a crash and
he jumps.
INSERT: THE PHONOGRAPH
RECORD on the floor in
pieces. Just next to
it we see Lilli's feet.
THE CAMERA ANGLES UP her
feet and legs and we see
Lilli with her arms out-
stretched, looking very
pathetic.

              LILLI   (sadly)
              It slip.

She gives Dave a look.
Dave comes into the picture.

              DAVE   (sourly)
              Now look what you went and
              done. Well...

He shrugs his shoulders.

              (CONTINUED)

64

Then he becomes cheerful
again.

                                DAVE (cont'd)
                                We'll just make an oven
                                better one and..who knows,
                                huh?

                            LILLI   (crossly)
                                I don't want to make no more.

                                DAVE   (as to a child)
                                Maybe you didn't understand.
                                I'm from the Apex Film
                                Company, A-p-e-x...the top!

                                LILLI   (nervously)
                                I don't care who you are, I
                                don't want to sing no more.

She takes the boy's arm.
                                Now come. We go to a movie
                                picture, yes?

                                DAVE   (sourly to the boy)
                                Will you explain to your
                                girl-friend that people give
                                their right eye and their
                                left..ear to have me so much
                                as listen to them?

                                LILLI   (indignantly)
                                I don't give nothing to have
                                you listen to me. I sing
                                very bad and you don't know
                                nothing.

                                THE BOY (gently)
                                I don't think you understand,
                                Lilli. This is the big
                                chance. This gentleman is
                                in a position to...

                                DAVE   (chiming in)
                                I could even have you meet
                                Mr. Apex himself.

                                LILLI   (furiously)
                                I never hear of Mr. Apex.
                                I don't want to see him. I
                                don't want to sing. I want
                                to go to a picture talking.

Suddenly she notices
the boy's expression.

CUT TO:

D-30   CLOSE SHOT...THE BOY

He is deeply puzzled at her
behavior.

                                THE BOY
                                I don't understand you,
                                Lilli...Why shouldn't you be
                                glad of a chance to...to...
                                make something of yourself
                                and..and...

CUT TO:

                                              LILLI   (quietly)
She turns to Dave.   Very well...I sing.

                                                   What you want me to sing?

                                              DAVE   (happily)
                                                       What do you know?

                                              LILLI   (acidly)
                                                       What do you know?

                                              DAVE
                                                       I don't suppose you could
                                                       sing from Rigoletto?

                                              LILLI
                                                       I could sing from anything
                                                       only I tell you...I am a
                                                       little bit nervous.

                                              DAVE
                                                       Just forget about me.

                                              LILLI
                                                       I will try. But naturally
                                                       such a big man and such a
                                                       big opportunitee make me
                                                       nervous. Play.
The boy sits at the
piano and Dave sticks
a record on the machine.
As he moves to one side,
THE CAMERA PANS with him.
He leans forward like a
cat watching a mousehole.
His face is all ears.

CUT TO:

D-32   THE BOY AT THE PIANO

Nervously he dries his
hands on his handkerchief,
then massages his finger-
joints. He strikes a chord.

CUT TO:

D-33   LILLI

She arranges her features
into the highclass sneer
of an amateur parlor performer
and places her hands under
the heart. She begins with
a very throaty note, then slips
into a headtone like a steam
whistle. Passing now through
a very inaccurate run, she
arrives at an extremely un-
pleasant trill. She makes this
doubly unattractive by cocking
her head on one side, smiling
archly and shooting it directly
into Mr. Horner's ear.

CUT TO:

kb

D-34   CLOSE SHOT...DAVE..

His face is a poem of
displeasure. A particularly
loud note comes over this
and he seems to dodge it.

CUT TO:

D-35   LILLI SINGING

She has reached the part
which is almost funny even
when well done. She is
having the time of her
life.

CUT TO:

D-36   THE BOY PLAYING...FROM
THE REAR...

He looks over his shoulder
and sends an embarrassed
and supplicating look past us.

CUT TO:

D-37   LILLI SINGING

She is seized with an over-
powering desire to laugh but
continues bravely. She leans
on the wall beside her and her
laughing eyes close to slits.

CUT TO:

D-38   DAVE...

He looks like an angry dog.

CUT TO:

D-39   LILLI

She steals a look at the
record, then finishes with
a note a full tone away from
where it should be. The buzzer
rings and Lilli dives into her
hankerchief, apparently in tears.

CUT TO:

kb D-40   DAVE AS THE BOY
            COMES INTO THE PICTURE..

                              THE BOY (angrily)
                                  That isn't a fair test.
                                  You get her all excited by
                                  talking about Boery and
                                  Gable and...and...Karloff
                                  and then you expect her to
                                  sing something that even a
                                  trained soprano is apt to
                                  go wrong on.
            CUT TO:

D-41   CLOSE SHOT...LILLI

        With laughing eyes she
        peeks over the handkerchief,
        then falls back into it.

        CUT TO:

D-42   THE BOY AND DAVE

                              THE BOY (furiously)
                                  Look what you've done to her.
                                  You've made her a nervous
                                  wreck. You and your
                                  Garbos and your Chaplins
                                  and your....
        CUT TO:

D-43   CLOSE SHOT...LILLI

        With an effort she looks
        up from the handkerchief
        and snuffles.
                              LILLI   (tearfully)
                                  Shall I...
                                     (she swallows a tear)
                                  ....do now the other side?
        CUT TO:

D-44   DAVE...

                              DAVE   (as politely as
                                          possible)
                                  I think one side is enough...
                                  Thanks a lot, folks.
        He starts out of the
        room.

        CUT TO:

D-45   FULL SHOT THE ROOM

                              THE BOY
                                  Don't you want to take it
                                  with you?
        He takes the record
        from the machine.

        (CONTINUED)

kb D-45 (CONTINUED)

THE BOY
    Some of tho notes woro
    vory....

DAVE   (magnanimously)
    Vory high...yes, sir.

He takes the record
without pleasure.

LILLI   (looking up)
    And loud;

DAVE
    Yos, ma'am,...your worst
    ononiy can't say you don't
    sing loud;

He forces a toothy
smile.

    Good night, folks...and
    thanks a million.

Ho exits; The boy
crosses to Lilli and
looks at hor with an
oxpression full of
compassion. Sho takes
one look at his face, then
throws hor arms around his
neck and buries hor head
against his chest;

THE BOY   (patting her on the
           back)
    Thoro, thore, thore...
    you'll got another chance;

CUT TO:

D-46   CLOSE SHOT...LILLI...

    She rolls one oyo up at
    hin, then closos it and
    shakes with laughter;

    FADE OUT
    FADE IN:

D-47   CLOSE SHOT...LILLI'S
        CHAUFFEUR SLEEPING..

    He is snoring gently; Prosently
    one seems to catch inside of
    him. He comes to with a start,
    looks at his watch, then looks
    up at something;

    CUT TO:

D-48   THE MARQUEE OF A MOVING PICTURE
        THEATRE..

    On it we read: "THREE FEATURES.
    ONE NIGHT OF LOVE. ONE HEAVENLY
    NIGHT. IT HAPPENED ONE NIGHT.
    ADMISSION 10¢. CHILDREN FREE."
    THE CAMERA ANGLES DOWN. On
    the sidewalk below we see a
    smaller sign reading: "NEXT
    WEEK: THE NIGHT WAS MADE FOR LOVE.   (CONTINUED)
    NIGHT AFTER NIGHT. WHAT A NIGHT!

kb D-48 (CONTINUED)

ALSO NEWSREEL. TIMELY
EVENTS. SUITABLE SHORTS
AND COLOR CARTOON. LADIES
FREE ON SATURDAY NIGHT. WATCH
THE NEWSPAPERS FOR 104-PIECE
FREE CROCKERY COMPETITION".
As some customers pass out,

CUT TO:

D-49 LILLI'S CHAUFFEUR

He sits upright and ready
for action.

CUT TO:

D-50 LILLI AND THE BOY COMING
OUT OF THE MOVIE PALACE..

Lilli puts her hand to her
forehead and shakes her head:

                    LILLI
                         Phew! It make you dizzy.

                    THE BOY
                         It isn't so bad when you
                         get used to it.

                    LILLI
                         I don't know who married
                         who---or why. I think I
                         go home now.

                    THE BOY
                         All right. Where do you
                         live?

                    LILLI
                         Uh...

She stops and frowns
slightly.

Out of the corner of   I have a room some place.
her eye she sees her
automobile.

                    THE BOY
                         Yes, but where?

                    LILLI
                         Oh, where?...You want to
                         kno where?

                    THE BOY (gently)
                         I don't see how I can take
                         you home if I don't.

                    LILLI
                         Oh, you don't take me home.
                         I get home very easy.

                    THE BOY
(CONTINUED)   How?

70

LILLI
    Oh I uh... I walk.

BOY
    You don't think I'm going to
    let you walk home alone, do you?

LILLI
    Oh, yes. I like to walk. It is
    very healthy and... and...I
    like it and you look very tired.
    so if you will just leave me
    here I will be all right and...
    and... Good night and thank
    you very much for a lovely
    evening.

THE BOY
    You know I'm not going to let
    you go home alone so you might
    as well tell me where you live.

LILLI   (with a trace of crossness)
    I don't remember.

THE BOY   (stupefied)
    You don't remember?

LILLI
    I forget.

THE BOY
    Then how're you going to get
    home?

LILLI   (crossly)
    I find it.

THE BOY
    How?

LILLI   (furiously)
    I walk.

THE BOY
    All right, we'll walk together.
    Where is it?

LILLI   (pointing vaguely)
    That way.

He looks puzzled.

THE BOY
    Are you sure?

LILLI
    Yes.

THE BOY
    All right, come on.

Lilli gives him a dirty
look, then starts out
of the picture very
fast. He goes with
her.

CUT TO:

D 51   LILLI'S CHAUFFEUR
        STANDING UP IN THE CAR

        He looks after the couple
        indignantly, then takes
        out his watch, looks more
        indignant still, and sits
        down and starts his motor.

        CUT TO:

D-52   THE FEET OF LILLI AND
        THE BOY

        They are walking very fast.

        DISSOLVE TO:

D-53   THE FEET OF LILLI AND THE BOY

        They are walking quite a lot
        slower. THE CAMERA ANGLES UP
        to their faces. The houses
        behind them are very poor.

                THE BOY
                  Are you sure it was this way?

                LILLI   (stubbornly)
                  Yes.

        He looks at her, then
        scowls ahead. They pass
        a ▬▬▬ pool parlor.

        CUT TO:

D-54   CLOSE MOVING SHOT AHEAD
        OF LILLI AND THE BOY

        We hear a raucous ▬▬▬ laugh.
        The boy takes a quick look at
        her, then looks ahead. Lilli
        steals a look at him, then also
        looks ahead.

        CUT TO:

D-55   LILLI'S CHAUFFEUR SCRUNCHED
        UP IN HIS SEAT WITH FEAR

        He looks around at the
        unsavoury neighborhood.

        DISSOLVE TO:

D-56   THE FEET OF LILLI AND THE BOY

        They are dragging along. Lilli
        stumbles once. THE CAMERA ANGLES
        UP and we see them looking very
        desperate. She hangs onto his
        arm for support.

                THE BOY   (persuasively)
                  You've got to live someplace.

                LILLI
                  Yes. I think we are coming...

        (CONTINUED)

72

D-56   CONTINUED

    Suddenly she sees
    something across the
    street. She points.

                LILLI   (continued)
                   I live there.

                THE BOY   (looking across the street)
                   Good.
    CUT TO:

D 57   LONG SHOT..A PRETTY LITTLE
       COLONIAL BUILDING FROM
       ACROSS THE STREET

    In the foreground we see the
    boy and Lilli starting across
    the street toward it.

    CUT TO:

D-58   LILLI AND THE BOY WALKING
       TOWARD US

    Suddenly he stops.

                THE BOY
                 But that's a... business...
                 establishment.

                LILLI   (desperately)
                 Yes...all right...my uncle
                 is in business.
    They start forward.

                 My uncle...he married my aunt.

    She gives him a look.

                 Shouldn't he?

                THE BOY
                 Oh, sure.
    CUT TO:

D-59   THE STEPS OF THE PRETTY
       LITTLE COLONIAL BUILDING

    Lilli and the boy come
    into the picture.

                LILLI
                 Now I am safe. Good night.
                 Thank you for everything and
                 a lovely walk.

                THE BOY
                 I enjoyed it.

                LILLI
                 Good. Good night.

                THE BOY
                 Are you working at the studio
                 tomorrow?

                LILLI
                 I think so, yes. I see you
                 then, hunh? Thank you very
                 much. Good night.

(CONTINUED)

                                              THE BOY
                                                    Good night.

                                              LILLI
                                                   Well?

                                              THE BOY
                                                   Aren't you going in?

                                              LILLI
                                                   Oh yes. Good night.

                                              THE BOY
                                                   Good night.

          She enters and closes
          the door after her.

          CUT TO:

D-60   INT. OF THE COLONIAL
       BUILDING
       ──────────────────

          We see the street and the boy
          outside. Lilli comes toward us
          a few feet then turns and
          watches the boy. He disappears
          from the doorway but is seen
          at the window. She waves to
          him.

          CUT TO:

D-61   THE BOY ON THE SIDEWALK OUTSIDE
       ───────────────────────────────

          He waves at Lilli whom we see
          through the window. On the
          glass is painted: "J.P.Smiley,
          Mortician." He raises his hat
          and hurries away.

          CUT TO:

D-62   INTERIOR OF THE COLONIAL
       BUILDING
       ────────────────────────

          Lilli stands in a panel of
          light which shines on the floor.
          She is peeking in the direction
          the boy disappeared. Into the
          panel comes slowly a black
          shadow. Lilli takes a step
          forward on tiptoe.
                                       MR. SMILEY'S VOICE (lugubriously)
                                            What can I do for you, my
                                            child...

          Lilli spins around.

          CUT TO:

D-63   LILLI LOOKING UP AT A
       VERY TALL MAN IN BLACK
       ──────────────────────

          She is tense with fear.

          (CONTINUED)

                                74

D-63   CONTINUED

> MR. SMILEY   (soaping his hands)
> ...in this hour of trouble and
> tribulation?

Lilli screams piercingly
and runs for the door.

OUT TO:

D 64   INT. COLONIAL BUILDING..
REVERSE SHOT

Lilli runs out of the place
and across the sidewalk. Her
car rolls into view. She leaps
into it and slams the door.
The car drives away full
speed.

*   FADE OUT   *

(End of Sequence "D")

D-65   (PROTECTION SHOT)
CLOSE SHOT..MR. SMILEY
LOOKING THROUGH THE WINDOW

His head is cocked to one
side, his mouth hangs open
and he looks very much
puzzled. On the plate
glass we read: "J.P.SMILEY,
Mortician."

FADE-OUT.

FADE IN:

E-1   CLOSE SHOT..VLADIMIR
       VON STARK

He looks inspired as he
sings. THE CAMERA STARTS
TRUCKING BACK.

                              VLADIMIR (singing)
                                   The Danube so blue, tra la,
                                        la la
                                   The blue of the blue, tra la,
                                        la la
                                   Tra la la yoo hoo, yoo hoo tra
                                        la...

By now THE CAMERA shows
Mr. Apex and Jasper also.

                              JASPER
                                   That's a great lyric.

                              MR. APEX (impatiently)
                                   All right, all right, Vladimir.
                                   We know how it goes and I don't
                                   like it anyhow. What I like is
                                   The Road to Mandalay.

                              VLADIMIR
                                   Mandalay is a song for basses...
                                   double basses.

                              MR. APEX (crossly)
                                   For nineteen thousand a week
                                   she ought to be able to sing
                                   anything.

                              JASPER
                                   How about Dixie? That makes
                                   a nice number and it's got
                                   a flag finish.
                                        (he sings offkey)
                                   "I want to be in Dixie,
                                   hooray hooray..."

                              VLADIMIR (angrily)
                                   Vot's dot got to do with
                                   the story?

                              JASPER   (belligerently)
                                   What's the Blue Danube got
                                   to do with it?

                              MR. APEX (with force and dignity)
                                   If you please. I'll make the
                                   decisions around here. She
                                   sings The Blue.. Danube
                                   and that's that. Now what
                                   kind of a dance does she do?

                              JASPER   (with great decision)
                                   A fan dance.

                              MR. APEX
                                   What?

(CONTINUED)

76

E-1   CONTINUED

VLADIMIR (sourly)
He's only yoking... and it
ain't funny.

Mr. Apex has crossed to
the door and opened it a
crack.

MR. APEX
Come in here, Lawrence.

A stout gentleman appears.

THE DANCE DIRECTOR:
LAWRENCE
Harya, boys?

He is followed by a
thin piano player.

Come in, Ernie.

MR. APEX
Lawrence, we want a dance for
The Blue Danube. Something
classy.

VLADIMIR
Someting fentestic.

JASPER
But at the same time very
simple.

LAWRENCE
Urm hmm.

He hums a moment, and
nods his head in three-
four time, then announces
quietly:

I got you.

VLADIMIR (aggressively)
You got what?

LAWRENCE (mildly)
I got the dance.

MR. APEX
Like that?

LAWRENCE (indignantly)
Why certainly.

He does the time step.

Nothing to it.

VLADIMIR
You said it.

LILLI'S VOICE (cheerfully)
Good morning.

They turn as she sweeps
into the room.

(CONTINUED)

E-1   CONTINUED

ALL TOGETHER
         Good morning. Good
         morning. Good morning. How
         do you do.

LILLI   (cheerfully)
         How is the story?

JASPER   (sourly)
         Magnificent.

LILLI
         The little girl goes now to
         Hollywood with the moving
         picture producer?

JASPER
         No, she isn't going anywhere
         with the moving picture pro-
         ducer. And neither is he.

LILLI   (in dismay)
         Why not?

VLADIMIR
         He's dead.

JASPER
         And buried.

MR. APEX
         To tell you the truth, my
         dear, we've made a little
         change in the story... and
         all for the best...

JASPER
         We hope.

MR. APEX
         It now takes place...

VLADIMIR   (beaming at her)
         In Vienna!

LILLI   (astonished)
         In Vienna!

JASPER   (with false amiability)
         In Vienna.

LAWRENCE
         And I got a great number for
         you: in six-eight over the
         three-four, you see.

Lilli looks at him blankly.

MR. APEX
         This is Mr. Langsome, our
         dance director.

LILLI   (bowing and smiling)
         Oh.

LAWRENCE
         It's very simple. There's
         nothing to it. Give me a vamp,
         Ernie. You see, I put you all

(CONTINUED)

78

E-1   C)NTINUED

LAWRENCE (continued)
        in pantalettes against some
        glass trees...

VLADIMIR
        In a pig's nose.

LAWRENCE
        Don't pay no attention to him,
        he's always like that. And it
        starts like this. These are
        the girls.

He rat-tat-tats up the
length of the office.

        And this is where you come in.

LILLI
        Me?

LAWRENCE
        It's very simple. It just
        looks hard.

He does an unbelievable
step down the length of
the office.

        Then here's some chairs come
        out of the floor...

He leaps onto a chair and
continues his dance.

                (yelling to Mr.Apex)
        Ain't that novel?

MR. APEX
        Be careful of that chair -
        it's an antique!

LAWRENCE
        I'm as light as a feather.
        Hot it up, Ernie.

He leaps onto the floor
and narrowly misses
Vladimir's foot. He
spreads his arms and
begins to twirl.

        Right in here we do the over-
        head stuff.
                (he speaks to Lilli)
        See? The camera's up there
        and you look like spools re-
        volving on your axes, see,
        like a knitting mill. Then
        we go into the mirror stuff,
        you see ten of me, see, and...

CUT TO:

79

MR. APEX'S OUTER OFFICE

Several secretaries sit
at their desks. Through
the door we hear Ernie's
music and Lawrence's yelling. The boy comes into the
picture holding a sheet of
music. He speaks to the
secretary nearest the door:

                    THE BOY
            I've got some music for
            Miss Pogany....they sent
            me down.

                    THE SECRETARY
            Well, go on in... I think
            they're giving a dance in
            there.

She picks up a telephone.

                    (into phone)
            I don't know, he just
            doesn't answer, that's all.

The boy takes the door
knob and opens the door:

CUT TO:

E-3   LILLI WATCHING THE
       DANCE DIRECTOR...

Suddenly she looks toward
the doorway. She takes a
step backward.

CUT TO:

E-4   THE BOY STANDING IN
       THE DOORWAY...

He frowns in amazement
as his eyes follow some-
thing higher and higher.

CUT TO:

E-5   MR. APEX'S DESK

Mr. Apex is leaning back
in his seat as far as
possible. As the dance
director climaxes his
number on the desk-top.
His final step is the one
where, with the exception
of a supporting leg, the
whole body is horizontal
in the air. The arms are
outstretched as in flight
or for swimming. With re-
sounding thuds on the desk-
top, he shifts his weight
from one leg to the other
while leaping high in the
air. Mr. Apex makes grabs at
various articles on his desk   (CONTINUED)

and suddenly sticks
his finger in his mouth.

                                    MR. APEX   (yelling at the top
                                                of his lungs)
                                          That's enough!

                                    LAWRENCE
                                          What?

                                    MR. APEX   (at the top of his
                                                lungs)
                                          We know how it goes. Get
                                          off my desk!

Lawrence stops and
climbs down. He mops
himself with a handkerchief
and speaks breathlessly.

                                    LAWRENCE
                                          That's...only...a rough
                                          idea.

He mops the back of his
neck. Mr. Apex is
concerned only with the
things on his desk. He
shakes a fountain pen,
and examines it closely.

                                    MR. APEX   (furiously)
                                          I think it's terrible!
                                          (then suddenly to the
                                           other end of the room)
                                          What do YOU want?

CUT TO:

E-6   THE BOY

He speaks nervously.

                                    THE BOY   (indicating the sheet
                                               in his hand)
                                          I have some music for
                                          Miss Pogany.

CUT TO:

E-7   MR. APEX BEHIND HIS DESK

He is examining a watch.
                                    MR. APEX
                                          Well give it to her!

He puts the watch to
his ear.

                                          What kind of dancing is
                                          that?
                                              (then to the Boy)
                                          There she is over..

He points and looks
puzzled.

CUT TO:

E-8   THE EMPTY WINDOW EMBRASURE

Mr. Apex strides into it.
                                    MR. APEX
                                          What's going on around here?

Absentmindedly he puts
the watch to his ear.
CUT TO:

LAWRENCE
    She was here a minute ago.

JASPER
    She walked out on you.

VLADIMIR
    I don't blame her.

LAWRENCE (to Vladimir)
    You should talk.

VLADIMIR
    You should dance.

MR. APEX (furiously to the boy)
    What are you standing
    around for? What do you
    want?

THE BOY
    I have some music for
    Miss Pogany.

MR. APEX
    Well....give it to me. Here.

He sticks it in
Vladimir's hand.

THE BOY
    Thank you.

MR. APEX
    You're welcome, you're
    welcome. I'm very busy.

The boy exits.

LAWRENCE (lamely)
    Anyway, gentlemen, that's
    my conception of it.

JASPER
    We'll be careful not to use
    it.

MR APEX
    We'll take it up with
    Miss Pogany.

LILLI'S VOICE
    I don't like it.

They turn suddenly.

CUT TO:

E-10   SHOT OF THE ROOM INCLUDING
      THE WINDOW...

Lilli is coming out from
behind the window curtain.

LILLI (apologetically)
    Something break.
      (pointing to the desk)
    I don't like to dance on
    a bureau.

(CONTINUED)

LAWRENCE
It was just an idea.

VLADIMIR
My idea goes like this:
The young girl dances with
her aunt ~~in the background~~

JASPER
why does she dance with
her aunt?

MR APEX
Why don't she dance with a
young fellow?

LILLI   (smiling)
So is better.

VLADIMIR (yelling a little)
She is dancing with her
aunt in the background.

MR. APEX (with a trace of
           irritation)
Why should she be in the
background, she's the star?

LILLI   (approvingly)
Yes.

VLADIMIR (a little louder)
Her aunt is in the back-
ground...she's in front
dancing with a young
fellow.

MR APEX
Well why didn't you say so?

VLADIMIR (at the top of his
           lungs)
I did say so and anyway it
don't start there. It
starts in a cab with her
aunt where she's going to
her first dance...it's
very foggy.

JASPER   (sourly)
Why?

VLADIMIR (spreading his arms)
Because it's Vienna?

JASPER
It's in London they have
the fogs.

VLADIMIR (exasperated)
All right, make it London...
or make it snow...or make
it oatmeal, what do I care?
All I'm telling you is she's
in a cab with her aunt?

(CONTINUED)

83

MR. APEX
>It could be a sleigh..

VLADIMIR (at the top of his
>lungs)
>It could be a gyroscope!
>Whatever it is, she sits
>there with her aunt.

MR. APEX
>Why does it have to be her
>aunt? Why can't it be
>some nice young fellow in
>a uniform? Give it some
>class.

VLADIMIR (as loud as he can)
>Why don't you let me fin-
>ish? All I'm telling you
>is: SHE SITS IN SOMETHING
>SOMEPLACE WITH SOMEBODY!

DISSOLVE TO:

E-11--69
>THE BLUE DANUBE PRODUCTION
>NUMBER AS OUTLINED BY
>MR. STURGES.

F A D E   O U T

END OF SEQUENCE "E"

84

"SONG OF JOY"

SEQUENCE "F"

FADE IN:

PROJECTION ROOM SHOOTING
TOWARD THE SEATS... DARK

The beam from the projector
passes above our heads. The
lights come up and we see
Messrs. Apex, Jasper, Lawrence
and Vladimir looking at us very
solemnly. They are deep in
thought. After a moment Mr. Apex
speaks:

> MR. APEX
> It's too good for them.

> VLADIMIR (rising angrily)
> What do you mean it's too
> good for 'em? I got all my
> soul in dot number.

> MR. APEX
> That's what I mean.

> VLADIMIR
> Hunh?

> JASPER
> That's the trouble with it.

> VLADIMIR (furiously)
> Who ast you?

> MR. APEX
> Gentlemen, PLEASE!

> LAWRENCE
> What you shoulda had is you
> shoulda had a nifty soft-shoe
> in there.

> VLADIMIR
> And what you should have is
> you should have a shoe some-
> where and it shouldn't be
> soft it should be HARD!

> LAWRENCE (furiously)
> Who says so?

> MR. APEX
> GENTLEMEN! SILENCE! All I
> want to know is does it fit?
> If it fits we can always cut
> it out later. How about it?

> JASPER (jerking his thumb)
> Ask him. He wanted it in.

> VLADIMIR (majestically)
> YES, and I don't give no ex-
> planation. Art is its own
> explanation. All I do is put
> beauty IN. YOU can explain it
> out.

CONTINUED

F-1.   CONTINUED

>JASPER
>Einstein couldn't explain this
>picture.

>VLADIMIR
>What does he know?

DISSOLVE TO:

F-2   CLOSE SHOT...A KITCHENETTE
       TABLE

We see some lumps of steak,
a can of paprika, two large
red onions and an iron kettle.
Lilli's hands are peeling a
garlic. We hear her humming
to herself.

CUT TO:

F-3   THE BOY AT HIS WORK TABLE

A student's lamp is shining onto
a lot of music. He is copying
a song. Presently he looks up.

>THE BOY
>How is it coming?

CUT TO:

F-4   LILLI IN KITCHENETTE

We pick her up as she is
crossing to the stove with
the pot of goulash. She puts
it down and licks her fingers.

>LILLI
>Wonderful.

She smiles and goes
toward the door.

CUT TO:

F-5   THE BOY AT HIS WORK TABLE..
       LILLI COMING TOWARD HIM

>LILLI   (leaning over his shoulder)
>For that old Pogany?

>THE BOY
>No. Just something....
>   (he laughs nervously)
>...it's no good anyways..it's
>just.....

>LILLI   (impatiently)
>What is it?

>THE BOY
>It's for you.

>LILLI
>For me a song?

CONTINUED

F-5   CONTINUED

                                    THE BOY
                                        You'd hardly call it a song...
                                        it's just....

                                    LILLI   (delighted)
                                        Well, play me. I always want
                                        for somebody to write for me
                                        a song and now somebody do
                                        and he is afraid for to play.
                                            (She pushes him toward
                                             piano)
                                        Play me.

        CUT TO:

F-6   SHOT...THROUGH PIANO AT
        BOY WITH LILLI LEANING
        ON HIS SHOULDERS

                                    THE BOY
                                        It's no good...it's just...

                                    LILLI   (severely)
                                        All right. It is no good...
                                        it is rotten...it is stoopid...
                                        but you wrote it for me..so
                                        PLAY.

        The boy sings the verse
        and first chorus of FOR
        YOU ALONE.

                                    LILLI   (as he finishes)
                                        All for me?

                                    THE BOY
                                        All for you.

                                    LILLI
                                        You got your nerve to say me
                                        things like that.

                                    THE BOY   (hastily)
                                        Naturally in a song you sort
                                        of put things...you know...for
                                        the rhymes.

                                    LILLI   (very wisely)
                                        Ohhh...you don't mean it!

                                     THE BOY   (lamely)
                                        Of course I mean it. I
                                        didn't mean to say that. It's
                                        just a sort of.....

                                    LILLI   (laughing at him)
                                        Play me more.

        He laughs nervously and
        plays the second chorus
        of the song. As he sings she
        sings in harmony with him.
        When he finishes he looks
        away from her, then
        speaks with an effort.

        CONTINUED

                          THE BOY
                              Anyway...that ought to give
                              you some sort f idea anyway..
                              of how I f

                          LILLI   (solemn)
                              Are you proposing to me in
                              marriage?

                          THE BOY   (rising hastily)
                              Oh no. I was just...uh...just
                              sort of uh...uh....

                          LILLI   (accusingly but with
                                      laughing eyes)
                              What you propose then?

                          THE BOY   (indignantly)
                              Oh NO...I didn't mea...as far
                              as that...marriage would be
                              uh...naturally.. All I meant
                              was I wasn't...proposing
                              marriage.

                          LILLI
                              Why not?

                          THE BOY   (stupidly)
                              Why not?

                          LILLI
                              Yes, why not?

                          THE BOY   (beginning a long ex-
                                      planation)
                              Well you don't just...ask...
                              like that, do you?

                          LILLI
                              Why not? If you want some-
                              thing...you ask.

                          THE BOY   (stupidly)
                              You...you ask.

He steps near her.

                          LILLI
                              You ask and then...
                                  (she laughs)
                              I say no.

                          THE BOY
                              Naturally...

Suddenly he looks up
frowning.

                              Why?

                          LILLI
                              That, I cannot tell you. But
                              I will tell you something.

                          THE BOY
                              What?

                          LILLI
                              You are very sweet.

CONTINUED

                              88

He steps closer and she
puts her hands on his shoulders.
Slowly he leans down to her
and she kisses him. After a
second she puts her arms around
his neck and hugs him to her.

DISSOLVE TO:

F-7   A SHINY BOWL OF
        GOULASH

Lilli's hands come into
the picture, seize a ladle
and fork and scoop up some
goulash. The boy's hands
come into the picture with
a plate on which we see some
gravy and part of an onion.

        CUT TO:

F-8   LILLI AND THE BOY
        AT THE TABLE

                              THE BOY   (happily)
                                  I never knew goulash could
                                  be so good.

                              LILLI
                                  You flattering me.

                              THE BOY
                                  If...if...we were...I mean if
                                  you and I uh...got together
                                  I mean...we'd have goulash
                                  every night..if I was working.

He smiles lamely.

                              LILLI   (entering into the
                                          spirit of the thing)
                                  If you wasn't working, I
                                  could work.

                              THE BOY   (with a superior smile)
                                  Oh no.

                              LILLI   (gently)
                                  Why not? A woman is to
                                  help her...husband.

She smiles at him

                              THE BOY   (still superior)
                                  Not that way. She makes his
                                  home for him, takes care of
                                  the...the little...offspring
                                  and like that, but she doesn't
                                  .....
                                      (he makes a gesture of
                                        the hand)
                                  ...Not mine, anyway.

CONTINUED

F-8   CONTINUED

        LILLI   (critically)
            To be proud is very good,
            but you don't make the wife
            eat always only pota toes
            just because inside you feel..
            so masculine.

       THE BOY (with a trace of irri-
               tation)
            My wife doesn't have to
            eat only potatoes.

        LILLI
            I don't mean exactly potatoes.
            But why should you make a
            woman live in this room when
            maybe if she helped too you
            get two rooms.

       THE BOY   (coldy)
            Well, this isn't upstairs
            over...anyplace like you
            live.

        LILLI   (quickly)
            I move- ed.

       THE BOY
            I don't blame you. How
            about your uncle?

        LILLI
            I no speak to him no more.

       THE BOY
            Good.

        LILLI   (returning to subject)
            Suppose you marry an actress.
            You think she give up acting
            just because you feel so
            lord and master?

        THE BOY   (with conviction)
            An actress? I wouldn't
            marry an actress if she was
            the last thing to get married
            to.

        LILLI   (with false amiability)
            Oh ho.

        THE BOY   (apologetically)
            I don't mean you, Lilli. I
            don't consider you an actress.

        LILLI   (smiling angrily)
            You don't.

CONTINUED

                              THE BOY (gently)
                                 Not yet.

                                 LILLI   (furiously)
                                    Ah ha! Suppose you marry
                                    an opera singer?

                              THE BOY (with contempt)
                                 An opera singer! I'd just
                                 as soon be married to a
                                 hyena. An opera singer is
                                 the bottom of everything. I
                                 know too much about them.

                                 LILLI   (rising furiously)
                                    You know too much about them!
                                    You don't know nothing and
                                    YOU are the bottom of every-
                                    thing, you conceited, you.

She grabs her hat and
bag.
                                    And I cook dinner for you
                                    with my own hands!

                              THE BOY   (lamely)
                                 Well, I can't help it. I
                                 wouldn't be found dead with
                                 an opera singer.

                                 LILLI   (furiously)
                                    You wouldn't be found dead
                                    with an opera singer! Any
                                    opera singer found dead with
                                    you would be crazy! You
                                    hear me? Co-co!

She taps her head and
slams out of the room.
                              THE BOY   (thunderstruck)
                                 Aren't you...aren't you
                                 going to finish your
                                 goulash?

        DISSOLVE TO:

F-9   CLOSE SHOT...A GLITTERING
        BOMBITA TOLEDANA

        Held by a waiter on a silver
        platter. I am assured that
        this is a very showy dessert
        what with stuck-in fruits,
        whipped cream and fancy business.

        CUT TO:

F-10   LILLI AND THE WAITER

        She is in her living room
        in a sumptuous apartment hotel.
        She sneers at the bombita toledana.

        CUT TO:

                                    91

F-11   MR. MAGNOLIUS AND MME.
       SCHNORTZ

      We see them across the be-
      silvered and beflowered
      table. The bedamask is
      dazzling.

                       MAGNOLIUS (smiling ~~reproach~~
                           fully in some
                           language)
           Quetah.

                  MME. SCHNORTZ (in another lan-
                              guage severely)
           Apostok cunyadi yarosh?

      CUT TO:

F-12   LILLI AND THE BOMBITA
       TOLEDANA

                  LILLI   (exasperatedly)
                      Sn-yet!
      She throws her napkin on
      the table, rises and stamps
      out of the room.

      CUT TO:

F-13   LILLI'S BEDROOM

      This is very voluptuous
      and lacy. She enters
      angrily, grabs a male
      doll from the bed, throws
      it across the room, pauses
      at a bookcase, shortly ex-
      amines five books which she
      drops on the floor, one after
      the other, then flops herself
      on the bed. After a moment.

      CUT TO:

F-14   CLOSE SHOT..THE BOY WORKING
       AT HIS TABLE

      He sighs, throws down his pen
      and stamps over to the piano.
      THE CAMERA PANS with him. He
      seats himself, then, very angrily,
      bangs out the first four bars of
      his tune to Lilli.

      CUT TO:

F-15   LILLI ON HER BED

      Sneeringly she sings:

                  LILLI   (singing sneeringly)
                      This is not a love song in
                       the popular wein.
                      Da da da da you alone.
                      (she glares)

F-16   THE BOY AT THE PIANO   F-9

>He bangs out the next four
>bars.

CUT TO:

F-17   LILLI ON HER BED

                              LILLI
                         Da da da da da da da da DA
                              da da
                         Da da da da DEE da da
                         When you're around me, dear..

At this point the image
of the boy playing
FADES IN in DOUBLE
PRINTING over the SHOT
of Lilli. At the same
time his piano playing
FADES IN.

                         ...Then love has found me,
                         dear
                         Something surround me, dear
                         But you da da da dee da da da
                         Da da DA da.

Together they

                    FADE OUT

               End of Sequence "F"

                         93

FADE IN: OFFICE OF MR APEX

G-1   CLOSE SHOT..MR. APEX

Mr. Apex is very much the
big executive: severe and
unjust but at the same time
kindly.

                              MR. APEX
                                 That you don't do your work
                                 on time, I forgive. You're
                                 only human...so am I.
                                       (he smiles an executive
                                        smile))

       CUT TO:

G-2   CLOSE SHOT...THE BOY

His fingers work nervously.
Anxiously he smiles back.

       CUT TO:

G-3   MR. APEX

                              MR. APEX
                                 That you don't do your work
                                 on time because it's spring-
                                 time and you're writing
                                 love songs to extra girls I
                                 forgive...so am I.
                                       (he gives him a short
                                        smile)

       CUT TO:

G-4   THE BOY

He smiles back but with
more anxiety.

       CUT TO:

G-5   MR. APEX

                              MR. APEX   (smiling)
                                 But...I say BUT....

The smile drops off
his face like a wash-
rag.
                                 WHEN you sit down with my
                                 money and don't do your
                                 work on time to write love
                                 tunes to extra girls that
                                 are NON-COMMERCIAL....

He points to a piece of
music.
                                 ...and won't make a dime like
                                 it says here: "I'll never
                                 make a dime on it"....
                                       (he smiles wolfishly)

       (CONTINUED)

                              94

                                        MR. APEX (cont|d)
                                        Then I don t forgive...and
                                        you're fired.

        CUT TO:

G-6   two SHOT..MR. APEX AND
        THE BOY

        The boy leans over the desk
        angrily.

                                   THE BOY
                                        Where did you get that?
                                        That's mine..it's private.

                                   MR. APEX
                                        It was here between the un-
                                        finished work. Maybe the
                                        work was private too...that's
                                        why you didn't finish it.

                                   THE BOY
                                        That didn't have anything to...

                                   MR. APEX
                                        From now on you'll have more
                                        time for your amusements.
                                        Your business won't interfere
                                        with it.

                                   THE BOY
                                        That only took a couple of
                                        minutes.

                                   MR. APEX
                                        It was my minutes and anyway
                                        don't give me excuses. This
                                        is harder on me that it is on
                                        you...don't break my heart.

                                   THE BOY
                                        But Mr. Apex....

                                   MR. APEX
                                        You're fired. Now get out of
                                        here like a gentleman.

                                   THE BOY (furiously)
                                        You'll be very sorry for this
                                        some day...

                                   MR. APEX
                                        I'm sorry already...Close
                                        the door after you.

        The boy turns around and
        hurries out. Mr. Apex
        sneers after him.
                                        Non-commercial!

        CUT TO:

                                    95

G- 7   THE BOY'S OFFICE

He comes in disgustedly.
He takes a few personal
things from the drawers
and puts them in a pile
and begins to unhook his
diplomas. They are very
dusty, so he cleans them
off as he takes them down.
Presently, while cleaning
one with his handkerchief,
he stares across the areaway
toward Lilli's window. He
looks unhappy for a second
then frowns and rubs his
diploma vigorously. After
another second he looks unhappy again and goes nearer
the window. He looks, then
whistles a call. As there
is no answer he whistles
again. While whistling the
third time his face lights
up with hope.

CUT TO:

G-8   EXTERIOR LILLI'S WINDOW

It opens and Mme. Schnortz
sticks her head out and frowns.

                    MME. SCHNORTZ
                    HUnh?

CUT TO:

G-9   THE BOY IN HIS OFFICE

He pretends that he was
whistling a tune and changes
his call into a rather un-
pleasant melody.

CUT TO:

G-10   MME. SCHNORTZ IN THE WINDOW

She closes the window majestically.

CUT TO:

G-11   THE BOY

He opens his mouth to say
something, but the window is
already closed. He picks up
his belongings including the
diplomas, takes one last look
around and walks out slowly.

CUT TO:

G-12   CLOSE SHOT..VLADIMIR

He is arguing.

OUT TO:

VLADIMIR
   Yes, but I don't feel dot
   you feel it. Dis is love.
   Dis is yoy. Dis picture is
   called De SONG of JOY.

G-13   CLOSE SHOT...LILLI

She is dressed in a
charming costume of the
1870 period and looks
anything but joyful.

VLADIMIR'S VOICE
   Vot does yoy mean except
   happiness, vot does happiness mean except yoy?

LILLI   (resentfully)
   Why don't you leave me alone?
   You think I'm a child?

She taps her chest.

   I feel very happy. I am
   full of yoy. Now leave me
   alone.

CUT TO:

G-14   CLOSE SHOT..VLADIMIR

In the b.g. we see the camera
crew waiting.

VLADIMIR
   Den laugh!

Cut TO:

G-15   CLOSE SHOT..LILLI

She cackles at him.

CUT TO:

G-16   CLOSE SHOT. VLADIMIR

VLADIMIR
   Vot for of a laugh is dot?
   Smile a coupla times and
   SING...sing vit de heart,
   not only vit de teet.
         (he yells over his
          shoulder)
   Gimme some lights!. Gimme
   some music. Now once more,
   please.

We hear an orchestra
begin to play.

         SOUND: ORchestra
                playing.

VLADIMIR
   And wit wollum..wit woice..
   wit werve.

CUT TO:

97

                              LILLI
                                Maybe you like to sing it
                                yourself?

                              VLADIMIR
                                Maybe you tink I couldn't.

                              LILLI
                                Why don't you leave me alone?
                                I sing but I don't sing
                                how you tink, I sing how me
                                I feel.

                              VLADIMIR
                                All right...but try to feel
                                good for a coupla minutes.

                              LILLI
                                How can I when you stare me
                                in the face all the time?

                              VLADIMIR
                                Maybe I should climb into
                                the camera perhaps?

                              LILLI
                                Behind it is good enough.

Vladimir throws his
hands in the air and
stamps off left. Lilli
turns and walks off
right.

CUT TO:

G-18   THE CAMERA AND THE CAMERA
        CREW

Vladimir comes into the picture.

                              VLADIMIR
                                Okay, roll 'em.
He flops into his director's
chair. The music grows loud.

CUT TO:

G-19   AN OLD-FASHIONED GARDEN SET

Lilli walks in swinging her
hat. Very beautifully she
sings the song: MY LOVE.

CUT TO:

G-20   A BALCONY OUTSIDE THE
        SECOND-FLOOR EXTRA DRESSING
        ROOMS

The boy is talking to a girl
inside the screen door.

                            THE BOY
                              It has to be around here
                              somewhere, because from wher'
                              I am, used to be..it was
(CONTINUED)   just across the way.

G-20   (CONTINUED)

                                        THE GIRL
                                          What was it again?

                                        THE BOY
                                          Lilli Bushmiller. Bushmiller.
                                          A bush in front of a miller.

The girl shakes her head.
Suddenly she looks up
brightly.

                                        THE GIRL
                                          You don't mean Lilli Burn-
                                          dorfer. Oh no, her name was
                                          Gertrude.

                                        THE BOY
                                          Are there any more dressing
                                          rooms down this way?

                                        THE GIRL
                                          Oh no, only Miss Pogany and
                                          people like that.

The boy turns and starts for
the stairs which we see
nearby.

   CUT TO:

G-21   THE BOTTOM OF THE STAIRS

   Lilli comes into the picture
   and starts to climb up. She
   looks unhappy.

   CUT TO:

G-22   THE SECOND FLOOR LANDING

   The boy comes into the picture,
   goes down a step, then pauses
   and looks up toward the third
   floor. Not wishing to overlook
   anything, he turns around and
   climbs slowly toward the third
   floor. As he passes out of the
   picture Lilli appears from below, reaches the second landing
   and walks past us. Mme. Schnortz's
   head appears, puffing.

   CUT TO:

G-23   INT. LILLI'S DRESSING ROOM

   She walks in slowly and closes
   the door on Mme. Schnortz seen
   in the b.g. with make-up box.
   Lilli goes to the mirror and
   touches up her make-up. She
   pauses and looks through the
   window curtains, then crosses
   to the window, lifts the curtain a little and peeks.

   CUT TO:

G-24   THE BOY'S WINDOW

We see only the back of
somebody working at the
desk.

CUT TO:

G-25   LILLI'S WINDOW FROM OUTSIDE

She opens it slowly, looks out,
smiles, then whistles a call.

CUT TO:

G-26   THE BOY'S WINDOW

The back comes to life and
a frightful-looking young
man sticks his head out of
the window.

                              THE YOUNG MAN
                                   You paging me, Toots?

CUT TO:

G-27   CLOSE SHOT..LILLI IN HER
WINDOW

                         LILLI   (in dismay)
                              Where is...where is who be-
                              long there?

CUT TO:

G-28   THE FRIGHTFUL-LOOKING YOUNG
MAN

                         THE YOUNG MAN   (happily)
                              Oh, he doesn't work here
                              any more. He's gone. I
                              work here now.
                                   (he gives her the eye)
                              What're you doing for dinner?

CUT TO:

G-29   LILLI IN HER WINDOW

                         LILLI   (furiously)
                              You....

She slams her window so
hard, a pane of glass
flies out.

CUT TO:

G-30   THE BOY WALKING ON A
STUDIO STREET

The glass crashes just behind him and he turns to
look at it. He looks up
once, then walks away.

DISSOLVE TO:

G-31 EXT. THE EXTRA GATE

Loads of pretty girls are
coming out and the boy
stands in the f.g. looking
at each one. The studio
policeman touches him on
the shoulder.

THE POLICEMAN
What do you think you're
doing?

THE BOY (nervously)
I'm just looking for a friend.

THE POLICEMAN
Well, just..look out how you
look.

He plants himself beside
him.

CUT TO:

G-32 CLOSE SHOT..LILLI'S CHAUFFEUR

He is eating a hot dog. As
he sees somebody coming, he
sticks the remaining half of
it into his mouth and tries to
look dignified. Lilli hurries
into the picture .

LILLI
You know where I have dinner
last night?

THE CHAUFFEUR (through the hot
dog)
Last night?
(this is unintelligible)

LILLI
What?

With a tremendous effort
the chauffeur swallows
what he has in his mouth
and nearly strangles.

THE CHAUFFEUR (in a very small
voice)
No.

LILLI (indignantly)
Didn't you follow me?

THE CHAUFFEUR
I had a flat tire.

LILLI
Well..find it: it was,...
something Court ,

THE CHAUFFEUR (dismally)
Something Court?

LILLI
Yes..that I remember.

CUT TO:

101

G-33   EXT. EXTRA GATE

                    The pretty girls continue
                    to come out as the boy
                    and the policeman watch.
                    The studio chief of police
                    comes up behind the policeman
                    and taps him on the shoulder.

                                        THE CHIEF OF POLICE (severely)
                                            What do you think you're
                                            doing?

                                        THE POLICEMAN (pointing to the
                                                        boy)
                                            Oh I was just..he was
                                            looking uh...

                    As the boy watches the two
                    policemen Lilli's car comes
                    out the studio gate and
                    passes three feet behind him.
                    She is, unfortunately, giving
                    the chauffeur instructions, and
                    does not see the boy.

                                        THE CHIEF OF POLICE
                                            (to the policeman)
                                            Just remember you're married,
                                            that's all.

                    DISSOLVE TO:

G-34   CLOSE SHOT..THE VESTIBULE
        OF A CHEAP APARTMENT HOUSE

                    By the light of a match the
                    chauffeur is reading the names
                    on the brass plates. He comes
                    to the end, throws away the
                    match and walks out.

                    CUT TO:

G-35   INT. LILLI'S LIMOUSINE NIGHT

                    The door hangs open.
                                        THE CHAUFFEUR
                                            No, ma'am.

                                        LILLI   (lighting a match)
                                            But he must be some place.
                    She brings the match near
                    the open telephone book on
                    her lap.
                                            Something Court.

                                        THE CHAUFFEUR
                                            How many more courts are
                                            there?

                                        LILLI   (DISgustedly)
                                            Millions and millions.
                                            Everything is called Court.
                                            It would take years.
                    The book slides off
                    her knees.

                    DISSOLVE TO:

G-36 <u>CLOSE SHOT..THE BOY</u> AT THE FUNERAL PARLOR

                  THE BOY
                    I know she moved..but where?

    CUT TO:

G-37   <u>MR. SMILEY</u>

                  **MR. SMILEY (amiably, as he soaps
                       his hands)**
                    To Australia.

    CUT TO:

G-38   <u>TWO SHOT..THE BOY AND
       MR. SMILEY</u>

                  THE BOY
                    To Australia! When?

                  MR. SMILEY (placidly)
                    In 1910 when she married
                    that sheep raiser..but
                    that's no business...he got
                    out of it.

                  THE BOY (happily)
                    That isn't the niece I mean.
                    You must have another niece..
                    Lilli?

                  MR. SMILEY (pulling his eyebrows)
                    Lilli?

                  THE BOY
                    Yes, Lilli.

                  MR. SMILEY (having his little
                       joke)
                    No Lilli..you don't mean
                    lilies?

                  THE BOY
                    But she had a room up-
                    stairs.

                  MR. SMILEY
                    Somebody's playing jokes on
                    you. You know: like call up
                    the aquarium and ask for
                    Mr. Fish?

                  THE BOY (thunderstruck)
                    You think so?

                  MR. SMILEY (confidentially)
                    Sure, they do it all the
                    time.

                  THE BOY (desperately)
                    But I saw her come in here?

                  MR. SMILEY (after a pause)
                    Did you see her come out?

  (CONTINUED)

G-38   (CONTINUED)

The boy backs away,

                              THE BOY
                                  I guess,..I'm sorry to have
                                  troubled you,

                              MR. SMILEY
                                  It's a pleasure. Come in
                                  any time for a chat,

                              THE BOY   (backing away)
                                  Thanks..you bet...I will,

He turns and hurries out.

                         FADE OUT

                  End of Sequence "G"

SEQUENCE "H"

FADE IN:

H-1   THE PIANO END OF
MR. APEX'S OFFICE

**Ernie is at the piano,
the dance director lingers**
in the background, and
around the instrument we see
Lilli, Mr. Apex, Vladimir
and Jasper each holding a
song manuscript, each reading
from it solemnly. After a
moment's silence Mr. Apex
puts his in front of Ernie.
Ernie plays and Mr. Apex
sings without conviction.

          APEX (singing)
          Mandy
          Mandy
          The sun shines up
          The sun shines down...

The other three give
him a look, and his
voice trails off. He
takes the song off the
piano and throws it on
a chair.

         JASPER
         Here's a little jewel.

In a cracked voice without
accompaniment he sings:

          (singing)
         On the sea of life
         We'll build a ship just
          right for two
         A little rendezvous
         Where we can parlez-vous.

         Each wave will seem to say:
         Take your pleasure while
          you may
         Because...

         LILLI
         It make you a little sea-
         sick, yes?

         JASPER
         More than a little, my
         child.

         VLADIMIR (more to himself)
          (singing)
         I'm dancing with you in my
          dreams
         And it seems
         That my schemes
         Were all beams from the moon
          up above
         That witnessed our love.

         JASPER
         And so on.

         (CONTINUED)

MR. APEX (to Jasper)
Thero's no use being too
critical. You've got to
sing about something and
we need a **lift** in this
picture.

VLADIMIR
Some life.

JASPER
Plenty of life.

LAWRENCE
Something with some taps
in it.

VLADIMIR
Who let you in?

MR. APEX
Gentlemen, that isn't
getting us anywhere.

LILLI
I could sing from Rigoletto.

MR. APEX
I was thinking of something
more...American.

LILLI
Oh.

VLADIMIR (enthusiastically)
Don't move. It's here.

MR. APEX
Something **light.**

VLADIMIR (silencing him with a
          gesture)
The New World Symphony:
          (he immediately begins
          to sing)
Goin' home, goin' home,
tra la la la la.
Tra la la, tra la la,
I'm just tra la la."

MR. APEX
Nothing like that at all.

VLADIMIR
That's light.

JASPER
Like pig iron.

Mr. Apex slaps the
music on the piano,
then turns to Lilli.

MR. APEX
Can **you** suggest anything,
Miss Pogany?

LILLI
I'm not, how you say, I am
not enough familiar...YES.
          (CONTINUED)

106

JASPER   (happily)
        Well, for heaven's sake!

MR. APEX   (happily)
        What's it called?

LILLI
        I forgot what he call it.

MR. APEX
        Well what's it about?

LILLI
        I don't exactly remember.

MR. APEX   (nonplussed)
        Well uh...

LILLI
        It's about love.

MR. APEX · (relieved)
        Fine, fine, just what we're
        looking for. Something
        commercial with a little tug
        in it. Who wrote it?

LILLI
        A young man called ....
        ....

MR. APEX   (repeating)
        ....
                (he repeats it again)
        ....
        Wait a minute. I know that
        name. Why certainly.
        That's the fellow I fired.

LILLI   (icily)
        Oh, you fire him.

MR. APEX
        I should say I did. He was
        fooling away my time with a...
        a thing...wait a minute.

He crosses to his desk,
rummages in the papers
and produces the boy's
song.

        Wait'll you hear this.
                (reading sneeringly)
        "Mine is not a song for sale
        It's just a non-commercial
           wail
        A low-falutin' lyric to your
           eyes

        And though I've spent some
           time on it...my time..
        I'll never make a dime on it..
        I hope to tell you he won't...
        So here it is: a love note
           in disguise."

LILLI   (coldly)
        That is the song I sing.
                (CONTINUED)

107

MR. APEX   (woofling)
　　Wh-w-wha-What do you mean
　　that's the song you sing?

LILLI
　　That is what I mean.

MR. APEX
　　B-bu-but we can't put a
　　thing like that in a picture.
　　Explain to her, Jasper.

JASPER
　　Don't drag me in.

MR. APEX
　　But that isn't a song at all,
　　it's a..a..a..it insults
　　everybody and here it says...

He points.

　　"If they don't like it, the
　　heck with 'em." You can't
　　use profanity in songs..OR
　　in pictures.

LILLI   (quietly)
　　That is the song I sing.

MR. APEX   (repeating as one
　　　　　mesmerized)
　　That is the song you sing.

JASPER   (amiably)
　　That is the song she sings.

VLADIMIR   (at the top of his
　　　　　lungs)
　　SO SHE SINGS IT!

He turns his back to
Lilli and speaks with
gestures.

　　We can always....

With his fingers he
simulates scissors, cutting
and with both hands does a
throw-away gesture.

MR. APEX   (as to a child or
　　　　　lunatic)
　　Why, certainly. Of course you
　　sing it, my dear. That's
　　probably a very nice song..
　　in its way.

LILLI
　　No. It is rotten...but I
　　like it.

She smiles at them.

　　You tell me when, yes?

She exits. Ernie reaches
for the song and with one
hand picks it out unenthusiastically.
Mr. Apex clutches his head.

　　　　　　　(CONTINUED)

108

H-1   (CONTINUED 4)

                              LAWRENCE (mildly)
                                  You could do great taps to
                                  that.

                              VLADIMIR (pleadingly to Mr. Apex)
                                  Why do you let dis individual
                                  poison my life.
      DISSOLVE TO:

H-2   A FAT WOMAN IN FRONT OF
      A MICROPHONE — ON SOUND STAGE AT APEX STUDIO
                              THE FAT WOMAN
                                  ....something now.
      She consults a paper
                                  We call it a preview, but
                                  it's really a pre-hearing
                                  of a number from the new
                                  Apex film "Song of...
                                      (she turns to the
                                      second sheet of her
                                      notes)
                                  Joy."
      CUT TO:

H-3   MR. APEX, JASPER AND THE
      PUBLICITY MAN AROUND THE
      RADIO IN MR. APEX'S OFFICE
                              THE FAT WOMAN'S VOICE
                                  They're all on the stage,
                                  ready, and as they make it
                                  we give it to you. I see
                                  the maestro raising his
                                  baton...take it away,
                                  Eddie....

                              MR. APEX
                                  And take it far away.
      He swings on the publicity
      man.
                                  Why did you have to pick
                                  this piece of cheese to...

      From the radio comes
      the overture music.   SOUND: Radio--overture
                                              music.

                              PUBLICITY MAN
                                  But Mr. Apex, this is a
                                  new gag.

                              MR. APEX
                                  It gags me all right.

                              JASPER   (reaching for the
                                              dial)
                                  Say, the cubs are playing
                                  the..
      He twists the dial as
      we

      CUT TO:

FADE IN:
LILLI'S HANDS HOLDING A
DESK-TYPE TELEPHONE

Over this we hear the overture music quite strongly.
The receiver is lifted out of
the picture.

CUT TO:

H-5   LILLI SITTING AT A GRAND PIANO

She is dressed as a young man
and wears a blond wig.

                    LILLI   (into telephone)
                    Hello. Is that you?

CUT TO:

H-6   NINETY-DEGREE MIRROR SHOT..
       LILLI IN A BEAUTIFUL NEGLIGEE

She sits on a satin pouf and
holds a lacquered telephone in
her hand.

                    LILLI   (into telephone)
                    Yes, darling, who is it?

CUT TO:

H-7   LILLI AS A BOY AT THE
       PIANO

                    LILLI
                    It's me...and I have a
                    message for you.

CUT TO:

H-8   LILLI IN THE NINETY-DEGREE
       MIRRORS

She lies back on the pouf
langorously.

                    LILLI
                    From who you have a message?

She arranges her back
hair.

CUT TO:

H-9   LILLI AS A BOY AT THE PIANO

                    LILLI
                    From me.

Holding the telephone
with the left hand she
strikes a chord with the
right and sings.

                              (CONTINUED)

110

H-9   (CONTINUED)

LILLI   (singing FOR YOU ALONE)
"This is just to tell you
that I love you
And the spell you've wound
around my heart
Is driving me insane.
This is not a love song in
the popular vein
'Cause it's meant for you
alone.
I don't give a hang..."

CUT TO:

H-10   THE FEMALE LILLE SMILING

Over the phone we hear the
other Lilli singing:

THE OTHER LILLI'S VOICE
"If little girls don't
learn to bang
It out on cheap pianos for
their mamma's joy.

Lilli smiles as she
listens.

CUT TO:

H-11   LILLI AS A BOY AT THE
PIANO

LILLI
"This is not a love song for
the great hoi polloi
'Cause it's meant for you
alone.
When you're around me, dear...'

As she sings she rises
and starts across the
screen.

CUT TO:

H-12   THE FEMININE LILLI IN
HER ROOM

She sings.

LILLI
"Then love has found me,
dear..."

As she sings: she crosses
the screen in the opposite
direction from the masculine
Lilli.

CUT TO:

H-13   MED. LONG SHOT...A SMALL
CIRCULAR STAGE

It is two feet above the ground
level and about fourteen feet
in diameter. It is divided in
the middle by a wall on one side
of which we see the masculine Lilli
with her piano and on the other side
the feminine Lilli and her voudoir.

CONTINUED

111

They are walking toward
the partition and we hear
them sing in harmony: THE TWO LILLIS (in harmony)
                             "Pink dreams surround me,
                                 dear
                             But the words won't come
                             You strike me dumb
                             So I'm humming...

They lean their backs
against the partition.

CUT TO:

H-14   CLOSE SHOT..THE TWO LILLIS
        WITH THEIR BACKS TO EACH OTHER
        LEANING AGAINST THE PARTITION

The masculine Lilli sings and
the feminine Lilli sings
obligato.
                             THE TWO LILLIS
                             "Something strictly personal
                             I wrote the tune, the
                                 verse'n' all
                             To pacify the maelstrom in
                                 my heart
                             This is just to tell you
                                 that I fell from the start
                             Fell for you and you alone."

THE CAMERA DRAWS BACK
rapidly, the little
circular stage revolves
and brings into view a
full jazz band. If this
is a well-known band, all
the better.

CUT TO:

H-15   CLOSE SHOT..THE LEADER

As his music blares out

CUT TO:

H-16   A CHEAP RADIO NEXT TO A COFFEE URN — DINER IN HOLLYWOOD

The music diminishes in volume.
A counter man in white comes into
the picture.

                    THE BOY'S VOICE
                        Coffee.

                    THE COUNTER MAN
                        Coming up.

As he goes to the urn with
a cup

CUT TO:

H-17   THE BOY ACROSS THE COUNTER

    He looks disconsolate. He slaps
a newspaper on the counter and
starts to read. The music comes
through very gaily, the counter
man puts the coffee in front of
him and the boy puts some sugar
in it. As he stirs it, he looks
**vaguely up at the radio once, then
picks up his coffee cup. As he is**
about to drink it, he lowers it a
few inches and frowns at the radio,
then puts the cup back to his lips.
He starts to swallow, then nearly
strangles as his melody comes
through clearly. He slams the cup
down on the counter and wipes the
coffee off his chin.

                THE BOY   (nearly speechless)
                  The dirty...the dirty
                  crooks !

    He goes out of the place at
a run.

    CUT TO:

H-18   THE COUNTER MAN

               THE COUNTER MAN
                 Hey, how about that...

    The music from the radio
becomes louder. He puts
his hands on the counter
and looks disgusted.

    CUT TO:

H-19   SHOT INTO TWO MIRRORS
        FACING EACH OTHER

    Photographed through one
clear spot this will look
like a long corridor. Lilli
dressed as a boy steps forward
and we see a hundred of her.
She sings:

               LILLI   (singing)
               "Mine is not a song for sale
               It's just a non-commercial
                  wail
               A low-falutin' lyric to
                  your eyes...

    CUT TO:

H-20   MR. APEX, the PUBLICITY MAN
        AND JASPER AROUND MR. APEX'S
        RADIO

    The publicity man has his hand
on the knob. Mr. Apex slaps his
thigh, apparently at the word:
"non-commercial". Through the

                         (CONTINUED)

radio we hear:

                              VOICE OF LILLI (singing)
                                "And though I've spent some
                                  time on it
                                I'll never make a dime on
                                  it...

                              MR. APEX
                                Hoar, hoar.

CUT TO:

H-21   SHOT INTO TWO MIRRORS
       FACING EACH OTHER

       Lilli as a boy has her
       back to us and the back
       is reflected all down the
       corridor. (I think this
       is possible). Into the
       picture steps the other
       Lilli in a lovely gown.

                              LILLI THE BOY (singing)
                                "So here it is: a love note
                                  in disguise.

CUT TO:

H-22   CRANE SHOT..CLOSE ON
       LILLI

       She stands on a circular
       platform thirty inches in
       diameter and five feet high
       which stands on an eight-foot
       circular platform three feet
       high and resting on the original
       fourteen-foot platform we saw in
       Scene H-13. The small platform
       does not revolve but the others
       do, As Lilli sings, the crane
       moves back and we see first four
       couples dancing around her little
       platform in an exaggerated collegiate
       manner.

                              LILLI   (singing)
                                "If my rhythm doesn't fit
                                  collegiate feet, the heck
                                  with it
                                The matter is indifferent to
                                  me.
                                They don't have to shake their
                                  feet to my melody
                                'Cause it's meant for you
                                  alone.
       By now the CRANE has brought
       into view the next level down.
       On this we see an assortment
       of plumbers with their tools
       and their helpers. Blow-torches
       roar, wrenches wrench and hammers
       clang as they work on an assortment
       of plumbing fixtures.

                              CONTINUED

114

                                         LILLI   (singing)
                                            "This is not a number written
                                            so the tired plumber can
                                            remember it and whistle it
                                            at noon.

                                         He can go and wipe his pipes
                                             to some other tune
                                         Mine is meant for you alone.

                    THE CRANE brings into view
                    now the bottom part of the
                    last platform and we see
                    that it is surrounded by toy
                    pianos two feet high. At
                    each piano sits a little girl
                    making tinkling music.

                    CUT TO:

H-23   MED..CLOSE SHOT..UP AT A
       CAMERA ON A CRANE...

                    On a little seat we see
                    Vladimir waving his arms
                    violently. The music of
                    the jazz band blares forth.

                    CUT TO:

H-24   A SERIES OF MONTAGE EFFECTS

                    The music is very hot and we
                    see short flashes of: a little
                    girl dancing on top of a
                    piano...a line of collegians
                    doing a fantastic stop,..Lilli
                    singing with her head thrown
                    way back...a chorus of plumbers
                    dancing like elephants...the
                    hands of a pianist playing
                    very hot music...a mother in
                    pince-nez and old-fashioned
                    blouse beating time for a
                    little girl at an old-fashioned
                    upright piano...the legs of
                     Lilli, presumably, doing a
                    remarkable step.

                    CUT TO:

H-25   MED.CLOSE...LILLI AS A BOY
       SURROUNDED BY A GROUP OF VERY
       STOOGEY-LOOKING CROONERS...

                    They look very refined as they
                    hum with her.
                                         LILLI   (singing)
                                            "This is not a crooner's
                                            croon
                                            It's what you'd call a pri-
                                            vate tune...
                    CUT TO:

                                  115

CLOSE SHOT...LILLI AS A
GIRL SITTING IN HER BOUDOIR

    She is listening at the tel-
    ephone as we hear:

                  LILLI'S VOICE (singing)
                   "Where I can tell you
                   things I'm dreaming of...:

CUT TO:

H-27   LILLI AS A BOY AT THE PIANO

    She sings into the telephone
    and the other music FADES down.

                LILLI   (singing)
                "This is just to tell you
                  that my heart's full of
                  love
                All for you and you alone,"

DISSOLVE TO:

H-28   MR.APEX..JASPER..AND
       VLADIMIR MOPPING HIS
       HEAD..MR.APEX'S OFFICE..

              MR. APEX
                Okay, that's out. Now where
                are we?

              JASPER   (amiably)
                Just where we were.

              VLADIMIR
                It wasn't so bad.

              MR. APEX
                Let's stick to business.
                Time is flying and...let's
                see what we've got so far.
                We've got her singing the
                Ave Maria.

              JASPER
                That's out.

              MR. APEX
                Oh yes. Is it?

              JASPER
                Why certainly. You remember.

              MR. APEX
                Oh yes.

He frowns.

                Well, we've got her singing
                that goodbye song with the
                boy there under the tree.

              VLADIMIR
                But that's out.

(CONTINUED)

                                         MR. APEX
                                             Oh yes. We changed the
                                             story.

He looks more cheerful
now.   But we've got The Blue
                                         Danube.

                                         JASPER
                                             But you don't like it.

                                         MR. APEX
                                             I don't like it, I don't
                                             like it, who am I?

                                                 SOUND: Telephone bell.

The phone rings and
he answers it.   (into phone)
                                             Why thanks, Harry...is that
                                             so? No, no, we're not
                                             keeping it in the picture..
                                             She just wanted to sing it.
                                             No sense in publishing it
                                             at all..it's out. Goodbye,
                                             Harry.
                                                     (he returns to Jasper
                                                      and Vladimir)
                                             Now let me see, where were
                                             we? Oh yes. We've got
                                             The Blue Danube and then
                                             we've got...

The phone rings and he
answers it.   SOUND: Telephone bell.
                                                     (into phone)
                                             What?....No, we're not
                                             interested in publishing it.
                                             No, no, just for the broad-
                                             cast, it isn't in the
                                             picture...fine, but we don't
                                             feel the same way about it.
                                             Goodbye.

He hangs up.   Now, We had the Blue Danube
                                             and...
The phone rings and he
picks it up.   SOUND: telephone bell.
                                                     (into phone)
                                             What?.....Five thousand? Why
                                             I can get ten thousand from
                                             any publisher, what are you
                                             talking about? Who do you
                                             think we are?...No...Take
                                             it up with the music de-
                                             partment.

He hangs up.   The nerve of some people.
                                             Now: From the Blue Danube
                                             we went to...

The phone rings. He
pushes the button on
his dictograph.   (into the dictograph)
                                             I don't want to be disturbed
                                             all the time by these music
                                             people. Tell them to get
                                             in touch with the...music
                                             department.

He returns to Jasper and
Vladimir.
(CONTINUED)

H-1.1A

He frowns.

MR. APEX
After The Blue Danube came
uh....

What have we got after The
Blue Danube, Jasper?

VLADIMIR
She sings "My Love".

MR. APEX
Then after that we had uh...
.hat have we got besides
The Song of Love, Jasper?

JASPER
We've got The Blue Danube.

MR. APEX
I know that. We've got
The Blue Danube and the
love song and...

JASPER
The Blue Danube.

MR. APEX
Are you being funny?

JASPER
You don't hear me chortling,
do you?

CUT TO:

H-29   THE INFORMATION DESK
AT THE STUDIO GATE...

A young man stands behind
it. The Boy hurries up
to the desk, pants a couple
of times, then speaks fer-
ociously.

THE BOY
I want to see Mr. Apex and
I want to see him quick.

THE YOUNG MAN BEHIND THE DESK
Who shall I say, President
Roosevelt?

THE BOY
No. Just say the man who
wrote that song.

THE YOUNG MAN
That song.

THE BOY
That's it.

The young man picks
up a telephone.

CUT TO:

H- 30 MR. APEX, JASPER AND
       VLADIMIR
——————————————————————

Mr. Apex looks thunder-
struck.

                    MR. APEX
                    But this is terrible. You
                    told me she was going to
                    take singing lessons in Paris.

                    VLADIMIR
                    London.

                    MR. APEX
                    Wherever it was, and then she
                    was going to...do something or
                    other until she got her big
                    chance to ---to---sing some-
                    where.

                    VLADIMIR
                    That's right.

                    MR. APEX
                    Well, where is it?

                    JASPER
                    We haven't come to that yet.
                    What we've been trying to fig-
                    ure out is how you tie The Blue
                    Danube onto what comes next.

                    MR. APEX (exasperated)
                    Well, what comes next?

                    VLADIMIR
                    We don't know yet.

Mr. Apex slaps his desk.

                    MR. APEX
                    Vladimir! Jasper! Time is
                    leaking away. You've got to
                    keep shooting. Shoot anything.

                    JASPER
                    That's what we've been doing.

                    MR. APEX (pounding his desk)
                    Well....where is it?

                    JASPER (furiously)
                    You threw it all out.

                    MR. APEX
                    All right, I'll give it all
                    back to you.

                    VLADIMIR (almost in tears)
                    But it don't fit no more...

CUT TO:

H-31   THE INFORMATION DESK
         THE BOY AND THE YOUNG MAN
         BEHIND THE DESK

                      THE YOUNG MAN BEHIND THE DESK
                        He's in conference and he
                        won't see anybody about music
                        and anyway he's gone home for
                        the day.

                    THE BOY   (angrily)
                        All right, but you tell him he
                        can't get away with it. Not
                        with me. I'll be back, and I
                        won't come alone. I'll get
                        lawyers and subpoenas and I'll
                        make him sorry he was ever born.
                        You just tell him that
                        from me.

                    THE YOUNG MAN
                        You bet I will.

        The boy turns and stamps
        out.

        CUT TO:

H-32   IE. APEX, JASPER AND
         VLADIMIR

                  MR. APEX
                      Well, what are we going to
                      do?

                  JASPER
                      Why didn't you leave us alone?
                      You would have had a nice
                      little story where she came to
                      Hollywood but in the meantime
                      the producer had to get out of
                      town and....

                  MR. APEX
                      I don't want any Hollywood
                      stories.

                 JASPER   (at the top of his lungs)
                      All right! You're not getting
                      one. Rejoice!

                MR. APEX   (to Vladimir)
                      Why don't _you_ say something?
                      You're always talking and
                      now for once....

                VLADIMIR   (sadly)
                      What can I say except I
                      told you so?

                MR. APEX
                      You told me so!

                VLADIMIR
                      Pictures that begin on Friday,.
                      I told you.

      CONTINUED

:B

CONTINUED

> JASPER
> If there was only some way
> you could tie...I mean connect
> what we've got by some sort
> of a...love story or something.

> LILLI'S VOICE
> Can I come in?

CUT TO:

H-33 SHOT OF THE DOOR OVER
THE GROUP

Lilli comes toward them.

> LILLI
> You like the song?

> MR. APEX
> I thought it was...beautiful,
> my dear. Simply beautiful.

> LILLI
> Thank you. Did anybody come
> to see you about...the song?

> MR. APEX
> No. .. couple of people called
> up.

> LILLI
> Did the compositor of the
> song, the man who write it,
> call up?

> MR. APEX
> No, he didn't call up.

> LILLI   (sadly)
> Oh. I thought maybe...he
> call you up.

> MR. APEX
> No.

> LILLI
> Well, I am glad you like the
> song. What come next?

> MR. APEX
> We're just..putting the final
> touches to it.

> LILLI
> Oh. Well...Good night.

> THE THREE MEN
> Good night.

Lilli goes out sadly.

> JASPER
> You see, if we had a little
> love story, then she could
> have come to Hollywood and
> we'd show pieces of the picture
> she's working in and those

CONTINUED

H-33 CONTINUED

                              JASPER   (continued)
                                   pieces would be...the pieces
                                   we've got.

                              MR. APEX (after a pause)
                                   Magnificent!

                              JASPER
                                   No, not magnificent but we
                                   could save the pieces.

                              VLADIMIR
                                   And I got a wonderful piece
                                   we could stick in.

                              JASPER
                                   Hold on, boys.

                              VLADIMIR (putting his hand over
                                        his eyes)
                                   Don't move.
                                        (he speaks emotionally)
                                   For years I had it in my
                                   heart to do one ting and I
                                   never find a place for it
                                   because it's too big to be
                                   little...and too little to
                                   be big.

Mr. Apex and Jasper
exchange looks.

                                   For fifteen years I been
                                   waiting and now I tink you
                                   are in a position where I
                                   can do the ambition of my
                                   life. You got to have some-
                                   thing,...
                                        (he shrugs his shoulders)
                                   It don't fit, it don't fit,
                                   but dot don't matter because
                                   nothing in our picture fit
                                   anyway.

He beams at Mr. Apex
who does not beam back.

                              MR. APEX (in a small voice)
                                   This is going to be terrible.

                              VLADIMIR
                                   No, it's going to be wonder-
                                   ful. It's going to be big;
                                   it's going to be immense.

He stretches his arms...
                                   It's going to be...
He taps his heart...
                                   Apex.

Mr. Apex shakes his head
as if he'd received a jolt.

                                        (very quietly)
                                   I'm going to interpret it.
                                   I'm going to do it from the
                                   inside out.

CONTINUED

H-33   CONTINUED

                              J..SPER   (throwing it away)
                                 That'll be novel.

                              MR. ..PEX
                                 No novelties, please Vladimir.

                              VLADIMIR (as in a trance)
                                 I see miles of pushta..

His voice gets lower and
lower, and Mr. ..pex and
Jasper lean forward to
listen to him.
                                       Willages...and willages by
                                       de tousand.

.. spasm crosses Mr. ..pex's
face.
                                       Horses...mountains...soldiers..
                                       cannons and blood. I see a
                                       whole people pushing up...up..
                                       and up for freedom. I see,.

                              MR. ..PEX
                                 But how can you explain all
                                 that in....

                              VL..DIMIR (Gently) ·
                                 Mr. ..pex. Liszt's Hungarian
                                 Rhapsody...don't need no ex-
                                 planation.

        SLOW DISSOLVE TO:

H-34 -- H-121   THE HUNG..RI..N
RH..PSODY ..S OUTLINED BY
MR. STURGES

        DISSOLVE TO:

H-122 .. STUDIO STREET...NIGHT

Lilli appears, still panting
and with a shawl thrown around
her shoulders. Suddenly she
stops just in front of a window
with Venetian blinds. Some light
comes through the blinds. Lilli
calls the Boy's name.

                              LILLI...! (the boy's name)

The Boy hurries into the
picture. In his right hand
he holds a summons.

                              THE BOY
                                 Lilli!

They take each other's
hands.
                                       I've been looking for you
                                       every place. I waited at the
                                       extra gate...

CUT TO:

H-123   INTERIOR OF JASPER'S
        OFFICE

This is just the other side
of the Venetian bl   Be
see him with the   him
him. His hat is a the
of his head, his feet on on
his desk and beside him then
sits a bottle of liquor and a
tumbler. He holds a pencil in
his hand and is looking sourly
at some paper on a board he
holds in his lap.

                            THE BOY'S VOICE
                                I looked all over the lot...
                                I even went to that under-
                                taker's...

Jasper's head comes up
with a snap.

                                ...He told me you'd gone to
                                Australia.

                            LILLI'S VOICE (cooingly)
                                But...(the
                                I've been

Jasper rolls his eyes as
he recognizes the voice.

                                I've been doing extra in
                                Hungarian Rhapsody.

Jasper rises to his feet,
hurriedly tiptoes to the
window, knocks his hat off,
and peeks through the Venetian
blinds.

        CUT TO:

H-124   LILLI AND THE BOY IN FRONT
        OF THE VENETIAN BLINDS

                            LILLI   (putting her arms on his
                                       shoulders)
                                I'm so happy to find you
                                again. They told me you was
                                fired.

                            THE BOY (angrily)
                                That's what I'm here about.
                                Those crooks stole my song..
                                that song I wrote for you
                                alone...

        CUT TO:

H-125   INTERIOR JASPER'S OFFICE

He does a silent dance of joy,
clutches his head with enthusiasm,
then returns to his peephole.

                            THE BOY'S VOICE
                                I've got a subpoena. I'm
                                going to stick 'em in
                                jail.
CONTINUED

                                124

H-125 CONTINUED

                              THE BOY (continued)
                                   just found out they let
                                   me old Pogany sing it.

Jasper throws his arms
in the air and bites
his fingers ecstatically.
He literally flies away
from the window in a spring
dance, then hurries back to
his peephole.

CUT TO:

H-126 LILLI AND THE BOY IN FRONT
       OF THE VENETIAN BLINDS

                              LILLI
                                   Then they must pay you for it.

                              THE BOY
                                   I don't want their measly
                                   fifty dollars. That's mine...
                                   I mean yours. It was private.
                                   You know what it meant.

                              LILLI   (gently)
                                   Yes, but...maybe they would
                                   give you five thousand.

                              THE BOY   (dumbly)
                                   Five thousand?

                              LILLI
                                   Maybe more, but anyway enough
                                   for you and me so

She looks away...
                                   You know.

                              THE BOY   (ecstatically)
                                   Lilli!

                              LILLI
                                   Only...you got to let me do
                                   a little extra work sometimes.

CUT TO:

H-127 JASPER NEXT TO THE VENETIAN
       BLINDS IN HIS OFFICE

He looks as if he were going
insane.
                              THE BOY'S VOICE
                                   You know I will...but you'll
                                   never have to now.

                              LILLI
                                   ...(The Boy's name)

                              THE BOY
                                   We'll fly to Yuma. What do
                                   we care for money.

                              LILLI
                                   Of course.
CONTINUED

H-127 CONTINUED

       THE BOY'S VOICE
        Lilli, I forgot to ask you.
        Will y   arry me?

       LILLI'S VOICE
        Of course.

       JASPER (at the top of his lungs)
        HOORAY!

   CUT TO:

H-128 LILLI AND THE BOY
   IN FRONT OF THE VENETIAN
   BLINDS

       LILLI (frightened)
        What was that?

       THE BOY
        Just a projection room.
         (then rapidly)
        Listen, I'll see Apex and if
        I get it I'll meet you at
        the extra gate in fifteen
        minutes..

       LILLI (excitedly)
        Yes.

       THE BOY
        And then we fly to Yuma.

       LILLI
        Yes.

       THE BOY
        And we take a taxi from here
        to the airport, what do we
        care?

       LILLI
        Yes.

       THE BOY
        Goodbye until then.

       LILLI
        Goodbye, darling.

  They kiss and run off
  on opposite sides. Im-
  mediately a door behind
  them opens and Jasper
  appears doing the war dance
  and the Indian war whoop. He
  nearly falls down, then gallops
  down the street.

  CUT TO:

H-129 MR. APEX'S OFFICE

    Mr. Apex and Vladimir
are facing each other with
their hands raised to heaven.

                           VLADIMIR
                             Yes.

                         MR. APEX
                             No.

    There is a wild war whoop
and Jasper enters doing
the war dance.

                         JASPER
                             Give it to him. It's worth
                             every nickel of it. Give
                             him a thousand more and if
                             it isn't worth it I'll pay
                             you back.

                         MR. APEX
                             Who? What?

                         JASPER
                             When he comes in...and asks
                             for it...You're not paying
                             for the song, you're paying
                             for the story. Listen!

                         VLADIMIR
                           What are you...

                         JASPER (without stopping)
                           She came to Hollywood but the
                           studio didn't know she was
                           coming. She met the boy but
                           she didn't tell him she was a
                           star. You made him rich and
                           now they're going to get
                           married and he still doesn't
                           know who she is. It's a
                           natural. It's immense. With
                           a story like that you could
                           stick in Custer's Last Stand
                           and the Battle of Manila Bay
                           and it would fit.

    The phone rings as
Mr. Apex and Vladimir
are staring at each other.
Mr. Apex picks up the telephone and frowns and says:

                         MR. APEX
                             Who?

    Jasper snatches the
receiver out of his
hands.

                         JASPER (at the top of his lungs)
                           SEND HIM IN...SEND HIM IN ON
                         A PLATTER!

H-130   THE BOY AND LILLI
        IN THE CABIN OF AN
        AIRPLANE

        They sit very close, side
        by side. Jointly they hold
        ~~ok and smile at it. The~~
        ~~noise of the airplane sounds~~
        like part of the Hungarian
        Rhapsody.

        DISSOLVE TO:

H-131   THE LIVING ROOM OF A
        PREACHER'S HOUSE IN YUMA

        We see only a kindly middle-
        aged woman sitting at a harmonium.
        She is looking back over her shoulder
        and her hands are at attention
        on the keys.

                            THE PREACHER'S VOICE
                            ...and have declared the same
                            by the joining of hands. I
                            pronounce that they are man
                            and wife. Those whom God hath
                            joined together, let no man
                            put asunder. Amen.

        The woman at the harmonium
        starts to play the wedding
        march and one note is pain-
        fully flat.

        CUT TO:

132   LILLI AND THE BOY COMING
        TOWARD US

        As they pass THE CAMERA...

        CUT TO:

H-133   LILLI AND THE BOY IN
        THE PREACHER'S VESTIBULE

        Very quietly and very happily
        they kiss.

                            THE BOY   (tenderly)
                            You're my own little wife.

                            LILLI   (gently)
                            And nobody know. .

        Very quietly he opens
        the door and they step
        out.

        CUT TO:

H-134   EXT. OF THE PREACHER'S
          DOOR

          Lilli and the Boy come out
          quietly. The instant they
          are outside, many things happen
          simultaneously. Fifty flash-
          light bulbs explode. Five
          undred people together yell
          scream Fifty photographers
          : of this way please."
          Up a little higher." "Turn
          your head to the right." "Come
          down a step." The Apex Film
          Company's brass band blares
          forth with Sousa's March,
          while the local band plays
          "There'll be a Hot Time in
          the Old Town Tonight." The sirens
          of motor-cycle cops are heard.
          Boys yell: "Extra!"

          CUT TO:

H-135   PANNING SHOT OF WHAT LILLI
          AND THE BOY SEE

          They see the photographers.
          The newsreel men, little boys
          yelling "Extra," the two bands
          playing against each other,
          the crowd held back by the
          police. Motorcycle cops ride
          up to the steps followed by a
          large limousine out of which
          steps Mr. Apex, Vladimir and
          Jasper. Mr. Apex almost falls
          down in his hurry to get up the
          steps.

          CUT TO:

H-136   THE GROUP ON THE STEPS

          The clergyman and his wife
          peek out the door. Lilli
          looks very gracious but the
          boy looks completely thunder-
          struck. Mr. Apex, Jasper and
          Vladimir hurry into the picture.
          Vladimir throws his arms around
          Lilli and kisses her on both
          cheeks.

                            VLADIMIR
                              Lilli!

                        LILLI
                              Vladimir!

          Mr. Apex presses a huge
          bunch of roses into Lilli's
          arms.

                       MR. APEX
                            Miss Pogany.. I am the proud-
                            est and happiest man on
                            earth.

          He grabs the boy's hand.

                            And you, my boy, you're a
                          great song writer.

          We hear a loud tooting of
          an automobile horn.
          CUT TO:

II-127   SHOT FROM THE PORCH
          AT LILI'S AUTOMOBILE

          It comes to a Tom Mix stop and
          the chauffeur looks up at us
          completely idiotically.

          The door flies open, Mr. Magnolius
          leaps out and Madam Schnortz falls,
          weeping, into his arms. With a
          handkerchief to her nose she starts
          towards us

          CUT TO:

II-138   GROUP ON THE PORCH

          LILLI and THE BOY are completely
          obscured by the crowd of people
          trying to get at them. It looks
          like an old-fashioned football game.

          CUT TO:

II-139   LILLI AND THE BOY

          The sound of the crowd is muffled
          by the mass of people around them.

                         THE BOY (Ruefully)
                              Well...it looks like I
                              married an opera singer after
                              all.
                         (he chuckles)

                         LILLI (With the expression
                              people use while shrugging
                              their shoulders)
                              Yes...
                         (She raises her eyebrows,
                         and then has a happy thought)
                              ...but I don't sing ALL the
                              time.

          The finale music grows louder.

                    T H E   E N D

Mr. Big Takes a Break: An Introduction to the Screenplay for *Nothing Doing*

Jay Rozgonyi

If you'd been a Hollywood insider in the late 1940s, reading the trade magazines and following the industry news, you would have thought that Preston Sturges was on the cusp of an exciting new chapter of his career. In September of 1948, *Screenland* magazine reported that Sturges was writing a script that "kids the pants off" Greta Garbo and her whole career—and that he was successfully wooing Garbo herself to appear in it. Then, in January of 1949, *Showman's Trade Review* reported that Sturges was following up his just-completed 20th-Century Fox contract with a two-picture deal at MGM; a week later, the same paper announced that the writer/director was preparing an original script for Clark Gable, titled *Mr. Big of Littleville*. Finally, in March, *Variety* published a notice that Sturges had agreed to write the book for Cole Porter's successor to his stage smash *Kiss Me Kate*, based on the Greek myth of Amphitryon.

In the end, not one of these projects came to fruition, and unfortunately, Sturges would write and direct only one more film in the remaining ten years of his life. Thankfully, however, the screenplay for *Mr. Big of Littleville* exists to offer us a glimpse of Sturges' creativity during this period. While *Mr. Big* may not be in the same class as *The Palm Beach Story* or *The Miracle of Morgan's Creek*, it's a Sturges conception through and through, with a blend of themes, characters, and situations familiar to any fan of his work.

In early 1949, Sturges was coming off a two-picture deal with 20th-Century Fox that had not been particularly successful. *Unfaithfully Yours* was a brilliant film, but it had been adversely affected at the box office when, just before its release, star Rex Harrison became embroiled in a scandal revolving around the suicide of his girlfriend, Carole Landis (Harrison also happened to be married at the time). Sturges followed this up with *The Beautiful Blonde from Bashful Bend*, a Western farce that featured a less-than-stellar Sturges script. Throughout production of the film the director and studio head Darryl F. Zanuck continued to battle, and the unhappy star, Betty Grable, bad-mouthed the film upon its release. The film was a flop. In addition, Sturges' Hollywood restaurant and dinner theater, The Players, was deep in debt. In dire financial straits, Sturges was at that moment most interested in obtaining some cash, and he therefore accepted MGM's offer to write a script for Clark Gable in return for $50,000—even though there was no accompanying offer for him to direct the film.

Preston Sturges worked on *Mr. Big of Littleville*—later retitled *Nothing Doing*—throughout the spring and early summer of 1949, and in early August submitted the version of the script that you're about to read. Its premise, its characters, and many of its scenes are pure Sturges, and the first two-thirds of the script reads like an inspired addition to his comedy catalog. But that inspiration peters out near the end as the writing falls back on a standard Hollywood will-he-or-won't-he scenario, with the main character seemingly ready to walk away from the woman who adores him. Because Sturges saves the day somewhat with a clever comic coda, *Nothing Doing* is a satisfying if ultimately imperfect screenplay from the great writer and director.

The film tells the story of Charles "Big Kim" Kimble, an overwhelmed tycoon whose empire spans construction, banking, oil, and manufacturing. When troubling memory lapses send him to a psychiatrist, he receives an unusual prescription: six months in a small town with no business, no wealth, and no women. Selecting West Bismarck at random, Kimble (under the alias "Mr. Jones") finds himself at a dilapidated hotel run by war widow Peggy Jones and her precocious 8-year-old son, Butch. Kimble's attempts at relaxation are quickly tossed aside thanks to the creativity and business instincts that made him a success in the first place, but the edict of "No Women" starts to pose a bigger problem.

This basic storyline, of a person being transplanted to a wholly different environment and finding him- or herself through the experience, should be familiar to fans of Sturges' work. He used it to various degrees in *Easy Living*, where working girl Jean Arthur is thrust into lavish surroundings and have others mistakenly believe that she's a banker's mistress; in *Remember the Night*, where jewel thief Barbara Stanwyck delights in the simple joys of a small-town Christmas; in *The Beautiful Blonde from Bashful Bend*, in which sharpshooting saloon singer Betty Grable is forced to masquerade as a modest schoolteacher; and most notably in *Sullivan's Travels* and *The Sin of Harold Diddlebock*.

It's in these last two films that we see the most direct connections to *Nothing Doing*, as in both cases Sturges introduces highly successful men whose years of doing the same work have caused them to lose their creative spark. John L. Sullivan, a Hollywood director famous for his hugely popular comedies and musicals, decides that such work isn't meaningful enough and that he needs to suffer the harshness of life on the road so he can make a serious drama. And Harold Diddlebock, a spectacular college football hero, is fired from his job after twenty years of spiritless toil. In both cases, these men are forced into extraordinary new circumstances that test their mettle—and that lead to them redis-covering the original talents that made them celebrated in the first place. In *Nothing Doing* you'll see echoes of Sullivan's and Diddlebock's personal journeys in Big Kim's trek from corporate figurehead, some of whose employees are not even sure he really exists, to single-handed savior of West Bismarck.

This focus on business was also not new to Sturges in the late 1940s. He had explored the idea of powerful and noteworthy leaders—men who labored hard, moved beyond their humble upbringings, and came to domi-nate their industries—quite directly in dramatic works like The *Power and the Glory* and *Diamond Jim*, as well as in the comedy *The Great McGinty*. In *Nothing Doing*, Sturges again turns to a comedic framework and this character type. While the script doesn't trace Big Kim's entire early life, we do get a picture of a man who began in less than auspicious circumstances (his parents were circus performers and he ran away from them at age 14); who, before building his industrial empire, held a variety of jobs in a variety of places ("bridge stiff" in Quebec, gambler in Arizona, and barnstorming everywhere, for instance); and who is clearly an opportunist when it comes to business decisions (starting new manufacturing divisions whenever the firm requires something they don't already make) and people (especially attractive women, as evidenced by his juggling of dates and paramours). When we encounter him at age 39, he's been fabulously successful in busi-ness, but his achievements have also pulled him further and further away from the traits that led to his success in the first place.

Sturges explored that theme—of how businesses and individuals can lose the inspiration that created their initial success—not only through the life of Big Kim, but also in 1947's *The Sin of Harold Diddlebock* and in the early 1930s stage play *A Cup of Coffee*.

He later rewrote *A Cup of Coffee* as 1940's *Christmas in July*, keeping the same essential storyline, but only the play—and not the later film—bears such a direct connection to Big Kim and *Nothing Doing*. In rewriting the play for the screen, Sturges both moved almost all of the action outside the walls of the Baxter Coffee company and shifted all focus away from the firm's president and his two sons and squarely onto the character of Jimmy MacDonald (played by Dick Powell). In fact, Sturges reduced the three Baxters in the play to one character, doing away completely with Ephraim ("Eph") Baxter, the aged founder of the company, and therefore the subplot regarding his diminished role at the firm. It's in this subplot of the play that we find echoes of *Nothing Doing*, as Big Kim resembles Eph in many ways.

Throughout *A Cup of Coffee*, Ephraim Baxter appears as a one-note curmudgeon: he's pushed around in a wheelchair by an attendant, blows a shrill whistle whenever he wants attention or to be moved, and more often than not drifts off to sleep in the middle of conversations. What he represents, as the founder of Baxter Coffee who still comes to the office every day and tries to exert his control, closely parallels *Nothing Doing's* Big Kim. In many ways, Eph is exactly what Big Kim would turn in to if Kim didn't get the chance to rediscover himself in West Bismarck. While not nearly as aged nor as frail as Eph, Kim is certainly well on his way to becoming him prior to his six-month vacation.

We first see Eph, as he arrives at the coffee warehouse for another day of work, through the disdain and resentment that his two sons have for him. They are more than willing to push aside the old man so they can modernize the business. But Ephraim will have none of it; "If you knew what I did to get a start in this business," he shouts back at them, "you couldn't sleep at night." Despite seeming like the geriatric patriarch, Ephraim at one time clearly knew how to play a very clever game in the world of business. Against his sons' better judgement, he champions the unorthodox character—and misinterpreted slogan—of Jimmy MacDonald, and in the process revives in himself the imagination that had made him a success years ago.

Like Eph, Big Kim is still leading the Kimble companies, but he too is in a rut. He still spouts the same stories and lines that served him well decades before, and he probably still thinks that the unsaleable Kimble Car is the best on the market. As with Eph, though, Big Kim will regain his creativity by the end of the script.

The obvious connection between *Nothing Doing* and *A Cup of Coffee* is limited to the characters of Big Kim and Ephraim. The overall plot of *Nothing Doing*, however, does display strong similarities to the story elements of another mid-1940s work, *The Sin of Harold Diddlebock*. Both scripts feature a protagonist who achieved acclaim while still a young man: for Big Kim it was the start of his many businesses, and for Harold it was the college football heroics that landed him a job at the E. J. Waggleberry Advertising agency. But both men have also seen twenty-plus years of work dull their original capacities for ingenuity and creativity. In each film, the protagonists will be forced to reclaim their brilliance and re-establish their success.

Big Kim receives his wake-up call, of course, when he consults with Dr. Rothmuller after not being able to remember his actions for days on end (pp. 152-161). For Harold Diddlebock, the jolt arrives when he is dismissed by Mr. Waggleberry for going absolutely nowhere in twenty-two years at the firm. Although he used to be "full of zing, full of zest, full of zowie," as his boss puts it, Harold now not only makes the same mistakes every year but also offers the same apologies for them. For the first time in his life Harold visits a bar and, in the company of his eccentric new friend Wormy, partakes of a specially concocted Diddlebock Cocktail. Miraculously, the drink serves as the equivalent of Big Kim's journey to West Bismarck—a trip to a type of place (in one case physical and in the other alcohol-induced) that neither man has visited before, and that provides the incentive for a return to his long-lost sense of creativity.

The details for Big Kim and Harold are different, of course, but we can see similarities as they each frantically propel themselves into efforts to think their ways out of their respective situations. Just as Big Kim's bouts of amnesia ultimately send him to West Bismarck, Harold's "mad Wednesday" ends with him possessing a circus that he can't recall purchasing. (Interestingly, Big Kim also turns to plans for a circus-like midway to revive the struggling town.) For both, a woman who's been overlooked despite being around for the entirety of the story completes their happiness. More important, though, both men are faced with the challenge of "selling"—either literally or figuratively—something that initially has no takers. Whether it's the circus that Harold finds himself stuck with, or the town with resources that no one but Big Kim recognizes, the basic situation is exactly the same: a visionary needs to come to the rescue, and in return he is rewarded with a renewed belief in his own ingenuity and insight—along with major business success and, naturally, love.

It's hard not to speculate, of course, on what a filmed version of *Nothing Doing* might have looked like. The Preston Sturges of 1949 undoubtedly conceived his screenplays with the directing process in mind, so even though he was only hired to write this script for Clark Gable, he naturally would have drawn on his directing skills as he wrote. On paper *Nothing Doing* is fully identifiable as a true Sturges comedy, full of his characteristic dialogue, physical comedy sequences, and idiosyncratic characters. It also makes use of a favorite Sturges plot conceit and a basis for comedy—setting up a character as fish out of water.

Among its particular strengths, *Nothing Doing* supplies a number of opportunities for Sturges' trademark style of physical comedy. Shortly after Big Kim's arrival in West Bismarck, for example, the industrialist tries to explicitly fulfill Dr. Rothmuller's prescription of relaxing on a porch, in a rocking chair, while puffing away on a pipe (pp. 179-183). Naturally, he chooses the wrong rocking chair, and quickly finds himself in a heap with chair parts all around him. A short time later, Big Kim meets Peggy and Lucas and attempts to help them fix a broken faucet in the kitchen (pp. 185-192). In this lengthy scene Sturges specifies some of the shots ("CLOSE SHOT – MR. KIMBLE UNDER THE SINK – REVERSE as the water shoots into his face from the leaking pipe") and provides cues as to what the comic acting should convey ("The two big men look at each other like strange male dogs"). Highlighting the importance of the scene to Sturges, these directorial details imply that it would have been carefully shot and timed for maximum effect.

Pay close attention, too, to Sturges' skill at conceiving, shooting, and editing lightning-paced scenes of chaos with snatches of great dialogue. One such example is when we see the tumult of the morning after Big Kim's nighttime trip to the Carriage Works (pp. 223-232). As Peggy wakes up to a clamor, she finds that the hotel is already being torn apart and that the new Kimble Cross Country Car is coming to life on Old Bob Zooky's drafting board. There's a palpable sense of energy and purpose that comes through in the script. The action moves rapidly, characters are introduced quickly and haphazardly, and comic lines overlap one another—in other words, this is vintage Sturges, reminiscent of similar whirlwind scenes such as the circus bidding free-for-all in *Harold Diddlebock* or Trudy giving birth in *The Miracle of Morgan's Creek*.

In a number of Sturges' films the main characters are not particularly distinctive or interesting in and of themselves; protagonists like John L. Sullivan (*Sullivan's Travels*), Jimmy MacDonald (*Christmas in July*), and Tom Jeffers (*The Palm Beach Story*) are better described as people whom things happen to than as catalysts for action. Sturges instead used supporting and bit-part characters to drive the action and deliver the laughs. And while Big Kim is not as bland as Hopsy Pike in *The Lady Eve*, for instance, he's also not the dynamic Harold Diddlebock, either. But Sturges fills the pages of *Nothing Doing* with several supporting roles that jump out at you as you read the script. By far the best of these is Dr. Rothmuller, the European doctor whom Big Kim consults for his troubles—and who struggles the entire time not to strangle the famous businessman out of frustration. Sturges gives Rothmuller some high-sounding yet ultimately meaningless medical dialogue and instills in him a supercilious edge that is only fully appreciated at the very end of the script. Bookending the story with Big Kim's visits to Dr. Rothmuller, Sturges makes these scenes a highlight of the screenplay.

While not quite as cleverly drawn, the character of Old Bob Zooky, the former carriage designer put to work on the Cross Country Car, is also classic Sturges. Most of the humor comes from Old Bob's inability to hear and his misunderstanding of what people are saying to him, an easy point of focus as well as a trait that inevitably recalls the Wienie King in *The Palm Beach Story*. But there's more to Old Bob than his hearing impairment: he also spends his time painting postcards of the old carriages he used to design. With that degree of depth to the character, one has to believe that Sturges as a director would have cast the role with care and made the most of Old Bob's memorable comic scenes. The same can be said for Madame Zaza, the midway fortune teller who appears only briefly in the script as the kind of typically cynical side character that was present in so many Sturges films (e.g., the lawyer in *The Miracle of Morgan's Creek* who states, "I'll sue anyone, at anytime, for anything"). In rehearsals and during filming Madame Zaza's character had the potential to be refined and amplified until she became a comic highlight.

Nothing Doing is not a Sturges masterpiece on the order of *The Palm Beach Story* or *The Miracle of Morgan's Creek*. But in the screenplay he does mine themes and explore characters that were related to (and sometimes derived from) the great work he had previously done. The story played to his strengths—characters who are taken out of their familiar element, plots revolving around crazy schemes, and ideas for inventions that took advantage of Sturges' own experiences in business and manufacturing. In regard to the latter, the Kimble Cross Country Car is a silly manifestation of a very real trend that Sturges seemed to have sensed: the post-war desire for families to get on the move and on the road. The place where *Nothing Doing* disappoints, however, is in its lack of interesting characters for Big Kim to play against. With little action that takes place outside of West Bismarck, the inhabitants of the town must provide almost all the engagement and charm—and despite the few good small character roles described above, the other people Big Jim meets are not that dramatically appealing. The sweet and caring Peggy is supposed to be a contrast to the women Big Kim interacts with or talks about in the beginning, but the blandly written role would have required a very skilled actress (and some on-set improvisation) to make her charming enough to fulfill her purpose. As Big Kim's competition for Peggy, though, the character of Lucas Stone is dull and dull-witted—an easy rival for Kim to thwart. If the small town is supposed to allow Big Kim to find a part of himself that he's lost in the big city and in big business, a slightly more formidable (or at least funny) antagonist would have served the story much better.

Another interesting miss on Sturges' part is the character of Butch. Sturges essentially never included children in his movies (with the possible exception of Emmy in *The Miracle of Morgan's Creek*, though she's a 14-year-old who is clearly more adult that her elders); it's not surprising, then, that he didn't quite know what to do with an eight-year-old child. The Sturges universe is an adult one in which children either don't exist or play any role other than waiting to grow up to become adults; perhaps this explains why Butch is simply a nice, average kid without any distinct personality. Not turning a child into a fully Sturgean character with idiosyncrasies and sardonic dialogue feels like an unfortunate missed opportunity.

Overall, though, *Nothing Doing* is an inventive script that could have made an engaging comedy, especially if Preston Sturges had directed it. A diverting comedy rather than an inspired classic, *Nothing Doing* features many of Sturges' tried-and-true themes and characters as well as comic touches — and with its references to post-war opportunities, the draw of old-time entertainment, and the desire to pack up the family and head out on the road, was also subtly aware of the spirit of its time.

NOTE:

Please see
inside of
cover for
changes and
additions.

NOTHING DOING

TEMPORARY
COMPLETE

From:

Preston Sturges

8-23-49

SUMMARY: No. 1
                        NOTHING DOING

                   (Script dated: 8-23-49)

Due to the excessive expense of re-running entire
script merely in order to obtain consecutive page
numbers, the script with its changes will not be
re-run, but herewith in front and back of the script,
you will find a summary of the total number of pages
in the script.

                        Total number of pages in script
                        including revisions to date, and
9-8-49   based on 63 lines per page: 129

                        Script completed: 9-8-49

NOTHING DOING

AFTER MAIN TITLES...FADE IN:
MONTAGE

Past a sign on a roof, we look down at the
yards of a great Construction Company. Considerable earth-moving and concrete-mixing
machinery is in evidence. The left hand
corner of the sign is embellished with the
capital 'K' enclosed in a square pulley or
sheave block which is the trademark of the
great Kimble Construction Company and its
allied companies. Next to the trademark we
read, of course, THE KIMBLE CONSTRUCTION
COMPANY. This dissolves to a HIGH CAMERA
SHOT of an oil cracking plant. The CAMERA
PANS over the plant and comes to rest on a
sign beginning, as before, with the 'K'
trademark. The rest of the sign says: THE
KIMBLE OIL COMPANY. We dissolve again, this
time to a HIGH CAMERA SHOT of an oil tanker
docking in a busy harbor. As its whistle
blows lustily we cut to a CLOSE SHOT of the
House Flag of the vessel. It consists of
the capital 'K' enclosed in the pulley block.
We PAN now to a SHOT of the building of a
great bridge. A heavy truck grinds into the
SHOT. On its side we SEE the 'K' in the square
pulley block. Again we dissolve, this time to
a test air field past a wind sock. As the
CAMERA PANS we read, in huge letters on the
roof: THE KIMBLE AIRCRAFT COMPANY. As a
large plane roars off dissolve to: a tanker
under construction in a shipyard. An arc-
welding outfit is wheeled between us and the
vessel. It bears the familiar 'K'. Dissolve
to the same 'K' enclosed in the pulley block
but this time in chromium and enamel. It
moves away from us and we find that it was
attached to a Kimble car on an assembly line.
Another car takes the place of the one just
gone and stops with its trademark in exactly
the same place. Having by now made our point,
I hope, we merely show THE KIMBLE NATIONAL
BANK AND TRUST COMPANY past its letterhead
in an active typewriter and then, for the
last time, go to a capital 'K' about a foot
high, surrounded by its customary pulley block
and stencilled on some canvas. As it pulls
away from us we find outselves looking at a
helicopter in flight.

141

INT. HELICOPTER   11

Here we find Big Kim himself, yelling at Long
Suffering Bamberger, the world's greatest
secretary. As they argue, the pilot gazes
stoically down through his fish bowl at the
thousands of ants, a hundred feet below them,
crawling over, under, and around the unbelievable Appohatchee Dam, his boss's latest on-
slaught upon the bosom of Mother Nature.

                    Big Kim (bellowing)
Friday! What do you mean it's Friday?

                    Bamby (shrugging)
What do I mean it's Friday? It's Friday.

He plays a few chords on his stenotype.

                    Big Kim
Quit taking your own dictation will you? How can
this possibly be Friday when I'm supposed to be at
a doctor's in New York on Tuesday.

                    Bamby
You're just making it worse.

                    Big Kim (to the pilot)
What day is today?

                    The Pilot (with distaste)
If it's all the same to you Boss settle it between
you will you?

                    Big Kim (after a hunted look)
Take me back to the plane.

                    The Pilot
Yes sir.

DOCTOR ROTHMULLER IN A LONG WHITE COAT AND   12
HIS NURSE - MISS SIMPSON

                    Dr. Rothmuller (tapping his
                wristwatch)
Who does he think he is, General...Grant?

                    Miss Simpson (soothing him
                prettily)
General Grant is dead, Doctor...Mr. Kimble is a
very busy man...President of so many corporations...

                    Dr. Rothmuller (indignantly)
And I am a pool room loafer, I suppose...with nothing
to do but shoot a....a...pair of sevens in the...the
...side pocket!

142

Miss Simpson
I think you've got your games a little mixed up,
Doctor...you're probably thinking of ice hockey or....

12
CONT'D
(2)

Doctor Rothmuller (putting on
his hat)
I have no time for games...and nobody plays them on
me neither...nobody plays pussy in the corner with
me Monday, Tuesday and Wednesday if he is president
of twice so many corporations.

Miss Simpson
And Thursday, Doctor...today is Friday.

Dr. Rothmuller (stupefied)
Friday! You know what?.

Miss Simpson
What?

Dr. Rothmuller (thoughtfully)
I'm getting more like my patients every day...maybe
I should see a doctor.

Miss Simpson
What do you mean "getting?"

BIG KIM'S OFFICE IN HIS PRIVATE PLANE   13

Through the window we see the helicopter,
its blades still turning slowly. In front
of this we see Mr. Kimble hurrying toward
us followed by Bamby and his stenotype.
Just outside the window Mr. Kimble mutters
"New York" to his pilot, then disappears.
We hear a door bang and Mr. Kimble comes into
the cabin, sits down and picks up the telephone
receiver. The pilot passes between him and
ourselves on his way into the nose of the plane.

Big Kim (into the phone)
This is N.C. 45163...that's right...45163...I want
New York...Butterfield 372721...I'll hold it.

A VERY PRETTY STEWARDESS IN THE DOORWAY OF   14
THE OFFICE - BEHIND HER WE SEE BAMBY SORTING
HIS PAPERS

The Stewardess (crossing to
Mr. Kimble)
Can I do anything for you, Mr. Kimble?

Big Kim (looking her over)
Plenty Baby...that's right Butterfield 372721...

Now noticing that the plane is beginning to
move, he pulls the girl down into the seat
beside him and puts his forearm over her lap.

                    Big Kim
You always want to put your belt on when taking off
or landing...remember that.
          (now into the phone)
I am holding it.
          (now back to the girl)
What are you doing when we get to New York?

                    The Stewardess
Oh, are we going to New York? The kind of life
I lead, how could I be doing anything?

                    Big Kim
Good, I'll tell you what I'll do I'll break a
couple of business appointments.

                    The Stewardess (smiling faintly)
With the blonde....or that new Spanish girl?

                    Big Kim
What do you want to notice things like that for?
I've just got to see a doctor for a few minutes.
then we'll take in a little show...then go dancing...
and then...

                    The Stewardess (after a slight
               pause)
Don't you think we're high enough up now to take
that belt off my knees?

                    Big Kim (looking at her knees)
I'm sorry...I was a little absent-minded...I'll tell
you what you do...if you'll get a couple of glasses
and some ice and a bottle of bourbon and hurry back
see? Tell Bamby to take a sleep...he looks tired.

                    The Stewardess (rising and
               smoothing her skirts as she exits)
Yes sir.

                    Big Kim (into the telephone)
Hello....hello....the Kimble Construction Company?...
Who is this, Margie?

SWITCHBOARD OF THE KIMBLE CONSTRUCTION COMPANY   15

Manhattan gleaming behind her head, we see a
very pretty phone operator.

                    Margie (into the telephone)
Well snap my garters if it isn't "C.K." himself.
How are you, "C.K."...and where are you?

                    144

BIG KIM AT THE TELEPHONE IN HIS PLANE   16

                    Big Kim
I'm fine thanks...I'm on my way in...now I'll tell
you what I want you to do...there's a brain guy
on Madison Avenue...a doctor called Rothmuller.
R for razzberry...O. .T...H...M for Moses...U...
double L...ER...you call him and tell him I'll be
a little late...I'll make it as close to four this
afternoon as I can...right now I'm passing Minnesota
...and tell Jake to wait for me...I'll see him when
I'm through at the doctor's.

MARGIE AT THE TELEPHONE   17

                    Margie
I've got it...anything else?

BIG KIM AT THE TELEPHONE   18

                    Big Kim (after making sure the
               stewardess is not within hearing)
Yeah...You know that certain blonde party at the
Rhinelander number? Well, you tell her I've been
delayed, see? Make it Oklahoma...I won't be in for
several days, see? I'll call her when I get in...
then call that room number at the Waldorf...you got
it? Tell her I'm delayed in Mexico for a few days...
then if that girl gets in from Hollywood...I'm in
Texas, see? You don't know just when I'll be back...
I guess that's about all, Honey...I'll be seeing
you...save a date for me, will you?
                    (he laughs, hangs up, then notices the
               pretty stewardess arriving with the drinks)
Sit down, Baby, sit down.

He pulls her down beside him.

DR. ROTHMULLER AND MISS SIMPSON IN THE DOCTOR'S   19
OUTER OFFICE

The wall clock indicates five minutes to five.

                    Dr. Rothmuller (tapping his
               wristwatch)
Four o'clock, huh.

                    Miss Simpson (soothingly)
He'll be here.

145

                    Dr. Rothmuller (putting on his   19
            hat and beginning to unbutton his coat)   CONT'D
But I won't...and if he ever should come...which he   (2)
won't...which to me is a matter of total indiffer-
ence...

        He removes his white coat and puts on his
        overcoat, forgetting to put on his suit coat.

                    Dr. Rothmuller
Tell him to take his trade elsewhere...

                    Miss Simpson (handing it to him)
You forgot your coat.

                    Dr. Rothmuller (removing his
                    overcoat)
What does it matter? Tell him to go to Hellman...
or Wolfan...or Zimbalist...or to a chiropractor...
they like to wait...Wait a minute I got a better
idea: tell him to take his business over to a
phrenologist on Third Avenue...in a vacant store
with a picture of the bumps on the window...tell
him that...that will fix him...good afternoon.

        He turns and meets Big Kim face to face, the
        door still closing behind him.

                    Big Kim (pleasantly)
Good afternoon to you...I'm sorry to be a little
late...my name is Kimble...there was quite a lot
of traffic on the bridge.

                    Dr. Rothmuller (indignantly)
A little late! You happen to know what day this is?

                    Big Kim (laughing ruefully)
If I knew that I wouldn't be here.

                    Miss Simpson (very pleasantly
                    after looking him over)
Welcome to the club...the doctor thinks it's yesterday.

                    Big Kim
I hope you'll still be able to take me...I've just
flown twelve hundred miles to get here.

                    Dr. Rothmuller (taken aback)
Twelve hundred miles! Well...if Miss Simpson is
foolish enough to be late for her supper...I guess
my soup will keep too.

                    Miss Simpson (warmly)
Miss Simpson is quite foolish enough.

                    Big Kim (confidentially)
You don't know how much I appreciate this, Miss
Simpson...or you either doctor.

146

                    Miss Simpson (leading him off)   19
If you'll follow me, Mr. Kimble..I'll take your   CONT'D
history first.   (3)

                    Dr. Rothmuller (looking after
               them sourly and beginning to put on his
                  white coat over his overcoat)
Millionaires...bah!

BIG KIM AND MISS SIMPSON IN A LITTLE CUBICLE   20
                    Miss Simpson (drawing a printed
               form to her)
It's plain Charles Kimble, isn't it, or is there a
middle initial?

                    Big Kim (removing his hat)
Plain Charles, thank you...age thirty-nine...not
married.

                    Miss Simpson (smiling)
I see you've been to the doctors before...have you
ever been married?

                    Big Kim
What does that matter?

                    Miss Simpson
It might matter a great deal, Mr. Kimble...this is
a history for a psychiatrist...not an income tax
report...the seat of all your troubles...if you
have any...might lie in an early and mistaken union
with...your washlady.

                    Big Kim (grimly)
I married a...lady when I was nineteen...one day she
met a guy who was richer than me and seemed to be
going places, so she...went along for the ride...I
haven't tried the arrangement since.

                    Miss Simpson (busy writing)
A little gun shy, huh?

                    Big Kim (looking back over the
               years)
There wasn't any gun play...I didn't even hit the
guy...he did me a favor.

                    Miss Simpson
It's always nice to look on the cheerful side of
things...now your occupation, please...I know you're
the famous Big Kim of course...with the big K on
everything but...

147

                    Big Kim   20
I'm a kind of a builder...dams...housing projects...   CONT'D
bridges...   (2)

                    Miss Simpson (rather pleased
                        with herself)
Masonry or suspension?

                    Big Kim (smiling faintly)
Masonry, suspension, cantilever, bascule, revolving,
jack-knife, draw, elevator, rolling span, swing
span, arch span, vertical lift, or what kind would
you like?

                    Miss Simpson (apologetically)
I'm sorry. There doesn't seem to be anything the
matter with your memory.

                    Big Kim
That's where you're wrong...that's why I'm here.

                    Miss Simpson
I see...we'll come to that presently...now: is
that all you do? Build bridges, dams and housing
projects?

                    Big Kim (almost with distaste)
No...we make a lot of the stuff we use to build with
...otherwise you're apt to run short sometimes or
get your throat cut...you have to have control...
so we started making tractors and our own earth-
moving machinery...and from there it was just a step
into automobiles...

                    Miss Simpson
Oh I've heard of the Kimble automobile...I even took
a demonstration...but I didn't like that phonetic
transmission or whatever you call it...I'm so sorry.

                    Big Kim (unenthusiastically)
It's all right with me...biggest car in the world
for the price...of course from automobiles and
tractors it was just one jump into planes and flying
equipment...everybody got into that...

                    Miss Simpson (slightly bug-eyed)
I see...airplane manufacturer.

                    Big Kim
Then the boys wouldn't let us have enough gas...wanted
to hog it all for themselves...so we gave them a little
run for their money...

                    Miss Simpson (looking up from her
                        writing)
The oil business?

148

                    Big Kim
That's right...only we didn't have any pipe lines
like the big combines...so we had to bring ours
around by boat, only we couldn't buy any boats...
so I built some.

            Miss Simpson (quite dazed)
You built some boats.

                    Big Kim
Yeah...naturally, once you got a ship yard you
keep on building boats...so we wound up with a
fleet.

                    Miss Simpson
I really feel sorry for you.

                    Big Kim
You should...we had so darn many payrolls and so
darned many places...the next thing happened we
had to open a little bank...and then that began to
spread.

            Miss Simpson (smiling)
You're really breaking my heart.

                    Big Kim
Oh I know...you're thinking how marvelous it must
all be...but it isn't...besides all I've told you,
there're a lot of little pains in the neck we had
to get to keep the other ones going: little short
line railroads...little ball bearing factories...
little synthetic rubber plants that stink up the
countryside...all kinds of little stuff.

            Miss Simpson (obviously too
          little to bother writing down)
...we'll just skip them...now where were you born
please?

                    Big Kim
You better just put Zanesville, Ohio...I was really born in a rowboat on the Muskingum River the
night the bridge washed out at Zanesville...they
were trying to get my mother over to the hospital
from the railroad yards...the lion tamer was rowing.

                    Miss Simpson
I beg your pardon?

                    Big Kim
My father was a razor-back with the Sells Floto
Circus...Ulyssus S. Kimble. My mother was an
equestrienne with the show who kinda married be-
neath her...the old man got a gander at her one
night and followed the circus right out of town...
been a book salesman, he said...but by the time I
got to know him he was working very steady as a
lush...till one morning about two o'clock he fell
                              (continued)

149

                    Big Kim (continued)
off the train going through ●klahoma...and we
never heard of him again.

                    Miss Simpson
Oh, I'm so sorry.

                    Big Kim
It didn't seem to bother anybody very much.

                    Miss Simpson
Then I won't worry about it either. Now: are you
aware of any nervous diseases in your family...such
as insanity, epilepsy or anything of that nature...
do you remember whether any of your relatives
suffered from dizziness for instance?

                    Big Kim (laughing)
Well my father sure suffered from it most of the
time...but my mother had to be very steady in her
line of work...so I'd say it was a kind of a stand-
off...you know, standing on a galloping horse with
a girl on your shoulders and another one on top of
her.

                    Miss Simpson
I should say she did! Now before we dispose of
him forever, would you say that your father was an
alcoholic?

                    Big Kim (with distaste)
I don't think a son ought to talk about his father
that way...I'd just say he was an exceptionally
heavy drinker...with his fair share of D.T.'s and
let it go at that.

                    Miss Simpson
Splendid. Now forgive this next question, but to
the best of your knowledge and belief, were you
ever dropped on your head as a child?

                    Big Kim (laughing)
I don't think so, but if they ever let the old man
hold me there's no telling what he might have
dropped me on.

                    Miss Simpson
Let's hope he didn't...Now: have you suffered any
severe falls or head injuries since childhood?

                    Big Kim (thoughtfully)
Well I got black-jacked one time in Arizona...but
that wasn't anything...and then there was that
time I was a bridge stiff in Quebec and the whole
thing fell down...

                    Miss Simpson (horrified)
Into the water, I hope.

                              150

                    Big Kim (laughing)
We reached the water all right, but we had to go
through quite a lot of ice to get to it.

                    Miss Simpson
Did you hit your head?

                    Big Kim
To tell you the truth I was really too busy to
notice...I had quite a swim.

                    Miss Simpson
You've had quite a life.

                    Big Kim
I've enjoyed it...I ran away when I was fourteen...
to go barnstorming with some kid flyers...everybody
said we'd wind up in jail...but instead of that we
wound up in the money...a few of us at least...we
kind of flew into a lot of different businesses.

                    Miss Simpson
I see...at least I think I see. Now tell me: how
do you sleep?

                    Big Kim (surprised)
Well, just in the tops of my paja...

                    Miss Simpson (hurriedly)
I mean how much...how many hours...how thoroughly.

                    Big Kim (laughing)
I never seemed to be around to find out...I guess
I sleep all right...I never thought much about it
...I can sleep if I've got the time...or not sleep
...it doesn't seem to make any difference.

                    Miss Simpson
I see...now this complaint...this trouble you're
seeing doctor about...how long have you had it?
When did you first notice it? If you can remember...

                    Big Kim
Just the other day...I was having a little conference with the Board of Directors of a little airplane parts firm we bought into out in Glendale,
California...

                    Miss Simpson (writing busily)
Yes?

                    Big Kim
I sat down with them at eleven o'clock on a Tuesday morning...they started the usual stuff...and
a fellow got up and started pointing out the usual
graphs on the wall...about the usual prospective
business conditions...

                              Big Kim (he pauses a little
                          and his eyes, close slightly)
The next thing I remember: I was playing roulette
...I was just raking in thirty-two thousand dol-
lars...it was ten o'clock at night...I was in Reno,
Nevada...and it was Friday.

                          Miss Simpson (bug-eyed)
Thirty-two thousand...dollars?

                          Big Kim
I lost it back later and more besides.

                          Miss Simpson
I see, you have all my sympathy...Now by any chance
...excuse my asking this, but it has to be asked,
had you been drinking heavily at the time this...
lapsus occurred?

                          Big Kim (amused)
At eleven o'clock in the morning! No, no...I
never touch it till five o'clock in the afternoon
...except maybe a couple of shots when I first get
up...just as an eye-opener.

                          Miss Simpson
I see. Now were you ever able to find out that
happened between that Tuesday morning and that
Friday night?

                          Big Kim
That's what scares me...nothing happened! Everybody saw me every day...I went right on dictating
letters...sitting in at conferences...signing
stock certificates...nobody noticed anything...
only I wasn't there...

                          Miss Simpson
You weren't...

                          Big Kim
No...that's what I'm here to find out...where was
I?

                          Miss Simpson (putting her
                      pages together and rising)
I see.

DR. ROTHMULLER'S EXAMINATION ROOM   21

    Big Kim wears only a pair of shorts and a
    short operating gown that ties in the back.
    The doctor is examining and dictating, Miss
    Simpson, in the background, takes the notes.

                              152

                    Dr. Rothmuller (feeling Big
               Kim's left eyebrow)
Left supraorbital ridge overly prominent...did you
get kicked by a horse maybe?

                    Big Kim
I used to do a little fighting between jobs...I
even wrestled one time I was really broke...
Kangaroo Kimble.

                    Dr. Rothmuller (continuing
               his examination)
Aha! Very natural...left ear slightly cabbaged...
posterior cervicle muscles prominent...nose broken
twice...

                    Big Kim
Three times.

                    Dr. Rothmuller
What's the difference? Now stick out your tongue,
to the left...to the right...back in the middle,
to the left again...in the middle, to the right...
normal...now close your eyes...stand up...put your
hands over your head and touch your toes...put
your feet together...raise your arms straight out
in front of you...keep your eyes closed...Romberg
negative. Stick your left hand out as far as you
can to the side...keep your eyes closed...now
touch the end of your nose with your left index
finger...now do the same with the right...negative.
Now open your eyes, sit down in this chair...cross
your legs...

          With the edge of his hand he hits both of Big
          Kim's knees, then, when they have jerked prop-
          erly, he spins him around in the chair a few
          times then looks into his eyes.

                    Dr. Rothmuller
No nystagmus.

                    Big Kim
Well, that's good news.

                    Dr. Rothmuller
How do you know?

          Now he picks up a rubber hammer and hits Big
          Kim's elbows and the sides of his wrists.

                    Dr. Rothmuller
Lie down.

First he raises each of the big fellow's legs   21
high in the air, then raises one foot, and   CONT'D
putting the point of the hammer against the   (3)
heel, suddenly jerks it upward toward the toes.

          Big Kim (exploding in giggles)
WOW !

          Dr. Rothmuller
Nothing to laugh at.

He has a hard time catching the other foot,
but finally succeeds and gives it the same
treatment. This time Big Kim's reaction is
so violent that he falls off the table and
lands on the back of his neck.

          Dr. Rothmuller (paying no
        attention to the fall)
Babinski negative.

          Miss Simpson (hurrying forward)
Did you hurt yourself?

          Dr. Rothmuller (philosophically)
He's a wrestler...they _like_ to fall.

          Big Kim (coughing slightly)
I'm all right...thanks.

          Dr. Rothmuller
You can get dressed now.

    DR. ROTHMULLER LOOKS UP FROM THE HISTORY

    as Big Kim enters, tying his tie.

          Big Kim
You find out anything?

          Dr. Rothmuller
Plenty...sit down.

Now he goes over to the big man, grabs his
head and examines it carefully, with special
reference to the profile, before continuing:

          Dr. Rothmuller
So you have no recollection of anything from that
Tuesday listening to those schnooks until Friday
raking in the mazuma...and you have no idea where
you were, except everybody saw you all the time
and said you looked very natural?

          Big Kim
That's right.

                              Dr. Rothmuller   21
I know where you were,   CONT'D
                                                                (4)
                              Big Kim
You do?

                              Dr. Rothmuller
Oh yes...you were taking a little vacation from
yourself...you bore yourself...you are a big bore.

                              Big Kim (surprised)
I am?

                              Dr. Rothmuller
The biggest...to yourself...maybe some women like
you...but from yourself you need a holiday...

     He starts walking around the room.

                              Dr. Rothmuller
From yourself and all this hoking-pocus...in German
we call it qvatch...which has pushed you so high up
the income tax...but which has done so little else
for you. You see, Mr. Krumble-Krimble-whatever it
is...your soul has taken already a holiday from you
for a few days without any permission whatsoever...
like a dog jumping against the door to go out...it
could not tell you more clearly what it wants.

                              Big Kim
Now wait a minute Doc all that happened to me was...

                              Dr. Rothmuller (interrupting)
You wait...there is nothing the matter with you or-
ganically in any way, Mister whatever it is...all
your nerve centers and tracts are normal...you are
even a very fine specimen, my nurse tells me...but
you are not, unfortunately, the intellectual type...
that primitive, sloping forehead...those ears to
warn you of approaching danger...that prognathous
jaw...those prominent supraorbital ridges to protect
the eyes...they tell their own sad story...did you
ever hear of the Missing Link?

                              Big Kim (feeling his head)
Who?

                              Dr. Rothmuller (outlining Mr.
                    Kimble's profile with his finger)
Pithecanthropus Erectus, the dandy of the Stone Age
looked a great deal like you, Mr. Kimble...which is
why you should have remained a fighter, or a wrestler, or a bear chaser, or a policeman...unfortunate-
ly you didn't...you decided instead to burden your
mind with thoughts...for which it was completely un-
suited...now you are beginning to pay the penalty.

                    Big Kim (not liking this
         at all)
Now wait a minute...

                    Dr. Rothmuller
Look: the soup at my club is already curdling...
I don't want to wait even half a minute or enter a
debate with you...if you don't know a Neanderthal
skull when it looks back at you from the mirror...
it is too late for me to teach you.

                    Big Kim (looking for a mirror)
I see.

                    Dr. Rothmuller
You don't, but it doesn't matter...I am going to
give you my opinion and then go home...what you do
with it is of no interest to me. How long you live...
or don't live...how long your mind stays healthy...
or doesn't...is entirely your own business and I
have no interest in business...no scientific loss
is involved.

                    Big Kim
Thanks.

                    Dr. Rothmuller
You're welcome...now listen carefully: you probably
won't understand but I will try to tell you anyway...
your mind is divided into two parts...the prosence-
phalon in the front, which we will call Mr. A...and
the rhombencephalon in the back, which we will call
Mr. B...Mr. A is your conscious, Mr. B is your sub-
conscious...Mr. A decides that you need a new car and
buys it...but Mr. B drives it for you because he is
in much closer contact with your nerves, your muscles,
your glands and your whole body generally...a dog can
wiggle his ears but Mr. A can not...he has to ask Mr.
B to do it for him.

                    Big Kim
I can wiggle my ears...

                    Dr. Rothmuller
Naturally...exactly what I'm talking about...you
can probably hold onto a tree with your feet too...
everything primitive comes very natural to you because you are more B than A.

                    Big Kim
Like a dog.

                    Dr. Rothmuller
Exactly...and to business conferences you react
exactly like a dog...you look out the window...you
chew your pencils...you scratch yourself...you wish
you were chasing a chicken.

                         Big Kim
Is that so...

                      Dr. Rothmuller
Positively. Now: you understand, _everybody_ is
made up of Mr. A and Mr. B, but in the high intellectual type...

                         Big Kim
Is that in again?

                      Dr. Rothmuller
Oh yes...in the high intellectual type, Mr. A learns
to control Mr. B...to hold him in check and use him
to his advantage like a good partner. But in the
low primitive type...

                         Big Kim
Like me, I suppose...

                      Dr. Rothmuller
Correct...Mr. B grows stronger than Mr. A...he can't
stand what Mr. A is doing...he is bored to the point
of insanity...he want OUT...

                         Big Kim
Huh.

                      Dr. Rothmuller
If your Mr. A were of the intellectual type he
would understand the principles of delegating
authority and the bigger his business became...the
smaller his job would become...

                         Big Kim
You think so.

                      Dr. Rothmuller
I know so...but being of the suspicious primitive
type...trusting no one because he thinks no one can
do as well as him...which is horse nonsense because
I can show you small children with a much higher IQ.

                         Big Kim
Huh...

                      Dr. Rothmuller

Oh yes...he exists in a vicious circle...slipping
always further behind, left always full of thoughts
half thought...deeds half done...correspondence
half answered...because there aren't enough minutes
in the day for him...his conscience packed with self
accusations...details half remembered...he suffers
from such an internal traffic jam that the place is
uninhabitable for Mr. B...he screams so loud to
go away...that one day he goes away...

                    Big Kim (distressed)
Now wait a minute, Doc, will you?

                    Dr. Rothmuller
What's the use. I have been trying to explain to
you why it was imperative for Mr. A to stop doing
what he is doing and give Mr. B a vacation before
he takes you away forever...I didn't expect to make
sense.

                    Big Kim (bitterly)
Naturally not...to a mind like a policeman's....
but this vacation idea is all wet in my case, you
see...because I just can't get away.

                    Dr. Rothmuller (sarcastically)
Of course...you are too important...you think.

                    Big Kim (ignoring this)
Couldn't you just give me some medicine or some
kind of treatment?

                    Dr. Rothmuller (smiling falsely)
You mean like cold baths and hot blankets? Not
yet...that comes later!

                    Big Kim (irritably)
I didn't mean that at all! I meant...injections or
something.

                    Dr. Rothmuller
Injections of what...applesauce?

                    Big Kim
You're supposed to be the doctor.

                    Dr. Rothmuller (pointing to the
              diplomas around the room)
Get a...load of those if you doubt it...look:
Mister Millionaire...you are going away in any case
...willingly...unwillingly...compos mentis or non
compos mentis...who cares.

                    Big Kim (frightened)
You mean...the booby hatch?

                    Dr. Rothmuller (indignantly)
Who's talking from booby hatches? That would be
the worst place...your whole life is a booby hatch
anyway...you'd meet all your friends there and have
conferences...and dictate memos to each other...to
see how fast you can forget them. No, no, Mr.
Krumble, when I say you are going away I mean this:
the other day you woke up in Nevada...four days
gone...the next time you might wake up in China...
four years gone.

                    Big Kim (after a pause)   21
How long would this little...vacation have to be?   CONT'D
                                                              (8)

                    Dr. Rothmuller
Not long...maybe six months...

                    Big Kim (yelling)
Six months ! Why I haven't any more chance of getting off for six months...

                    Dr. Rothmuller (raising a fin-
                        ger)
Six months minimum ! Away from EVERYTHING...from
everything you do and everybody you know...so that
by yielding to this urge to get away...we may remove the urge...and triumph by weakness...like the
Chinese.

                    Big Kim (very sourly)
If I wanted Chinese advice I could of gone to an
herb doctor.

                    Dr. Rothmuller
And get a very nice recipe for bird's nest soup...
look: I've already told you I don't care what you
do with it afterwards...do you want to listen to my
advice or don't you?

                    Big Kim
All right...pour it on.

                    Dr. Rothmuller
You find a little town some place...a village or
what used to be called a hamlet...where you have no
branches...no connections...no offices...not even
one small factory...and you go to this hamlet by
train...like everybody else...not by balloon or
something...and when you get off this train you are
alone...naked...

                    Big Kim (startled)
You mean a nudist camp?

                    Dr. Rothmuller
I mean without an oriental retinue...to remind you
who you think you are and pump up your importance...
no valets...no secretaries...no first, second and
ninth assistants...no major domos, masseurs, private
doctors or any other domestics...also you are not to
use your name which is so unforgettable...and you
are to take along just enough money to live, a man
among men for six months...none of this giant among
the pygmies business ! How much could you stagger
along on for six months?

                    Big Kim (with distaste)
I don't know...I don't spend much personally...may-
be a hundred thousand...

159

                    Dr. Rothmuller (snorting)   21
Hah! I will allow you <u>six</u> thousand and not one   CONT'D
kopeck more.   (9)

                    Big Kim (horrified)
For six months!

                    Dr. Rothmuller
You won't starve...better people than you have lived
sometimes even a year on six thousand dollars...
sometimes even a lifetime or two! Nun alzo: when
you get to this hamlet...<u>incognito</u>...try to forget
who you are...become a member of the community...
try to exchange <u>your</u> tempo for <u>theirs</u>...which is a
much better one...try to learn to slow down...to
change your pace...to give your poor head a chance
to catch up with your feet...on this treadmill where
you are running so fast...toward the undertaker.

                    Big Kim (sourly)
What do I do when I get to this hog hollow...this
Yap's Corners?

                    Dr. Rothmuller
Find a porch with a rocking chair on it...sit down
in it...light a pipe and learn to rock.

                    Big Kim (in horror)
A pipe!

                    Dr. Rothmuller (complacently)
A pipe and a rocking chair...they are the great
allies of these psychiatrists...
                    (he pulls a prescription pad toward him
                    and starts to write.)
I'll write them down for you so you won't forget...
maybe we can throw in a little gardening.

                    Big Kim
For six months!

                    Dr. Rothmuller (writing)
A hamlet...six months...incognito, that means you
don't mention your name...

                    Big Kim
Thanks.

                    Dr. Rothmuller (writing)
Only six thousand dollars and no more...positively
no phone conversations, memos or letters to anybody in any of your organizations and...oh yes...
and one thing more...

                    Big Kim (narrowing his eyes)   21
What now?   CONT'D
                                                        (10)
                    Dr. Rothmuller (stretching the
        words as he writes them)
No...women.

                    Big Kim (in horror)
No women.

                    Dr. Rothmuller
You heard me.

                    Big Kim
For six months.

                    Dr. Rothmuller (amiably)
That's right.
            (he rises and places the prescription
            in Mr. Kimble's hand)

                    Big Kim
Nuts to you.
            (he slips the prescription in his pocket,
            picks up his hat and strides out of the
            office.)

                    Dr. Rothmuller (looking after him)
And to you, Mr. Krumble...Miss Simpson.

                    Miss Simpson (coming in)
Yes doctor? What did you have to scare the poor
devil to death for...he's sort of cute in a kind
of homely way.

                    Dr. Rothmuller (ignoring her)
You will kindly add five hundred dollars to my
regular fee in this case...when these great men
say nuts to me...it's two fifty per unit.

                    Miss Simpson
Yes doctor.

Suddenly she turns and gives him a look.

MARGIE, THE KIMBLE PHONE OPERATOR AND JAKE   22
KRAMER, THE PARTNER IN CHARGE OF THE NEW
YORK OFFICE

Behind them we see the glass entrance doors
and through these the elevator landing on
the seventeenth floor. Jake wears his hat
and the look of a man who has wanted to
leave for some time.

161

                    Jake (irritably)
Are you <u>sure</u> he said to tell me he'd be in <u>this</u>
afternoon? I've got a dinner engagement.

                    Margie
Who hasn't.

                    Big Kim (coming in the door
               behind them, sullen and distraught)
Hello Jake...hello Margie...I'm sorry to keep you
waiting so long...but that doctor is quite a
blabber-mouth...come in the office a minute, will
you?

                    Jake (forcing a smile)
Why certainly, Kim...I certainly didn't have anything more important to do...hahaha!

     They start moving toward Kim's office and will
     eventually pass through the huge combination
     drafting room and business office, fortunately
     deserted at this hour except for two young men
     working overtime on a five foot model of a
     hydro-electric plant. On the far side of the
     office we see the bookkeeping and cashiers'
     departments.

                    Big Kim (holding back to
               speak to Margie)
Did that little uh...that new stewardess from my
plane call up?

                    Margie (with a faint smile)
Oh yes...she is on ice...and I took care of the
other ones...do you want me to wait a few minutes
in case anything went haywire?

                    Big Kim
Just a few minutes, Margie, thanks...I sort of
stranded her here...she didn't have any date.

                    Margie
If she looks like she sounds, that wouldn't be any
problem...all she'd have to do would be go down
to the lobby and cross her legs...

                    Big Kim (turning to go)
She might be an old dame with legs like a saw
horse.

     He walks out of the SHOT.

                    Margie (beaming)
That's right, she might....or cross-eyed.

                    162

JAKE - WAITING FOR MR. KIMBLE   23

This is near a model two young men are working on.

                    Big Kim (coming down the
            aisle)
Beejack Project?

                    Jake (proudly)
That's right.

                    Big Kim (moving out of the SHOT)
I'll see it when it's finished.

                    One Young Man Working On the Model
In just a few mmminutes...

                    The Other Young Man
Is that the big boss?

                    One Young Man
Yyes...

LONG SUFFERING BAMBERGER AT THE TELEPHONE   24
IN MR. KIMBLE'S OFFICE

                    Bamby (desperately into the
            telephone)
But Miriam...listen once for a minute, will you...
who's trying to catch who? Gum shoeing! Who's gum
shoeing? Is it my fault if I work for a...I'll
call you later!

This last as he looks over his shoulder.

THE PRIVATE OFFICE   25

Big Kim and Jake come in. The big fellow goes
directly to a double door, which, as he opens
it, reveals a complete clothes closet with
shelves for haberdashery, a bath and shower.

                    Big Kim (starting to undress)
Go on out, Bamby, will you...I want to talk to Mr.
Kramer.

BAMBY - CROSSING WITH SOME PAPERS IN HIS HAND   26

                    Bamby
A Senora Madriga who says she's the mother of a
Senorita Madriga, Felice Consuella Guadalupe,
called from south of the border to say...

                    Big Kim (continuing to change
                         his clothes)
It's a lie...take it up with the legal department...
and go on out of here...I want to talk to Mr. Kramer.

                    Bamby (happily)
Can I have the whole night off?

                    Big Kim
Yeah...go on, will you?

                    Bamby (leaving the SHOT)
Now if I just had something to do for a whole night.

                    Big Kim (watching Bamby leave)
Jake: What would you do if I dropped dead for awhile?

                    Jake (startled)
For awhile.

                    Big Kim
Maybe six months.

                    Jake
What are you talking about, suspended animation?

                    Big Kim (irritably)
What are you talking about? I'm asking you a hypo-
thetical question...as the President of this outfit
I have a perfect right to ask you what you'd do if
I croaked all of a sudden.

                    Jake
That you have.

                    Big Kim (loudly)
All right, I just croaked...I'm stiff on the floor
...with my tongue hanging out...what do you do now?

                    Jake (after a few helpless
                         gestures)
Well, I...I'd...send for an embalmer I suppose...
or would you rather be cremated?

                    Big Kim (still louder)
I'm not talking about all that stuff...you're already
back from the graveyard...you can have had me stuffed
for all I care...or mold my ashes into a set of
souvenir...ash trays...WHAT DO YOU DO NOW?

                    Jake (after a slight pause)
Go home to dinner...I'm late already.

                    Big Kim (with forced calm)
Look: Jake...all I'm asking you is: Do you think
you and the boys could hold things fairly well together if I had to disappear for say...six months?

                    Jake (confidentially)
You mean on account of that Spanish dame?

                    Big Kim (barking)
It has nothing to do with dames.

                    Jake (worried)
They didn't get you on that income tax thing?

                    Big Kim (loud again)
They did not get me on that income tax thing.
Because I don't horse around with that income tax
thing...like some people I could mention!

                    Jake (relieved)
Then what do you mean can we run things while you're
away? In the first place they practically run themselves...all except that lousy automobile company you
started that'll run us into the ground!...in the second
place who do you think has been running things while
you were doing your little disappearing act? If I
don't...

                    Big Kim (interrupting)
I'm not talking about little things, Jake...I know
how competent you are...and the rest of the boys
...but what would you do if something big came
along while I was away? Something big like...

                    Jake (thoroughly aroused)
Something big like what?

                    Big Kim (pointing toward the
                        outer office)
Maybe something like the Beejack Project! What
would you do if something like that came along?

                    Jake (boiling)
Well exactly what I did...we were running into a
penalty...you were flying around someplace with
some new air hostess or other...so I broke ground
yesterday!

                    Big Kim (somewhat displeased)
Oh you did.

                    Jake
Well what was I supposed to do...burst into tears?

165

Now they turn, as the two young men bang their
way into the office with the model.

                    Big Kim (watching them scurly)
What's that supposed to be?

                    1st Young Man Working On The Model
Why the Bbbeejack Project...you said you'd llook at
it when it was fffinished...

                    Big Kim (bellowing)
All right, I've <u>looked</u> at it...TAKE IT OUT.

                    The Two Young Men (together)
Yyyes sir.

    As they hurry out backwards the young man
    furtherest from us catches his heel in the
    soft carpet and sinks gently to the ground,
    without injuring the model however.

                    Big Kim (glaring after them)
The Beejack Project.
        (then to Jake:)
I'm going away for six months...doctor's orders...
something the matter with my nut...or at least
 there could be if I didn't go away...I'm not
supposed to write or talk to any of you and you're
not supposed to get in touch with me...I'll leave
you a power of attorney and get me six thousand
cash in the morning...that's all I'm supposed to
take with me...I hope there'll be a little something left here when I come back.

                    Jake (affectionately)
There'll be plenty left, Charlie...you see, you're
an instigator...a starter-upper...the head guy on
the camping trip who can start the fires by rubbing the sticks together or whatever they use but once
those fires are started we can keep them going...you
don't have to worry your head about that...and you
have been getting a little irritable lately Charlie
...I'll be frank with you.

                    Big Kim (narrowing his eyes)
Is that so!

                    Jake
Yes you have, Charlie,..and if six months doesn't
quite do it...take <u>eight</u> months...take a <u>year!</u>

                    Big Kim (growling)
That's really very generous of you.

                    Jake
Don't mention it, Charlie...I'll get you the money
in the morning...now I'm <u>really</u> late for dinner...
Good night.

He hurries out.

                 Big Kim (muttering after him)
You're late for dinner...you tramp...you didn't
have a pail to eat out of when I picked you up...
if it wasn't for me...
         (suddenly he looks at his watch and
         yells:)
You're late for dinner...Holy Mackerel!

    Ceasing to be sorry for himself, he leaps
    into his trousers, shoves a necktie and a hand-
    kerchief into his coat pocket, a Western bank-
    roll into his pants and hurries out to keep
    his date with the pretty little stewardess.

                     DISSOLVE TO:

BIG KIM AND THE BEAUTIFUL STEWARDESS IN A   27
NIGHT CLUB

    They are sitting on a banquette, a champagne
    cooler on the table in front of them. He is
    toying with her hand. The music is very
    pretty. The lights are dim.

                 Big Kim (a little sorry for
        himself)
I sure hate to leave all this...you'll probably be
married with nine children by the time I get back.

                The Beautiful Stewardess (softly)
Would you like me to go with you, Kim?

                Big Kim (with a helpless gesture)
This is supposed to be for a rest, Honey.

    The beautiful girl gives him a double-take,
    then busts out laughing.
                     FADE OUT:

FADE IN: 28
LONG, HIGH SHOT OF THE GRAND CENTRAL STATION -
DAY

    The Information Booth in the middle is clearly
    visible.

THE INFORMATION MAN IN GRAND CENTRAL STATION   29
PAST BIG KIM'S SHOULDER

                Information Man
How was that again?

BIG KIM AND A NEGRO PORTER PAST THE INFORMA-   30
TION MAN

     Big Kim
I said...what have you got in the way of hamlets?

     Information Man
Hamlets?

     Big Kim
That's right.

  INFORMATION MAN PAST BIG KIM   31

     Information Man (after a moment's
    concentration)
To be, or not to be...that is the question...
whether 'tis nobler in the mind...

  BIG KIM AND THE PORTER PAST THE INFORMATION   32
  MAN

Mr. Kimble is looking at the Information Man
with considerable displeasure.

     The Information Man's Voice
...to suffer the slings and arrows of outrageous
fortune...

As Big Kim opens his mouth to insult him, the
Porter picks up the soliloquy, and Mr. Kimble
glares at him instead.

     The Porter (mellifluously)
...or to take arms against a sea of troubles...and
by opposing...end them...

     Big Kim (glaring from one to
    the other)
Give me that book over there...
    (he reaches across the counter for a big,
    fat book, flops it open at random and jabs
    a pencil on the page)
What does that say, right there?

     The Information Man (squinting)
I'll really have to put my glasses on for that one.

He begins to do so.

     Big Kim (throwing some money
    on the counter)
All right, that's a hamlet...get me a one-way ticket
to it...and meet me in the pipe shop over there.

       168

32
CONT'D
(2)

                    The Porter (picking up the
        money)
Yes sir.

                    Big Kim (departing)
And save your television skit for somebody who
likes television.

                    The Porter (looking after him)
Yes sir.
        (then to the Information Man)
Probably got a stomach ache.

                    The Information Man (philos-
        ophically)
Or a toothache...man is subject to many aches...now
let me see what we've got here.

        They both bend their heads down.
                              DISSOLVE TO:

A WORM-EATEN RAILROAD SIGN ON TOP OF A   33
PASSENGER SHED. WE READ: WEST BISMARCK
ELEVATION 2 FT.

        We hear a train coming to a stop.

COMBINATION PASSENGER AND FREIGHT TRAIN ROLLS   34
TWENTY FEET TO A STOP

        Big Kim, suitcases beside him, magazines under
        his arm, stands on the lowest step of the lone
        passenger car. He looks around dubiously, then
        steps to the ground and puts his suitcases
        down beside him.
                    The Conductor's Voice
All aboard!

        The locomotive answers with a pleasant whistle
        and the train moves on.
                    Butch's Voice
Carry your bags, Mister?
                    Big Kim (looking past the
        CAMERA)
Huh.

A NICE LOOKING LITTLE BOY OF EIGHT IN FRONT   35
OF THE DESERTED AND DILAPIDATED STATION

His hair cut explains his name. The shadows
of the cars and the noise of the train continue
on during the first part of this scene.

                    Butch (coming forward to join
          Mr. Kimble)
Can I help you carry your bags?

                    Big Kim (gravely)
Oh sure.

                    Butch (happily)
You a stranger in town?

                    Big Kim
Well, I didn't grow up here.

                    Butch (trying to lift the bags
          without success)
You got bricks in there?

                    Big Kim
No...mantelpieces...I always carry a couple of
them around...you know, in case it gets cold.

                    Butch
I'll bet you're just teasing me.

                    Big Kim (laughing and picking
          up the suitcases)
You carry the handle and I'll take the rest of it
and we'll be all right.

                    Butch
All right.

     THE CAMERA MOVES WITH THEM

                    Big Kim
Now tell me about your fair city...where is it? I
don't smell it.

                    Butch (raising his nose)
Smell what?

                    Big Kim
The herring factory! I presume a town called
Bismarck has a herring factory.

                    Butch (puzzled)
I don't know what you're talking about...we don't
have any factories here any more...there used to
be a carriage works but that's closed now.

170

                    Big Kim (stamping his feet)
And just when I could use one too...how far is the
hotel in this boneyard? I suppose there's a choice
of one.

                    Butch (evasively)
Not very far.

                    Big Kim (a slightly suspicious
              look)
About how far?

                    Butch
Well it might seem further to me because my legs
are shorter.

                    Big Kim (his suspicions deepen-
              ing rapidly)
Never mind that stuff...I asked you a frank question and I want an honest answer...I didn't happen
to wear my suitcase carrying shoes today.

                    Butch (reluctantly)
About two miles.

                    Big Kim
What!

     He dumps the heavy suitcases on the ground
     and glares down at the little boy.

                    Butch
Walking is good for you.

                    Big Kim
When I want any health advice from you I'll ask for
it...is there a cab in this graveyard?

                    Butch
You mean like a taxicab?

                    Big Kim (vehemently)
Any kind of a cab...at this point I'm not fussy.

                    Butch
No sir...Mr. Richardson used to have one...but the
bottom fell out of it...he takes care of the ceme-
tery.

                    Big Kim
Well, I'm certainly glad to hear it...I mean that
they bury the people around here...I was afraid
they just left them sitting on the front porch...
rocking.

                    Butch (laughing)
Gee you're funny.

                              171

                    Big Kim (picking up the suit-
            cases)
Well...let's get going.

                    Butch
Yes sir.

                    Big Kim (stopping suddenly and
              looking past the CAMERA)
Say...

                    Butch (following his gaze)
What?

        A SURPLUS JEEP ACROSS THE STREET

        It is battered but complete down to the
        shovel on the side and the winch on the front.

        BIG KIM AND BUTCH - LOOKING AT THE JEEP   37

                    Big Kim
Does that look as cozy to you as it does to me?

                    Butch (happily)
It looks super.

                    Big Kim (stamping his feet)
Then follow me.
                                    DISSOLVE TO:

        BIG KIM AND BUTCH IN THE JEEP AS IT DRIVES   38
        DOWN THE STREET

                    Big Kim (listening to the
              terrible motor noise)
Sure purrs like a kitten, don't she?

                    Butch (laughing)
You make me laugh all the time...what's your name?

                    Big Kim (stalling for time)
Oh, my name...let me see now: Jones.

                    Butch (delighted)
No fooling! That's my mother's name and my father's
name too...what's your first name?

                    Big Kim (disgustedly)
Smith...what's yours?

172

                    Butch
Butch...my real name is Ocla E. Jones, Junior...
but they call me Butch because my hair is cut that
way.

                    Big Kim
I see...what does your father do...I suppose his
name is Ocla E. Jones, Senior.

                    Butch (a little evasively)
He's still in the army on an island some place...
hehasn't come back yet.

                    Big Kim
What's the name of the island?

                    Butch (looking straight ahead)
Tarara...

                    Big Kim (after looking at the
            little boy out of the corner of his eye)
That's down in the South Pacific some place, isn't
it?

                    Butch (looking straight ahead)
That's right.

                    Big Kim
I see....
            (then suddenly looking past the CAMERA)
Holy Moses! Look at that joint.

                    Butch (a little worried)
That's the Ogden House...the hotel I'm taking you
to.

LONG SHOT - A RAMSHACKLE SMALL TOWN HOTEL   39

    It is complete with gingerbread work, broken
    railings and missing balustrades. The jeep
    pulls up in front of it and dies a quivering
    death. Big Kim and Butch start to get out.

LONG SHOT - THROUGH THE DOORS OF THE HOTEL   40
AT BIG KIM AND BUTCH GETTING OUT OF THE JEEP

    As they come toward us with suitcases, the
    CAMERA pulls them into the ancient lobby.

                    Big Kim (looking around with
            very little pleasure)
You sure this is the best hotel in town?

                            173

                              Butch
You didn't say anything about the best hotel...
besides it's the only hotel...it has to be the
best.   MO..THER!

                    Big Kim (suspiciously)
Your family connected with this?

                    Butch (brightly)
Oh yes...we own the hotel...grandma does the cooking.

                    Big Kim
I got you...and you certainly got me...
          (he puts down his suitcases)
I'll try the porch before I make up my mind...I got
to have rocking chairs.

                    Butch (leading the way)
I'll show you the good one.

THE PORCH OF THE OGDEN HOUSE   41

     Mr. Kimble and Butch come out and stop at a
     rocking chair.

                    Butch
Here it is.

                    Big Kim (looking at it dubiously)
You say this is the good one?

                    Butch
Some of the others came off the rockers a couple
of times.

                    Big Kim (lowering himself
               tenderly into the chair and trying it
               gingerly)
Six months of this and I'll be a little off my own
rocker.

                    Butch (happily)
You going to be with us six months?

                    Big Kim (rising)
That's the theory.

                    Butch
We never had anybody for six months before except
Mr. Stone...I think he gets special rates...would
you like the room next to him?

                    Big Kim
You say he plays the cornet?

                              174

                    Butch
Oh no...he's just a friend of my mother's...he
lends money, I think.

                    Big Kim
Good! I'll put the bite on him for a few C's...
now let's take a look at the cells - the rooms.

                    Butch (leading the way)
Yes sir.

     Now there is pounding on iron.

                    Big Kim (clocking his head)
Blacksmith shop upstairs...or is that a rock
crusher?

                    Butch
I guess my mother's trying to fix the bathroom
again.

                    Big Kim (gallantly)
Ah...may her efforts be attended with success...
let's go.

     The CAMERA PANS with them as they walk into
     the lobby and together, as before, pick up
     the suitcases.
                                    DISSOLVE TO:

BIG KIM AND BUTCH COMING INTO ROOM   42
NUMBER SEVEN IN THE OGDEN HOUSE

     It contains an iron bed, a night table, a
     bureau, a wash stand with a pitcher, chipped
     basin and slop jar, and a rocking chair.
     Across the door to the adjoining room there
     is attached a pole for hanging clothes. Next
     to the hall door a speaking tube complete with
     whistle comes up from the floor. Under the
     window, a bucket contains some twenty feet
     of knotted rope, one end of which is attached
     to a big ring in the frame.

                    Big Kim (putting down suitcases)
Very neat...neat but not gaudy.

     He puts down his suitcases and crosses to
     the speaking tube into which he whistles.

                    Big Kim
Where does this go...to the engine room?

                    Butch
That goes to the lobby...in case you need something.

                            175

                    Big Kim
I see..and they pump it up to you through this...
like hot soup or something.

                    Butch
Oh no, you just ask for it.

                    Big Kim
What will they think of next!

          Now he crosses to the bucket under the window
          and lifts up an end of the rope. The CAMERA
          PANS him over.

                    Big Kim
And this is to hang yourself with, I suppose...
after eating one of the hotel's dinners.

                    Butch
It's to shinny down in case of fire...it's lots of
fun.

                    Big Kim
I'll be looking forward to it.

          He laughs and goes to the bureau and unpacks
          his bags functionally but unfussily by turn-
          ing them upside down and dumping their contents
          into the drawers. Three suits he hangs on
          the rod. The cans of tobacco he puts on the
          top, next to them a few pipes, cleaners,
          lighters and pipe tools.

                    Big Kim
You a pipe smoker?

                    Butch
No sir.

                    Big Kim
You're missing something.

          Butch laughs and Mr. Kimble picks up the two
          suitcases and tries to shove them under the
          bed. One of them strikes an obstruction.
          Now he exchanges a look with Butch, then
          reaches under the bed and pulls out a wire,
          cage trap about two feet long by ten inches
          square.

                    Big Kim
What's this for? Gophers, I hope...

                    Butch
No sir...my mother says all old hotels have rats...
that some hotels are just more honest than others.

                    Big Kim   42
Then this is the most honest hotel in the world...   CONT'D
bar none...and your mother must be a very remarkable   (3)
woman...I look forward to meeting her.

                    Butch
Oh she is...I'll tell her you're here.

                    Big Kim
Good...you do that.

          He watches the little boy go, laughs at the
          room, then crosses to the bureau. Here he
          puts on a golf cap and from a box full of new
          pipes, tries several in his face to see how
          they look. After this, he opens a number of
          tobacco pouches, including one in which each
          opening of a zipper reveals more zippered
          compartments until the whole thing hangs
          loosely in a dilapidated chain of leather
          pockets, and one of those Englishman's, made
          of magnificent tie silk, which unwinds
          almost to his knees before giving up its
          tobacco. He fills this from a pound can,
          spilling only a little of it on the floor,
          then loading all his pockets with pipe clean-
          ers, pipe scrapers, special blowtorch lighters
          for pipe smokers, and all the other apparatus
          of an apprentice pipe smoker, he picks up
          two Book-of-the-Month novels, provided with
          paper cutters, and gets ready to go downstairs.
          He reacts once more to the pounding.

                              DISSOLVE TO:

BUTCH BEHIND THE HOTEL DESK

          He is trying to put a ten cent airplane
          together. Now he looks up and smiles.

                    Butch
Hello.

          Mr. Kimble coming downstairs with his books
          and smoking equipment. This is to the
          accompaniment of pounding from above.

                    Big Kim
Must have that horse almost shod by now...or are
they building a boiler?

          The CAMERA PANS him over to the desk.

                    Big Kim
Going to do a little reading...
          (he points to the toy airplane)
What's that?...a P-31?

                      177

                         Butch
No, Aeronca...but it doesn't go together very well.

                    Big Kim (pointing)
I think that fits on to there..Where's the cement?

                         Butch
Here.

                    Big Kim (working)
That's better...then this fits on to here...and
that folds over like that on the dotted line...

                    Butch (delighted)
Oh gee...

                         Big Kim
Then this slips under here...and we put a little
cement there...and there we are.

                         Butch
Were you a flier one time when you were young.

                    Big Kim (after a slight pause)
Yeah...I've done a little flying.
                    (now he looks with displeasure at his
                    books, then at his wristwatch)
I don't suppose there's a little brokerage office
in this town.

                    Butch (innocently)
A what? Wheeeee!
                    (this last as he pretends that his plane
                    is flying)

                         Big Kim
How about a little gambling house?...although I
suppose that's a silly question...is there a bowling
alley?

                    Butch (vaguely)
A bowling alley?

                         Big Kim
Where they bowl Recreation Center? Shuffleboard...
Ping Pong...Turkish Bath...Pool Parlor...There's
gotta be a Pool Parlor.

                         Butch
There used to be one I think.
          (then as Mr. Kimble turns away dejectedly)
We have baseball.

                         Big Kim
When?

                         Butch
Fourth of July.

Big Kim (turning to go)
Okay...the books.
　　　　(he sighs as he looks at them and exits)

Butch (flying his plane)
Wheeee...brrrrrr...

MR. KIMBLE ON THE PORCH OF THE OGDEN HOUSE   44

He counts the chairs to find the good one, then
sits in it cautiously. N w, spreading out his
apparatus, he goes to work on a pipe. He fills
it too tightly so that when he tries to light
it with the blow torch lighter it won't draw.
Now he takes it apart, sucks through it and on
the third suck is rewarded by a mouthful of
tobacco he has considerable trouble getting rid
of. The pipe being still plugged up, he blows
through it as hard as he can and the tobacco
sprays all over the porch, except what gets in
his eye, leaving the bowl as clean as a whistle.
Having wiped his eye and sneezed, he starts again.
Unwinding the pouch to the floor, he fills the
pipe, lights it with the blow torch and when it
is going well, inhales a great cloud of smoke
which nearly strangles him. Recovering from this,
he puts his apparatus neatly away and starts cutting the pages of his novel with a dull paper
cutter. At one point, the paper proves to be
so strong and the cutter so dull, a whole chapter
comes out in his hands rather than submit to
having its pages cut. Now he discovers that the
pipe has gone out and this time the blow-torch
lighter refuses to work. He takes it apart with
the screwdriver that came with it, retrieves the
parts that fall and roll on the porch, and re-
assembles it in a slightly new form. This time
it lights and shoots a long thin flame straight at
his nose, rubbing his nose, he twists part of the
lighter around, holds it horizontally and sets
fire to his cap.

MRS. LANE IN THE DOOR OF THE HOTEL   45

She is a somewhat severe looking lady in her
middle fifties, at the moment slightly dishevel-
led and marked with grease. She holds a Stillson wrench in her hands and a wad of oakum. She
watches Mr. Kimble in surprise.

MR. KIMBLE BEATING OUT THE SPARKS FROM HIS CAP   46

MRS. LANE IN THE DOORWAY OF THE HOTEL

She looks back over her shoulder and her
daughter, Mrs. Jones, peeks out. The latter
carries a h mmer, pliers, more oakum and a
faucet, but despite wearing overalls and being
also covered with grease, she is a lovely thing
to behold. After a look at Mr. Kimble, she examines herslef in a pocket mirror and immediately
retires to repair her appearance.

                    Mrs. Lane (to Mr. Kimble)
You got a bee in your bonnet?

     MR. KIMBLE WORKING ON HIS CAP   48
                    Big Kim
Oh hello...no I just had a little...misunderstanding
with this thing...I'm Mr. Jones the new guest here...
your little boy shanghaied me at the station...I'm
in Number Seven.

     MRS. LANE IN THE DOORWAY
                    Mrs. Lane
And I hope you'll be very happy with us Mr. Jones...
I'm Mrs. Lane, Butch's grandmother, and...
               (seeing her arrive out of the corner of
               her eye:)
This is my daughter, <u>Mrs.</u> Jones

                    Mrs. Jones (looking even pre-
               ttier than before)
How do you do, Mr. Jones...
               (THE CAMERA PANS her over to him)
This is quite a coincidence...I hope it doesn't
start a scandal...I'm Butch's mother.

                    Big Kim (shaking hands warmly)
Well what do you know.

                    Mrs. Jones
Won't you sit down?
               (she seats herself in the good rocker)

                    Big Kim (seeing the whole six
               months through entirely new eyes)
With great pleasure.

     He sits.

                         180

                    Mrs. Jones (rocking)
It really is strange, our both being called Jones...
my name could just as easily have been Brown.

                    Big Kim (laughing)
Mine too.

                    Mrs. Jones
Are you going to be with us long? Butch said something about six months but I'm sure he misunderstood.

                    Big Kim (charmed)
Well that was kinda the idea...and the more I look
over the...prospects here the better they look.

                    Mrs. Jones
I'm so glad...I hope you're not looking for work
because I'm afraid...

                    Big Kim
No, no...nothing like that.

                    Mrs. Jones
Were you thinking of opening a business maybe?

                    Big Kim
Anything but.

                    Mrs. Jones
Or buying a farm? There are lots of them for sale.

                    Big Kim
I'm just here for a,...a kind of a slowdown...I'm
supposed to take it sort of easy for about six
months...you know: a rocking chair...a pipe...
          (he glances at the prescription from
          his pocket)
...a little incognito...I mean gardening and,..uh...
          (he scowls at the paper and puts it away)
that's about all...just a kind of a slow-down.

                    Mrs. Jones (happily)
Well we'll certainly take the best care of you...
I'll take your temperature...and see that you smoke
your pipe...and put a little rug over your knees
while you're in your rocker...and you certainly
could go a long way before you'd find a town any
slower than this one.
          (she puts her hand on his forehead:)
You don't feel hot.

                    Big Kim
Look: I think I gave you an entirely false impression...it's just this doctor's idea...

                    Mrs. Jones (interrupting
              soothingly)
I know, I know...and I can tell just what kind of a
patient you're going to be just by looking at you...
but there isn't any sense in going to a doctor and
paying him a lot of money and then not doing what
he tells you to do...now did you think to bring
your slippers and a bathrobe, and a hot water bag?

                    Big Kim (firmly)
I did not.

                    Mrs. Jones
Naturally...I'll get you some in Peruvia....now how
would you feel about breakfast in bed?

                    Big Kim
Well that all depends...

                    Mrs. Jones
It would be very good for...I'll bring it up
myself.

                    Big Kim
Then I want it.

                    Mrs. Jones (laughing)
Yes, I can tell exactly what kind of a patient you're
going to be...What did you do before you were sick?

                    Big Kim (scowling)
I'm not sick...I just...I was a kind of a builder,
I guess you'd call it...in a small way naturally.

                    Mrs. Jones (hopefully)
You mean like a carpenter?
              (then her face falling:)
Not that you can do anything like that now, of course.

                    Big Kim (violently)
What do you mean I can't do any? If I can do gardening, I can do carpentering can't I? It's the same
thing...you don't think I'm going to spend six months
in a rocking chair just with a pipe in my kisser, do
you?...

                    Mrs. Jones (calculatingly)
Can you plumb too?

                    Big Kim (almost gruffly)
I've done a little plumbing in my time...and a little
plastering too.

182

                    Mrs. Jones (ecstatically)   49
Oh how heavenly...to have a plumber-carpenter-plast-   CONT'D
erer living right here in the <u>hotel</u> with me...you   (4)
don't know what it's like being a woman.

                    Big Kim (laughing gaily)
I think you got something there.

        He rocks back roaring with laughter, the
        chair collapses into so much kindling wood
        and Mr. Kimble lands on the flat of his back.

                    Mrs. Jones (hurrying to his
              assistance)
Oh dear! I'm so sorry Mr. Jones...did you hurt
yourself?

                    Big Kim (sitting up and
              laughing)
No...I just didn't pick the good one that time.

        Mrs. Jones helps him to his feet, without
        either of them noticing that one of the rockers
        is still attached to the seat of Mr. Kimble's
        pants.

                    Mrs. Jones (distressed)
I can't tell you how sorry...

                    Big Kim
Forget it...I'll buy a little glue and fix these
up for you.

                    Mrs. Jones
Oh that is so kind of you

                    Butch's Voice
Mommie.

                    Mrs. Jones (turning)
Yes Darling...

    BUTCH IN THE DOORWAY   50

                    Butch
Grandma says now the water's running all over the
kitchen.

        He exits hurriedly

                        183

MR. KIMBLE AND MRS. JONES   51

                         Mrs. Jones (defeated)
Oh...rats!

                         Mr. Kimble (laughing)
Maybe I can help you.

                         Mrs. Jones (ecstatically)
Oh would you Mr. Jones?

                         Big Kim
Sure.
                    (he takes a step, then discovers the
                    rocker attached to the seat of his pants)
Wait a minute...I'm taking some of the furniture
with me.

                         Mrs. Jones (hurrying behind him)
Oh dear.

         She tries unsuccessfully to loosen the rocker.

                         Big Kim (directing the maneuver
                    over his shoulder)
Try to unhook it...it's probably pinched in there...
in a crack in the wood or something...just give it
a little yank...

                         Mrs. Jones (worried)
There might be a nail.

                         Big Kim (manfully)
There wouldn't be a nail in that part of the chair...
Just yank it a little...not too hard...but a little
harder than...
                    (there is a loud tearing sound and the
                    seat of Mr. Kimble's trousers comes down
                    in a flap.)

                         Mrs. Jones (nearly in tears)
Oh now look what I've done.

                         Big Kim (holding himself to-
                    gether)
Oh that's all right...I never cared much for this
suit anyway...it was always a little...

                         Mrs. Jones
You're such an angel...I'll pin you up.

         She does so.

                         Big Kim (laughing)
Not let's take a look at the plumbing.

184

Mrs. Jones
Do you want to change your trousers first?

Big Kim
Maybe I'd better change after the plumbing.

MRS. LANE AND BUTCH - IN THE KITCHEN   52

The handle has just come off the cold water
faucet in the sink and a strong stream of
water is splashing merrily from the sink onto
the floor. Butch and his grandmother are trying to pound the handle back onto the faucet

Mrs. Lane
It just won't do it...the teeth are all gone.

Butch
Hit it again...why don't you?

Mrs. Lane
We'll just break it like we did that other one...
what did you do with the screw that's supposed to
hold it on?

Butch
I lost it.

MR. KIMBLE AND MRS. JONES COMING INTO THE   53
KITCHEN

Big Kim (the portrait of
self assurance)
Well, well...what's our little problem here?
(the CAMERA PANS him over to the sink
and he spins the useless handle)
The first thing to do in a case like t is is find
the shut-off valve...it's usually under the sink
...
(he dives through the spray and squats
under the sink)
Here it is...anybody got any pliers?

Mrs. Jones (bending a little
and ducking the spray)
Where are the pincers mother?

Mrs. Lane
What did you do with the pincers, Butch?

Butch
I don't remember.

                    Mrs. Lane (taking a Stillson   53
              wrench off the table)   CONT'D
Would a monkey wrench do?   (2)

        She hands it to him.

                    Big Kim (laughing)
This is called a Stillson wrench...it'll do fine.

        He starts adjusting it.

                    Mrs. Jones (kneeling close to
              him)
I tried twisting that thing one day but I couldn't
budge it.

                    Big Kim
I'll budge it....
                    (He gives a yank and nothing happens.)
...but it's a little rusty at that...
                    (He readjusts his wrench)
...you ought to have a plumber look over all your
pipes.

                    Mrs. Jones
He won't come any more.

                    Big Kim (grunting and trying
              again)
Why not?

                    Mrs. Jones
He wants to be paid in cash.

                    Big Kim (indignantly)
In advance.

                    Mrs. Jones (meekly)
No...for the other times...besides he says my pipes
are past repairing.

                    Big Kim
That's just a racket...we'll have this fixed in no
time.
                    (He heaves hard on the wrench without results)
It's rusty all right...but that's why you have wrenches
with long handles...

                    Mrs. Jones
You're terribly kind.

                    Big Kim (bracing his foot
              against the foot of the sink)
With enough leverage it has to come... nothing
can resist leverage.

          He arches his back and grunts with the effort.
          He is quite right about the leverage because
          the shut-off valve comes out of the pipe by
          the roots. A geyser of water shoots out from
          under the sink and Mr. Kimble falls flat on
          his back. Butch jumps up and down in glee
          but Mrs. Jones manages to suppress her laugh-
          ter. The water is now shooting across the
          kitchen at a great rate.

                    Mrs. Jones (helping Mr. Kimble
              to his feet)
Did you hurt yourself?

                    Big Kim (popping his thumb
              into his mouth)
Not at all... now give me a...a towel or something... a couple of towels.

                    Mrs. Lane (handing them to him)
Here.

                    Big Kim
And some wire.

                    Mrs. Jones
Get some wire, Butch... there's some in the backyard.

                    Big Kim
I don't know how much good this'll do but...

          He dives under the sink and, partly with his
          body and partly with the towels, momentarily
          controls the stream of water.

MR. STONE COMING THROUGH THE DOOR FROM THE   54
LOBBY

          He is a large rurally-prosperous looking man,
          a little older than Mr. Kimble.

                     Mr. Stone
What's the trouble, Peggy... the pipes again?
              (he starts for the sink)
Let's find the shut-off valve... Who's that?

          He bends down to have a better look at the
          stranger under the sink.

                    187

Mrs. Jones
Oh Mr. Jones, this is Mr. Stone.

CLOSE SHOT MR. KIMBLE UNDER THE SINK -   55
REVERSE

Water is spraying in his face as he wrestles
with the broken pipe. Mr. Stone's face appears behind him as he bends low.

Big Kim (without looking around)
What did you say?

Mr. Stone (stretching forth a
big hand)
My name is Stone... how are you?

Mr. Kimble turns to look at him, then takes
his hand off the pipe to shake. A solid stream
of water hits Mr. Stone right between the eyes.

FULL SHOT - THE KITCHEN   56

Mrs. Jones
Look out, Lucas, you'll get all wet.

Mr. Stone (wiping his glasses)
Too late to tell me now... Where did you find this
plumber?

Without waiting for a reply, he goes over
and bends down behind Mr. Kimble.

Mr. Stone
If you can't shut that valve off, there's porbably
another one in the cellar.
(in reply he gets a solid stream which
splashes off the end of his nose)

MR. KIMBLE - UNDER THE SINK FROM THE BACK   57

Big Kim (coming out from under
the sink)
If you'd like to take a crack at it brother... it's
all yours.

The CAMERA brings him in to a position opposite
Mr. Stone. The two big men look at each other
like strange male dogs.

Mrs. Jones (hastily)
This is Mr. Stone, Mr. Jones... who has been so very
kind to us all.

                    Big Kim (looking him over)   57
Oh yes... the cornet player.   CONT'D.
                                                            (2)
                    Mr. Stone (puzzled and faintly
            irritated)
How's that?

                    Big Kim (snapping his fingers
            and laughing)
Oh no...I remember: the money lender!

                    Mrs. Jones (in hasty response
            to Mr. Stone's look)
I don't know what Mr. Jones is talking about, Lucas..
            (then to Mr. Kimble)
Mr. Stone has been very, very kind...
            (then to Mr. Stone)
Mr. Jones is the new guest in the hotel, Lucas.

                    Mr. Stone (looking him over
            sourly)
Oh...practicing without a license, huh?

                    Big Kim (narrowing his eyes)
I've already told you it's all yours...if you need
a little practice.

                    Butch (rushing in full speed
            with some wire)
Here's all the wire I could find.
            (he slips onto the wet floor into a
            sitting position)

                    Big Kim (yanking him to his
            feet)
You hurt yourself?...'course you didn't.
            (he takes the wire)
Thanks, now unless Mr. Stone wants to take over...
Where is the cellar? We'd better find that other
valve before the joint floats away.

                    Mrs. Jones (stooping over to
            open a trap door)
It's right here, Mr. Jones.

                    Mr. Stone (to Mrs. Jones)
Let me help you.
            (he moves forward and bends over. Mr.
            Kimble having had the same idea at the
            same time, does the same thing and the
            two gentlemen crack their heads together
            like two billy goats.)

                    Big Kim (recovering first)
You're a big help.
            (he goes down three steps)
We got a flashlight?

                    189

                    Mr. Stone
I got one in my car...only my battery's weak.

                    Mrs. Jones (picking up a box)
I'll hold matches for you.
          (she follows him down the steps)

                    Big Kim (disappearing into the
          cellar)
All right you'd better start scratching.

      And after one nervous smile at Mr. Stone,
      Mrs. Jones disappears also.

                    Mr. Stone (to Mrs. Lane)
Fellow going to be here long?

                    Mrs. Lane (nervously)
I don't suppose so, Lucas..just over night, I guess.

                    Mr. Stone
Paid in advance?

                    Mrs. Lane
I don't really know....I don't suppose so.

                    Mr. Stone
Better be careful...that's a very low type...notice
them ears?

                    Mrs. Lane
No I didn't, Lucas.

                    Mr. Stone
Like a gangster...I seen 'em in the movies...could
be a fugitive from justice.

                    Mrs. Lane (putting her hand to
          her heart)
Oh my gracious.

      MR. KIMBLE AND MRS. JONES - IN THE CELLAR   58

      This contains apple barrels with and without
      apples, potatoe bins, old crates, a coal bin
      and lots of preserves in Mason jars on rickety
      shelves. Water is coming through the floor
      above in several places including the edge of
      the trap door opening.

                    Big Kim
We'll find the pipe and follow it and someplace
there has to be a valve.

                    Mrs. Jones (lighting a match)
Of course there has to be, Mr. Jones.

                    Big Kim (starting over a barrel)
I think I can see it.

                    Butch (appearing at the top of
          the stairs)
Can I come down too, Mummy?

                    190

                Mrs. Jones (turning to her son
         match in hand, so that Mr. Kimble is
         deprived of all light)
No, darling, not now. You go back up to Grand-...

                Big Kim (disappearing behind
         the barrels)
WOW!

                Mrs. Jones (coming forward,
         match in hand)
Mr. Jones, are you all right? You go back upstairs
this very instant, Butch! Mr. Jones!
         (a stream of water puts out her match)
Darn it!
         (now she lights another match)
Mr. Jones, did you hurt yourself?

                Big Kim (rising from under a
         pile of detritus which falls to all sides
         of him)
Well....I didn't do myself any good, but...
         (he chuckles)
Now where's that wrench?...There it is.

    He bends over to pick it up and we HEAR a long
    tearing sound.

                Mrs. Jones (distressed)
Did you tear your suit again?

                Big Kim (in the darkness)
At this point it really doesn't matter.

                Mrs. Jones (struggling with the
         wet matches)
Can you see what you're doing?

                Big Kim
No!

                Mrs. Jones
Well, wait till I get a match going.

                Big Kim (panting)
I'm all right. I've got a hold of...

    His sentence is not completed because of a new
    CRASH eight times worse than the first one.

                Mrs. Jones (terrified)
Mr. Jones! Are you all right? Help! Mother!

                Mrs. Lane (coming down the steps
         with an old stable lantern)
For heaven's sakes, Peggy, what are you doing down
here...taking the hotel apart?

                    Mr. Stone (appearing with his   58
              weak flashlight)   CONT'D
Amachoor!   (3)

        Butch follows behind him.

                    Mrs. Jones (taking the lantern
                · from her mother)
Hurry up!

        The CAMERA PANS them forward as they peel
        away the wreckage, finally REVEALING Big
        Kim, black with coal, streaming wet, his
        suit torn to shreds, but otherwise unhurt.

                    Big Kim (laughing)
        I couldn't answer you...I had a mouthful of tomatoes...
                    (he spits and makes a face)
        I guess they were quinces...you got quite a supply
        down here.

                    Mrs. Jones
        I'm terribly glad you're all right.

                    Big Kim
        I'm fine...now let me have that lantern.

        He reaches over for it, then bends down to get
        the wrench and again bumps heads with Mr. Stone,
        who gets the wrench first and with his flashlight
        shuts off the valve.

                    Butch (who had run up the stairs
                    to see what was happening)
        It's off! It's off! It's stopped!

                    Mr. Stone (modestly)
        It's nothing...no trouble at all when you know what
        you're doing.

                    Big Kim
        Why you...

        A small stream of water squirts him in the eye.

                    DISSOLVE TO:

        MR. KIMBLE SEATED IN AN OLD-FASHIONED BATH   59
        TUB WITH WOODEN SIDES

        He is scrubbing his hair with soap. Now he
        ducks down into the water to rinse himself,
        then reappears. After this he turns on the
        faucet to add some hot water. Having enough
        hot water he tries to turn the faucet off. It
        will not turn, of course. Mr. Kimble merely

gives it a pitying look, however, then
reaching down to the floor beside the tub,
INVISIBLE UNTIL THE CAMERA TIPS with him,
he picks up the wrench and turns off the
water.

59
CONT'D
(2)

DISSOLVE TO:

MRS. JONES - IN FRONT OF THE MIRROR IN HER   60
BEDROOM

She now wears a very pretty cotton frock. She
puts the finishing touches to her make-up,
thinks for a moment, then goes to a closet
and from a moth bag takes first two and finally three men's suits. With the suits over
her arm, she leaves the room.

MR. KIMBLE IN HIS BEDROOM   61

He has just put on another suit and at the
moment is arranging his tie rather carefully.
Now he puts his bank roll in his pants pocket,
then frown slightly at the paper he has picked
up.

INSERT: DR. ROTHMULLER'S PRESCRIPTION

It is rumpled, but still readable, especially
the last item: NO WOMEN. There is a knock
on the door.

Big Kim's Voice
Yeah?

MRS. JONES COMING IN CARRYING THE SUITS   63

The CAMERA PANS her over to Mr. Kimble

Mrs. Jones
I can't tell you how sorry I am about your lovely
suit, Mr. Jones...
        (she picks it up from the foot of the bed,
        then drops it like a dead cat)
...I just don't know what to say...

Big Kim (laughing)
Forget it, will you? I never liked that suit
anyway, and...

                    Mrs. Jones (nearly on the verge   63
          of tears)   CONT'D
You're just being terribly kind but...my insurance   (2)
has expired along with everything else...and I
want you please to take these to make up, at least
a little bit, for your beautiful one. Of course,
they're not exactly the latest style...but they're
not a bit of good to me...and he was about your
size...or almost your size...I believe.

                    Big Kim (embarrassed)
I appreciate your great honesty, Mrs. Jones, but
you've got to believe me...

                    Mrs. Jones (putting the suits
          on the bed)
But I really don't need them, Mr. Jones...the
moths will have them long before Butch can ever
get any use out of them...and it's just sentimental
nonsense anyway...when you've got something to face
...the sooner you face it and wash it out of your
heart the better off you are.

                    Big Kim (indicating the suits)
Butch's father?

                    Mrs. Jones
That's right...he was killed at Tarawa...Butch
doesn't know of course.

                    Big Kim
I'm sorry.

                    Mrs. Jones
Thank you...I bough this hotel with the ten
thousand they give you...It seemed a good idea
at the time...then the Carriage Works closed...
and everybody went away...but I certainly didn't
mean to thrust my troubles upon you.

                    Big Kim
The joint in hock?

                    Mrs. Jones (smiling ruefully)
Oh yes.

                    Big Kim
That schmo downstairs who's been so very, very,
kind...got the mortgage?

                    Mrs. Jones
That's right, but he's been very patient...he's
waited and waited so long for his money...I don't
suppose he really can wait much longer.

                    Big Kim
Why not...is he going someplace?

                    194

                    Mrs. Jones (laughing)   63
I'm afraid I sort of took him over the jumps a   CONT'D
little bit...while he was making up his mind about   (3)
the mortgage...I think he sort of thought he was
going to marry me some day...I'm afraid I sort of
let him think so.

                    Big Kim
Well, that's natural.

                    Mrs. Jones
A widow with a little boy doesn't stop at much
I guess...
          (she laughs into his eyes)
Be careful if you ever meet one.

                    Big Kim
Thanks for warning me.

                    Mrs. Jones
You're welcome. I'll see you at dinner...I hope.

                   · Big Kim
Yes, Mam...It's the only place anyway, isn't it?

                    Mrs. Jones
I'm afraid so.

                    Big Kim
I'll see you at supper.
                              DISSOLVE TO:

MR. KIMBLE AND MR. STONE - IN THE OGDEN HOUSE   64
DINING ROOM

     They are at either end of a nine foot table.
     Mr. Stone has already finished and is picking
     his teeth. He glares at Mr. Kimble and hiccups.
     Mr. Kimble takes another mouthful of a peculiar
     looking dish, chews it pensively, swallows and
     also hiccups.

               Mrs. Jones (coming brightly into
          the SHOT near Mr. Stone bearing coffee and
          pie)
Did you enjoy your supper Lucas?

                    Mr. Stone (gravely)
Very tasty...I think.

195

                    Mrs. Jones
I'm so glad.
                    (she starts toward Mr. Kimble, then
                    pauses and looks back at Mr. Stone,
                    who is still shaken from a tremendous
                    hiccup)

                    Mr. Stone (apologetically)
Something I et no doubt...OOIP!

                    Mrs. Jones (moving on)
No doubt.

        The CAMERA takes her to Mr. Kimble's end
        of the table.

                    Mrs. Jones (sweetly)
I hope you enjoyed your first supper with us, Mr.
Jones.

                    Big Kim (charmingly)
Very....unusual...OOIP...excuse me...what were they
called again...those little things we had.

                    Mrs. Jones (sweetly)
Mock snipe...they're made out of pork rind and beef
heart.

        The smile freezes on Mr. Kimble's face and
        he smothers a hiccup in his napkin.

                    Mrs. Jones (trying to ignore
              the hiccup)
They're what you call an economy dish...Mother
got them out of the Woman's Constant Companion...
she made the beaks out of toothpicks.

                    Big Kim (lowering his napkin)
They sure fooled me.

                    Mrs. Jones
I'll tell her.

                    Big Kim (raising and lowering
              his napkin)
You have them often?
                    (he puts the napkin back up)

                    Mrs. Jones (slightly apologeti-
              cally)
Only about once a week...Butch is very fond of them.

                    Big Kim
Good.

        (he puts his napkin back up)

                            196

MR. STONE AT HIS END OF THE TABLE   65

> Mr. Stone
> Had 'em twicet last week...what did you say them
> beaks was made outen?

MR. KIMBLE AND MRS. JONES   66

> Big Kim (before Mrs. Jones
>   can answer)
> Pork hearts! Pork hearts and beef gizzards!
>   (he puts his napkin to his mouth)

MR. STONE AT HIS END OF THE TABLE   67

> Mr. Stone (sourly)
> Very funny...ha...ha...ha.
>   (suddenly he puts his napkin to his
>   mouth)

BIG KIM AND MRS. JONES   68

> Mrs. Jones (hurt)
> Didn't you like it at all?

> Big Kim (gallantly)
> Well of course I did...you know how it is when you
> eat something for the first time...

> Mrs. Jones
> Mother's always finding little things like that...
> you know...little novelties?

> Big Kim (dismally)
> You say she's always finding them?

MR. STONE AT HIS END OF THE TABLE   69

> Mr. Stone
> 'Bout six times a week...the other day I eat out.

MR. KIMBLE AND MRS. JONES   70

> Mrs. Jones
> You know that isn't true, Lucas...she just finds
> a little something every so often.

197

MR. STONE AT HIS END OF THE TABLE   71

                    Mr. Stone
Every too often if you ask me.

        MR. KIMBLE AND MRS. JONES   72

                    Big Kim
Have you ever considered installing a professional
cook in this institution?

                    Mrs. Jones (sitting down
            dejectedly and lighting a cigarette)
We were going to do all things like that when
the hotel grew but....

                    Big Kim (with finality)
Nothing will grow on mock tripe.

                    Mrs. Jones
Snipe.

                    Big Kim
That's right...did the hotel ever do well? I
mean since you bought it?

                    Mrs. Jones
It started to...we had as many as four in a bed...
I don't mean all at once...you know...two on the
day shift and two on the night shift...

                    Big Kim
That must have been a little rough on the springs.

        MR. STONE AT HIS END OF THE TABLE   73

                    Mr. Stone
You'll find out....you're lucky you're leaving in
the morning.

        MR. KIMBLE AND MRS. JONES   74

                    Big Kim
Who's leaving in the morning?

                    Mrs. Jones
Mr. Jones is going to be with us for six months,
Lucas...Isn't that wonderful?
                    (then to Mr. Kimble)
Oh everything was really buzzing around here...
till the Carriage Works closed.

                            198

MR. STONE AT HIS END OF THE TABLE   75

                    Mr. Stone (alarmed)
What's he going to do here for six months?

MR. KIMBLE AND MRS. JONES   76

                    Big Kim (to Mr. Stone)
What's that got to do with you?
                    (then to Mrs. Jones)
What kind of carriages were they making?

                    Mrs. Jones (smiling)
Oh they haven't made carriages there since before
I was born...They made gun stocks for the army...
and some caisson wheels I think...These hills are
full of good hardwood...that's why my grandfather
...I mean my great-grandfather started the works
here in the first place...He was a German coach-
builder.

                    Big Kim
No fooling.

MR. STONE AT HIS END OF THE TABLE   77

                    Mr. Stone
A Heinie.

MR. KIMBLE AND MRS. JONES   78

                    Mrs. Jones
His name was Herman Oppenschlopper...That's why
the town is called Bismarck...Bismarck was somebody very important in Germany when my great-grandfather left there...I don't remember exactly what
he did.

MR. STONE AT HIS END OF THE TABLE   79

                    Mr. Stone (sourly)
Was a musician...I hear lot of his pieces....

MR. KIMBLE AND MRS. JONES   80

                    Big Kim
Who owns the works now...any of it come down to
you...or to Butch?

                    199

                    Mrs. Jones (In some embarrass-
            ment)
Oh no...that all went a long time ago...I believe
Mr. Stone owns them now...don't you Lucas?

    She rises and starts gathering some dishes.

    MR STONE AT HIS END OF THE TABLE   81

                    Mr. Stone
Yep...for all they're worth...got 'em for the taxes.

    MR. KIMBLE AND MRS. JONES   82

                    Big Kim
That's too bad...why don't you make something down
there?

    MR. STONE AT HIS END OF THE TABLE   83

                    Mr. Stone
Something like what? I'm no manufacturer.

    MR. KIMBLE AND MRS. JONES   84

                    Big Kim
How do I know? If these hills are full of hardwood...
make something out of hardwood.

                    Mrs. Jones
Wouldn't that be wonderful?

    MR. STONE AT HIS END OF THE TABLE   85

                    Mr. Stone
Don't use it no more...all they want now is tin and...
and...coronmium.

    MR. KIMBLE AND MRS. JONES   86

                    Big Kim
What are you talking about? How about...chairs...
tables...baseball bats...nut bowls...clocks...
butcher blocks...axe handles...motorboats...pianos...
xylophones...ZITHERS!

                    Mrs. Jones (laughing)   86
Mother used to have a zither.   CONT'D
                                                         (2)
        She exits toward the kitchen.

        MR. STONE AT HIS END OF THE TABLE   87
                    Mr. Stone
Look...you want to start a zither factory...I'll
rent you the place nice and cheap.

        MR. KIMBLE AT HIS END OF THE TABLE   88
                    Big Kim
I don't want to start a zither factory...I don't
want to start any kind of a factory...I'm here
for a rest...I'm just trying to give you an idea.

        MR. STONE AT HIS END OF THE TABLE

        In the background we see Mrs. Jones come back
        into the dining room.
                    Mr. Stone
Don't need no ideas...we're getting along all right.

                    Mrs. Jones (coming up behind
            him)
You want some more coffee, Lucas?...or you Mr. Jones?

                    Mr. Stone (shaking his head)
Keeps me awake.

        MR. KIMBLE AT HIS END OF THE TABLE   90
                    Big Kim
You want to take a run out to the Works and show it
to me?

        MR. STONE AND MRS. JONES   91
                    Mrs. Jones (slightly nervously)
You mean me...or Mr. Stone?

201

MR. KIMBLE AT HIS END OF THE TABLE   92

                    Big Kim
I certainly don't want to go for a ride in the
moonlight with Mr. Stone...I thought since your
great-grandfather built the place...he might
let you show it to me.

        MR. STONE AND MRS. JONES   93

                    Mrs. Jones (still more
            nervously, stealing a look at Mr. Stone)
Well I...uh...

                    Mr. Stone
No concern of mine...but it seems to me the daylight's
the best time to see things.

                    Mrs. Jones (still nervously)
Maybe some...other time, Mr. Jones...but thank you
very much for asking me.

                    Mr. Stone (in a better humor)
Want to play a game of checkers?

        MR. KIMBLE AT HIS END OF THE TABLE

                    Big Kim (somewhat sourly)
Never played it...How does it go?

        MR. STONE AND MRS. JONES   95

                    Mrs. Jones (happily)
I'll show you...and we'll play against Lucas.

        She walks to the wall behind her to get the
        board.

        MR. KIMBLE AT HIS END OF THE TABLE   96

                    Big Kim (rising)
Okay.

        The CAMERA PANS him to Mr. Stone's end of the
        table, where he arrives at the same time as
        Mrs. Jones with the checkers.

                    Mrs. Jones (noticing his cigar-
            ette)
Shouldn't you be smoking your pipe?

                            202

Big Kim   96
I can't smoke it all day long...my mouth feels   CONT'D
like a cuspidor now.   (2)

                    Mrs. Jones (laughing as she sits
              down and starts arranging the checkers)
You only smoked it once today.

                    Big Kim (sitting next to her)
Once was enough...
        (he fingers one of the checkers then addresses
        Stone:)
How much are we playing for?   .

                    Mr. Stone (horrified)
You mean money?

                    Big Kim
Certainly I mean money...You don't think I'm going
to sit here all evening and look at your kisser for
nothing do you? I might play with a pretty woman...

                    Mr. Stone (severely)
I never gamble for money.

                    Big Kim
Then let's forget it...I'll get a book

                    Mr. Stone (narrowing his eyes)
Besides...how can you play for money if you've never
played before?

                    Big Kim
She's played before...probably plays better than
you do.

                    Mrs. Jones (hastily)
Oh no I don't...he's very good.

                    Big Kim
I'd still take a chance on you...anyway I never
gamble for free...It's like swimming in an empty
swimming pool.

                    Mrs. Jones (disappointed)
I'm sorry.

                    Mr. Stone (looking Mr. Kimble
              over shrewdly)
How much do you want to play for?

                    Big Kim (instantly)
Make it easy on yourself brother...how much have
you got?

                    Mr. Stone (virulently)
About as much as you've got, I guess...and then
some.

203

                    Big Kim
Okay...we'll shoot a thousand...shuffle up the...
things.

                    Mrs. Jones (stupefied)
A thousand dollars.

                    Mr. Stone
Don't let him bluff you, Peggy...he never seen a
thousand dollars.

                    Big Kim
Have it your way.
          (he shoves the board away and turns to Mrs.
          Jones)
How about a cup of coffee?

                    Mrs. Jones (relieved)
You were just joking, weren't you?

          She pours his coffee and looks into his eyes
          and smiles.

                    Big Kim (smiling at her)
I guess so.

                    Mr. Stone (completely out of
               the party)
You want to play for a thousand dollars, huh?

                    Big Kim
I don't want to play at all...you started this
project.

                    Mr. Stone (incensed)
You drive in here in a fifty dollar jeep...

                    Mrs. Jones (shocked)
Lucas !

                    Mr. Stone (too far gone to
               stop)
...and right away you start talking big...Mr. Big
in Littleville...givin' advice...Why don't you
build factories...Why don't you...

                    Mrs. Jones (worried)
Lucas ! Mr. Jones is a guest in the hotel the
same as you.

                    Mr. Stone
Oh no he ain't ! Who loaned you the money to
keep goin'? Who paid your taxes for you? Who
brought groceries to you?...Before the government come through with that...blood money?

                    Mrs. Jones (aghast)
Lucas, Mr. Jones is a stranger here...

               Mr. Stone
Yeah...a stranger putting on the dog...You want to
gamble for a thousand dollars, huh? Put up your
money.

               Big Kim (quietly)
Not now I don't.

               Mr. Stone (triumphantly)
I'll bet you don't!

               Big Kim
Now it's two thousand...You missed the boat.

               Mr. Stone (with a snarling
          laugh)
You think you can bluff me, huh?

               Big Kim
I know I can bluff you.

               Mrs. Jones (trying to make
          peace)
Mr. Jones is only joking, Lucas.

               Mr. Stone (albeit a little
          nervously)
He never even saw two thousand dollars.

               Big Kim (amused)
Just for that, it's three thousand.

               Mr. Stone
For a game of checkers!

               Big Kim
For a game of checkers...

               Mr. Stone (shrewdly)
And I suppose if I said "yes" to three, it
would jump up to four.

               Big Kim
Why don't you say "yes" and find out.

               Mr. Stone (again cautious)
Because I ain't seen the color of your money yet.

               Big Kim (mimicking him)
I ain't seen yours. neither.

               Mr. Stone
Yeah...but everybody knows I got it...I ain't no
fly-by-night that blows into town and talks big
...what I got I can prove.

                Big Kim (with a semblance of   96
          dejection)   CONT'D.
I guess you win.   (5)

                Mr. Stone (slightly mollified)
I guess I do.

                Mrs. Jones (sighing with
          relief)
Now let's all have a cup of coffee...and talk
about the weather.

                Mr. Stone (pursuing his victory
          a little further)
And let this be a lesson to you, Peggy...when
strangers come around and start talking big.

      He starts sipping a cup of coffee.

                Big Kim (laughing, to Mrs.
          Jones)
I was going to shoot him for your mortgage.

      Mr. Stone starts strangling on his coffee.

                Mrs. Jones (laughing and
          patting Mr. Stone on the back)
That was terribly sweet of you but...

                Mr. Stone (recovering his
          voice with wheezes and also his fury)
WHAT DO YOU MEAN IT'S TERRIBLY SWEET OF HIM!
          (he coughs)
He never even saw fifty-two hundred dollars.
          (he strangles again)
Sure! He says: "I'll bet you fifty-two hundred
dollars"...and if he wins, he wins! But suppose
he loses? Where do I come out?

                Mrs. Jones (again trying to
          make peace)
Lucas! Mr. Jones is only...

                Mr. Stone (interrupting with
          renewed fury)
Listen Mister! You like to bet, huh? Well I'll
bet you fifty-two hundred dollars you haven't
GOT fifty-two hundred dollars.

                Mrs. Jones
Lucas, please.

                Lucas
Try that on your harmonium.

                Big Kim (with a great
          semblance of nervousness)
You mean all in...cash?

           Mr. Stone (triumphantly)   96
YES I MEAN ALL IN CASH! We don't take no checks CONT'D.
from no strangers.   (6)

           Big Kim (looking overly
        embarrassed)
That's quite a lot of cash.

           Mrs. Jones (sympathetically)
Well of course it is Mr. Jones, this has all...

           Mr. Stone (having another
        thrust at his victim)
It's quite a lot of cash for them as ain't got it.

           Mr. Kimble (reluctantly to
        Mrs. Jones)
You heard him make that bet?

           Mr. Stone (answering for her)
YES SHE HEARD ME!

           Big Kim
I don't like to do this to this poor hick...

           Mr. Stone
I ain't so poor...and you'll find out how much of
a hick I am...Put up or shut up!

           Big Kim (stirring his coffee
        in simulated embarrassment)
It's like taking candy from a child...

           Mrs. Jones (gently)
I really think the joke has gone far enough.

           Big Kim
You do?
    (then after a look at Mr. Stone)
You got any smelling salts in the house?

           Mr. Stone (slightly tense)
Don't pay no attention to him, Peggy...This is
all part of the bluff.

           Mrs. Jones (putting a hand on
        Mr. Kimble's shoulder)
Mr. Jones...

           Big Kim (smiling)
Of course I changed my trousers this afternoon...
    (he feels the outside of his pocket and
    frowns)
I might have left it on the bureau...

                         Mrs. Jones (embarrassed)
Or you might have mislaid it.

                         Mr. Stone
Watch him sweat! If he left it on the bureau we'll
give him two minutes to go and get it, won't we Peggy.
                    (he cackles)
He left it on the bureau all right...a bureau about
nine thousand miles from here...a bureau nobody ain't
ever seen.

                         Big Kim (putting his hand in
                              his pocket)
No by golly...I didn't leave it on the bureau...

                         Mrs. Jones (putting her hand
                              on her heart)
Mr. Jones you're just killing me.

                         Big Kim (quietly)
I'm really not trying to...now before I take my
hand out of my pocket, I want you to remember three
things: That he suggested the bet...that he made
the terms...and that there's a sucker born every
minute...You got that?

                         Mrs. Jones (her teeth chattering)
Yyyyes...

                         Big Kim
Now I'm going to give him one last chance to eat
crow, apologize and call off the bet.

                         Mr. Stone (highly nervous)
Put up your dough and, stop talking so much.

                         Big Kim (shrugging)
You asked for it...
                    (he pulls a huge roll of bills out of his
                     pocket and throws it on the table in front
                     of Mr. Stone.)

                         Mrs. Jones (startled)
Lucas!

                         Big Kim
Count it yourself.

          He lights a cigarette. Mr. Stone stares dumbly
          at the money...still too stunned to understand
          what has happened to him. With limp fingers
          he scatters the money a little, then examines
          one note a little more closely, although with-
          out much hope.

                         Big Kim (reading his thought)
If you think they're queer, take 'em to the bank.

                              208

Suddenly Mrs. Jones breaks under the strain.   96
She buries her face in her hands and starts   CONT'D
to sob.   (8)

                    Big Kim (patting her on the back)
What are you crying about?

                    Mrs. Jones (lifting her face,
               streaming with tears)
I...I don't know.

     Mr. Stone gives her a blank look.
                                        DISSOLVE TO:

     MR. KIMBLE AND MRS. JONES IN THE JEEP - NIGHT   97

     She looks very pretty with a fluttering scarf
     around her head and seems somewhat recovered.
     Mr. Kimble's arm is protectingly around her
     shoulders.

                    Big Kim
Feel better now? Nothing like a little air.

                    Mrs. Jones
Oh so much...I don't know why I behaved like such
an idiot...I've never seen anything like that thing
that just happened before...don't I really owe
Lucas anything anymore...or am I just dreaming?

                    Big Kim
Well that all depends on how you feel about certain
things...he lost all right...only you're not supposed to bet on a sure thing...that is if you're
a gentleman you're not...and I sure knew how much
I had in my pocket.

                    Mrs. Jones
I see.

                    Big Kim (cheerfully)
Of course, on the other hand, I'm not a gentleman...
so that leaves the whole matter open again.

                    Mrs. Jones
I think you're very much of a gentleman.

                    Big Kim
Who me?...no no...my head is in the wrong shape...
you ever hear of Pithecanthropus Erectus?

                    Mrs. Jones
That's a kind of a melon, isn't it?

                    209

                    Big Kim
No...that's me...I'll tell you all about it sometime.
...it turns out I've got two heads...with a Mr. B.
in the back one who doesn't like Mr. A who lives
in the front one and is always complaining to the
janitor or something...it's all very scientific.

                    Mrs. Jones (ignoring that which
               she does not understand)
Where did you get all that money?

                    Big Kim
All what money? Oh all that money! I uh...I won
it in a crap game.

                    Mrs. Jones
I see.

                    Big Kim
That's how I can afford to take six months off.

                    Mrs. Jones (slightly puzzled)
But you didn't expect to spend all that in just
six months, did you?...at least not around here.

                    Big Kim (hastily)
Of course not.

                    Mrs. Jones (pursuing her thought)
But you told me you were a kind of a carpenter...

                    Big Kim
Can't a carpenter get in a crap game? Besides I
didn't say I was a carpenter...I said I was a
kind of a builder.

                    Mrs. Jones (still with her own
               thought)
I knew you weren't of course...your hands were too
soft...are you a gambler?

                    Big Kim
What do I look like to you.

                    Mrs. Jones
...a traveling salesman maybe...or, possibly a
dentist.

                    Big Kim
Cash or credit?

                    Mrs. Jones (looking into the
               distance)
They say confidence men are awfully attractive too...
they have to be in their line of business.

                    Big Kim (amused)
Have I got your confidence?

                    Mrs. Jones
Except you wouldn't ever have come here in the first
place...there isn't anything in the whole town worth
taking.

                    Big Kim
You looked in a mirror recently?

                    Mrs. Jones
Now you sound more like an ice man.

                    Big Kim
I carried a little ice in my time.

                    Mrs. Jones
You're still carrying it...
                    (then after a laugh)
Would you like to see the carriage works? It's
just down the street here to the left.

                    Big Kim
But I thought you said you didn't want to go tonight.

                    Mrs. Jones
That was on account of Lucas...I didn't think it was
wise to upset him...it's been that way for quite a
little while...I used to have quite a few callers...
they'd come over from Peruvia...and even further...
you know: we'd all sit around on the porch and talk...

                    Big Kim
I know.

                    Mrs. Jones
But after talking to Lucas for a while...they all
sort of faded away...

                    Big Kim
He has a very warm personality...like a muskrat.

                    Mrs. Jones (laughing)
Poor Lucas...it's the next turn to the left.
                                        DISSOLVE TO:

EXTERIOR THE OLD BISMARCK CARRIAGE WORKS -   98
IN THE MOONLIGHT

Beside the name on the front of it, there is
a Prussian Eagle and the date 1881. To one
side we see the gleaming millpond. Now we
hear the sound of the jeep and the CAMERA
PANS to catch it as it comes to a stop in
front of the shadowy works.

                    Big Kim
So this is it, huh? Very spooky!

                    Mrs. Jones
Would you like to go inside?...I think it's open.

                    Big Kim
Sure.

        He gets down from the jeep and goes around to
        the other side to help Mrs. Jones down.

                    Mrs. Jones (leading him to the
              door)
It all works by water...a big paddle wheel...and
they say it works just as well right now as when
my great-grandfather built it.

                    Big Kim
No fooling...

        He swings open the door, which sounds like a
        sound effect in a radio ghost story. She
        takes his hand and leads him in. We follow
        them a little bit and see behind them cob-
        webbed draped vistas, ancient work benches
        and much machinery on either side of moonlit
        alleys.

        TRUCKING SHOT AHEAD OF MR. KIMBLE AND MRS. JONES 99

        They wander through the plant looking overhead
        and right and left.

                    Mrs. Jones
Can you picture this all full of wood shavings...
and the men making beautiful carriages for elegant
ladies all over America...and my great-grandfather
in the middle...hollering at everybody with that
accent he had?

                    Big Kim (mildly interested)
Too bad they're not making anything here now...
with all this floor space and that wood growing
all over...even the machinery's all right...
probably as good as the Romans had...and they
conquered the world.

                    Mrs. Jones (pointing)
There were still a couple of old carriages here...
the last time I was here...there they are!

                    212

AN OLD BUGGY AND A TALLY-HO   100

They are very dry and cracked at the joints
but their elegance is still apparent.

MR. KIMBLE AND MRS. JONES COMING TOWARD US   101

He raises a cigarette lighter.

                    Mrs. Jones (pointing to the
          buggy)
Think of all the families that started in that
buggy...the lovers didn't have to keep their eyes
on the road...the old mare did it for them.

                    Big Kim (without thinking)
A plane is very nice that way, too.

                    Mrs. Jones (giving him a long
          look)
Is it?

                    Big Kim
I mean as far as not having to keep your eye on the
road...it don't bring you back by itself.
               (now he points to the tally-ho)
What's that thing?

     The CAMERA PANS them over to it and he examines
     it by sticking the lighter through the glassless
     windows.
                    Mrs. Jones
They were called tally-hos, I think...People used
to go to the races in them and have their lunch on
top...or to picnics...if the weather was good they
rode on top and if it started to rain...

                    Big Kim (beginning to be
          interested)
...they moved inside! Quite a gag at that! Look
at those seats...

                    Mrs. Jones
I think they made into a bed...in case of a long
trip or something.

                    Big Kim (almost to himself)
Sure...you could have double steering and controls...
a roller canvas over the top...

                    Mrs. Jones
What did you say?

213

                    Big Kim   101
I was just thinking outloud...you'd have good   CONT'D
vision, too...   (2)
          (then suddenly opening a compartment
           in the back)
Say what do you know? An ice box.

                    Mrs. Jones (proudly)
Great-grandfather seems to have thought of everything...

                    Big Kim
He sure did...you know what? I'd like to have one
of these.

                    Mrs. Jones
Well you can probably have that one awfully cheap.

                    Big Kim
I didn't mean that...I don't suppose there're any
of the old carpenters still around...coach builders...
or whatever you call them?

                    Mrs. Jones (surprised)
Plenty of them...Mother's known them since she was
a little girl...of course I don't actually think
they're great-grandfather's men...probably their
sons and grandsons...

                    Big Kim
But they'd still know the craft...it would have
been passed on to them...and then I'd need a
designer...

                    Mrs. Jones (interrupting)
Oh, but there is one! Old Bob Zooky who actually
worked with my great-grandfather...or maybe it
was only my grandfather...he makes colored postcards of the old carriages now...all by hand.

                    Big Kim
You know where he lives?

                    Mrs. Jones (thoughtfully)
I think out by the air port someplace...

                    Big Kim (astonished)
What air port?...

                    Mrs. Jones (proudly)
Oh we had one during the war...for important people
to fly in and out...it's just a field on the other
side of town really but they called it the air port...
we even had a general at the hotel once.

                    Big Kim (amused)
No fooling.

                    Mrs. Jones (sorry to say it)   101
I'm afraid he's in jail now.   CONT'D
                                                       (3)
                    Big Kim
No fooling.

                    Mrs. Jones
There wasn't any fooling about it at all.

        Mr. Kimble starts to laugh. Suddenly a roar-
        ing is heard and Mrs. Jones jumps into the
        protection of his arms. The roaring is fol-
        lowed by a great swish, which is followed by
        slapping noises and screaming like sirens as
        the rusty overhead jackshafts begin to turn
        and the old plant comes to life.

THE HUGE UNDERSHOT WATERWHEEL   102

        It gains momentum in the moonlight and throws
        silver sparks high into the air.

MOVING SHOT UP AT THE SHAFTING IN THE OLD WORKS 103

        We go from side to side then pan DOWN onto some
        of the humming machinery. The PANNING SHOT
        ends on Mr. Kimble holding a protective arm
        around Mrs. Jones as they watch all this.
        Suddenly Mrs. Jones looks past the CAMERA and
        screams. Mr. Kimble follows her gaze and holds
        her tighter.

A HUGE BLACK FIGURE WALKING TOWARD US AGAINST   104
THE MOONLIGHT

        As it gets close, its face is suddenly illumin-
        ated by a slanting ray and we recognize Mr. Stone.

    MR. KIMBLE AND MRS. JONES - PAST MR. STONE   105
                    Mrs. Jones (frightened)
Lucas!

    MR. STONE - PAST MR. KIMBLE AND MRS. JONES   106
                    Mr. Stone (coldly)
Thought while you were down here...you'd like to
see how everything works...

                         215

MR. KIMBLE AND MRS. JONES - PAST MR. STONE   107

                Mrs. Jones
Well, that was very thoughtful of you, Lucas.

MR. STONE - PAST MR. KIMBLE AND MRS. JONES   108

                Mr. Stone (taking a paper out
        of his pocket and handing it to Mrs. Jones)
And here's your mortgage... I'll be movin' out
tomorrow... thought you'd better take it.

MR. KIMBLE AND MRS. JONES   109

                Mrs. Jones
Hadn't we better talk it over, Lucas? There's no
hurry about anything and...

MR. STONE - PAST MR. KIMBLE AND MRS. JONES   110

                Mr. Stone (bitterly)
Nothing to talk over...your friend here pulled a
fast one on me...and I'm paying off...it'll all
come home to roost.

MR. KIMBLE AND MRS. JONES - PAST MR. STONE   111

                Mrs. Jones (tendering Mr. Stone
        the mortgage)
I don't want you to feel that way, Lucas...I don't
want to take this from you.

                Big Kim (taking the mortgage
        from her and forcing it into Mr. Stone's
        hand)
Look; I was just kidding you, see?...I knew how
much I had in my pocket so there was no guess work
about it...and a bet is supposed to be a guess...
you give Mrs. Jones six months to catch up on her
payments...and the use of this place for six months...
with an option to buy for what you paid for it plus
six per cent on your money for the time you held
it...and that thing is all yours and nobody's been
hurt and we'll all feel better.

216

                    Mrs. Jones   111
Much better Lucas.   CONT'D
                                                        (2)

    MR. STONE   112

                    Mr. Stone (suspiciously after
              looking at the mortgage in his hand)
What she want the works for?

    MR. KIMBLE AND MRS. JONES - PAST MR. STONE   113

                    Big Kim (aggressively)
What do you care what she wants 'em for? Maybe
to give a tea party in... they're not doing you
any good are they? And you're still getting the
squarest shake any sucker I ever saw get.

    MR. STONE   114

                    Mr. Stone (indicating the
              mortgage)
How do you feel about this Peggy?

    MR. KIMBLE AND MRS. JONES - PAST MR. STONE   115
                    Mrs. Jones
I'd feel a great deal better about it, Lucas.

                    Mr. Stone
Well then... if you really think it's only right
and proper... and the bet really shouldn't have been
made anyway... and you'll be careful not to burn
this place down... why I guess...

                    Big Kim (interrupting)
Oh! And one thing more: You can't move out of the
hotel... you've got to stay there at full rates...
that's part of the deal... and from now on we serve
mock tripe twice a day!

                    Mr. Stone
You the manager there now?

                    Mr. Kimble (starting out with
              Mrs. Jones)
No... the janitor... and don't stay out too late...
we don't want to give the joint a bad name!

                            217

They pass out of the picture and the CAMERA   115
rests on Mr. Stone, who looks after them with   CONT'D
an expression of deep puzzlement and suspicion.   (2)
An ancient piece of machinery chooses this
moment to make a SOUND which starts like the
chattering laugh of a South American monkey,
then changes into a sort of Bronx cheer. Mr.
Stone acknowledges this by a look off to one
side, then looks back straight into the CAMERA.
                                   DISSOLVE TO:

MR. KIMBLE AND MRS. JONES DRIVING ALONG IN THE   116
MOONLIGHT

Mr. Kimble appears to be in deep thought.

                    Mrs. Jones (after looking at
               him a couple of times)
What did you want the carriage works for?

                    Big Kim
Just a little idea I got... you can't tell how it
might work out... our principal problem is to get
some guests into that hotel of yours...

                    Mrs. Jones (ruefully)
Wouldn't that be something!

                    Big Kim (frowning)
I wonder if a nice little... but I don't suppose
gambling is legal in this state is it?

                    Mrs.Jones
Oh my no.

                    Big Kim
Naturally... anything that adds to the joy of living...
what we need is some kind of an attraction... it does-
n't matter what it is... just something to bring people
close to the hotel... it could be a balloon ascension
or a two headed calf... we'll get that lot next to the
hotel and put something on it they have to come to see...
wrestling bears... a pie baking contest... a night in a
Turkish harem... I dunno... we'll buy a billboard and see
what's available.

                    Mrs.Jones
What kind of a billboard.

Big Kim

That's a trade paper for showpeople.. my mother
used to be with a circus... we'll pick out a sure-
fire attraction... or wait a minute: we might put
in a whole bunch of 'em.. permanent pitch concessions
with booths in between for the farmers... ring men..
Madame Zaza the fortune teller knows all sees all
and <u>tells</u> all...a little fun house.. a shooting
gallery... have your picture taken with Harry Truman...
a baseball pitch.. and then every other booth: the jams,
the jellies, the pickles, the green tomatoes... and all
that kind of stuff the rubes are always putting up in
glass jars... when the concessions get stale you change 'em.

Mrs.Jones (delighted)

A county fair!

Big Kim

That's right... a sort of little county fair.. what's
the matter with that? You put in a little pony ride..
a little real steam railroad...

Mrs.Jones

Oh wouldn't Butch love that!

Big Kim

So would everybody else.. a merry-go-round...

Mrs.Jones (fearfully)

But wouldn't that all cost a <u>terrible</u> lot of money?

Big Kim

They pay <u>you</u>... that's why they're called concessions...
and you hold out a few of the good ones for yourself...
the beer.. the soda pop and the hot dogs!

Mrs. Jones

And hope they'll get thirsty.

Big Kim

You sell 'em salted nuts! And keep 'em standing around
in the sunlight! Then we wangle one of the bus lines
to go through here instead of wherever they're going...
and things will really begin to crackle.

Mrs.Jones (frightened)

I...I... it still sounds awfully expensive...

Big Kim

You never want to think that way... or nothing would
ever get done. <u>Do</u> it first and look for the money
<u>afterwards</u>... like the government does!

Mrs.Jones

It makes me a little dizzy.

                    Big Kim   116
So is the government... anyway we'll do most of   CONT'D
the work ourselves.. we'll find some third grade   (3)
lumber and some second hand bricks..for the barbecue...

                    Mrs.Jones (happily)
I know where there're some.. from an old bakery that
burned down.. and Butch has a wheelbarrow.

                    Big Kim
That's the spirit.. or we can use this thing.. then
we'll slap a little paint on the hotel... fix up the
chairs.. and there you are! Now where's that air
field? I want to take a look at it.

                    Mrs.Jones
Tonight?

                    Big Kim
Look Honey.. I'm only going to be here for a short
time... I've got to work fast.

                    Mrs.Jones
You haven't forgotten you're here for a rest have you?

                    Big Kim (in surprised indignation)
Well what else am I doing?
                              DISSOLVE TO:

EXT. SECOND FLOOR WINDOW - THE OGDEN HOUSE   117

    It is slightly open and Mr. Stone is peering
    down past the CAMERA.

HIGH CAMERA SHOT OF WHAT MR. STONE SEES   118

    The Jeep comes to a stop in front of the hotel.
    Mr.Kimble gets out and comes around to help
    Mrs.Jones. As he holds his arms out to her,
    they pause, their faces quite close together.

EXT. MR. STONE'S WINDOW   119

    He leans forward and glares bitterly.

CLOSE SHOT - MR. KIMBLE AND MRS. JONES   120

                    Mrs. Jones (looking into his
            eyes)
I don't know why but...when you blew into town...
you seemed to bring a lot of fresh air in with you.

                    Big Kim (amused)
Might be hot air.

                    Mrs. Jones
I don't think so...anyway all I know is...I'm
terribly happy.

                    Big Kim (huskily)
Are you?

                    Mrs. Jones
I am.

        In reply, Mr. Kimble leans forward and kisses
        her fully on the lips for a kiss of the legal
        length.

EXT. MR. STONE'S WINDOW   121

        He opens it jerkily to see better.

CLOSE SHOT - MR. KIMBLE AND MRS. JONES   122

        They break out of the kiss.

                    Mrs. Jones (breathlessly)
Well that was a nice thing to do!

                    Big Kim (helping her out of
            the Jeep)
I'm sorry...you got a little too close to the machinery
that time...you want to watch that.

                    Mrs. Jones
I will...I wouldn't want anything to happen to you.

        Now she laughs, forgives him, and takes his
        arm as they walk into the hotel and disappear
        into the shadows. The CAM   FOLLOWS them.

MR. STONE LEANING OUT OF THE WINDOW   123

        He snatches his head back inside, bumps it
        violently, then tries to close the window
        which now sticks. He starts pounding it

                        221

outwards with the heels of his hands to loosen
it. On the fourth pound the window flies out
past the CAMERA and lands crashingly in the
street.

123
CONT'D
(2)

DISSOLVE TO:

VERY PRETTY SHOT OF BUTCH SLEEPING IN THE
MOONLIGHT

124

A wedge of light falls on the child.

MRS. JONES IN THE DOORWAY FROM HER ROOM

125

She is lit from the back, and her negligee
although probably not a very rich one, looks
very lovely. The CAMERA PANS her over to
the far side of the little boy's bed and goes
down with her as she kneels quietly and looks
at him. She smoothes his hair, then kisses
him on the forehead. The child smiles in his
sleep.

Mrs. Jones (in a whisper)

Everything is going to be all right, little man...
everything is going to be all right.

Her eyes glisten as if with tears. The
child moves, sighs contentedly, then opens
his eyes and speaks sleepily.

Butch

Good night, Mommie.

Mrs. Jones (taking him in her
arms)

Good night, my darling.

She holds him close to her bosom and rocks
him to sleep.

FADE OUT:

FADE IN:
A BIRD SINGING IN A TREE - MORNING MUSIC

126

DISSOLVE TO:

A VERY PRETTY SHOT OF MRS. JONES IN BED

127

She smiles languorously. From below we hear

222

muffled pounding and the cracking of breaking
wood.

            Mrs. Lane's Voice (sharply)
Peggy!

The smile fades on Mrs. Jones' face.

MRS. LANE SHAKING HER DAUGHTER - IN THE LATTER'S   128
BEDROOM

            Mrs. Lane (ominously)
Peggy...wake up!

            Mrs. Jones (opening her eyes)
Good morning, Mother...what's the matter?

            Mrs. Lane (sharply)
Good morning...though I don't know what's good about
it...if you want to save your hotel, you'd better
come downstairs quick...you hear that?

            Mrs. Jones (sitting up in vague
         alarm as she hears the pounding)
What's that?

            Mrs. Lane
Your new boarder is taking the hotel apart.

            Mrs. Jones (swinging her legs out
         of bed)
Oh, how wonderful! When did he start?

    During the rest of the scene she dresses and
    possibly takes a quick shower, the cutting
    back and forth between the two women taking
    care of the propriety of the SHOTS.

            Mrs. Lane
Wonderful! He got me up at the crack of dawn to find
old Bob Zooky your grandfather's designer for him
who's been in his third childhood for twenty years...
then Zooky dug up old Jim Tandy for him, the old fore-
man with the red nose...then they took Butch and all
got into the Jeep of his and all went over to Peruvia
to buy tools..wheelbarrows...I don't know what all...
and a motorcycle for Butch he'll probably break his
neck on.

            Mrs. Jones (in horror)
A motorcycle!

            Mrs. Lane (grudgingly)
Well, it isn't a real one...but it's dangerous enough!

            Mrs. Jones (severely)
You shouldn't do things like that to me.

                         Mrs. Lane
Then the whole parade came back from Peruvia
with a truckload of lumber behind them...and a
couple of old tramps they found in the lumber yard
sitting on top of it pretending to be some of your
grandfather's old carpenters...that I don't think
would know a saw from a corkscrew!

                              Mrs. Jones (enthusiastically)
But this is all part of a plan, Mother...

                         Mrs. Lane (snorting)
A plan to land us all in the street! You know what
they are planning right now?

                         Mrs. Jones (laughing in anticipation)
What?

                         Mrs. Lane
Moving my kitchen into the backyard!

                         Mrs. Jones (delighted)
Whatever for?

                         Mrs. Lane (hissing the words)
Because they want to put a saloon in its place...
they bought old man Schultz'that was a disgrace to
the community...complete with brass rails and spit-
toons!...and probably a chute to slide the drunks
out on.

                         Mrs. Jones
Won't that be gay?

                         Mrs. Lane
Gay! Your father would roll over in his grave.

                         Mrs. Jones
Probably do him good...and grandfather would be
sliding down the chute all day.

                         Mrs. Lane (darkly)
I don't know what's come over you Peggy but wait
til Lucas sees all this!

                         Mrs. Jones
Hasn't he seen it yet?

                         Mrs. Lane
He walked through the lobby like a man in a nightmare
...looking neither to right nor to left.

                         Mrs. Jones
What did he say?

                         Mrs. Lane (ominously)
Nothing.

                    Mrs. Jones
                    Mrs. Lane (challengingly)
What?

                    Mrs. Jones (with great force)
Nothing!
                              DISSOLVE TO:

OLD BOB ZOOKY IN THE MIDDLE OF THE DINING ROOM   129

He has arranged himself a temporary drawing
table and is serenely making free hand draw-
ings in the bedlam of pounding and a cloud of
plaster dust. He wears a large, old-fashioned
hearing aid with a head set like a wireless
operator's.

INSERT: OLD BOB'S HANDS WORKING ON A DRAWING   130
OF A MOTORIZED TALLY-HO.

Around the one he is working on are several
others, some completed, some abandoned, half-
finished.

OLD BOB   131

He looks up from   drawing board and squints
around the room, looking for someone.
                                              9-

MR. KIMBLE AND JIM TANDY   132

Mr. Kimble is on the last lap of sawing a nine-
foot archway through the wall of the dining
room. Jim Tandy is working just ahead of him
with a small sledge hammer, knocking off the
plaster in the path of the saw. This is where
the plaster dust and most of the noise is coming from.

TWO OLD CARPENTERS - WITH WRECKING BARS   133

They are breaking out another archway already
sawed by Mr. Kimble in the end of the dining
room giving on the side toward the vacant lot.
A few seconds after we come to them, their efforts are rewarded by the whole section falling
out with a crash.

                    Big Kim (back over his shoulder)
Nice work, boys.

                    Jim Tandy
We got a little life left   yet...special for
building bars.

                    Old Bob Zooky (coming into the
               SHOT)
You want a compound curve on the tonneau or just a
plain simple one? Compound is twicet as elegant.

                    Big Kim (to Tandy)
What's he talking about?

                    Jim Tandy
The curves of the body...I think you'd be happier
with compound.

                    Big Kim (to Old Bob)
All right, make it compound.

                    Old Bob
You're the boss, but I think you re making a mistake.

                    Big Kim (hollering)
I SAID COMPOUND.

                    Old Bob
How was that?

                    Jim Tandy (indicating the double
               curve with a hand movement, but speaking
               softly)
Compound.

                    Old Bob (who has understood the
               hand movement)
Why didn't he say so in the first place?

                    Big Kim (pointing to a huge micro-
               phone on the old gentleman's vest)
You got any batteries in that thing?

                    Old Bob (after looking down)
Perfect...'course, it ain't the latest model...
               (he cackles happily)
But come to think of it, I ain't, neither...when do
I get that chassis to measure?

                    Big Kim
I'll get it for you today...meanwhile figure on a
hundred and forty-four inches.

                    Old Bob
What'd he say?

                    Big Kim

        In pantomime, Jim Tandy tells old Bob he will
        write it for him.

                    Old Bob (grumbling)
All right, but all you have to do is speak in a low
clear voice...this thing could hear a pin drop.

        He looks from one to the other suspiciously.

                    Jim Tandy
He's a little deefer on some days than others, but
wonderful with a pencil.

                    Big Kim
I wonder where we could find a good ear trumpet...

                    Butch's Voice (like a bugle)
Here he is! Here's Mr. Peabody.

                    Old Bob (turning)
Which Peabody is that...Ed? Hello, Ed.

        They all turn and look at the new arrivals.

BUTCH AND MR. PEABODY   135

        They are coming through the new opening in the
        end of the room. Butch is riding his motor-
        cycle by pushing his feet along on the floor.

                    Butch (happily)
I went to get him on my motorcycle...Brrrrrrrr...
putt-putt-putt...Brrrrrrrr...putt-putt-putt...
squawk, that's the horn.

        By now the CAMERA has brought them into the
        SHOT with the others.

                    Old Bob
Sounds just like one, too...you got a nice, clear
voice.

                    Big Kim
Like a steam whistle.

                    Jim Tandy
There's your ear trumpet.

                    Big Kim
Sure.
            (then, to Mr. Peabody)
How are ya? My name is Jones. I believe you own
this vacant lot next door here, don't you...the one
with all the tin cans on it?

                       227

                    Mr. Peabody   135
That's right...finest lot in town...been kep up   CONT'D.
nice, too.   (2)

                    Big Kim
Maybe you ought to have your glasses checked...I'm
thinking of renting that one...or the one on the
other side of the hotel...or any one of those in
back for six months to a year with an option to
buy...you own them all?

                    Mr. Peabody (worried)
No...all own is this one...but it's the best one...
finest lot in town.

                    Big Kim
That's too bad...well, I ll get in touch with the
other owners and find out which one will give us
the best deal and then contact you later.

                    Mr. Peabody
How much you willing to pay? Might be gold under
that dirt.

                    Big Kim
Yeah...and oil under the gold and diamonds under the
oil...maybe way down at the bottom, some uranium...
I'll tell you what I ll do...

        A HUGE OLD COLORED MAN AND HIS BOY - IN THE   136
        DOORWAY TO THE LOBBY

                    The Colored Man
Anybody here expecting a saloon?...We got it on
the truck.

        MR. KIMBLE AND HIS GROUP   137

                    Big Kim
Bring it in.

        THE COLORED MAN IN THE DOORWAY   138

                    The Old Colored Man
Gonna need a little help...I ain't had my Wheaties
yet today.

        BIG KIM AND HIS GANG   139

                    Big Kim
All right, front and center, everybody out!

                    Old Bob
What'd he say?

                    Butch
He said "everybody out"...they need some help.

                    Old Bob
Glad to give 'em a hand.

                    Big Kim (to Butch)
You stick around, boy.

    They all start out.
                              DISSOLVE TO:

    MRS. JONES COMING DOWN THE STAIRS   140

    She looks very lovely in her cotton morning
    frock. She stops a few steps from the bottom
    and claps her hands with glee.

                    Mrs. Jones (ecstatically)
Good morning!...wherever did you find it?

    HIGH CAMERA SHOT - THE LOBBY - SHOOTING   141
    TOWARD THE FRONT DOOR OF THE HOTEL

    Here we see Mr. Kimble, Jim Tandy, Old Bob,
    Mr. Peabody, the two old carpenters, the
    two colored men, and a screaming Butch,
    struggling in with a medium sized old-fashion-
    ed bar, complete with brass rail. In the
    street behind them we see a dilapidated horse
    truck bearing the rest of the equipment: a
    back bar, some swinging doors, some old saloon
    tables and a dozen Douglas chairs. Half
    visible between the legs of the chairs we
    see the traditional oil painting of a nude
    lady.

                    Big Kim
Easy does it, boys...up she comes... don't strain
yourselves.

                    Old Bob
What did he say?

                    Butch (well into his role of
            interpreter)
He said, "don't strain yourself."

                    Old Bob
Never fear...I'm as strong as a horse.

                    229

MRS. JONES ON THE STAIRWAY   142

  The CAMERA brings her forward as she takes a
  place next to Mr. Kimble and also helps.

      Mrs. Jones
Good morning.

      Big Kim (happy and sweating)
Hello there...getting a little head start.

      Mrs. Jones (happily)
I should say you are.

      Butch (noticing his mother)
Mommie, Mommie, wait 'til you see what Mr. Jones
got me.

  He rushes out to the hotel porch.

      Mrs. Jones
Everything is so exciting...I'm sure my grandfather
must have stood at this one half his life.

      Big Kim
Then it ought to be lucky.

      Mrs. Jones
I think anything you do will be lucky.

      Butch (riding into the SHOT)
Mommie, look...Brrrrrrrr...putt-putt-putt...
Brrrrrrrr...putt-putt-putt...

      Mrs. Jones (getting on one
    knee beside her son as the bar moves on)
It's just lovely, darling...so real looking.

  Suddenly she stands up, looks past the CAMERA,
  and speaks severely:

      Mrs. Jones
Mr. Jones!

  MR. KIMBLE HELPING WITH THE BAR   143

      Big Kim
Yes, Mrs. Jones   By the way, where are those
bricks you said you knew about? I want to start
moving them over here and then I've got to get
over to Petunia to see about...

MRS. JONES AND BUTCH   144

    She comes forward accusingly and the CAMERA
brings her into the SHOT with Mr. Kimble.

               Mrs. Jones
Have you had any breakfast yet?

               Big Kim
To tell you the truth I don't remember...now we'll
bring the rest of the stuff...

               Mrs. Jones (taking his hand)
The rest of the stuff can wait...you come with me
and have your breakfast.

               Big Kim (after a slightly
          sheepish look around)
Yes, mam.

    He starts away.

               Old Bob
What'd he say?

                    DISSOLVE TO:

MR. KIMBLE, MRS. J   S AND THE TWO COLORED   145
MEN - OUTSIDE THE OGDEN HOUSE

    The Jeep is near one of the new openings in
the hotel dining room and they are unloading
from it the last of some brick. Mrs. Jones
wears a big pair of canvas gloves. We HEAR
much hammering and sawing from the hotel.

               Big Kim
Don't hurt yourself now.

               Mrs. Jones
This is fun.

               Big Old Colored Man
Yes mam...,you wouldn't be needin' a bartender for
this new cocktail loungy y all is buildin'? You
gimme the job and I'll lay this brick for you awful
cheap.

               Big Kim (sweating at his work)
We'll talk about it later...we really ought to have
a truck for this...
        (he snaps his fingers as he remembers
        something:)
...pile those up right along side the hotel...I'll
be right back...
        (then to Mrs. Jones:)
You want to ride over to Petunia with me?

Mrs. Jones
I'd love to...it's called Peruvia.

Big Kim
Hop in.

The Jeep zizzes out of the SHOT.

The Old Colored Man
Hot dog! Ain't he a ball of fire?

His Boy
Yeah man...makes me weary just a'lookin' at him.

DISSOLVE TO:

THE KIMBLE DISTRIBUTOR IN PERUVIA   146

Behind him we see a window with a big KIMBLE
written backwards. Through the window we see
a lot full of Kimble chassis. He is a des-
perate looking little man with a round face
that wrinkles up like a baby about to burst
into tears.

The Distributor (whiningly)
Why do you want to borrow a Kimble one and a half
ton chassis...why don't you want to buy one? Why
doesn't anybody want to buy one? They're cheap...
they got four wheels...they run good...they got
everything every other car has plus phono-pusic
transmission...but nobody never wants to buy one...
do they smell bad or something...is there something
their best friend ought to tell them?

Big Kim (severely)
I happen to be working on a body idea...
          (the Distributor takes a quick look at
          Mrs. Jones)
...that might come out all right and do you a lot
of good...I won't drive it...I won't hurt it in
any way...you can chain it to the floor if you like...

Distributor (shaking his head)
Nobody will want to steal it.

Big Kim (frowning at him)
I'll even pay you a little rent if you like but I
don't want to sink any dough in it because I got a
lot of other things to sink it in.

232

                    The Distributor (really looking   146
              as if he were blubbering)   CONT'D
Always the same answer! People sink money in Cadil-   (2)
lacs don't they...and Buicks and Fords and Chevvies...
even in Lincolns! But nobody never sinks nothing in a
Kimble...with that big "K" on the front of it! Go
ahead...help yourself...take one! They're not doing
me any good...or anybody else either! They just sit
there getting older and older and stiffer in the joints
...and the next thing that happens I have to buy a
batch of new ones...to hold on to my distributorship!

                    Big Kim (sourly)
You have all my sympathy...thanks...make out a re-
ceipt will you?...and tie a box on it...I'll take it
right now.

                    The Distributor
You do it...I don't even want to look at one.

                    Mrs. Jones
Why do you want a Kimble, Mr. Jones?

                    The Distributor (before Mr.
              Kimble can answer)
You see what I mean? Even for nothing she don't
want you to have it.
                                        DISSOLVE TO:

A HAND HOLDING AN ADVERTISEMENT IN THE BILLBOARD   147

It reads:

              MIDWAY CONCESSIONS WANTED
              Permanent pitches for small
              county fair-type attraction.
                    No grifters!
              Write or wire Mrs. Jones
                 The Ogden House
                 West Bismarck

The reader's thumb hides the state.
                                        DISSOLVE TO:

THE TWO COLORED MEN BUILDING THE BARBECUE GRILL   148

It is about three-quarters done. They look
quite happy at their work.
                                        .DISSOLVE TO:

                        233

THE TWO OLD CARPENTERS   149

They are panelling the wall behind the bar
with random width knotty pine.
                                        DISSOLVE TO:

MR. KIMBLE AND MRS. JONES   150

He is sawing a piece out of the porch railing
to give access to the steps to the fair ground.
In the background Jim Tandy and a new carpenter
are starting the erection of some booths. Still
behind them a man with a small bulldozer is level-
ling the midway.
                                        DISSOLVE TO:

MR. STONE AND MRS. LANE - IN THE LOBBY OF THE   151
OGDEN HOUSE

They look around sourly at what is going on,
then exchange a look.
                                        DISSOLVE TO:

A BEAUTIFUL WASH DRAWING LABELLED: THE CROSS-   152
COUNTRY

Over this are projected the shadows of Mr. Kimble,
Old Bob and a stranger. Mr. Kimble's hand points
out various parts of the drawing.

                    Big Kim's Voice
You get the idea? We've slid the engine back to here
and it's accessible through these louvers and of
course through a big hatch on the flying bridge...

MR. KIMBLE, OLD BOB AND A SHARP LOOKING STRANGER 153
- IN THE CARRIAGE WORKS

They are bending over Old Bob's drawing board.
About five old carpenters are visible and the
overhead shafting is spinning merrily.

                    Big Kim
...dual controls, of course, inside and on top...then
down here breakfast nook...seats forming double bed
...kitchen and ice box...The Cross-Country Car.

                    The Stranger
Remarkably interesting idea...gets around the trailer
laws...you can ride in it.

234

                         Old Bob
What did he say?

                         Big Kim
Nothing.

                         The Stranger
Certainly a design patent...and possibly more...
possibly much more...the upper and lower controls
would cinch it...they would cinch it but good!
          (now he looks past the CAMERA)
And this is it in the flesh...

                         Big Kim (leading the way)
That's right.

          The CAMERA takes them over to the gleaming
          nearly finished Kimble Kross-Kountry Kar.

                         Big Kim
Beautiful wood in these hills...coming out very very
nice.

                         The Stranger
It certainly is...what make of car is that?

                         Big Kim
A Kimble.

                         The Stranger
That lemon...it wouldn t do them any harm to get
hold of an idea like this...

                         Big Kim
I might sell it to them.

                         The Stranger
They should be very grateful...
          (he pulls a notebook out of his pocket)
Now what name do you want this taken out under Mr.
Jones?...just your own?

                         Big Kim
That's right.

                         The Stranger
And the initials?

                         Big Kim (laughing)
Oh yes...let me think a minute...

                         The Stranger
Sir?

                         Big Kim (with an effort)
Make it...Ocla E. Jones...Junior...

                         Old Bob   153
What did he say?   CONT'D
                                                           (3)
                         Big Kim (shaking his head)
He never opened his kisser.

                         Old Bob
Well, if he don't like it...there's plenty of people
that will...yes sir!

                                        DISSOLVE TO:

          MRS. JONES AND BUTCH PAINTING ONE OF THE   154
          BOOTHS ON THE MIDWAY

          Butch is none too skillful. Behind them we
          see a medium amount of activity: farmers and
          their wives tacking bunting and arranging
          homemade preserves...pitch men working on their
          set-ups...some men assembling a merry-go-round
          in the distance. The local general store
          owner is talking to Mrs. Jones.

                         The Store Owner
But I already got a store Peggy...what do I want to
open another one here for...and give you part of the
profits?

                         Mrs. Jones
Because this is where the people are going to come,
Ezra...and once they're here Mr. Jones says...it
isn't that they want to buy...they have to buy...
you just put in a little hardware and a couple of
tractors...and you'll find out.

          At this moment an elderly village spinster
          and a dark Oriental lady covered with spangles
          come into the SHOT

                         The Spinster (nearly in tears)
Peggy...I had my booth all picked out for my crochet
work and when I got here Madame Zaza had already
moved into it with a stuffed owl and a lot of dirty
old cats and things!

                         Madame Zaza (very profession-
               ally)
I should sweat on the sunny side from morning till
night? Look, dearie, I've been in this game too
long.

                              236

Mrs. Jones (embarrassed,   154
        holding her head)   CONT'D
There must be some friendly way of....   (2)

She is interrupted, and turns at the SOUND of
an automobile horn followed immediately by the
bawling of all kinds of farm animals.

A LARGE DILAPIDATED TRUCK PULLING A TRAILER   155

It is grinding up the midway. On the side of
it we read: Finnegan's Famous Farm Freaks.
The rest of the space is taken up by naively
painted animals: a two-headed chicken, a six-
legged calf, Siamese pigs, a unicorn, etc., etc.
A cow with reindeer's antlers sticks its head
out of the window and whinnies. A handsome
blonde lady, looking something like Mrs. Abe
Lastvogel, starts wedging herself out of the
front seat.

                    Mrs. Finnegan
Well, we made it...and not a minute too soon...one
more day in that truck and you could put me in the
show....
            (a calf bawls behind her and she
            turns her head ferociously)
Shut up!

MRS. JONES, BUTCH, THE SPINSTER & MADAME ZAZA   156

                    Mrs. Jones
How do you do, Mrs. Finnegan...I hope you'll be very
happy with us...I suppose you'll be wanting a room in
the hotel like all the other concessions...we're making
professional rates...

                    Madame Zaza
Hello, Minnie...

MR. AND MRS. FINNEGAN IN THE TRUCK   157

                    Mrs. Finnegan
Well now ain't that handy...right next to the pitch.

                    Mr. Finnegan
Super! I hope there's a little bar in the joint.

237

MRS. JONES, BUTCH, THE SPINSTER & MADAME ZAZA   158

                    Mrs. Jones
Oh my yes.

                    Butch (pointing suddenly to
                the side of the truck)
Look at the two headed chickens!

THE TRAILER BEHIND THE TRUCK   159

A cow with reindeer's antlers sticks its
head out between the curtains and whinnies.

MRS. LANE IN THE LOBBY OF THE HOTEL   160

She is behind the desk and we are SHOOTING at
her past a group of carnival people all talking
at once. There is also much hammering and
sawing.

                    Mrs. Lane (pushing her hair back)
One at a time, please...everybody will be taken care
of...there's room for everybody!

                    A Woman (pushing into the SHOT)
Where are the sheets for room fourteen...what do we
sleep on the linoleum?

                    Mrs. Lane
Everything will be taken care of...
            (she hollers past the CAMERA)
We're out of sheets.

MR. KIMBLE AND A PRINTER   161

The latter is holding a big tack card against
the wall of the lobby for the haggard Mr.
Kimble's approval. The card reads:

            The Bismarck County Fair
            Come One Come All!
            Bring The Kiddies!
            Door Prizes! Free Gifts!
            Farmers' Exchange
            Opening Sunday

                    Big Kim (looking back at Mrs. Lane)
All right I'll get some...

                    Mr. Finnegan (coming into SHOT)
Excuse me, brother...but where could a party get a
little shot around here...my tongue is hanging out!

238

Big Kim   161
The bar won't be open for three days...   CONT'D
                                                (2)
                    Mr. Finnegan (in horror)
Three days!

                    Big Kim
I'll take care of you in a moment.

                    Mr. Finnegan
Thank you brother.

                    Big Kim (turning to the printer)
Okay...now can you get me somebody to tack 'em
around?

                    Mr. Finnegan
I'll give you a hand.

                    DISSOLVE TO:

MR. KIMBLE ON THE MIDWAY - NIGHT   162

By the light of a gasoline lantern, he is hammering away on the construction of still another
booth. Some slight activity is going on in the
background...and other gasoline lanterns flicker
in the darkness. A calf bawls.

MRS. JONES - LOOKING AT HIM   163

She looks worried. She has a little shawl over
her shoulder and is carrying a cup of coffee.
Now the CAMERA takes her over into the SHOT with
Mr. Kimble.

                    Mrs. Jones
I brought you some coffee, Jonesey...but you've really
got to come to bed...you're wonderful, but you're supposed to be here for a rest...I'm afraid you're going
to drop dead.

                    Big Kim
I never felt better in my life...I've just got to
get this blasted thing finished...

                    Mrs. Jones (softly)
Well you don't have to get it finished tonight.

                    Big Kim (ominously)
Well...I darn near have to get it finished tonight.

                    Mrs. Jones (sensing danger)
Why?

239

                    Big Kim (avoiding her eye)
You'll get a big laugh out of this...

                    Mrs. Jones (still more frightened)
Out of what?

                    Big Kim (laughing)
This'll kill you...we're out of dough.

                    Mrs. Jones (seizing his arm)
Jonesey! You mean all that big roll...of hundred
dollar bills...

                    Big Kim (laughing)
And then some...I owe a little too.

                    Mrs. Jones
Then what are you laughing about?

                    Big Kim (still laughing)
Struck me kinda funny, that's all...we'll have to
hock something...

                    Mrs. Jones
What is there left to hock?
          (Mr. Kimble does not answer)
I told you this was going to cost a lot of money...
but you wouldn't listen to me...you said "do like
the government does...spend it first...and look for
it afterwards"...now we're afterwards and you see...

                    Big Kim (interrupting politely)
Lucas in?

                    Mrs. Jones (astonished)
Lucas! He's usually in by this time...but I should
hardly think that...

                    Big Kim
Look: you've got to get it from where it is...you
can't get it out of a turnip...Stone owns that air-
field, doesn't he?

                    Mrs. Jones
I-I think so...I think he got it for the tax ...

                    Big Kim
Like he got everything else...come on...

          He takes her hand and drags her toward the
          hotel so rapidly she spills half the coffee.

                              DISSOLVE TO:

240

MR. STONE IN HIS BEDROOM   164

He wears a ratty looking bathrobe over his
night shirt. He is sitting on the bed.

                    Mr. Stone (looking past
            the CAMERA)
How do you know I <u>want</u> to sell the air port?

MR. KIMBLE PAST MR. STONE   165

He is leaning on the chiffonier.

                    Big Kim
Because you're a smart business man and you own the
land around it...which will increase in value...
also because I'm going to take an option at three
times what you paid for it.

                    Mr. Stone
Huh! What do I have to do to get paid <u>this</u> time?

                    Big Kim
I'm going to give you a great opportunity...instead
of just exercising the option on the works and shut-
ting you out forever...I'm going to let you become
a part of this great expansion...a founder...a useful man...a bond holder...

MR. STONE - PAST MR. KIMBLE   166

                    Mr. Stone (narrowing his eyes)
Go on...

                    Big Kim
Instead of allowing outside capital to come in and
complete this venture...strangers who have taken
no risk but who now move in for the cream...I'm
going to let <u>you</u>...
            (Mr. Stone turns to ice)
...put up the completion money...

MR. KIMBLE - PAST MR. STONE   167

                    Big Kim
And increase your sale price on the works to fifteen
thousand dollars...which does not begin to represent
its value!

MR. STONE HOLDING ONTO THE BED   168

                    Mr. Stone
Wait a minute...are you trying to borrow fifteen
thousand dollars from me on something that I own...
that only cost me twenty-seven hundred in the first
place?

        MR. KIMBLE

                    Big Kim (pleasantly)
What you paid for it has nothing to do with its
value...I don't think you appreciate the potentials
of that plant...its nearness to the hardwood stands
...its unlimited free power...its machinery built
to last FOREVER!

        MR. STONE HOLDING ONTO THE BED   170

                    Mr. Stone
You don't have to sell it to me...I own it!

        MR. KIMBLE   171

                    Big Kim
Only technically because I own the option...which
I will most certainly exercise...what I'm offering
you is a magnificent big mortgage at six per cent.

        MR. STONE - ON THE BED   172

                    Mr. Stone (beginning to yell)
On my own property!

        MR. KIMBLE   173

                    Big Kim (gently)
But it won't be your property any more because the
first thing I'm going to do is pay you off!

        MR. STONE - ON THE BED

                    Mr. Stone (yelping and tapping
            his chest)
With my own money!

                    242

MR. KIMBLE   175

     Big Kim (a little more
  forcefully)
Well what's the matter with your own money...it's
just as good as anybody else's and look what you
get: a big mortgage on a going concern...a
tremendous increase in the safety of your hotel
mortgage...and three imes what you paid for the
air field...a huge profit!

MR. STONE ON THE BED   176

     Mr. Stone (rubbing his chin)
I think you're batty.

MR. KIMBLE BY THE CHIFFONIER   177

  During this scene the CAMERA takes him over to
  Mr. Stone so that he can shake a forceful finger
  under his nose.

     Big Kim (beginning pleasantly)
Maybe you're right...but when you see that long line
of bodies rolling out of that old carriage works...
and all that machinery spinning and the joint jumping with workmen...and men sleeping four in a bed
in this hotel again...it's nearly full right now...
and the bar downstairs three deep with business...
and the midway pulling them in like flies from all
over the state...don't forget I've got options on
all the ground around the hotel too...you'll think
you were batty not to come in on the ground floor
while I was here holding the door open for you...
ANYTIME AFTER TONIGHT YCU'LL HAVE TO COME UP THE
FIRE ESCAPE!

     Mr. Stone (sweating slightly)
Is that so...how do you know all these things are
going to happen like you say?

     Big Kim (delivering the final
  thrust)
Because they're happening right now all around you...
haven't you got any eyes in your head...don't you
realize what that cross-country body means to the
American motoring public? You've certainly sneaked
down there enough times at night to find out! DON'T
DENY IT! Now I'm just going to ask you one question:
Do you want in or out? This is your last chance!

  Mr. Stone opens his mouth to speak...his lips
  move...but nothing comes out.
        DISSOLVE TO:

MRS. JONES IN HER BEDROOM   178

She has put on a dressing gown and is visible
through the half open door, twisting her hands
nervously. Now she looks up at the SOUND of
a door closing and rises slowly and looks past
the CAMERA.

THE DOORWAY OF MRS JONES'S ROOM   179

Mr. Kimble appears out of the darkness, leans
against the doorjamb and looks at her in amusement. Now he winks.

MRS. JONES PAST MR. KIMBLE   180

Her lips are trembling slightly as she comes
forward.

                    Mrs. Jones
Don't tell me...you got it...

                    Big Kim
Why not?

                    Mrs. Jones
Oh Jonesey!

She bursts into tears of relief and sobs
against his chest.

                    Big Kim (putting his arm around
           her and patting her)
There there there...

From outside one of Finnegan's freaks lets
out a doleful moo. Mr. Kimble turns slowly
in the direction of the SOUND.
                              FADE OUT:

FADE IN:

LONG SHOT THE LITTLE MIDWAY IN FULL BLAST   181

The SOUND is a mixture of calliope music, a
village band, the cracks of rifles, gongs
being hit by pellits, the whistle and bell
of the miniature railroad, the hoarse voices
of barkers and the little bell used by Madame
Zaza. All this is interlarded with a strident
police whistle.

244

A SERIES OF SPOT SHOTS OF THE VARIOUS   182-
CONCESSIONS   186

When we have seen enough come-ons, jellies,
vegetables, homemade bread, pies and cakes,
crochet and quilt work and children flying
by on the little train and the merry-go-
round....

THE STREET IN FRONT OF THE HOTEL   187

The village constable, whistle in mouth, is
having one hell of a time with the traffic.
This is not aided by the presence of a large
bus.

MRS. JONES IN FINNEGAN'S FREAK SHOW   188

She is looking at her son who is looking at
a two-headed calf which is looking at her son.

                    Mrs. Jones
Why don't you go and look at something else, darling? You've been looking at this one all day...
you'll wind up with four eyes.

The double-headed calf moos at Butch who moos
back at it. Mrs. Jones sighs and starts looking at somebody else. She starts threading her
way through the crowd, toward the hotel.

THE BAR OF THE OGDEN HOUSE   189

It is jammed with people and noise.

THE COLORED BARTENDER IN A BEAUTIFUL WHITE   190
COAT - NEXT TO HIM PERSPIRES HIS SON IN
ANOTHER WHITE COAT

                    The Bartender
            (in response to a blast of incomprehen-
            sible orders)
Yassuh...yassuh...comin' right up...
            (he mops his head with a bar towel)
Willie...we didn't know when we was well off...

                    Willie (without expression)
Hot dawg...,

245

R. KIMBLE AND MR. STONE - SIDE BY SIDE AT   191
THE BAR

They are surrounded by activity of which they
are totally unconscious. They are stiff as
planks.

                    Mr. Stone (punctuating with
          hiccups)
Yes sir...Ooip...the most remarkabola..I mean remarkabule...thing I ever seen...

                    Big Kim (staring straight ahead)
S'nuthing...

                    Mr. Stone (looking at him
          indignantly)
What duya mean...s'nuthing? S'th'mos'remarkabule...
remarkabole thing I ever...s'wonderful!

                    Big Kim (straight ahead)
S'nuthing...make mine with plain water this time...

                    Mr. Stone (looking around in-
        , dignantly)
What duya mean it's...s'nuthing? S'th'mos'remarka-
abule...Ooip...why with your brains and my money...
we could set the world on fire!
          (Mr. Kimble turns jerkily to look at him
          then looks back at the bartender)
Ya hear me?...

                    Big Kim (to the bartender)
Where's the ice?
          (the bartender's hand comes into the
          SHOT and shakes his glass to show the
          ice in it)
Oh...
          (now he turns slowly to Mr. Stone)
You talkin' to me?

                    Mr. Stone
I don't care what they say about you...I know everybody thinks you're a crook...but all I gotta say
is...if you're a crook...what we need in this world
is more crooks.

     He slaps the bar and knocks his glass over.

                    Big Kim (turning slowly)
Like you?

                    Mr. Stone (emphatically)
Exactly!

                    Big Kim (turning slowly away)
S'nuthing...

                         246

MRS. JONES COMING THROUGH THE CROWDED BAR   192

Suddenly she is accosted by a little man in
spectacles.

                    The Little Man
Oh Mrs. Jones I'm the new bookkeeper....we're fall-
ing rapidly behind and I have a few questions...
Mr. Jones is hardly in a condition...

                    Mrs. Jones (urging him away)
I'll see you in a few minutes...I've got to take
care of something.

                    The Little Man (departing)
Certainly Mrs. Jones.

          Mrs. Jones now comes forward and the CAMERA
          pulls her into the shot with Messrs. Kimble
          and Stone.

                    Mrs. Jones (putting a hand on
               Mr. Kimble's shoulder)
How do you feel now Jonesey?

                    Big Kim (turning slowly to her)
S'nuthing...

                    Mrs. Jones
How would you like to come and sit in a nice rocking
chair...and get a little air...it's about time you
sat in that rocking chair...

                    Big Kim (making a feeble joke)
Rocking chair! The whole joint is rocking...
          (he laughs feebly and looks at Stone)
You hear that one?

                    Mr. Stone (on the verge of
               tears)
Nobody offers me rocking chairs...I could be out
all alone in the snow and...

                    Mrs. Stone
I'll take care of you in a minute Lucas...
          (now she helps Mr. Kimble off the stool)
Suppose we have a nice little nap?

                    Big Kim
Zat a promise?

                    Mrs. Jones (leading him away)
Nice and easy now...just lean on me a little...

          As they move away the CAMERA centers on Mr.
          Stone.

Mr. Stone (looking after them   192
       indignantly)   CONT'D
Rocking chairs! Rocking chairs my...   (2)

He does not get to say the word "foot because he falls off the bar stool at this
point and disappears behind the bar like so
much pig iron.
                 DISSOLVE TO:

THE DOOR INSIDE IRS. JONES S DARKENED ROOM   193

About all   can see is that it is a bedroom.
There is a KNOCK on the door, then a wedge
of light falls on the bed and the CAMERA goes
up to Mrs. Jones bearing a breakfast tray which
also contains a few pill bottles.

             Mrs. Jones (sitting on the bed
          with the tray in her lap)
Good morning...good morning!

There is a movement among the pillows, a couple
of dolls are pushed to one side and Mr. Kimble
appears.

             Big Kim
What? Huh...OOOOOOh!

He sticks his tongue out, makes a face, then
clutches his head.
             Mrs. Jones (sweetly)
How do you feel now?

At this point we get a blast of the calliope
music as the merry-go-round gets its morning
oiling.

             Big Kim
Oh nooooo...say what did I toss into myself last
night...or did I fall out of a window on my head?

             Mrs. Jones (laughing and putting
          some pillows gently under his head)
You gave the bar quite a start...in fact I think
it's almost paid for...everything's going wonderfully...we don't know how much we took in yesterday
...the bookkeepers are days behind...now here's
some coffee...and some bromoseltzer...and some ana-
cin...and some alkabromo...and if that isn't
enough...

             Big Kim (suddenly worried)
Say...where am I?

                    Mrs. Jones (laughing)
Oh this is my room...you were bound and determined
you were going to sleep in it...and you were so
sweet about it...I just let you sleep in it...
            (then in reply to a look)
I slept with mother...oh you were all wound up...
you said I was the prettiest girl you'd ever seen
in your whole life...that you'd been in love with
me from the first moment you laid eyes on me...
and that one day I would have millions...tens of
millions...

                    Big Kim (chuckling)
The things a guy will say.

                    Mrs. Jones (back to normal)
Yes, they're really something aren't they...and there
ere four gentlemen downstairs from the Kimble Automobile Compay to see you.

                    Big Kim (sitting bolt upright and
            spilling his coffee)

                    Mrs. Jones (grabbing a napkin)
Now look what you've done!
                                    DISSOLVE TO:

THE PORCH OF THE OGDEN HOUSE   194

    Four strangers, young and with brief cases,
    are waiting: Messrs. Kempenard, Shook,
    Coblentz and Jaffney, the brain trust of the
    Kimble Automobile Company.

THE DOOR FROM THE LOBBY   195

    Mr. Kimble, somewhat hastily dressed, and wear-
    ing his golf cap down to his nose, peers around
    the doorjamb and squints suspiciously at the
    young men. Deciding that he has never seen
    them before, he comes out slowly and the CAMERA
    takes him over to a position behind them where
    he takes another look.

                    Mr. Kempenard (noticing him
            suddenly)
Oh...Mr. Jones I presume?

                    Big Kim (suspiciously)
Yeah...

                    Mr. Kempenard (rising and
                shaking hands)
Mr. Jones...I am Mr. Kempenard...<u>Dick</u> Kempenard...
in the engineering department of the Kimble Automobile Company...you've heard of the Kimble Automobile I trust.

                    Big Kim
I certainly have...you mind if I sit down?
                (he sits in Mr. Kempenard's chair and
                touches his head slightly)
That's that lemon nobody wants isn't it?

                    Mr. Shook (jovially)
Far far from it, Mr. Jones. Those are just rumors
put out by jealous rivals...I'm Mr. Shook of the
sales department.

                    Mr. Jaffney
Rumors we are going to make them   Mr. Jones.
I am Mr. Jaffney of the advertising department.

                    Mr. Coblentz
And without any salt and pepper either...I am
Mr. Coblentz of the new projects department, Mr.
Jones.

                    Big Kim
How are ya...well the company seems to be well
represented...what's this Kimble like anyway?

                    Mr. Kempenard (laughing confi-
                dentially)
To tell you the truth I don't think there is any
such person.

                    Big Kim (startled)
Huh?

                    Mr. Shook
We think he s just a figment of the advertising
department's imagination...

                    Mr. Coblentz
A legendary figure...

                    Mr. Jaffney
A trade mark...

                    Big Kim
You mean you've never even seen him?

                    Mr. Kempenard
I don't think <u>anybody's</u> ever seen him.

                    Big Kim (removing his cap and
          looking around)
Well what d'ya know...wh t brought you boys to
Bismarck?

                    Mr. Kempenard (looking to the
          others politely)
Shall I do the talking gentlemen?

                    Big Kim (holding his head)
Is this going to be a long talk?...because I've
got a little headache this morning...

                    Mr. Kempenard
I can make it as long or as short as you like,
Mr. Jones...you have made a little invention...
the Cross-Country Car that we know everything
about...we at Kimble want it...and we are going
to have it!

                    Mr. Coblentz
Right...

                    Big Kim (looking around)
Is that so!

                    Mr. Kempenard (firmly)
That is so...we don't mean by bludgeoning methods,
Mr. Jones, such as some firms who shall be nameless
use...

                    Mr. Coblentz
Mr. Kempenard is the man who put the pope's noses
on the Cadillacs...they swiped it.

                    Mr. Kempenard (mildly)
Let's say they purloined it...but by the weight of
sheer logic...the future of the Kimble Car...

                    Big Kim (interrupting)
How did you know about this gag of mine.

                    Mr. Coblentz
It's very simple really: any man who's interested
in a Kimble...<u>we're</u> interested in...

                    Mr. Shook (jovially)
After all there aren't so many of you.

                    Mr. Kempenard (warningly)
Arthur...

                         Mr. Coblentz
So we sent a little man over from Peruvia to find
out what was happening to our little chassis...and
then a few more of us dropped in from time to
time...

                         Big Kim
By parachute?

                         Mr. Jaffney
By plane...there's a little field about a quarter
of a mile from here.

                         Big Kim
Oh you know about that too do you...

                         Mr. Kempenard (pleasantly)
Oh we know about everything...the hardwood stands...
the old coach builders...how much you optioned the
plant for...and just about how good your patent
is...which happens to be fairly good.

                         Big Kim
You know something?

                         Mr. Kempenard
What?

                         Big Kim
You're not a bad bunch of boys at that...you might
do something with that car yet.

                         Mr. Coblentz
You'll find out.

                         Big Kim (taking command of the
                            situation)
Okay...you can have the plant for what I paid for
it plus fifty thousand dollars...I've got a few
other things to pay off.

                         Mr. Coblentz (interrupting)
Now just a minute...

                         Mr. Kempenard
If you don't mind...

                         Big Kim (also interrupting)
You just listen to me for a minute, buddy...I've
got a little headache...fifty grand profit on the
plant...twenty-five dollars royalty on each body...
and I want them made right here in West Bismarck.

                              252

Mr. Coblentz
Well now <u>there</u> Mr. Jones...

Mr. Kempenard
It presents a little problem in transportation.

Mr. Jaffney
We've talked it over pretty thoroughly.

Mr. Shook
<u>Very</u> thoroughly....

Big Kim
Oh you have...well it presents <u>no</u> problem in transportation which is why I just bought that air field...
which you are going to buy back from me at a slight
profit...because I have still a few <u>other</u> things to
take care of.

Mr. Kempenard (laughing politely)
You seem very sure of yourself.

Big Kim
You'd be surprised how sure I am of myself! Now
I'll tell you why there's no transportation problem...
you ever hear of the Kimble Airplane Company?

Mr. Coblentz
Well certainly...although we are not actually closely
allied...

Big Kim
You're closer than you think! Now in case you don't
know it the Kimble Airplane Company builds freight
planes...and in case you're not familiar with planes...
freight planes have to get a test flight just like any
other plane...the test flights will be to here...on
the way down they bring a few chassis for local distribution...on the way back they carry a load we
have built flat...in panel form...with just that in
mind.

Mr. Coblentz (stupefied)
You seem to have made quite a study of the problem...

Big Kim (suddenly snapping his
fingers and getting to his feet)
Wait a minute!
(the four young men rise and gather around
him)
We might be able to connect the air field directly
to the plant...so you wouldn't have to transship...
the planes would come in over there, land...and taxi
right through the town...to the front door of the
works!

The four young men exchange looks as if they
were listening to a lunatic.

Mr. Kempenard (gently)
Excuse me but you're a little ahead of us there...
just how would you get the planes through the town?
They're very big you know.

Big Kim (pointing to it)
By building an airway...I think Stone owns most of
the land between here and the field anyway...and
this village green isn't doing anybody any good...

Mr. Kimble and the four young men start FADING
very slowly, and their figures are replaced by
SHOTS of the building of the airway. Mr.
Kimble's voice continues as we see the arrival
of some earth-moving machinery at the station,
a crane lifting a big tree, houses moving left
to right, houses moving right to left, thirty
workmen with tool boxes and suitcases getting
off the train, steamrollers and concrete mix-
ers at work, a cavalcade of trailers crawling
into town, the construction of a market, more
workmen getting off a train, more bulldozers
at work, a SHOT of great activity in the
Carriage Works and finally a large freight
plane, bearing the Kimble K, coming in for a
landing.

Big Kim
....all we need is room enough down the middle for
the flying box cars...and we're in...just means
moving a few trees...a couple of dozen houses and
putting in a few safety gates...then you roll it
down...it doesn't even have to be very flat because
nobody's going to take off from it...put a light
surface on it...and there you are! And I'll tell
you something else it'll do it'll be the first town
in America you can come right into the middle of
with an airplane...to go to the movies or do your
shopping!

His voice is replaced by MUSIC until the end
of the construction MONTAGE.

DISSOLVE TO:

MR. KIMBLE ON THE PORCH OF THE OGDEN HOUSE   196

At last he is sitting in the rocker and smoking
his pipe. He seems quite peaceful and contented
due no doubt to the fact that there is hammering
and sawing to the right of him, calliope music
and the noise of a shooting gallery to his left,
and airplanes in front of him. An unusually
loud jazzing of a motor attracts his attention.

254

FULL SHOT THE AIRWAY   197

The street in the foreground is full of traffic:
Pedestrian and automotive. A small building on
one side of the SHOT sells ice cream and novelties,
another building is in process of erection from
the other side of the shot, a handsome small plane
is taxiing by on the airway, four or five still
smaller ones are taxiing around like water bugs
in the background. A field master is directing
the taxiing airplane traffic with a whistle. A
couple of gasoline trucks shoot by. A porter
comes toward the hotel leading some guests and
carrying their hand baggage.

MR. KIMBLE ON THE PORCH

He watches all this placidly, but he does not
seem quite as cheerful as we would expect him
to be.

THE DOORWAY INTO THE LOBBY OF THE HOTEL   198

Mrs. Jones appears, some papers in her hands.
Behind her the lobby is full of activity. The
porter and the guests go by her and she bows
to them. Now she locates Mr. Kimble and the
CAMERA takes her over to him.

                    Mrs. Jones (affectionately)
There you are! In your rocking chair at last...and
smoking your pipe.

                    Big Kim
I thought I ought to do it at least once...sit down
a minute...you haven't been doing much sitting either.

                    Mrs. Jones (sitting close to him)
I certainly never felt better...isn't it wonderful
to be active all the time!

                    Big Kim
Yeah...I never felt better either...the little trouble
I had before I came down here...is certainly all gone...
I guess that doctor was right.

                    Mrs. Jones
You mean the one who told you to take a rest?

                    Big Kim
Yeah.

                    Mrs. Jones (patting his head)
You're so funny...you make me laugh just as much now
as the first day you got here.

                         Big Kim (smiling wanly)   198
I'm glad...   CONT'D
                                                              (2)
                         Mrs. Jones (uneasily)
What's the matter Jonesey?

                         Big Kim
Nothing...
                    (he points to the papers in her hands)
...what you got there?

                         Mrs. Jones (looking down)
Oh it's just about the new wing on the hotel...d'you
want me to see about financing it through that bank
that's coming in...or shall I ask Lucas to increase
the mortgage? He said he'd be delighted to...he's
made so much money he doesn't know where to put it.

                         Big Kim (avoiding her eye)
I'll tell you what I'll do Peggy...I'll make you a
present of that new wing...

                         Mrs. Jones (astonished)
A present of it! I don't think you have any idea
how much it's going to...

                         Big Kim (interrupting gently)
Oh yes I have...and I'd like very much to make you
a present of it...a sort of going away present...
it'll cheer us both up...
                    (Mrs. Jones turns and looks at him miserably)
...they called me this afternoon...that was that long
distance call I got...they're coming to get me...

                         Mrs. Jones (alarmed)
Who's coming to get you? Did you do something that...

                         Big Kim (laughing a little)
No...no...just some of my partners and Bamby...I
guess...my secretary...probably with a bunch of
mail that high...I suppose they had to find out
where I was sooner or later...

                         Mrs. Jones (still stunned)
But I don't understand...

                         Big Kim (explaining gently)
My six months are up honey...I've got to get back
to work...I've got income tax...I've got...I've got
a lotta pains in the neck...

                         Mrs. Jones (nearly on the verge
                              of tears)
And you're going away?

                         Big Kim (slightly on the defensive)
Well you always knew I was...I told you all about it
the first day I got here...that it was just for a
six months...rest...I never made any secret about it.

Mrs. Jones (miserably)
I know you didn't...but I...people can change their
minds sometimes can't they? At least you've got
the right to...hope they will anyway...

Big Kim
Hope they will anyway what?

Mrs. Jones
Change their minds...

Big Kim
You mean about staying here? Peggy I haven't got
any more chance of staying here than...than...

Mrs. Jones (defensively)
Oh I'm not a romantic girl of sixteen you know I...
I know how wonderful you've been...taking this poor
miserably little town and this poor miserable little
hotel...and turning them into...you've only got to
look around ! But even so...I don't think you have
the right to just...

Big Kim (slightly aroused)
What do you mean I haven't get the right? I've
got to get back to work...you mean because....I
kissed you that time?

Mrs. Jones (coldly)
Which time...you've been kissing me for six
months...
     (now she loses her calm)
...and I...I wish you'd kissed me a lot more !

Big Kim
So do I...but that doesn't...I mean you're a very
very pretty girl...

Mrs. Jones (working herself up)
And now after six months of of of...

Big Kim
Of what?

Mrs. Jones
Well of...having breakfast...and dinner...and supper together...and working side by side all day,...
and...and...going for rides in the moonlight
together...you just want to give me a...wing on
the hotel...and beat it ! Well let me tell you something Mr. Jones...there are some women you don't
treat like that...and I'm one of them...I wouldn't
have been trying to run this poor broken-down excuse for a hotel with just my mother and my son...
and trying to do my own plumbing and everything...
if I was the type of girl you can just...believe me
Mr. Jones...mink coats aren't hard to get...they're
hard to avoid !

                    Big Kim
Who's talking about mink coats?

                    Mrs. Jones (aroused)
I am...I suppose you've bought quite a few of them
in your time...as little going away presents...

                    Big Kim (coldly)
In every style...wrap-arounds...double-breasteds...
stoles...capes...muffs...brown ones...blue ones...
and for all I know maybe some green ones...

                    Mrs. Jones
Well you're not going to buy me one...and I just
wish I could figure out some way to put everything
you've given me in one big pile and then hit you
over the head with it...in my family, Mr. Jones...
the women don't accept expensive presents from
gentlemen!

                    Big Kim (indignantly)
Well this is a nice time to tell me...after I've
worked eighteen hours a day for six months...
horsing around with your plumbing fixtures...
electricuting myself on your lousy fuses, carpentering, wall papering...I've done everything but
make the beds!

                    Mrs. Jones (snuffling)
I thought those were...engagement presents...

                    Big Kim (in righteous indigna-
          tion)
Engagement presents! You mean a janitor service!
A guy who gets engaged buys a ring, doesn't he,
with a sparkler in it? And then he comes around
in a hard collar and says something doesn't he...
some exact words?

                    Mrs. Jones (miserably)
I suppose so...

                    Big Kim
Did I ever say those words?

                    Mrs. Jones (weeping lightly)
I thought you were too busy...

                    Big Kim
You can say that again!

                    Mrs. Jones (through her tears)
I thought we were building all this for us...to
share together...you...and Butch...and I...I
thought...Butch was going to have a father...

                         Big Kim (in mounting indignation) 198
Now let's be fair about this: Butch is going to get CONT'D
twenty-five dollars royalty on every Cross-Country (5)
body we build...and we're going to build thousands
of them...I took out the patent in his name...he
needs a father like he needs a hole in his head...
you've got your hotel free and clear...practically
speaking...in good shape...and all the ground around
it...you've got money in the bank...you've got an
automobile...even your mother has one...so now it
turns out I"m behaving like a heel...a cheap drummer
...a welsher...and a fly-by-night...

                         Mrs. Jones
That's your own description...

                         Big Kim
You've made it clear enough...all right! You win...
get ahold of old doctor whats-his-name and we'll
get spliced before I go...

                         Mrs. Jones
You really mean that?

                         Big Kim
I really do...of course when you'll be seeing me
the next time is something else again...

                         Mrs. Jones (coldly)
I'm really touched...that's as pretty a proposal as
any woman ever had...thank you very much...

                         Big Kim (with the same reading)
You're entirely welcome...

                         Mrs. Jones (beginning her diatribe)
Only I wouldn't marry you, Mr. Jones...

                         Big Kim
My name happens to be Charles Kimble.

                         Mrs. Jones (wound up)
Whatever it happens to be...I suppose you have something to do with that lousy car...but I wouldn't
marry you if you were the last chance in pants...
and it was either you or life in a women's club!

                         Big Kim (somewhat relieved)
Well...you can't say I didn't ask you...

                         Mrs. Jones
No...you're entirely in the clear.

                         Big Kim (gently)
Look, Peggy...now that you know who I am...t whole
thing ought to be much easier for you to understand
...I have to move around so much...I have to go to so
many con...

259

                    Mrs. Jones (interrupting)
I never heard of you...except your name is the
same as...

                         Big Kim
Never mind the car...you ever hear of the Octogan
Building in Washington...the biggest in the world?

                       Mrs. Jones
No....

                         Big Kim
Well...I built it...you ever hear of the Alexander
Hamilton Bridge over the Delaware Water Gap?

                    Mrs. Jones (resentfully)
Should I have?

                    Big Kim (not making much head-
              way)
I built that too...how about the Appohatchee Dam
that makes the Appohatchee River run backwards?

                       Mrs. Jones
Does it? I didn't even know it ran forwards....

                    Big Kim (controlling himself
              admirably)
The...uh...Kimble Oil Company? That sails its
own tankers all over the world...and builds them
besides?

                       Mrs. Jones
Besides what?

                         Big Kim
Well you've certainly seen the Kimble Aircraft!
That's what's flying in and out of here every day!
There's one coming for me in a few minutes! Then
there's the Kimble First National Bank and Trust
Company....the Kimble Rubber and Novelty Company
that makes hot water bags...you've got one in your
bed.

                       Mrs. Jones
Is that supposed to be a novelty?
              (then after a pause)
Look, Jonesey...or Mr. Kimble...or whoever you are
...I don't care who you are...it was you that I
liked...of course I understand now that you're a
big shot...a very big shot...and that a widow with
a little boy...in a little town...is very small-time
stuff to you...
              (she points out to the airway)
...here come your friends, I guess.

MR. KIMBLE'S PRIVATE PLANE   199

It bears the familiar K and is taxiing toward
us.

MR. KIMBLE AND MRS. JONES   200

                    Mrs. Jones (getting up)
I don't know enough words to thank you for every-
thing you've done...Jonesey...so I won't try to...
Goodbye...and God bless you.

        She bursts into tears and hurries away. Mr.
        Kimble starts to rise then sits down again
        and rocks despondently. After a moment of
        self-justifying thought, he starts to rock
        furiously. On the third rock the chair
        explodes into kindling and he lands heavily
        on the flat of his back.

                        DISSOLVE TO:

MISS SIMPSON IN A CORNER OF DR. ROTHMULLER'S   201
EXAMINATION ROOM

She is writing down the notes she hears.

                    Dr. Rothmuller's Voice (rapidly)
NORMAL! Now close your eyes...stand up...put your
hands over your head and touch your toes...put your
feet together...raise your arms straight out in
front of you...keep your eyes closed...ROMBERG NEGATIVE.

        Miss Simpson makes a note.

MR. KIMBLE AND DR. ROTHMULLER   202

        Mr. Kimble wearing only a pair of shorts has
        his arms stretched out toward the doctor like
        a somnambulist.

                    Dr. Rothmuller
Keep your eyes closed...now stick your left hand
out to one side...further...now touch the end of
your nose with your index finger...good...now do
the same with the right...NEGATIVE! You learned
to smoke a pipe?
                    Big Jim
A little bit.

                        261

                    Dr. Rothmuller
Now sit down and cross your legs...the other way...
          (he hits Mr. Kimble under both knee
          caps, then spins him around in the
          chair a few times and peers into his
          eyes)
...NO NYSTAGMUS.

                    Big Kim
Don't you ever get tired doing that?

                    Dr. Rothmuller (picking up a
          hammer)
Very...
          (he hits Mr. Kimble's elbows and the
     sides of his wrists)
...now lie down...
          (he draws the point of the hammer handle
          under each of Mr. Kimble's feet, from the
          heel to the toes)
...control yourself...

                    Big Kim
You ought to try it yourself sometime.

                    Dr. Rothmuller (wiping his
          hands on a towel)
BABINSKI NEGATIVE...okay...as usual you are in perfect health.

                    Big Kim (lighting a cigarette)
I'm glad to hear it...because there's just one minor
little thing that happened.

                    Dr. Rothmuller (not greatly
          interested)
So tell it...

                    Big Kim
I got back here one month ago...March fourteenth to
be exact...just in time to sign my tax returns...

                    Dr. Rothmuller
So?

                    Big Kim
Then we went into a little conference...I sat down
with a tableful of my partners...including one of
our bank presidents who began a little chat...

                    Dr. Rothmuller (shaking his head)
Those bank presidents...

                    Big Kim (accusingly)
...the next thing I remember...I was shooting craps
with the American Consul in Punta Arenas...I was in
Chile, South America...it was the twelfth of April...

                    Big Kim (cont'd)   202
and I had just rolled a pair of snake eyes!   CONT'D
                                                        (3)
                    Dr. Rothmuller (vaguely)
Some kind of South American game...

                    Big Kim (ignoring this)
I just got back this morning.

                    Dr. Rothmuller (lacking a better
          word)
Aha!

                    Big Kim
Aha is right!

        MISS SIMPSON AT HER LITTLE TABLE   203

                    Miss Simpson (sympathetically)
Oh I'm so sorry....

        MR. KIMBLE AND DR. ROTHMULLER   204

                    Dr. Rothmuller (pensively)
Very...very...interesting...

                    Big Kim (like an angry dog)
Yeah..lovely scenery down there...a little high up
but...

                    Dr. Rothmuller
Maybe you rested too much.

                    Big Kim (shaking his head)
I watched it.

                    Dr. Rothmuller
Nun alzo...all the time you were in this dust bowl...
this Bismarck..nothing similar to this in any way
happened...Mr. B. was dormant...not a word from him...

                    Big Kim
Not even a postcard...

                    Dr. Rothmuller
Aha! From this we deduce there must be something
in Bismarck that Mr. B likes...that smooths him...
that gives him a feeling of purring contentment...
what you would call: Gemütlichkeit!

                    Big Kim
That isn't what I'd call it...

                         263

                    Dr. Rothmuller (ignoring this,
              looking to the ceiling)
Maybe down there...in some rustic farmyard...he
found his, who knows, his...Lebens Gefahrtin...

                    Big Kim (sourly)
No fooling...

                    Dr. Rothmuller
Like you would say his...only English is so thin...
life's sweetheart-other half for always helpmeet-
partner...in one word...

                    Big Kim
That would be quite a trick...

                    Dr. Rothmuller (waving jokes
              aside)
Nun alzo...did you expose Mr. B...I mean did you
take him near anybody who smelt nice...he might
have fallen in love with?

                    Big Kim (avoiding his eye)
Well there's always somebody around I suppose...
that...

                    Dr. Rothmuller (pointing a finger
              like a district attorney)
But you, Mr. Kimble...I mean Mr. A...you didn't fall
in love of course...with any lady of the opposite sex...

                    Big Kim
I never fall in love...I got too much to do...I
don't mean I don't like people...and do anything
I can for them...

                    Dr. Rothmuller
...naturally...being of the low suspicious type...
you are afraid to give yourself...to trust yourself...
you fear love like the wolf fears the trap...no wonder
B hates you...you are denying him everything that is
his by right...he should hate you!

                    Big Kim (anxious to change subject)
Thanks...now could we...

                    Dr. Rothmuller
I don't mean it personally...the whole thing is im-
material to me...but men like you are the scourge of
mankind   you go constantly backwards...you revert to
type...you defeat progress...

      Mr. Kimble turns toward Miss Simpson for a
      sympathetic look.

      MISS SIMPSON - AT HER DESK IN THE CORNER
      She smiles and shrugs her shoulders a little.

Dr. Rothmuller

...you become great conquerors...great dictators...
great emperors...you build and build empires...
monopolies...little kingdoms of all kinds...but
everything you build always finishes the same...in
a blaze of nothing...because you never have the
most important quality of all: a heart with which
to love...and understand.
            (he rises and walks around a little)
There is no hope for you at all, Mr. Kimble...you
were condemned a long time ago...you were useful in
the Ice Age...but on Fifth Avenue? You fit like a
Sabre Tooth Tiger...I don't know how you lasted as
long as you did...you should have been dead long
ago...there will be no fee, Miss Simpson...I don't
like taking money from corpseses.

Big Kim (worried)

Now wait a minute...
            (he looks to Miss Simpson and then
            back to the doctor)
You mean there isn't any hope at all?

Dr. Rothmuller

Hope! While there's life there's hope...for an
intellectual man there wouldn't even be a problem
...but for you...maybe a few...

Big Kim (grasping at straws)

Maybe if I what?

Dr. Rothmuller

Maybe if you tried that place again...you might
get another six months respite...or maybe if you
could find out what Mr. B really wants and GIVE IT
TO HIM...it might complete his pattern...fulfill...
and give you both...emotional stability.

Big Kim

Yeah...but I'd have to go along on that deal...
and at this point of my life...I'm not much of a
bargain to anybody...

Dr. Rothmuller

I wouldn't let that part of it bother me too much...
if you are talking about a woman...because women
from the beginning of time have had to put up with
such a collection of schnooks...no man is very far...
below standard...

Big Kim (rising)

Thank you, doctor.

He starts out.

Dr. Rothmuller (suppressing a
grin)
You are welcome...Mr. A!

MISS SIMPSON - IN THE CORNER   207

She rises indignantly and the CAMERA takes her
over to Dr. Rothmuller.

Miss Simpson
What did you have to tell that poor devil all that
hogwash for...you know it isn't true...all he's got
is a mild neurosis...a kind of battle fatigue that...

Dr. Rothmuller (amiably)
Because in dealing with tigers you got to use hot
pokers! He's already cured...the six months proves
it...all he's got to do is keep on what he's been
doing which I suspect has to turn into a marriage...
which is exactly what a man like him needs! Quod...
Erat...Demonstrandum!

Miss Simpson (slightly mollified)
Then why don't you try it...if you think so well of
the institution?

Dr. Rothmuller (pointing to himself in surprise)
Me!...because I am of the high intellectual type...
what do I need anything like that for?

Miss Simpson puts her hands on her hips and
just looks at him.
DISSOLVE TO:

MRS. JONES - IN THE TAVERN ROOM OF THE OGDEN   208
HOUSE

She wears a very pretty, although simple dinner
dress. She looks rather dejected and does not
seem to be paying much attention to Mr. Stone's
voice, only half audible anyway over the bar
NOISES.

Mr. Stone's Voice
...three more air clubs starting the first...The Sky-
way...The Jolly Weekenders and The Cubs...

Mrs. Jones (coming to)
I'm sorry, Lucas...I didn't hear just what you said
...my mind wandered I guess.

MR. STONE AND BUTCH - PAST MRS. JONES   209

Behind their table we see much activity in the
Tavern Room. The old black bartender is
shaking them high.

                    Mr. Stone (gently)
I was saying Peggy that three more air clubs are
going to start to use our field...that means they'll
be here for the dances on Saturday nights... The Sky-
way... The Jolly Weekenders.. and The Cubs... there're
going to be some hot times around here.

                    Mrs. Jones (quietly)
I'm so glad Lucas.

                    Butch
Who's coming Mommie?

                    Mr. Stone
A lot of men in little airplanes...to spend their
money.

                    Butch
Can I be a pilot when I grow up Mommie? I want
to be a pilot and fly Pipers and Mustangs and
Aeroncas... I think they're super.. don't you
like airplanes Mommie?

MRS. JONES - PAST BUTCH AND MR. STONE   210

                    Mrs. Jones (ruefully)
Well if I said I didn't... I guess I'd be pretty
ungrateful... so I think I'll just say...

The words die on her lips as she sees something
past the CAMERA. Butch and Mr. Stone turn and
look in the same direction.

A FRENCH WINDOW - GIVING ON THE PORCH   211

Mr. Kimble stands here in a leather jacket.
He looks at Mrs. Jones for a moment then comes
slowly through the window and starts for her
table.

MRS. JONES, BUTCH AND MR. STONE - AT THE TABLE   212

Mrs. Jones gets slowly to her feet. Her lips
are slightly parted. Her eyes are full of tears.

                    Mr. Stone (not too   212
          enthusiastically)   CONT'D
Hello there.   (2)

                    Butch (suddenly shrieking)
Jonesey!

He rushes across the room past the CAMERA.

     MR. KIMBLE IN THE MIDDLE OF THE ROOM   213

     He bends down to receive the little boy and
     lift him safely into his arms.

                    Big Kim (patting the child)
Hello there soldier.

     Now he continues toward Mrs.Jones and the
     CAMERA pans him over to her.

                    Mrs.Jones (as they meet)
Oh Jonesey.

     She puts her left arm around his neck and
     moves very close to him in the little space
     left free by her son. Her right arm is
     around Butch. She hugs them both.

     MR. STONE - STILL AT THE TABLE   214

     He looks at this family group for a second,
     then shrugs, drinks his bitter coffee and
     puts the cup down.

     CLOSE SHOT MR. KIMBLE, MRS. JONES AND BUTCH   215
                    Mrs.Jones (crying)
You came back to me Jonesey.. you came back to me!

                    Butch
What's the matter with Mommie?
                              DISSOLVE TO:

     MR. KIMBLE'S LEGS - FROM THE WAIST DOWN   216

     They are marching up and down in front of the
     window of his old bedroom, Number Seven.

                         268

BUTCH SITTING ON THE EDGE OF THE BED   217

His legs dangle and his head turns slowly from
right to left as he watches the big man by the
window.

MR. KIMBLE - BY THE WINDOW   218

He marches up and down once or twice, then stops.

                    Big Kim
I don't know exactly how to start this... but as the
man of the family... I thought I ought to speak to
you first.. we might as well dive in and get it over
with.. what do you say?

BUTCH ON THE EDGE OF THE BED   219

                    Butch
I don't think I... understand exactly, Jonesey...

MR. KIMBLE BY THE WINDOW

                    Big Kim
I'm not sure I do either... but it sort of boils
down to this: how would you like to go fishing and
hunting with me up in the North Woods... I don't
mean just once in a while... I mean from now on and
it doesn't just have to be the North Woods.. it can
be Canada... Alaska...South Africa...almost any place...

BUTCH ON THE EDGE OF THE BED   221
                    Butch (stupefied)
Oh gee!

MR. KIMBLE BY THE WINDOW   222

                    Big Kim
All right... that's settled... now how about camping...
snow shoeing...skiing... you're still a little young
to fly... but we could get a nice little sailboat...
and get sick together in it.. how does that sound?

BUTCH ON THE BED   223
                    Butch
Oh gee!

                        269

MR. KIMBLE BY THE WINDOW   224

                    Big Kim
Good! I've been trying to tell you some of the
nice things first...because there are certain
times in our lives...not too many thank God...
when we just have to stick out our chins...and
take it...because there isn't any other way to
take it...I've discussed this with your Mommie
and we both know it's going to come as a terrible
shock to you...but there isn't any way around it.

BUTCH ON THE BED   225

                    Butch
What's going to be a shock to me Jonesey?

MR. KIMBLE BY THE WINDOW   226

                    Big Kim
What I'm going to talk to you about...because it
brings up the matter of your father...at Tarawa...
and believe me I hate to be the one to have to
bring it up...but I've got to...because I'm going
to ask your Mommie to marry me...Butch...you
understand?

BUTCH ON THE BED   227

          He looks at Big Kim for a moment, then over
          his shoulder like a conspirator. After this
          he gets down off the bed and crosses to Mr.
          Kimble. The CAMERA PANS him over.

                    Butch (after another look at
                    the door)
Come down closer, Jonesey.

          Mr. Kimble sits on the window ledge and
          looks at the little boy in perplexity.

                    Butch (after another quick
                    look over his shoulder)
My father is dead, Jonesey...he's never coming
back from Tarara...another kid told me a long
time ago...only I didn't want Mommie to know...

                    Big Kim (after a moment's
                    stunned silence)
But your Mommie knows Butch...she thought you didn't
know...

                         270

                    Butch   227
Everything's all right then.   CONT'D
                                                   (2)
                    Big Kim (after another little
          pause)
Would I be all right for you...do you think...as
your father?

                    Butch (solemnly)
Oh yes...I think Mommie would like that very much
too.

                    Big Kim
You do?

        THE DOORWAY OF THE ROOM   228

        Mrs. Jones is standing just inside...silhouetted
        against the open door.

                    Mrs. Jones (who has been eaves-
          dropping)
She most certainly would...Oh my darling!

        Crying a little she hurries forward and the
        CAMERA takes her over to the little group.

                    Mrs. Jones (getting on one knee)
You bet she'd like it very much too.

                    Big Kim
Then everything's all set up...we've got a deal on
here...Butch and I Canada and Alaska...

                    Butch
And South Africa...in a sailboat!

                    Mrs. Jones
That's what you think.

                    Big Kim
But we'll drop in to see you every once in a while...
won't we?

                    Mrs. Jones
You won't have to...because I'll be right there...
with a big chain on you...so you'll know where you
are...and who you belong to...

                    Big Kim (serious for one second)
You know what I told you...I may snap out of this...
and I may not...you're not getting any bargain...

                    Mrs. Jones
You let me be the judge of that.

The love theme swells then modulates into
big city music.

DISSOLVE TO:

A FIFTH AVENUE TRAFFIC POLICEMAN   229

He is squinting past the CAMERA in astonishment.
Now his look goes slowly up.

MR. KIMBLE, MRS. KIMBLE AND BUTCH   230

They are waving from the top deck of a Kimble
Kross-Kountry Kar. It is covered with streamers
and accompanied by the SOUND of cow bells. They
wave at the cop and a colored man in a chef's
hat waves from a window of the lower deck.

The CAMERA PANS the big vehicle past us. We
see the K on the back of it get smaller in the
distance. The cop watches it for a moment,
then turns back, looks straight into the lense
and scratches his head. The MUSIC swells because
we have reached:

THE END

When George Bernard Shaw and Preston Sturges Got Together: An Introduction to the Screenplay for *The Millionairess*

Jay Rozgonyi

In the fall of 1953, Preston Sturges was struggling. It had been four years since he'd completed his last motion picture, the financial and critical disappointment *The Beautiful Blonde from Bashful Bend*, starring Betty Grable. His first attempt at writing and directing a Broadway musical, *Carnival in Flanders*, had closed after a mere nine performances. With both money and work in short supply, Sturges was truly in need of a break.

That break came in the form of an offer from producer Lester Cowan, who, at the request of Katharine Hepburn, was eager to hire the filmmaker to adapt and direct a movie version of the George Bernard Shaw play *The Millionairess*. Hepburn had spent much of 1952 and early 1953 starring in the first London and New York productions of the 1936 comedy, which tells the story of a domineering heiress and her romantic pursuit of an Egyptian doctor from a vastly different culture and class, who seems immune to her wealth and commanding personality. Hepburn thought that Shaw's satiric portrait of London's upper class aligned perfectly with the Sturges worldview; one only had to look at *The Lady Eve* or *The Palm Beach Story* to see the similar ways he had presented (and lampooned) millionaires before. For Sturges, who had spent much of his youth in Europe and considered himself a cultured man, adapting one of England's greatest playwrights was a golden opportunity—one that would allow him to get behind the camera again and earn some much-needed money.

Sturges quickly accepted the offer and, still stationed in New York following *Carnival in Flanders*, began working on drafts of a screenplay and shuttling them off to Hepburn for feedback and approval. In the early weeks of 1954, he packed up his young wife, Sandy, and their year-old son, Preston, Jr., and headed to England where filming was to take place. And that's where the trouble began.

When Sturges arrived in England with his family, he quickly discovered that the regular progress Lester Cowan had been reporting had taken place only in the producer's mind. Sturges was thrilled to hear, for example, that Alec Guinness would be starring in the film, but when the filmmaker ran into the actor at a party and expressed his enthusiasm for their upcoming project, Guinness had no idea what Sturges was talking about. Undaunted, Sturges filled his time with rewrites and refinements to the script, as well as side trips in Europe to show Sandy where he had grown up. Unlike Sturges, however, Katharine Hepburn was not able to sit around and wait for Lester Cowan to get the project moving; because she was in high demand for both stage and screen roles, her time was tightly scheduled. And as the delays and Cowan's excuses piled up, Sturges watched his paychecks fall behind and his star's availability—or lack of it—increasingly become an insurmountable obstacle. Finally, by the time the calendar had turned to April, the production had completely fallen apart, and Sturges had added one more unrealized project to his growing list.

If any director from Hollywood's golden age can be considered an auteur—the clear author of his or her own films—it's Preston Sturges. For each film he set out to create he had his own unique vision. Shortly after arriving in Hollywood as a fledgling screenwriter in the early 1930s, he began clashing with directors over how his scripts should be filmed, and with producers over the rewrites they would inevitably assign to other writers on the lot. Once he began directing his own scripts in 1940 and gained control over his writing, he quickly entered into a multi-year feud with Paramount's studio head, Buddy DeSylva, over budgets, shooting schedules, and final cuts. Clearly his own man when it came to his film work, Sturges rarely adapted others' writing, and when he did, the final products tended to bear little resemblance to the source material. In short, he was unlikely to be a generous collaborator, or to respect the original material in any work he might be adapting.

And yet, that's exactly the case in the screenplay you're about to read. Shaw's *The Millionairess* seems to have brought out the best in Preston Sturges, fueling his creativity and transforming him into a virtual co-author with the playwright. Perhaps it was the edict from the Shaw estate forbidding him from changing more than 20% of the play's text (however that might be calculated), or perhaps it was simply the challenge of "collaborating" with such a noteworthy literary figure. Whatever the reason, in *The Millionairess* Sturges constructed a script that's both very faithful to Shaw's play—incorporating virtually all of its structure, its characters, and its dialogue—and adds layers of exposition and nuance that deepen those characters, their motivations, and their relationships. Shaw's work seems to have offered Sturges not a launching pad of an idea that he could run with and make his own, but instead a strong framework and foundation to be enriched and built upon. In the end, Sturges took this not-so-great work by an oh-so-great author and elevated it to become its own unique Sturgean blend of physical, visual, and verbal comedy.

Exactly how Sturges accomplishes this is worth examining, not only to marvel at his achievement but also to help refute the myth that he had somehow lost his touch after leaving Paramount in the mid-1940s. Katharine Hepburn was right to tap him as the perfect person to craft the screen version of this play, for as you'll see, the Preston Sturges who adapted *The Millionairess* had all of his powers at hand, as well as perhaps a new power: enough humility to become a "writing partner" to George Bernard Shaw.

To fully appreciate Sturges' work on this script, we need to understand the material that Shaw had provided. The play, which *Variety* called "transparently weak" in its review of the New York premiere in 1952, is uneven and less than fully developed, with two primary shortcomings. The first lies in its uneven chronological structure, as Shaw sets two of the four acts within a single day, the third a couple of days later, and then the final one at some unspecified time in the future (months? a year? Shaw isn't clear). Second, Shaw never quite provides his lead character of Epifania ("Eppy") with enough humanity, or offers hints of her below-the-surface grace, to make his ending believable. What Sturges does, though, is remedy both of these shortcomings, and in so doing produces a screen adaptation that far outshines his source material.

Sturges fills in the details of Eppy's character in an assortment of small ways, but the character development rests on Sturges' enhanced structure for the story, one that creates a far more seamless flow than in the original. Sturges relies on two strategies: adding new scenes that don't exist in Shaw's play and creating highly cinematic montage sequences that spell out and expand upon action that appears only as dialogue in the play. Following all of the details can be confusing, so it's worth spelling out the structure of Sturges script—and calling out his additions to Shaw's four acts.

- Prologue: Eppy and Alastair at home (*New scene #1*)
- Shaw's Act I: Eppy and the other characters at the lawyer's office (includes *New scene #2/Montage #1* of Eppy's upbringing; *Montage #2* of Alastair's money-making scheme)

275

- Montage of Adrian Blenderbland's life with Eppy (*New scene #3/Montage #3*)
- Shaw's Act II: Eppy, Adrian, and the doctor at the dilapidated inn
- Eppy at the doctor's clinic/Eppy and the doctor at the dilapidated inn (*New scene #4* at the clinic; *New Scene #5* at the inn)
- Shaw's Act III: Eppy at the sweatshop
- Eppy executing her takeover of the clothing business (*New scene #6*, including *Montage #4*)
- Shaw's Act IV (pt. 1): Most characters at the renovated inn/Eppy at the doctor's clinic (*New scene #7*, inserted in the middle of Shaw's Act IV)
- Shaw's Act IV (pt. 2): Eppy and the other characters at the renovated inn

It's also worth noting the primary characters as well: Eppy (the self-centered heiress); Alastair (her husband, from who she's seeking a divorce); Adrian (Eppy's boyfriend and presumptive new husband); Patricia (Alastair's girlfriend and fiancée); the doctor (who Eppy will fall in love with); and Sagamore (Eppy's lawyer). With this information as our reference guide, then, it's possible to dive into the specifics of the screenplay to see just how intricate and clever it is.

Additional Scenes

Sturges launches his reworking of the play with a manic, virtually wordless opening that supplies the film's opening credits while also establishing the first broad strokes of Eppy's character (*New scene #1*, pp. 283-285). Conceived as a single, extraordinary tracking shot that moves from room to room within Eppy's home, it calls for the camera to cleverly make stops at each room's door to display individual lines of the film's credits. Along the way, it moves past servants, maids, and kitchen workers, and we're treated to the raucous sounds of a battle that we never quite see — although flying objects occasionally make their way into the shot, and the chaos that's left in the battle's wake is revealed as we move from one room to the next. Sturges masterfully drops us right in the middle of a turbulent marital war and a high-energy comedy. The sequence makes clear, before we ever see Eppy and Alastair, that these people are incredibly wealthy — and prone to ferocious battles. It's a chaotic opening — similar to that of *The Palm Beach Story* in 1942 — that could have been created only by Sturges.

After largely following the details of Shaw's Act I, Sturges inserts another scene that has no parallel in the play, which he refers to in his script as *The Probation of Adrian Blenderbland* (*New scene #3/Montage #3*, pp. 311-314). This sequence also alters the time frame of Shaw's play: rather than moving directly to Eppy and Adrian's lunch at the inn as Shaw does in Act II, Sturges presents a series of scenes that further establish Eppy as a largely overbearing woman who drags Adrian along on her various excursions to exercise, eat, and shop, shop, shop. In all, Sturges shows the couple in more than twenty different settings, from gyms and pools and horse paths to jewelry stores, furriers, and restaurants. There is no dialogue whatsoever—it's purely visual storytelling and humor—and in each setting, Eppy drives the action with no regard for Adrian. Again, as with the opening credits, Sturges develops his own material to reveal the details of a romantic relationship, yet integrates that material into the original narrative while remaining true to Shaw's characters.

Sturges employs this same strategy again in Shaw's lunch-at-the-inn scene, where the playwright had packed one act with virtually an entire play's worth of action: Adrian proposing to Eppy; the two having a fight and Adrian gets injured; Eppy meeting the doctor; the doctor's character being generally defined; the respective marriage "tests" being described; Eppy falling for the doctor; and Eppy providing him with £150. But Sturges wisely decides to split all of this action into two scenes, with an unspecified amount of time in between, and to give Eppy the opportunity to leave the inn and visit the doctor's clinic (*New scene #4*, pp. 328-331). The characters now have extra time to interact, and they do so in a setting—the doctor's workplace—that establishes a striking contrast between the self-absorbed heiress and the man with selfless interests.

With the additional scene, Sturges not only fills in more of the doctor's character but also lays the foundation for the eventual turn-around in Eppy's selfish attitude. In the visually striking opening to the new sequence, Sturges does something that Shaw never directly does in the play: he deftly portrays the enormous gulf between Eppy and doctor. In a stark contrast to the earlier scenes in which Eppy fully dominates Alastair and Adrian, at the clinic Eppy is surrounded by poor and ailing refugees in dire need of help—and she is continually ignored by the one man who seems able to resist her will.

Sturges also cleverly follows this new scene with an expansion of the second half of Shaw's Act II (Eppy and the doctor at the inn), as Eppy, without invitation, simply follows the doctor back to the inn and sits down with him as he tries to eat dinner (*New scene #5*, pp. 331-338). Her actions fit with the Eppy we've come to know, and also minimize what seems, in the play, to be a sudden shift from self-centeredness to attraction to a selfless man. Although Sturges picks up the basic details from Shaw's Act II, he adds some dialogue and comic business and reinforces the doctor's commitment to his patients and his disdain for Eppy's seemingly singular focus on money (and herself). The scene also better explains the parallel promises that Eppy and the doctor made to their respective parents on their deathbeds. With a third scene between Eppy and the doctor, the attraction she feels toward the man seems more believable, and his façade of disinterest toward her begins to show some cracks. Once again, with only a minor reconstruction of these scenes and their action, Sturges makes a major improvement to the story, expanding and strengthening Shaw's material.

Working within the play's final act, Sturges introduces one more entirely new scene that finally induces us to empathize with Eppy. In Shaw's play, Alastair and Patricia arrive at the inn and hear the manager's story of its recent renovation; shortly thereafter Eppy unexpectedly arrives. In the screenplay, however, prior to Eppy's appearance, Sturges inserts a new scene that completes her evolution from being disagreeable to being far more sympathetic—a character whose fate we actually care about (*New scene #7*, pp. 357-360). The scene again takes place at the doctor's clinic, where Eppy demonstrates that she's no longer the selfish woman that we met in Sagamore's office. What's more, the scene sets up the finale to be much more satisfying than Shaw's conclusion, as Sturges allows us to experience firsthand what Shaw merely hinted at.

Montages

In the opening credit sequence described above, Sturges establishes the montage as a recurring motif. With the estate's restriction on alterations of Shaw's text, Sturges cleverly took brief spoken accounts of events and created fully realized sequences that make the story more cinematic and bring out more nuances in the main characters.

In the first montage, which occurs within Shaw's Act I, Sturges builds on a few lines of dialogue that explain Eppy's father's test for a prospective husband in order to show more fully how her upbringing led her to be the woman we're now encountering (*New Scene #2/Montage #1*, pp. 290-291). Here Sturges also moves beyond the stage origins by inserting visual humor with rapid edits between a number of morbid plays and operas that the young Eppy was forced to attend. As with the opening credit sequence, the montage displays Sturges' genius at comic storytelling, but more importantly for the story, it provides a glimpse into the origins of Eppy's behavior and her mixed feelings toward her father. Sturges is helping to mitigate one of the major flaws in Shaw's play— Eppy's seemingly inexplicable pursuit of the doctor. In the play, Eppy simply reveres her father and unhesitatingly follows his dictates regarding marriage, almost to the point where her admiration becomes unbelievable. In Sturges' sequence, however, Eppy's father harshly puts his daughter through some hellish experiences in order to make a point—a point that Eppy does not always appreciate. In addition to making Eppy more sympathetic, the montage paves the way for the story's resolution, in which Eppy relaxes her standards on the money-making test and accepts the doctor as her husband. If her previous attempts met with such failure, and her father's manner was as harsh as it seems, then marrying a man so dedicated to others certainly seems more credible.

Later in the scene at the lawyer's office (from Shaw's Act I), Sturges transforms what is essentially a monologue—this time featuring Alastair's account of how he turned £1500 into £50,000—into a flashback montage that's narrated in voiceover (*Montage #2*, pp. 303-307). Sturges introduces characters and settings that are not in the play, but the words we hear are Alastair's alone as he relates the details of his accomplishment. *"The action in this montage will illustrate the words said by Alastair,"* Sturges notes in his screenplay. *"Occasionally, when he repeats lines of dialogue, the lips of the characters on screen will form his words."* As with the previous sequence, narrated by Eppy, Sturges uses his directorial skills to bridge time (we see the action of the past as if it were happening right now) and to create comic contrasts between what Alastair is saying and what the audience perceives as having "really happened."

The sequence takes us from a bar to a bank to a London street, and after a brief return to Sagamore's office for an exchange between the main characters, back to Alastair's office and the theater, where the production he's backed inexplicably becomes a smash hit. Sturges adds his own comic spin to Shaw's straightforward account: "We took a theatre. We engaged a first rate cast. We got a play. We got a splendid production: the scenery was lovely; the girls were lovely; the principal woman was an angry-eyed creature with a queer foreign voice and a Hollywood accent, just the sort the public loves."

Perhaps Sturges' screenplay best displays his ingenuity, though, in his re-imagining of Shaw's sweatshop scene. He begins in the same spot as Shaw's Act III—as Eppy shows up at the sweatshop intending to simply take a job and earn the money she seeks. Rather than having another character dismiss Eppy as unqualified, however, Sturges shows us roughly forty shots that contrast Eppy's inept attempts to use a sewing machine with those of others in the shop, all set to music *"like the Anvil Chorus."* This brilliantly conceived set piece of visual humor again extends the action while at the same time reinforcing Eppy's complete inability to function in the real world. Having failed in her quest for money, Eppy leaves the basement sweatshop—and happens upon the truck driver who has arrived to pick up the finished clothes. Once again building on Shaw's handful of lines of dialogue, Sturges is off and running with his own whirlwind version of Eppy taking complete control of the clothes distribution business (*New scene #6* and *Montage #4*, pp. 343-352). With shifting locations, quick and pointed dialogue, and rapid movement through time, the sequence stands alongside some of the best work of Sturges' Paramount years. But more than that, it also reveals Eppy's business acumen and creative thinking, facets that moderate the selfishness of her character. Shaw only hints at this side of Eppy, mostly in Act IV when the inn's manager describes the mysterious woman who appeared one day and soon revitalized the entire operation. But Sturges, throughout the scenes he's been adding, has been building up to this revelation. The scenes depict a more vulnerable Eppy than Shaw ever portrayed—a character who is at least partially admirable. In the end, Sturges' more well-rounded version of Eppy makes his screenplay more satisfying, and Eppy's relationship with the doctor more believable.

For anyone who might think that Preston Sturges had lost his ability to write brilliant screenplays after leaving Paramount in the mid-'40s, *The Millionairess* serves as a resounding rebuttal. Amazingly enough for an adaptation—especially one that hews quite closely to the original work—the screenplay reads as if it came entirely from Sturges' creative mind. Besides the kinetic montage sequences, so typical of Sturges, the screenplay abounds with his signature small comic touches—the satyr who appears at the beginning, middle, and end of the action; the tinny intercom in the lawyer's office that is frequently used but rarely understood; and the inn's roof leaks that create a musical pattern as each drop hits a different pot—as well as the descriptions of physical comedy bits, written with a director's eye toward exactly how they should be filmed.

The ample amount of comic business, however, is not the only Sturges touch. The character of Eppy—specifically as Sturges develops her over the course of the script—harkens back to Lee Leander in *Remember the Night*, the self-centered jewel thief who is reformed by the prosecutor's love, and even Jean, the card shark in *The Lady Eve*, who initially aims to take advantage of the obtuse beer heir but ends up being transformed by her love for him. Similarly, the doctor shares some characteristics with John L. Sullivan in *Sullivan's Travels*: both men are so single-mindedly driven to "do good" that they can't see the value of what's staring them in the face (Sullivan's ability to make the world laugh, and the doctor's opportunity to have love along with the wealth to treat even more poor patients).

Finally, like other great Sturges scripts, *The Millionairess* offers up scene-stealing supporting character roles. The lawyer Sagamore, albeit a bit more than a minor character, could easily be cast and played as a harried and ineffectual solicitor, steamrolled by Eppy and largely befuddled by the crazy characters around him (think of a less extreme version of Franklin Pangborn). Sturges also expands the comic potential of the continually frustrated Adrian, who could be portrayed as a handsome but somewhat dim-witted—and certainly overwhelmed—character (a more serious Toto from *The Palm Beach Story*). And in smaller roles, Tim Goodenough, the inn's manager, and even the chauffeur had the potential to be turned into memorable onscreen characters thanks to Sturges' casting and directing magic.

There's no doubt that *The Millionairess* is a screenplay that truly deserved to be filmed. Its failure to make it to the screen can be viewed as perhaps the most tragic of the filmmaker's late-career missed opportunities, as it fully refutes the myth that Sturges lost his creativity after the Paramount years. As you're about to see, the following pages prove that with all of his wit and imagination intact in 1953 and 1954, he was still fully capable of delivering a sophisticated and brilliant comedy to rank among his best. The fact that Katharine Hepburn might have starred in the film only makes us wish even more that Sturges would have been able to bring this first-class screenplay to life. It's no wonder that Hepburn later called the unmade *Millionairess* the biggest disappointment of her career.

281

The shadowy figure of a swallow-tailed satyr with cloven
hoofs appears on the screen. Suddenly, to a burst of music,
his eyes light up. Now on the screen we read the following
words:

F O R E W O R D

THIS IS THE STORY OF THE IRRESISTABLE FORCE

THAT MET THE IMMOVABLE OBJECT. THEY COOPER-

ATED WITH THE INEVITABLE.

The satyr winks one eye.

282

T H E   M I L L I O N A I R E S S

by

BERNARD SHAW

Arranged for the Screen by Preston Sturges

The MAIN TITLES will be superimposed over appro-
priate shots in the following series of events: We pick up
a Rolls Royce coming toward us in front of a beautiful
house. The CAMERA pans with it as it comes to a stop and
winds up aiming straight at the traffic side door. The
kerb side door is now slammed so angrily that we hear a
tinkle of broken glass. Instantly the second credit appears on the door. When enough time has elapsed for us to
read it, the Rolls Royce pulls out of the shot and we see
the street door of the beautiful building at the end of a
slam. On this appears a credit. We dissolve to the lift
door banging closed and get a credit. The door of the
flat, the master bedroom door, and the mistress' bedroom
door, give us others. It is possible, of course, that
the reading time required for the credits might defeat the
intention of indicating the anger by these staccato re-
ports of the slamming doors. Now we hear another door slam
and a scream. We go into the kitchen full of servants.

1.   THE MOST LUXURIOUS PRIVATE KITCHEN IN LONDON   NIGHT
This should be an English product to make Americans gasp.
Besides the butler who has just entered, it contains a footman, a valet, a housekeeper, a cook, a scullery maid, a
ladies' maid, and two chambermaids. They all jump at the
sound of a heavy crash, and jump again as the bell goes off
startlingly.

> HOUSEKEEPER: (clutching her heart) She's calling for
> 'elp.
>
> FOOTMAN: More likely its 'im.
>
> BUTLER: No comments please...I think we'd better
> ...(we hear another terrible crash)...
> Yes, I think we'd better have a look.
>
> COOK: A little of this goes a long way with me.

And they start out of the kitchen...

2.   THE BEAUTIFUL DINING ROOM

Note: I hope all the rooms we are about to see can be extra
ordinarily well done as this single traveling shot must indi-
cate to us all of our heroine's wealth and inherited background. The CAMERA picks up the servants as they come fearfully into the dining room and precedes them as they start
across it toward the foyer. Suddenly the butler sees something past the CAMERA. He spreads his arms in alarm.

> BUTLER: (to the others) Duck!

Preceded by a wild crescendo of music a heavy candelabrum
whizzes into the room, smashes against a mirrored screen and
ricochets onto the sideboard. The screen bounces against
the wall, then falls forward onto the dining room table. The
servants duck, then hurry forward as the CAMERA leads them
into the foyer. Here they find a wall bracket hanging by its
wires and a console table turned over. As the Butler and the
Footman put the table back on its legs, the ladies' maid
plucks a sable cape from the floor just before the damaged

283

table collapses again. As the others move on into the living
room, the valet picks up his master's overcoat, his seriously
damaged opera hat and his stick suffering from a green tree
fracture. Suddenly he ducks and avoids being brained by a
potted plant which explodes on the wall behind them.

3. THE LIVING ROOM
Now, preceded by a tiny dog which appears from under a sofa,
the servants advance very much on the qui vive like the three
doughboys in "What Price Glory?". The Butler and the Valet
pick up some over-turned chairs, the ladies' maid picks up
her mistress' bag, gloves, and one shoe with a flapping heel.
The Valet picks up his master's winged collar and, with some
surprise, a front quarter of his white waistcoat, complete
with pocket watch. As they continue across the living room
the ladies' maid picks up the remains of her mistress' evening dress out of which there falls a bra. This latter she
conceals modestly and hastily. The Valet picks up his master's braces just as the Butler gives warning and a barrage
of books comes through the double door leading to the library.
The books fall where they may, the barrage ceases and the
servants move toward the library.

4. THE LIBRARY
The servants enter, picking up chairs and an occasional
table. In the middle of the room they pick up an over-turned
sofa which releases a table with a broken leg. Its contents
shower to the floor. As they continue toward it a couple of
billiard balls, a triangle, and a box of chalk are heaved into the room, doing whatever damage is useful to the shot.

5. BILLIARD ROOM
This is really chaos. Snooker balls, cues, chalk, ball
basket, bridges, and various other appurtenances strewn
around the floor making walking dangerous. The last intact
green shade crashes to the billiard table as the servants
reach it and proceed.

6. THE SECRETARY'S OFFICE
This room also has been wrecked by the tornado. The passing
servants pick up an adding machine, the insides of which pop
out, as it is returned to a desk.

7. THE HALL OF THE GREAT FLAT
The servants come into this, pause in puzzlement then enter
the master's bedroom.

8. THE MASTER'S BEDROOM
Obviously the hurricane has psssed through here as indicated
by some overturned chairs, bottles and the condition of the
dressing table. Through the doorway to the combination bathroom-gymnasium an Indian club is hurled and causes a pretty
musical effect as it destroys a crystal chandelier. The
lights go out leaving only a broad beam from the bathroom-
gymnasium.

9. THE BATHROOM-GYMNASIUM
This is a wonderful room containing everything an enormously
wealthy athletic gentleman could wish for. Naturally, among
other things there are some Indian clubs. The servants go
through here.

10. THE DRESSING ROOM OF THE LADY OF THE HOUSE
This is an unbelievably luxurious room dripping with mirrors,
perfumes and a fur floor. Once again the Butler gives the
alarm and all duck as a jewel case flies past their heads,
shatters a mirror behind them, then bursts open showering a
king's ransom in jewels onto the fur floor. The music stops
suddenly so that we hear the tinkle of the falling jewelry.
Into this silence comes a tremendous "Ugh", the sound of a
falling body, retreating footsteps, and the slamming of a
door. Now the servants hurry toward the bedroom, preceded by
the little dog.

11. THE MAGNIFICENT BEDROOM
This is the apotheosis, the bedroom to end all bedrooms
Near us is an enormous bed, although we do not see this until the entering servants cross to it. Now at last we see
the lady of the house, at least a little of her, consisting
of her stockinged feet and legs popping up over the far side
of the great bed. The little dog is yapping on the bed,
near her.

            THE LADIES' MAID: (in horror) Madam!

She seizes the nearest cover which is the throw at the foot
of the chaise longue and hastily drapes it over the recumbent
figure invisible to us. Now she scowls at the menservants.

                                          FADE OUT

FADE IN:

12. THE OFFICE OF JULIUS SAGAMORE - IN LINCOLN'S INN
     FIELDS - DAY
The stout Mr. Sagamore sits with his back to us, writing at
his desk. Now a buzzer sounds and he pushes a button on the
dictagraph.

            SAGAMORE: Yes?

We hear the tinny voice of the dictagraph complicated by
the fact that the man on the other end has a nasal voice and
comes from some part of England whose inhabitants are difficult to understand.

            SAGAMORE: Will I come down and what?

The dictagraph says something about a consultation in her
motor car.
            SAGAMORE: A consultation about a motor car? What
                       do I know about motor cars? What do they
                       want me to do, change the tyres?

The dictagraph says something about IN...not ABOUT.

            SAGAMORE: In a motor car!

Now he swings in his swivel chair and looks out a window.

13. HIGH CAMERA SHOT DOWN AT THE FABULOUS ROLLS ROYCE

14. SAGAMORE - IN HIS OFFICE
            SAGAMORE: Coming, my lad, coming!

15. THE LOWER OFFICE AND STAIRWAY OF MR. SAGAMORE'S OFFICE
His clerk and the Chauffeur we saw last night are here.

            SAGAMORE: (coming down the stairs) Now what's all
                       this about?

            CHAUFFEUR: If you'd be good enough to come out to
                       the car...

            SAGAMORE: Oh...certainly...Unusual, but certainly.

            CHAUFFEUR: (holding the door open for him) Thank
                       you, Sir.

16. THE STREET OUTSIDE MR. SAGAMORE'S OFFICE
Mr. Sagamore appears, followed by the Chauffeur and the CAM-
ERA pans them to the fabulous Rolls Royce. The Chauffeur
opens the door and Sagamore peers inside.

            SAGAMORE: Uh...you...uh...sent for me, Madam?

17. EPIFANIA - IN THE DEPTHS OF HER MOTOR CAR
She is in her early thirties, magnificently dressed in black.
She tries to speak, then dives into a large handbag for a
handkerchief.

                         285

EPIFANIA: (tragically, while producing from her
bag: a turtleneck sweater with an enormous diamond brooch pinned to it; a pair
of shorts, a small dog, a toothbrush and
a six-shooter which points directly at Mr.
Sagamore, and finally the handkerchief)
Are you...are you Julius Sagamore, the
worthless nephew of my late solicitor,
Pontifes Sagamore?

18.   SAGAMORE - IN THE OPEN DOORWAY OF THE CAR

SAGAMORE: (putting on his spectacles and dodging
the gun) I do not advertise myself as
worthless, Madam, but Pontifex Sagamore
was my uncle, and...

19.   EPIFANIA - IN THE DEPTHS OF HER MOTOR CAR

EPIFANIA: I naturally concluded that,as you had
been packed off to Australia, you must
be worthless. But it does not matter,
as my business is very simple. I desire
to make my Will, leaving everything I
possess to my husband. You will state
that it was his conduct that drove me
to commit suicide.

20.   SAGAMORE - IN THE OPEN DOORWAY OF THE CAR

SAGAMORE: (startled) Ah! Excellent! Of course..
quite so! But do you feel that the middle of the street is the very best place
for the composition of such a document?

21.   EPIFANIA - IN THE DEPTHS OF HER MOTOR CAR

EPIFANIA: (tragically) At this point I have no
feelings...We can do it here...or on the
roof...or in the window at Swan & Edgar's.
Get in...we'll drive about.

22.   SAGAMORE   IN THE OPEN DOORWAY OF THE CAR

SAGAMORE: (soothingly as to a lunatic) I can think
of nothing more delightful...but as I
might be visited by one, or even two other
clients this morning...would it be too
much to ask...(he points toward his office)

23.   EPIFANIA - IN THE DEPTHS OF HER MOTOR CAR

EPIFANIA: (putting the dog down) Solicitors' offices always stink of decayed leather...
However, if you're a slave to convention...

24.   SAGAMORE - OUTSIDE THE ROLLS ROYCE

SAGAMORE: (handing Epifania to the pavement) You
are indeed gracious...Do come up and sit
down.

EPIFANIA: (starting toward the building with him)
Sit down...stand up...what difference
does it make? Lead the way and don't
fuss...It is clear to you that every
penny is to go to my husband?

SAGAMORE: Quite...But for this it will be necessary
for me to know who your husband is.

EPIFANIA: My husband is a fool and a blackguard.
You will state that fact in the Will.

SAGAMORE: Splendid...And his name?

EPIFANIA: His imbecilic name is Alastair...Aden... MacMungo...Fitzfassenden.

SAGAMORE: (stopping dead) But then...good heavens! ...You must be...

EPIFANIA: Epifania Ognisanti di Parerga.

SAGAMORE: The wife of the tennis player and ex-amateur heavyweight boxing champion!

EPIFANIA: Obviously.

SAGAMORE: But we swim together every morning at the club! That is to say, I float mostly...

EPIFANIA: The acquaintance does you little credit.

SAGAMORE: I had better tell you that he and I are great friends, Mrs. Fitzfassenden.

EPIFANIA: Do not call me by his detestable name! Put me in your books merely as...

SAGAMORE: Epifania Ognisanti di Parerga, of course! (he bows) Your father was a very wonderful man, Madam.

EPIFANIA: (reverently) My father was the greatest man in the world! And he died a pauper. I shall never forgive the world for that!

SAGAMORE: A pauper! You amaze me. It was reported that he left you, his only child, thirty millions.

EPIFANIA: (indignantly) Well, what was thirty millions to him? He lost a hundred and fifty millions! He had promised to leave me two hundred millions! I was left with a beggarly thirty. The humiliation of it! It broke his heart.

She reaches for her handkerchief, which involves placing the revolver in her left hand.

SAGAMORE: You take my breath away, Madam.

EPIFANIA: (handkerchief business) As I am about to take my own breath away, I have no time to attend to yours.

POLICEMAN: (entering the shot) Excuse me, Madam... but have you a permit for that weapon?

EPIFANIA: (instantly and crushingly) Young man! I am entirely cognizant of the London County Council regulation covering the transport of firearms, which you will find under Article 461, Section II, Paragraph 6... obviously I have a permit. (to Sagamore) Lead the way.

They enter the building and the CAMERA moves on to the stupefied policeman, who reaches for his regulation book, opens it, looks after Epifania, then moistens a large finger.

DISSOLVE

25. SAGAMORE'S OFFICE
Sagamore ushers Epifania into the office, indicates a chair, then moves toward his own without stopping.

SAGAMORE: Pray sit down...while I make a few notes.

EPIFANIA: Sit down yourself...I have very little time.

SAGAMORE: (reminded) Ah, yes...the suicide...(then very cheerfully) I'd almost forgotten it. (now he opens a little filing box) Now, let me see.

EPIFANIA:	You understand that I am leaving every-thing...without exception... to this imbecile: all of my shares...all of my bonds...all of my jewelry...my properties in England...in Scotland...in South Africa...my ranches in New Zealand...my villa in Dauville...all of my motor cars...my racing stable...my yacht... everything.
SAGAMORE:	I understand perfectly, of course....and this is only a suggestion, but might not the punishment be still more severe...if youcut him off with a shilling?
EPIFANIA:	(diabolically) Oh, no...many people can adjust themselves to poverty...they have had so much practice. Very few can sur-vive wealth...His little mind will crack under the strain...He will glut himself to death and blow to pieces...like a horse let loose in a granary!
SAGAMORE:	(his eyes popping out of his head) Dia-bolical!
EPIFANIA:	Thank you...I have given it a great deal of thought.
SAGAMORE:	Which obviates my having to do the same. The matter is very simple, then...the Will is practically drawn...(he pulls a card out of the filing box and hands it to her)...leaving only one small, last, final matter to be attended to.
EPIFANIA:	(examining the card) What's this?
SAGAMORE:	(matter of fact) For the suicide. You will have to sign the chemist's book for the cyanide. Say it is for a wasp's nest. The tartaric acid is harmless; th chemist will think you want to make mem-onade. Put the two separately in just enough water to dissolve them. When you mix the two solutions the tartaric and potash will combine and make tartrateof potash. This, being insoluble, will be precipitated to the bottom of the glass; and the supernatant fluid will be pure hydrocyanic acid, one sip of which will kill you like a thunderbolt.
EPIFANIA:	You seem to take my death very coolly, Mr. Sagamore.
SAGAMORE:	I am used to it.
EPIFANIA:	Do you mean to tell me that you have so many clients driven to despair that you keep a prescription for them?
SAGAMORE:	I am acting only as your solicitor, Mad-am. You wish to commit suicide and I have done my best to help you do it as neatly and expeditiously as possible... without ruining the carpets. For this I shall charge your executors six and eightpence.
EPIFANIA:	You expect me to kill myself to make money for you?
SAGAMORE:	Well, it is you who have raised my expec tations, Madam. (then, after a slight-pause) There will be countless taxes to

288

SAGAMORE: (cont'd) to...appraisals..cemetery
plots...caskets...profusions of flowers.

EPIFANIA: You are an unmitigated hog, Julius Sagamore. You are not a man...you are a
rhinoceros with the soul of a fish...

SAGAMORE: ...and were it not for your imminent
demise, Madam, I should also congratulate
myself on the number of actions for
libel I should undoubtedly have to defend as your solicitor.

EPIFANIA: Then you are a rotten solicitor...because
I never utter libel. My father instruc-
ted me most carefully in the law of
libel. If I questioned your solvency,
that would be libel. If I suggested you
were unfaithful to your wife, that would
be libel. But if I call you a rhinocero
which you are, that is only vulgar abuse
I take good care to confine myself to
vulgar abuse. And I have never been
sued. Is that the law, or it is not?

SAGAMORE: (amiably) I really don't know...I would
have to look it up...But what does it
matter at this point? The prescription
will cure everything.

EPIFANIA: (tearing it up and throwing it in his
face) Damn your prescription. There;

SAGAMORE: (beaming) You see? It's infallible.

EPIFANIA: You are a heartless blackguard. My distress, my disgrace, my humiliation, the
horrible mess I have made of my life
seem to you merely funny. Well, I warn
you: I have no sense of humor. I will
not be laughed at.

SAGAMORE: But my dear lady, I don't know anything
about your distress...your disgrace...
or the whatever it is you've made of
your life...and I shouldn't dream of
laughing at a client with an income of
a million and a half.

EPIFANIA: Have you a sense of humor?

SAGAMORE: I try to keep it in check, but I'm
afraid I have a little. You appeal to
it somehow. Why don't you sit down?

EPIFANIA: My father warned me never to employ a
solicitor who had no sense of humor...

SAGAMORE: The dear, wise man...

EPIFANIA: ...otherwise I would walk out of here
instantly...

SAGAMORE: Please don't.

EPIFANIA: ...thus depriving you of a client...

SAGAMORE: Do sit down.

EPIFANIA: ...whose business would almost certainly
prove a fortune to you.

SAGAMORE: (gently) Of course it would...Now would
you sit down?

EPIFANIA: You seem to have one idea in your head,
and that is to get your clients to sit

EPIFANIA: (cont'd) talking, she moves toward a chair and sits down. The back snaps off and they both go over backwards. Howling with laughter but trying to conceal it, Mr. Sagamore hurries to her assistance. She takes a kick at the chair and wrenches herself loose from Sagamore) Oh, I Cannot even sit down in a chair without wrecking it! There is a curse on me. (then noticing Sagamore's laughter) Aye, laugh, laugh, laugh, fool! Clown!

SAGAMORE: (controlling himself and fatching another chair from the wall) My uncle's best fake Chippendale...(then placing the new chair forward) Now will you please sit down as gently as you can..and stop calling me names. Then, if you wish, you can tell me what on earth is the matter.

He picks up the broken back of the chair, puts it on another chair, then brings this one over for himself.

EPIFANIA: The breaking of that chair has calmed and relieved me somehow...I feel as if I had broken your neck...

SAGAMORE: Splendid. (he sits)

EPIFANIA: My father...(she pauses while, in some embarrassment, Mr. Sagamore removes the chair back from under him, then sits down)....My father was the greatest man : the world...I was his only child...his one dread was that I should make a foolish marriage and lose the little money he was able to leave me...

SAGAMORE:)hypnotized) The thirty millions... precisely.

EPIFANIA: Don't interrupt me...To prevent this, he started me on a safety program of theatel and opera-going...

DISSOLVE

26. MONTAGE OF DEATH SCENES IN THE PLAYS AND OPERAS MEN-TIONED INTER-CUT WITH SHOTS OF THE YOUNG EPIFANIA, IN-VARIABLY IN WHITE AND WEEPING, SITTING IN A STALL OR BOX NEXT TO A SINISTER, MONOCLED, BEARDED, EL GRECO CHARACTER, APPARENTLY HER FATHER.

EPIFANIA'S VOICE: ...demonstrating the perils of impul sive...or unplanned...romance. We saw "Romeo and Juliet"..."Tristan und Isolde' ..."Troilus and Cressida"..."Eloise and Abelard"..."Pelleas et Melisande"... "Aida"..."Othello"..."Madama Butterfly" ..."Tosca"..."Trovatore"..."Samson and Delilah"..."Siegfried"..."Pagliacci"... Antony and Cleopatra"...Then, fearing he might not have made his point sufficiently clear, he instituted a further o. post-graduate course of realistic examples of the same theme...

A BUILDING EITHER INSIDE OR OUTSIDE THAT IS VERY OBVIOUSLY A MORGUE

EPIFANIA'S VOICE: ...we visited a morgue...

INTERIOR A LUNATIC ASYLUM WITH A LADY LOOKING LIKE OPHELIA IN THE MAD SCENE

EPIFANIA'S VOICE: ...a lunatic asylum...

INTERIOR A BUILDING WITH A LOT OF YOUNG WOMEN IN UNIFORM

    EPIFANIA'S VOICE: ...a home for wayward girls...

THE NURSERY OF THE HOME FULL OF BABIES

    EPIFANIA'S VOICE: ...with many sad little reminders...

EPIFANIA PAST HER FATHER
She sits white and intense, listening to her father, who,
huge cigar in hand, is delivering a diatribe.

        EPIFANIA'S VOICE: I understood what he was hinting at
            and resolved to approach marriage only
            with the deepest caution. Finally he
            made me promise...(Epifania raises her
            hand)...that whenever a man asked me to
            marry him...I should impose a condition
            on my consent...Nobody but my father
            could have thought of such a real....in-
            fallible...unsentimental test...(she
            hoists her hand which had started to
            sink, back up again)...I was to give him
            one hundred and fifty pounds and tell him
            that if, within six months, he had turned
            that hundred and fifty pounds into fifty
            thousand, I was his. If not, I was never
            to see him again...I saw the wisdom of
            this...

Epifania lowers her hand a little sadly and the scene

                                    DISSOLVES

27. EPIFANIA AND A MIDDLE-AGED MEDITERRANEAN COVERED WITH
     ORDERS AND DECORATIONS

        EPIFANIA'S VOICE: ...only too clearly. All Europe was
            on its knees to me...(the gentleman falls
            to his knees...Daintily, Epifania re-
            moves a check from her bosom and the
            gentleman departs, backwards, leaving
            Epifania alone in the shot looking after
            him and hoping he won'tmake it.)

                                    DISSOLVE

28. EPIFANIA - IN THE SAME PLACE BUT A DIFFERENT DRESS PLUS
     A TIARA
She has a slight double-take for the new gentleman, and a
very handsome one this time; who arrives in the scene.

        EPIFANIA'S VOICE: ...I was like a princess in a fairy
            tale...offering all men alive my hand and
            fortune if they could turn myhundred and
            fifty pound check...(she produces one
            from her bosom, kisses it, and hands it
            to the young man, who departs emotionally
            ...into fifty thousand within six months.

                                    DISSOLVE

29. EPIFANIA - IN ANOTHER DRESS...WITH ANOTHER MAN
If we have run out of dresses, we will merely dissolve the
men to match the dialogue, each one getting his check...from
a less and less hopeful Epifania. In fact, she plucks her
last check from her stocking.

        EPIFANIA'S VOICE: Able men...brilliant men...younger
            sons of the noblest families...either re-
            fused the test...or failed. Why? Be-
            cause they were too honest...or too
            proud...

                                    DISSOLVE

-12-

EPIFANIA: (with a hopeless gesture, she concludes)
              ...Alastair succeeded.

SAGAMORE: Are you trying to tell me..that..Alastair
              turned a hundred and fifty pounds...

EPIFANIA: ...into fifty thousand in six months. I
              found myself tied for life to an insect.

SAGAMORE: But surely you were a consenting party?
              If you didn't like him, why did you even
              let him...

EPIFANIA: ...Boxing.

SAGAMORE: I beg your pardon?

EPIFANIA: His boxing fascinated me...he trained in
              the same gymnasium where I was studying
              judo...

SAGAMORE: Judo? Do you mean Hebrew?

EPIFANIA: (disgusted) Judo is the combat form of
              jiu jitsu...a kind of Japanese wrestling
              ...I could toss you through that window,
              for instance, as easily as a rotten apple.

SAGAMORE: (after looking out the window to see how
              far he would fall) Huh!

EPIFANIA: My father held that women should be able
              to defend themselves.

SAGAMORE: Ah...quite...now do go on, please...only
              break it to me as gently as you can...I
              have never had a client like you before.

EPIFANIA: You never will again.

SAGAMORE: I don't doubt it for a moment...so you
              married Alastair because he was a Japan-
              ese wrestler...

EPIFANIA: No, no...I saw him win an amateur heavy-
              weight championship...He has a murderous
              solar plexus punch...

SAGAMORE: And for this you married him...

EPIFANIA: Well, he was handsome...he stripped well
              ...unlike many handsome men...(then while
              Mr. Sagamore is hastily pouring himself
              a glass of water) I am not insuscep-
              tible to sex appeal...very far from it,
              in fact.

SAGAMORE: (glassy-eyed) Quite, quite...You need
              not go into details....

EPIFANIA: I will if I like. It is your business
              as a solicitor to know the details.

SAGAMORE: Oh...

EPIFANIA: I made a very common mistake. I thought
              that this irresistable athlete would be
              an ardent lover. He was nothing of the
              kind...all his ardor was in his fists.

SAGMORE: (uneasily) It was? Oh, dear.

EPIFANIA: Never shall I forget the day...it was
              during our honeymoon...when his coldness
              infuriated me to such a degree that I
              went for him.

292

EPIFANIA: Yes, but he knocked me out in the first exchange! (then after a slight pause) Have you ever been knocked out by a punch to the solar plexus?

SAGAMORE: (recoiling) Who, me?

EPIFANIA: (scientifically) It does not put you to sleep like an ordinary belt on the jaw... it stiffens you...but leaves you conscious.

SAGAMORE: Good heavens!

EPIFANIA: ...When he saw me rigid on the floor... with nothing moving but my eyes...he was horrified, he said.

SAGAMORE: (indignantly) Horrified! He should have been electrified...I mean cuted.

EPIFANIA: You don't understand...it was automatic. Boxers counter that way by instinct...I almost admired him for that.

SAGAMORE: But you still want to get rid of him..

EPIFANIA: I don't know what I want any more. I did when I came in but now you've confused me with your rotten jokes about tartaric potash and...This is a horrible state of mind. I am a woman who must always want something...desperately...and always get it.

SAGAMORE: (hypnotized) Precisely! An acquisitive woman! A maitresse femme! How splendid!

EPIFANIA: (tragically) I saw myself as the most wonderful woman in England....marrying the most wonderful man...I was only a goose...marrying a jack rabbit.

SAGAMORE: Surely not a goose, Madam...a swan, perhaps...a black one.

The buzzer rings.

SAGAMORE: (rising and starting toward the dictagraph) Excuse me...I hate to interrupt this...(The CAMERA goes with him. He starts for the table, trips on a rip in the carpet, then finally gets there right side up) Yes? (the dictagraph says something tinnily and incomprehensibly) Yes? Good heavens! (then back into the dictagraph) Hold everything calmly down there for a moment. (then ominously to Epifania) I regret to inform you that your... uh...husband...is downstairs at this very moment...not alone! They wish to see me.

EPIFANIA: (pointing a triumphant finger at him) Polly Seedystockings! Have them up at once!

SAGAMORE: Now, now, just a minute. Polly Seedy what?

EPIFANIA: (relishing her words) My husband's soulmate! The refined lump with whom he spends his lighter moments! Her name is Smith, but she signs her love notes "Seedystockings", as a hint, no doubt, that he is to buy her another dozen. (she hurries toward the mirror, removing objects from her bag, as she looks for her lipstick) We shall now see the sort of woman for whom he has deserted ME!

SAGAMORE:	(worried) You are sure you won't be... upset?
EPIFANIA:	(amused) By that crumpet? (then after a little work on her lips) I couldn't care less.
SAGAMORE	(pointing to the revolver in her left hand) I mean: you will control yourself?
EPIFANIA:	(waving the revolver in surprise) This? * wouldn't give her the satisfaction. (she drops the revolver and lipstick into her bag and starts eagerly toward him) Have them up, I tell...

Instead of saying "you", she trips on the rip in the rug and plunges straight into Mr. Sagamore's arms.

SAGAMORE:	(after a long look at her and a reaction to her perfume, leaning out of the embrace and reaching for the dictagraph) Well...send Mr. Fitzfassenden...and the lady....up. (then tenderly to Epifania) She must be extraordinarily seductive.
EPIFANIA:	(coldly) And why, pray?
SAGAMORE:	I mean to say...any woman...any man... would prefer to your extraordinary...
EPIFANIA:	(pulling away) Don't be an ass! I'll bet she comes in with a bow in her hair.

She now drapes herself like a Vogue model. After a slight double take at this, Mr. Sagamore arranges his cravat, then dabs his forehead delicately with his handkerchief.

31. THE DOORWAY OF MR. SAGAMORE'S OFFICE
Patricia Smith appears, followed by Alastair Fitzfassenden. She is a plump and jolly young woman with very pretty legs, an adorable smile and "feminine" written all over her. She wears a bow in her hair. Alastair is six feet two or three, elegantly dressed, if a shade loudly. He weighs fifteen stone. He has a beautiful profile and wavy hair.

EPIFANIA AND SAGAMORE
Seeing the bow in Patricia's hair, Epifania nods toward it for Mr. Sagamore's benefit. The latter's eyes bulge.

33. ALASTAIR AND PATRICIA

ALASTAIR:	(revoiling as he sees his wife) Eppy! What are you doing here? (then indignantly to Sagamore) Whydidn't you tell me?

34. EPIFANIA AND SAGAMORE

EPIFANIA:	(pointing to Patricia) Introduce the femme fatale.

The CAMERA brings them all into one shot.

ALASTAIR:	(menacingly) Now, listen, Eppy...
EPIFANIA:	Who is the female?
ALASTAIR:	She is not a "female".
EPIFANIA:	(charmingly) Really...how novel...
PATRICIA:	(going quietly to Sagamore) I am Patricia Smith, Mr. Sagamore.
EPIFANIA:	That is not how you sign your love notes, I believe...isn't it Sleazystockings?
ALASTAIR:	(ferociously) Now, look here, Eppy... don t start a row!

5
1

5-

EPIFANIA: (virtuously indignant) A row! I wan't even speaking to you...I was speaking to Greasystockings...

ALSTAIR: (striding toward her furiously) Why, you...

Patricia and Sagamore get between them hurriedly.

SAGAMORE: Mrs. Fitzfassenden! Mr. Fitzfassenden! (desolated to Patricia) I am so sorry, Miss Smith.

PATRICIA Oh, I don't mind...My grandmother goes on like that all the time.

EPIFANIA: (galvanized) Your grandmother! (then taking a menacing step toward Patricia) You dare to compare me to your...why, you

ALASTAIR: (leaping between the two ladies) I'm damned if I stand this.

EPIFANIA (striking the pose of a martyr) Yes: strike me! Show her your knock-out punch! Let her see how you treat women!

ALASTAIR: (baffled) Damn!

SAGAMORE: (from one to the other) Please...please ...please...why don't we all sit down?

He picks up the chair with the missing back.

PATRICIA: Hello. What's happened to the chair?

EPIFANIA: I have happened to the chair. Let it be a warning to you.

Sagamore places the chair for Patricia next to the table. Alastair shoves the broken chair back out of the way with his foot; fetches another from the wall, and is about to sit on it next to Patricia when Epifania sits on it and motions him to her own chair, so that she is seated between the two, Patricia on her left, Alastair on her right. Sagamore goes back to his official place at the table.

SAGAMORE: (settling himself behind his desk) Now that we are all cool and collected...

PATRICIA: (after a look at Alastair) Mr. Sagamore: don't you think Ally had better go? He's worn out...he's hardly slept all night...

EPIFANIA: (instantly and accusingly) How do you know that, pray?

PATRICIA: (miserably) I...well, I...do....

EPIFANIA: (rising and crossing to Sagamore) You hear that, Mr. Sagamore?

35. PATRICIA AND ALASTAIR
Patricia moves into the seat vacated by Epifania and takes Alastair's hand.

ALASTAIR: It was quite innocent, I assure you. Where could I go when she drove me out of the house with her vile...

36. EPIFANIA AND SAGAMORE
Mr. Sagamore opens his mouth to reply, then turns with it still open at an unexpected burst of laughter from Epifania.

EPIFANIA: (amused) You went to...her?

37. ALASTAIR AND PATRICIA

ALASTAIR: (with great dignity) I went to...Miss Smith. (then putting his arm around Patricia) I went where I could find peace, and kindness...to my good...sweet...darling.

295

PATRICIA: (quietly) Thank you, Dear.

38. EPIFANIA AND SAGAMORE

EPIFANIA: I have no sense of humor; but this strikes me as irresistably funny. (then to Alastair) You actually left _me_ to spend the night in the arms of Miss Seedystockings?

39. ALASTAIR AND PATRICIA
Patricia opens her mouth to speak but Alastair beats her to it

ALASTAIR: It was quite innocent...I...

40. EPIFANIA AND SAGAMORE

EPIFANIA: (pointing an accusing finger at Patricia) Was he in your arms or was he not?

SAGAMORE: (distressed) Must we know the exact position?

EPIFANIA: Yes. (then to Patricia) Now: was he or wasn"t he?

41. ALASTAIR AND PATRICIA

PATRICIA: (looking nervously at Alastair) Well... yes, of course he was...for awhile, I suppose...but not in the way you mean.

42. EPIFANIA AND SAGAMORE

EPIFANIA: (hopping off the desk triumphantly) Then he is even more of a sexless fish than I took him for.

SAGAMORE: (horrified) Mrs. Fitzfassenden!

He starts to strangle and pours himself a glass of water with a shaking hand.

EPIFANIA: (to Sagamore) Well, what would you call him? A man capable of flouncing out of the house when I was offering him a night of legitimate bliss...

At this point Sagamore strangles on the water and Epifania pats him.

43. ALASTAIR AND PATRICIA

ALASTAIR: (leaping to his feet indignantly) A night of legitmmate bliss! (he crosses into the shot with Epifania and Sagamore) You call potting me with a potted palm and tearing my best coat in two a night of legitimiate bliss, do you?

EPIFANIA: I suppose you didn't leave me unconscious on the floor!

ALASTAIR: Only to save my life, as Heaven is my judge!

EPIFANIA: It was still a filthy thing to do! You, at least, had your...Seedystockings to go to! _I_...had nobody. Adrian was out of town.

She gasps in horror at her admission.

ALASTAIR: (triumphantly) Ah, ha! You heard that, Mr. Sagamore!

SAGAMORE: (looking around miserably) Oh, dear, now who is Adrian? This is a new complication.

ALASTAIR: Only her lover.

SAGAMORE: Mr. Fitzfassenden!

EPIFANIA: Adrian Blenderbland is a gentleman with
                whom I discuss subjects beyond my hus-
                band's mental grasp...this gives us a
                wode range.

ALASTAIR: The great intellectual...always calls at
                meal times. Greedyguts, I call him. Per-
                sonally, I think he's in love with her
                cook. But if I call on Polly for an
                hour's peace, oh my!

SAGAMORE: (looking around helplessly) I'm not
                quite sure that I understand..all these
                ...these...

44. PATRICIA - PRESENTLY THE GROUP

PATRICIA: Q   (rising, speaking sweetly and joining the
                group. Adrian Blenderbland is Mrs. Fitz-
                fassenden's Sunday husband, Mr. Sagamore
                ...as dear, wise old Father used to call
                them.

EPIFANIA: She sets up a wise father...this is the
                end. (then turning to Patricia) And
                what are you, pray...a Sunday wife?

PATRICIA: No, I should say that you are the Sunday
                wife, Mrs. Fitzfassenden. I'm the one
                who has to look after his clothes...and
                his shirts and his ties...and his teeth
                and his eyes...and make him get his hair
                cut...

EPIFANIA: I thought the Government took care of all
                that.

PATRICIA: (ignoring this)...then send him back to
                you...all scrubbed and shined and spif-
                fied up...for Sunday.

EPIFANIA: Well, just spiffy up his ears a little
                more next Sunday, will you?

The CAMERA starts pushing in on Patricia.

PATRICIA: Oh, I know you're making fun of me..and
                it probably isn't up to me to say any-
                thing...But there are two sorts of people
                in the world...the people anyone can live
                with...and the people no one can live wit

45. CLOST SHOT EPIFANIA

PATRICIA'S VOICE: The people that no one can live with
                may be very good-looking...and vital...
                and splendid...and temperamental...and
                romantic...and jall that...(by turn Epi-
                fania has looked all these things)...and
                they can make a man or woman happy for
                half an hour when they are pleased with
                themselves and disposed to be agreeable..
                but if you try to live with them theh jus
                eat up your whole life running after them
                ...(Epifania frowns slightly and begins
                directing a look of great displeasure at
                this longwinded young lady)...or quarel-
                elling or attending to themone way or
                another...You can't call your soul your
                own.

EPIFANIA: 'ear, 'ear.

46. CLOSE SHOT PATRICIA

PATRICIA: (after acknowledging the interruption of the slight look) As Sunday husbands and wives...just to have a good tearing bit of love-making with...or a blazing row... or mostly one on top of the other...once a month or so...they're all right...But as everyday partners they are just...

47. CLOSE SHOT EPIFANIA

PATRICIA'S VOICE: ...impossible.

Epifania rises, crosses to Patricia and considers her for a moment before speaking.

EPIFANIA: Speaking of a good tearing bit of love-making...

48. SAGAMORE - LEAPING TO HIS FEET

SAGMORE: Mrs. Fitzfassenden, please!

49. EPIFANIA AND PATRICIA

EPIFANIA: (after looking resentfully at Mr. Sagamore) Well..if I'm the Sunday wife... what does that make her?

PATRICIA: (blandly) Well, I'm what dear wise old Father always called his...angel in the house.

50. ALASTAIR

ALASTAIR: Wiping away a tear) You are, dear. You are.

51. EPIFANIA

EPIFANIA: (to Alastair, starting to say "Oh Balderdash") Oh, Bal... (then to Patricia) You're what my dear wise old father always called a....

52. SAGAMORE

SAGAMORE: Mrs. Fitzfassenden...please! (the dictagraph buzzes. After listening to the customary incomprehensible tinny yammering) Good Heavens! (to the others in the room) Mr. Blenderbland is downstairs.

53. EPIFANIA AND THE OTHERS

EPIFANIA: Adrian! How did he know I was here?

54. SAGAMORE

SAGAMORE: Shall I have him up? One more or one less at this point...

55. EPIFANIA AND THE OTHERS

EPIFANIA: Certainly.

ALASTAIR: (to Sagamore) You understand, of course, that I am supposed to know nothing...of this stuffed shirt's relationship with my wife....WHATEVER IT MAY BE.

EPIFANIA: It is perfectly innocent, I assure you... so far. I am not yet convinced...that I love Adrian...Until now I have found him ...merely attractive.

ALSTAIR: (venomously) Especially with a mouthful of snails...au vin blanc! (to be pronounced: au vang blang)

-19-

SAGAMORE: (into the dictagraph) Then send Mr.
                 Blenderblard up.

56. EPIFANIA AND THE OTHERS

ALASTAIR: (to Patricia) You will now see the
                 blighter who did me the dirty with Eppy.

PATRICIA: (soothingly, putting her cheek close to
                 Alastair's) I can't imagine any man do-
                 ing that to...you, dear...with any woman.

She pats his hand.

EPIFANIA: I hope you will be able to restrain your
                 endearments...when he comes in.

There is a heavy knock on the door.

57. SAGAMORE

SAGAMORE: (coming around his desk) Come in.

58. DOOR OF THE OFFICE
Adrian Blenderbland, an imposing, rather handsome man in the
prime of life, magnificently tailored, hatted, boutonniered,
gloved and umbrellaed, enters healthily.

ADRIAN: Mr. Sagamore, I presu--- (then stopping
                 dead, looking around and removing his
                 hat) Well, hallo, hallo...hallo. (this
                 last one to Patricia) Where have we all
                 come from? Good morning, Mrs. Fitzfasser
                 den. How do, Alastair...Madam?

SAGAMORE: (indicating Patricia) Miss Smith.

PATRICIA: Pleased to meet you, I'm sure.

EPIFANIA: (pointedly) An intimate friend of Mr.
                 Fitzfassenden.

ADRIAN: (delighted) Ah, splendid. (he gives
                 Patricia another look, then beams know-
                 ingly at Epifania) Splendid. (then
                 looking around) Though I had hoped to
                 discuss a matter or two with Mr. Sagamore
                 privately...

SAGAMORE: Has the matter on which you wish to con-
                 sult me any reference to...uh...Mr. Fitz-
                 fassenden's family circle?

ALASTAIR: (vulgarly) And how it has.

ADRIAN: (distressed) Well...uh...in a manner of
                 speaking...why...uh...yes.

EPIFANIA: I will not be included in anybody else's
                 family circle...I concern myself alone.

ALASTAIR: Now she is off the deep end again. We
                 may as well go home.

EPIFANIA: The deep end! The deep end! What is
                 life if not lived at the deep end? Ala-
                 stair: you are a tadpole.

While saying this, she passes him and ruffles his pomaded
hair.

ALASTAIR: (his hair in ruins) Don't do that.

EPIFANIA: (coolly taking Patricia's handkerchief
                 and wiping her hands) Ugh. (then putting
                 the handkerchief back into Patricia's
                 pocket) Smooth it for him, Angel in the
                 House.

299

PATRICIA: (combing Alastair's hair with a comb she
               has taken from her bag) You shouldn't
               make a sight of him like that.

EPIFANIA: (over her shoulder) Don't forget to
               cover his bald spot.

PATRICIA: (defiantly, to Epifania) He has the most
               beautiful wavy hair.

EPIFANIA: Yes, it's waving goodbye.

59.   MR. SAGAMORE - HE IS JUST SITTING AT HIS DESK

SAGAMORE: (rapping politely to attract attention)
               Mrs. Fitzfassenden...if we could all just
               get together for one moment...(he recoils
               slightly at what he sees)

60.   THE GROUP
Epifania is just seating herself on Adrian's lap. In the
background Patricia, with small cluckings, is arranging Alastair's hair.

ADRIAN: (delighted) How witty you are! Really,
               you are the most enchanting...the most
               intoxicating...the most adorable woman
               on earth.

He lifts her hand and kisses it.

EPIFANIA: Not here, Adrian...If you're going to
               talk like that, take me where there is
               music...and we can be alone.

ALASTAIR: (vehemently) Do, for Heaven's sake! Be-
               fore she drives us all crazy!

61.   SAGAMORE

SAGAMORE: (his eyes popping out of his head)
               Steady! Steady! I hardly know where I
               am...You are all consulting me...but none
               of you has given me any instructions...
               Had you not better all be divorced?

62.   THE GROUP

EPIFANIA: Certainly not! I find it most convenient
               to be married...It is respectable...it
               keeps other men off...it gives me a free-
               dom I could never enjoy as a single
               woman! Besides, I have become accus-
               tomed to a husband...I will not divorce
               him unless I am absolutely certain of a
               satisfactory replacement. (Then pointing
               to Adrian) He might be perfect...but
               who knows?

ALSTAIR: Who, indeed?

EPIFANIA: (to Alastair) And you would starve to
               death! If you hadn't married me you'd
               be a rubber in a Turkish bath.

ALASTAIR: (violently) I made fifty thousand pounds,
               didn't I?

ADRIAN: (electrified) Who made fifty thousand
               pounds?

EPIFANIA: (ignoring Adrian) Yes, with the hundred
               and fifty pounds I gave you!

| ADRIAN: | But this is fascinating! |

ADRIAN: But this is fascinating!

ALASTAIR: Well, if you didn't want me, why did you give me the hundred and fifty?

ADRIAN: How long did it take?

EPIFANIA: (to Adrian) Six months. (then without a pause, to Alastair) Because you were young, you were well-shaped...I was excited by physical contact with you...

62. SAGAMORE

SAGAMORE: (nearly weeping) Is it necessary to be so very explicit, Mrs. Fitzfassenden? These fulsome details...

63. THE GROUP

EPIFANIA: You may be made of sawdust, Julius Sagamore! But I...am made of flesh and blood! Alastair is physically atractive. That is his sole excuse for existing.

ADRIAN: (still dumbfounded and interested in one subject only) But he did make fifty thousand pounds?

ALASTAIR: And by my own brains.

EPIFANIA: Your own brains! Your own folly, your ignorance, your criminal instincts, and the luck that attends the half-witted!

60. MR. SAGAMORE

SAGAMORE: (distressed) Mrs. Fitzfassenden, please!

65. THE GROUP

EPIFANIA: (not even hearing Sagamore) What you deserved was five years' penal servitude!

ALASTAIR: Five! Fifteen, more likely. And what did I get for it? Life with you was worse than any penal servitude.

EPIFANIA: It would have been heaven to you if nature had fitted you for such a companionship as mine.

ADRIAN: Of course...but how did he make the fifty thousand pounds? My own bank balance at the moment is somewhere about a hundred and fifty...and I should very much like to know how to make it up to fifty thousand...

66. SAGAMORE

SAGAMORE: (piously) Who wouldn't!

67. THE GROUP

EPIFANIA: Do not meddle with money, Adrian...you do not understand it...

ADRIAN: ...and I loathe it...but I have to have it! You see, my dear, you are so abominably rich..that even the most honorable man...on approaching you..feels like a needy...not to say seedy...adventurer.

ALASTAIR: Wait till she marries you...then see how you feel.

ALTERNATE VERSION

EPIFANIA: And you would have starved to death. If
                    you hadn't married me, you would be a rub-
                    ber in a Turkish bath.

ALASTAIR: (violently) I made fifty thousand pounds,
                    didn't I?

ADRIAN: (electrified) Who made fifty thousand
                    pounds?

ALASTAIR: (ignoring Adrian) You may say what you like
                    you were just as much in love with me as I
                    was with you.

EPIFANIA: Well, you were young, you were well-shaped,
                    and I was excited by physical contact with
                    you.

SAGAMORE

SAGAMORE: (nearly weeping) Is it necessary to be so
                    very explicit, Mrs. Fitzfassenden? These
                    fulsome details...

THE GROUP:

EPIFANIA: You may be made of sawdust, Julius Sagamore
                    But I...am made of flesh and blood! Ala-
                    stair is physically attractive: that is his
                    sole excuse for existing.

ADRIAN: (still dumbfounded and interested in one
                    subject only) But how did he make the fifty
                    thousand pounds? My own bank balance at
                    present is in the neighborhood of a hun-
                    dred and fifty...

EPIFANIA: With two race horses of mine that look very
                    much alike...he borrowed them and made a
                    little mistake. He made fifty thousand and
                    it cost me ten thousand to keep him out of
                    gaol. What he should have got was five
                    years' penal servitude.

ALASTAIR: Five! Fifteen, more likely! And what did
                    I get for it? Life with you was worse than
                    any penal servitude.

EPIFANIA: It would have been heaven to you if nature
                    had fitted you for such a companionship as
                    mine.

ADRIAN: (desperately) But I still do not understand
                    how he...

EPIFANIA: (interrupting) Do not meddle with money,
                    Adrian. You do not understand it...I will
                    give you all you need.

ADRIAN: (dejectedly) This fifty thousand pounds....
                    he invested it safely, I trust?

EPIFANIA: Oh, very safely...He bought a circus with
                    it.

ADRIAN: I beg your pardon?

ALASTAIR: (furiously) Well, how was I to know that
                    the Ministry of Health had condemned all
                    the animals?

68. SAGAMORE

    SAGAMORE: May I once again...

As nobody listens to him, he makes a helpless gesture and subsides.

    ADRIAN: (waving these interruptions aside) If I
                      gave Alastair my hundred and fifty pounds
                      might he, do you suppose...

    EPIFANIA: (drily) You would never see it again!
                      Don't worry about these things, Adrian...
                      I will give you all you need.

    ADRIAN: (in pain) No, no, please! Leave me the
                      poor man's luxury of paying for a million
                      airess' cabs...and flowers...and theater
                      tickets...and little lunches at the Ritz
                      ...besides lending her all the small sums
                      she always seems to be without...when we
                      are together.

    EPIFANIA: (confidentially) I will instruct my
                      bankers to send you a thousand on account.

    ADRIAN: (in pain again) But I don't want that! I
                      adore lending you money! It is only
                      that...as my comparatively slender re-
                      sources are dwindling at an appalling
                      rate...I would honestly appreciate some
                      lessons from Alastair...in the art of
                      turning hundreds into tens of thousands.

    EPIFANIA: (scornfully) Lessons from Alastair! Of
                      all the swindles...

    ALASTAIR: (resentfully) Well, it worked out all
                      right, didn't it? (then to the others)
                      But it was a near thing, I can tell you.

    ADRIAN: Do, please.

    ALASTAIR: Well, when she gave me this hundred and
                      fifty that had to be parlayed into fifty
                      thousand in six months...

    EPIFANIA   Pardon me while I lie down.

The CAMERA takes her to a leather couch on which she throws
herself, instantly disappearing in a cloud of dust.

69. CLOSE SHOT ALASTAIR

    ALASTAIR: ...The first thing I did was to drop into
                      this pub I know, where I met this Amer-
                      ican. When I mentioned my problem to
                      him...

70. EPIFANIA - ON THE COUCH

    EPIFANIA: After a hundred and fifty drinks...

71. CLOSE SHOT ALASTAIR

    ALASTAIR: Am I telling this or are you?

He resumes his story as a barroom starts coming in in an
eight-foot dissolve. In the barroom we see Alastair in a
contrasting suit of clothes. On the next stool there sits
a Broadway character, presumably the American. The action
in this montage will illustrate the words said by Alastair.
Occasionally, when he repeats lines of dialogue, the lips
of the characters on screen will form his words.

72. A FIRST-CLASS LONDON SPORTING BAR
Prints of bare-knuckle fighters, cock fights, dog fights,
and hunting scenes adorn the walls.

> ALASTAIR'S VOICE: This bloke jumped off his stool and
> said: "Why man alive, if you've got a
> hundred and fifty we can open a bank ac-
> count and get a cheque book!" I said:
> "What good is a cheque book? Listen to
> him!" This last was to the bartender.
> Then he said: "Are we partners...fifty-
> fifty, even-steven, or ain't we?" So not
> knowing just what to say, I said: "yes."
> What else could I say? So that very day
> we started in.

The barroom dissolves to the receiving teller (what the hell
is this called in England?) of a London bank.

> ALSTAIR'S VOICE: We lodged the money and received in
> return a book of one hundred cheques.
> "Now all we gotta do," said my partner,
> "is to decide what racket" I believe he
> called it, "we're going into...then hop
> in with both feet! Come on!"

As they leave the bank to the musical accompaniment, the
CAMERA pans over to a staid bank manager, who watches them go
in surprise and some alarm. The bank dissolves to a traveling shot down the London sidewalk. Alastair and the American
occupy the center of the shot and the latter is doing all the
talking. He seems full of confidence except once or twice
while passing a policeman.

> ALASTAIR'S VOICE: I gathered he had tried almost every
> line of endeavour...and did not approve
> of most of them...

We have just seen the American pointing to various business
establishments as they pass them, and holding his nose. Also
his lips have several times formed the verb: "stinks".

> ALASTAIR'S VOICE: Suddenly he stopped dead...and I fol-
> lowed his gaze through the glass front of
> a tea shop...he looked as if he had seen
> a ghost....

We cut from the two gentlemen on the street to a shot of a
slender old gentleman with a white beard, partaking of tea
and crumpets, in this inexpensive establishment. Feeling a
gaze upon him, the old gentleman turns slightly and looks
quizzically out the window. We cut to Alastair and the American through the plate glass wind ow, the London traffic
heavy behind them. The name of the establishment is visible
on the glass, but backwards.

> ALASTAIR'S VOICE: I had no idea, of course, who the
> old codger was, but my partner seemed in
> a state of violent excitement. He ordered
> me to wait where I was and rushed into the
> tea shop...I had not realized he knew the
> old gentleman, but suddenly there he was
> ...talking to him.

73. SHOT THROUGH THE PLATE GLASS - THE AMERICAN,
obviously a book agent at one time, forcing his presence and
some kind of proposition on the surprised, but not unamused
old gentleman. Suddenly the latter seems to make a proposition of his own...at the same time taking out a large gold
watch he places next to his crumpets.

> ALASTAIR'S VOICE: What they were talking about I had
> not the faintest notion, naturally. Sud-
> denly the old gentleman put his watch on

ALASTAIR'S VOICE: (cont'd) the table, my partner leaped
            to his feet and hurried out to where I
            was waiting...

The old gentleman watches the American go and looks through
the plate glass in amusement. The Shot changes to Alastair
and the American through the plate glass.

ALASTAIR'S VOICE: He said that we only had one minute
            for the opportunity of a lifetime and
            commanded me to write an immediate cheque
            for a thousand pounds as a down payment
            on the next play of the old gentleman's...
            whom he described as the world's greatest
            playwright. When I pointed out that we
            only had a hundred and fifty pounds, he
            replied that we had only forty seconds,
            and ordered me under pain of disaster to
            do what I was told. I wrote the cheque
            against the window...

Having seen the start of the cheque writing, we cut to the
old gentleman at his table. His attention is divided between
the cheque writing, his tea and his watch. Suddenly, to a
crashing musical climax, the hand of the American comes into
the shot and gives him the cheque...obviously in time. The
old gentleman looks at the cheque, puts his watch back into
his pocket, looks up at the departing American, then out the
window. We cut to what he sees: Alastair, through the window, mopping his forehead. The American now rushes into the
shot and pumps his hand up and down enthusiastically. We cut
back to a close shot of the old gentleman who laughs uproariously, then dissolves to Alastair and the American in the
lobby of a theater.

ALASTAIR'S VOICE: Immediately after that, he wanted to
            hire a theater...the first one we found
            vacant...When I asked desperately how we
            were to pay for these things, he replied:
            "With cheques, of course...that's why we
            have a cheque book!" And when I pointed
            out that the cheques must all be dishon-
            oured...he assured me calmly that none of
            them would be dishonoured...And when I
            asked, "How, in Heaven's name?" he said,
            "By kiting them, of course!"

During the last part of the shot of Alastair and the American
in the lobby, a big astonished head of Adrian with a background of Sagamore's office is slowly dissolved in.

ADRIAN: (completely mystified) But I don't un-
                derstand...what does kiting mean?

74. CLOSE SHOT EPIFANIA

EPIFANIA: He didn't understand it either.

75. ALASTAIR AND THE GROUP

ALASTAIR: What of it? Did it work or didn't it...
                (then shaking his head) ...but a real
                stinker of a job. So we took this
                theater...

ADRIAN: (interrupting) But how does it work?

PATRICIA: (looking admiringly at Alastair) Explain
                it to him, darling.

76. EPIFANIA - ON THE COUCH

EPIFANIA: Yes, do.

305

77. ALASTAIR AND THE GROUP

    ALASTAIR: (uneasily) Well...it's quite simple...
actually. A being a bit short of cash
gives B a slightly worthless cheque...
or is it B who gives it to A....No, it
was A who gave it to B. Then A goes to
C to borrow overnight, the amount that B
owes to A...no, I mean that A owes to B
...wait a minute , it's clearer this way
...It was D:!! D went to B and said...
let me begin again: A went to...

78. EPIFANIA - ON THE COUCH

    EPIFANIA: (quietly) Mr. Sagmore, would you be
kind enough...

79. MR. SAGAMORE - BEHIND HIS DESK

    SAGAMORE: (with distaste) The operation known as
"kiting" proceeds as follows: you pay for
something with a cheque...for which you
have not sufficient funds...preferably
after the banks have closed for the day..

80. CLOSE SHOT ALASTAIR

    ALASTAIR: That's right...It was within a few min-
utes of closing time.

81. SAGAMORE - BEHIND HIS DESK

    SAGAMORE: Of course...this leaves you safe until
the morning...before which you must in.-
duce a friend...or merchant...or hotel
manager to cash you a cheque for enough
to make good your previous cheque. But
now, on pain of eighteen months' hard
labor, you must induce another friend...
or merchant,..or hotel manager to cash
you a third cheque...in order to make
good the second cheque...which made good
the first cheque. Obviously, still another friend, or merchant or hotel manager must be induced to cash you a fourth
cheque to make good the third cheque,
which saved the second cheque which had
been deposited to cover the first cheque.
Of course, by now it has become a little
easier, as it is known that you have
cashed several large cheques...all of
which have been honoured. It is called
kiting because it requires that one
cheque, the last one, be kept always in
the air....until a new one can be flown
up to replace it. Of course, if the wind
should die...the penalties could be five.
...ten...or even fourteen years.

82. EPIFANIA - ON HER COUCH

    EPIFANIA: He should have got twenty.

83. CLOSE SHOT - ALASTAIR

    ALASTAIR: (ignoring Epifania) If you think that was
an easy job, just try it yourself: that's
all!

                             DISSOLVE

Theater office shared by Alastair and the American...Many
shots of cheque signing...depositing large amounts of money...
cashing large amounts of money...depositing again...more sign
ing...looking at clocks...falling back in one's chair with
relief...more signing...getting new pens..opening new ink
bottles...

> ALASTAIR'S VOICE: I dream of it sometimes: it's my
> worst nightmare. Why, my partner and I
> never saw that theater! Never saw the
> author again! Never saw that play! Never
> read it! Until the first night: we were
> signing cheques and kiting them all the
> time. It must have been a very unusual
> play...

84. SHOTS OF THE EXTERIOR OF THE THEATER WITH POSTERS OF
     THE PLAY
Which is called: "WHY?" "Controversial" "Puzzling""Profound"
"Tantalizing" "The most provocative play ever produced".

> ALSTAIR'S VOICE: ...because no one seemed to under-
> stand anything about it at all. The
> critics were baffled...

We see them looking just so...followed by members of the public in the same condition.

> ALASTAIR'S VOICE: ...which caused them to write re-
> views which could be interpreted in any
> way whatsoever. Thepublic went to see
> for itself. Not understanding a word of
> the play, they concluded it must be marv-
> elous...something far above their heads..
> and probably good for them. Then went
> their friends, who sent their friends,
> who sent their friends. We had a smash!

We see news vendors waving papers.

> ALASTAIR'S VOICE: It rained money in bucketsful.
> People came to buy the rights...

We see dark gentlemen waving cheques.

> ALASTAIR"S VOICE: I didn't know a right from a left...
> but it turned at there were all sorts of
> them: touring rights, translation rights,
> publication rights, stock rights, radio
> rights, television rights...They formed
> syndicates...they divided the world into
> hemispheres...hundreds of thousands were
> involved...But all I wanted was fifty...
> (in a slow dissolve, Alastair returns to
> us in person)...and Icleared out with
> that and came swanking back to claim
> Eppy's hand. She thought I was great.
> I was: the money made me great! I tell
> you I was _drunk_ with it! I was another
> man...

> ADRIAN: (dumbfounded) But this is remarkable! He
> was a great man. (then to Alastair) This
> money...you invested it safely, I presume.

85. EPIFANIA - ARISING AND JOINING THE OTHERS

> EPIFANIA: Oh, very safely...he bought a circus with
> it.

> ADRIAN: I beg your pardon?

> ALASTAIR: (furiously) Well, how was I to know that
> the Ministry of Health had condemned all
> the animals?

| EPIFANIA: | By looking at them! (then looking at the others) He was about to turn the wild beasts loose to eat up the countryside when I intervened. |

ALASTAIR: It took my last pound to bury the elephants.

EPIFANIA: And four hundred of mine...The net result of this great transaction was that instead of his being fifty thousand pounds to the good...I was four hundred to the bad...and married to him.

ADRIAN: Good heavens!

EPIFANIA: I've had to support him ever since...to thank me for which he now has the audacity to ask for a divorce.

ALASTAIR: I did not...that was entirely Sagamore's idea.

86. SAGAMORE - BEHIND HIS DESK

SAGAMORE: (dizzily) I haven't the faintest idea what anyone wants any more...One of you comes about a Will...another about a divorce...the third about a marriage... May I suggest that we return to the point?

87. THE GROUP

EPIFANIA: (coldly) And what is the point, pray?

88. SAGAMORE: BEHIND HIS DESK

SAGAMORE: (after shaking his head) The point is... the point is...you can obtain a divorce if you want one...Mr. Fitzfassenden, having admittedly...

89. THE GROUP

ALASTAIR: I did not! You wormed it out of me.

EPIFANIA: Oh, shut up! Try to remember the dignity of your position as my husband.

90. SAGAMORE - BEHIND HIS DESK

SAGAMORE: ...having admittedly left you and taken refuge in the arms of Miss Smith...

91. THE GROUP

EPIFANIA: ...Her arms...Ha!

92. SAGAMORE - BEHIND HIS DESK

SAGAMORE: ...could have nothing to say about it.

93. THE GROUP

EPIFANIA: Well, if you think I'm going to be dragged through the divorce courts and have my picture in the papers...(she points vaguely to Alastair)...with that thing! And have this vulgar story in letters this high...)she indicates two feet)...in every rag in London...."'ERE YOU ARE.' READ ALL ABOUT IT!" "HEIRESS GIVES ATHLETE THE FOOT!" "'ERE YOU ARE... READ ALL ABOUT IT."...you're crazy.

94. SAGAMORE - BEHIND HIS DESK

SAGAMORE: Then I am to forget the divorce?

95. THE GROUP

EPIFANIA: I will let you know in...(she looks spec-
ulatively at Adrian, who looks back at
her in some surprise)...three weeks should
cover the situation...Or let us say a
month! (now reaching into her bag and
bringing out the sneakers, the sweater,
the toothbrush and the revolver which she
puts on the desk) How much do I owe you
for this abortive consultation? And
what o'clock is it!

96. SAGAMORE - BEHIND HIS DESK

SAGAMORE: (dodging the gun in the event she is hold-
it in her fingers) Two pounds, thirteen
and fourpence...and it is ten minutes
past twelve.

ALASTAIR: (bitterly) I really think you might buy
a wristwatch, Eppy.

EPIFANIA: Why should I go the expense of buying a
wristwatch when everyone else has one...
and I have nothing to do but ask? (finding that she has no money, she brushes
the contents of her bag back into her
bag with one sweep of the gun, then turns,
pointing it unconsciously at Adrian) Can
you lend me two pounds, thirteen and fourpence, Adrian? (as Adrian puts his hand
into his pocket, she turns to Alastair)
I have not carried a watch since I lost
the key to my father's old repeater.(Then
turning to Adrian, counting money in the
palm of his hand) Never mind. (finally
turning to Mr. Sagamore) I have decided to
overlook your attempt to poison me, Mr.
Sagamore, and to appoint you as my family
solicitor...you may send your bill at the
end of the year. (She puts her gun back
into her bag)

97. SAGAMORE

SAGAMORE: (overcome) Oh, thank you, Madam!

98. THE GROUP

ALASTAIR: (bitterly) And don't forget to send a
county court summons along with it, Sagamore...or you will whistle for your money.

EPIFANIA: (virtuously) Naturally I always wait for
a summons...it is a simple precaution
against paying bills sent in twice over.

99. SAGAMORE:
Coming from behind his desk and joining the group.

SAGAMORE: (fervently) Quite, Mrs. Fitzfassenden...
an excellent rule.

EPIFANIA: You are a man of sense, Mr. Sagamore.

ADRIAN: (whose opinion has not been asked) My
father always used to say that in choosing
a solicitor...

EPIFANIA: ...Come along, Adrian, I must have some fresh air. (Adrian hurries over the tear in the carpet to hold her coat)... This orgy of domesticity has made the room stuffy...(then handing her bag to Adrian, she gets into her coat and starts for the door) Goodbye, Mr. Sagamore... Goodbye, Seedy...Take care of Alastair, for me...his good looks will give you a pleasing sensation down your spine.

PATRICIA: (violently and surprisingly) Oh, I know you all think him a fool...but he isn't! He is a dear, good boy and it just disgusts me the way you treat him! What would you be, may I ask, without your money?

EPIFANIA: Nothing! Nobody is anybody without money, Seedystockings. My dear old father taught me that. "Stick to your money," he said, "and all other things will be added unto you!" He said it was in the Bible...I have never verified the quotation but I have stuck to my money...and I shall continue to stick to it...Come along, Adrian.

ADRIAN: (starting to cross the room holding the bag) Cheerio!

At this exact instant his foot catches in the tear in the carpet, he does a magnificent swan dive and lands heavily on the floor. The revolver in the bag goes off, Patricia screams, Alastair leaps to his feet and Mr. Sagamore ducks behind the desk.

ALASTAIR: (helping him) I say, old chap...

100   EPIFANIA - IN THE DOORWAY

EPIFANIA: You know I have no sense of humor, Adrian, and that pranks like this annoy me...This is hardly a promising beginning...to a lifetime of conjugal bliss.

101.   ADRIAN - IN THE MIDDLE OF THE FLOOR

ADRIAN: (holding up the smoking bag) I am so sorry

ALASTAIR: Better luck next time, old chap. And if I can help with any advice, or bits of information...

ADRIAN: Thank you.

He starts to go and stops suddenly,feels at his chest and removes a crushed and dripping fountain pen from his waistcoat.

SAGAMORE: (picking up his pewter water pitcher as he notices that it has been doubly punctured) Oh, dear...oh, dear...

Then noticing the smoking bag, he pours water into it with a hissing sound. After awhile it is the bag that squirts the water, while continuing to smoke.

ADRIAN: (exiting) Quite.

PATRICIA: (miserably) What do we do now?

ALASTAIR: (dizzily) At this point I don't know,
               darling...Ten minutes of Eppy and...I
               just don't know.

SAGAMORE: (putting down his pitcher) We wait,
               obviously, until she has made up her
               mind...about the gentleman...She thought
               a month would suffice.

ALASTAIR;   Poor devil.

PATRICIA: I just hope he lives through it.

ALASTAIR: I lived through it, didn't I? And a
               lot more.

PATRICIA: You were an athlete, dear. (then to Mr.
               Sagamore) But you will stand by us,
               won't you, Mr. Sagamore...you'll save
               Ally from that awful woman...you'll save
               him for me?

SAGAMORE: I'm afraid I can't control her, Miss
               Smith. What's worse, I'm afraid she can
               control me...It's not only that I dare
               not offend so rich a client...it is that
               her will paralyzes mine...It's a sort of
               genius some people have...a mysterious
               personal force..and what to do...when
               brought face to face with it...I don't
               know any more than you do, my child.

We hear the slamming of a heavy automobile door. They turn
and look out the window.

102. HIGH CAMERA SHOT DOWN ON THE EXTRAORDINARY ROLLS ROYCE
To the cheerful accompaniment of a swirl of music, the car
pulls away.

103. ALASTAIR, PATRICIA AND SAGAMORE - IN THE WINDOW

               ALASTAIR: And there...but for the grace of God...
               go I.

                                        FADE OUT
FADE IN:

104. THE PROBATION OF ADRIAN BLENDERBLAND:
      ADRIAN ASLEEP
This is in his bedroom. The phone rings. He answers it in
horror, but this horror is nothing compared to the horror on
his face when he looks at his watch.

                                        DISSOLVE

105. AN ICY SWIMMING POOL AT A SPORTS CLUB - ADRIAN AND
      EPIFANIA
She enjoys the cold water more than he does.

                                        DISSOLVE

106. EPIFANIA IN THE RUBBING ROOM-THE CLUB
She is being pounded vigorously by an enormous masseuse.
She likes it.
                                        DISSOLVE

107. ADRIAN - ON THE OTHER SIDE OF THE PANEL
He is also being rubbed, but is enjoying it less.

                                        DISSOLVE

311

108. THE BREAKFAST ROOM OF THE CLUB - ADRIAN AND EPIFANIA
They are now in bicycle outfits. Adrian sits in front of a
huge breakfast which he is wolfing. Epifania waits impatiently on her feet, cup and toast in hand.

                                                    DISSOLVE

109. EPIFANIA AND ADRIAN - BICYCLING VIGOROUSLY
Epifania points exultantly to a tree, or a vista, and Adrian
meets with a slight mishap. He does not, however, break his
neck.
                                                    DISSOLVE

110. EPIFANIA IN A BANK VAULT
She is tearing coupons expertly and rapidly with the small
appurtenance provided therefor. Adrian sits in a small
chair with hat, gloves and umbrella. The little dog is on
his lap.
                                                    DISSOLVE

111. EPIFANIA - IN CARTIER'S
She has brought a few pieces to have the settings checked,
and one in which the central stone has fallen out...about
two hundred thousand pounds' worth altogether. Adrian sits
in a small chair with hat, gloves, umbrella and dog.

                                                    DISSOLVE

112. EPIFANIA - IN ELIZABETH ARDEN'S
Simultaneously, she is being manicured, pedicured, sham-
pooed and mud-packed. She is also making a phone call.
Adrianand dog sitting on an unusually narrow chair as the
booth is small.

                                                    DISSOLVE
113. EPIFANIA'S RIGHT FOOT
It is encased in a very pretty pump. Now her left foot
comes into the shot, wearing an enormously elaborate mule.
The salesmen arrive with more shoes, and still more and
still more. Adrian, as usual, sits in his little chair.

114. BIG HEAD - ADRIAN - HIS EYES CLOSED
They open. Now he looks startled.

115. EPIFANIA - IN A WONDERFUL HAT
This is quickly whipped off her and replaced by another. The
gentleman designer then tempts her with another which he
demonstrates on his own head. A pretty model demonstrates
another hat, a few more hats are brought in, then the CAMERA
pans to two more pretty models.

ADRIAN   DISSOLVE
Complete with dog, he sits on a small chair; as he looks
past the CAMERA and sighs:

117: EPIFANIA - AT A FITTING
The gentleman designer, his woman assistant, the vendeuse,
the woman fitter, her assistant and the assistant's assistant. Epifania wears something breathtaking. The usual
fitting business goes on and the CAMERA pans to Adrian complete with hat,stick and gloves, sitting on a very small
chair with the dog on his lap.
                                                    DISSOLVE
118. ADRIAN - AT THE FURRIER'S
He sits with dog in his usual small chair. His eyes are
beginning to roll up in his head.

119. EPIFANIA
She is looking without pleasure at some wonderful coats that
are being modelled for her. She tries one on but doesn't
like it. Now the proprietor comes in wearing a "be prepared
to be knocked dead" expression. He is followed by two men in
white furrier's coats, carrying a large muslin bundle. The

proprietor takes it from them and with an heroic gesture, empties an enormous quantity of Russian sable pelts around Epifania's knees.

DISSOLVE

120. A BARGAIN PLACARD
I do not know the exact wording of an English bargain sale sign, but that is what the placard is. The CAMERA comes down from it to a group of determined ladies, wrestling for the prizes.

121. ADRIAN - IN THE EDDY AT THE EDGE OF THE GROUP
He has been nearly destroyed by the rushing women, but is still there. A passing lady knocks his hat off with a bundle, but he retrieves it and looks around desperately. Now he sees his objective.

122. EPIFANIA - COMING OUT OF THE MELEE
Her hat is askew, her clothes are disarranged, but she is breathless and happy. Triumphantly she holds up a paper bag and from this removes and shows to Adrian a horrifying neck-tie she has bought him. As he looks at it in horror,

DISSOLVE

123. A DOZEN AND A HALF MARENNES VERTES
These, of course, are the beautiful green French oysters, probably the best in the world. They will be served with Mignonette sauce, a half of a lemon, a crystal container of roughly ground pepper and a stack of brown bread buttered. The dish is probably silver. The dozen and a half oysters are in front of Adrian...Epifania is content with six. Adrian is eating his oysters happily, drinking the juice out of each shell. Epifania sits with a newspaper open at the stock market page, talking to her broker over the telephone. Now, absent-mindedly, she spears an oyster, puts it in her mouth and chews on it. She stops instantly, feels around pensively for a moment with her tongue, then removes an enormous pearl from her mouth.

124. BIG HEAD - ADRIAN
He looks at her in stupefaction.

125. EPIFANIA'S RACING STABLE - ROLLS ROYCE IN BACKGROUND
Both she and Adrian wear tweeds. Some of her jumping horses are led around for her inspection. The trainer points to some improved condition above one of the horse's hooves. Epifania feels of it, then lifts the hoof to look under it. After this she asks Adrian if he would like to go for a little canter, and as he accepts reluctantly,

DISSOLVE

126. A COUNTRY FENCE - CLOSE SHOT
Through the rails we see Epifania and Adrian galloping toward us. The CAMERA pulls back and to one side as Epifania jumps the fence. It pans around to follow her, but she gallops away. A second later, Adrian's horse goes past the CAMERA, its saddle empty, its stirrups flapping. The horses gallop away.

DISSOLVE

127. A BEAUTIFUL SAILING YACHT COMING TOWARD US...PROBABLY A CUTTER

128. EPIFANIA - AT THE TILLER
She is exulting in the sport and the beautiful day. The CAMERA pans to Adrian in a yachting outfit. He is already seeing double and getting ready for the old heave-ho.

DISSOLVE

313

ADRIAN ASLEEP - IN HIS BEDROOM
The phone rings. He answers it in horror, but this horror
is nothing compared to the horror on his face when he looks
at his watch.

DISSOLVE

130. ADRIAN - AT THE SIDE OF THE ICY POOL
He puts his hands over his eyes and jumps in.

DISSOLVE

131. ADRIAN - RIDING ON A BICYCLE
Suddenly he hears something and seems wo say "What?"

132. EPIFANIA - ON A BICYCLE - FROM THE BACK
She points in a different direction from the previous shot.

133. ADRIAN - RIDING THE BICYCLE
He goes down like a ton of pig iron.

DISSOLVE

134. ADRIAN - ON A HORSE
He has one foot in the stirrup. He looks around gloomily,
then climbs aboard.

DISSOLVE

135. EPIFANIA - TRYING ON A MAGNIFICENT HAT

136. ADRIAN - ON A SMALL CHAIR
He is in his usual pose, complete with dog, hat, gloves and
umbrella.

DISSOLVE

137. A MAGNIFICENT RADIO AND TELEVISION SALON
Epifania is looking at some extraordinarily expensive models
of colour television sets. The same entertainment is visible
in three tubes As she looks from one to the other.

138. ADRIAN - IN HIS CUSTOMARY SMALL CHAIR
He sits complete with hat, dog, boutonniere, gloves and um-
brella. On the wall behind him, a placard says: "YOU BE THE
JUDGE! WHY NOT LET US INSTALL A NEW SUPERCOLOUR TELEVISION
SET IN YOUR OWN HOME ON THIRTY-DAY FREE TRIAL?"

THE CAMERA PUSHES IN ON ADRIAN, ENDING UP IN A BIG HEAD WITH
THE WORDS BEHIND HIM: "ON THIRTY-DAY FREE TRIAL?"

FADE OUT

139. EPIFANIA'S ROLLS ROYCE IN A DOWNPOUR - NIGHT
From a high angle we see it grinding along the bottom of a
ravine that looks like a torrent. Picking its way through
the detritus with a powerful spotlight, it yaws...it skids...
its wheels chatter...it plows bravely ahead.

140. CHARLES, THE CHAUFFEUR
He is apparently enjoying himself as he drives with one hand,
and alternately aims the spotlight and wipes the rain out of
his eyes with the other. Now the speaker beside his ear
comes to life with

    EPIFANIA'S VOICE: It's only about a hundred yards
        more, I think, Charles.

    CHARLES: (cheerfully) Yes, but it's that last
        'undred that's the 'ardest, Madam...as
        the shark said to the channel swimmer...

    EPIFANIA'S VOICE: Then give her the gun.

    CHARLES: Then fasten your lap straps, please, and
        'ang on.

With this he thunders his motor and takes a firm grip on the
wheel with both hands.

141. HIGH CAMERA SHOT - EPIFANIA'S ROLLS ROYCE
It leaps forward.

142. INTERIOR OF THE ROLLS ROYCE
The effect of the sudden move is continued here by throwing
Epifania and Adrian violently backwards and upwards. They
are in full evening dress. Adrian's silk hat is pushed into
the shape of a concertina. As they bounce forward:

    ADRIAN: (looking at his hat) I say, this is im-
                     possible...we must be off the road.

    EPIFANIA: (amiably) No...it's just a little bit
                     rough.

They are now thrown back by another bump.

    ADRIAN: (recovering his hat from under him)
                     A little bit what?

    EPIFANIA: Bumpy.

    ADRIAN: Ch...bumpy...Yes, quite a little bit...

Suddenly they grab each other as a wild and rocking skid begins.

143. CLOSE SHOT - CHARLES, THE CHAUFFEUR
He fights the wheel happily.

144. HIGH CAMERA SHOT - THE ROLLS ROYCE
It slithers from side to side of the road.

145. INTERIOR - THE ROLLS ROYCE
Epifania and Adrian are hanging onto various straps and handles. Various possibilities suggest themselves with the fur
robe.

    ADRIAN: (politely) You're sure that the dinner
                     at the end of this rainbow is worth forty
                     miles in full evening dress over the
                     roughest road I have ever been shot over
                     ...on the worst night of the year?

    EPIFANIA: (laughing) It's very romantic.

    ADRIAN: (worried) Not the cooking, I trust.

    EPIFANIA: (laughing) Of course not.

    ADRIAN: (making his little joke) What was it
                     called again: The Cleft Palate"?

    EPIFANIA: (laughing) No, Silly, The Cloven Hoof.

    ADRIAN: Ah, yes. I was unable to find it in The
                     Guide to Good Eating.

    EPIFANIA: (dreamily) My father used to bring me
                     here.

    ADRIAN: (vaguely) Oh.

    EPIFANIA: (her eyes twinkling) And tonight is a
                     very special occasion...

At this moment, another tremendous bump in the road throws
them backwards and upwards.

146. EXTERIOR OF A DILAPIDATED RIVER INN..THE CLOVEN HOOF...
    NIGHT

Skidding wildly, the Rolls Royce comes to a slithering stop
into the shot and a slushing stop. The Chauffeur steps out
into the mud, practically does the big split, then pulls himself up and goes cautiously around the car, hanging onto it.

315

147. CLOSE SHOT - THE OFF SIDE OF THE ROLLS ROYCE
The Chauffeur comes into the shot and opens the door, revealing Epifania and Adrian sitting on the floor. Adrian's
collar pops open.

          EPIFANIA: (cheerfully) Well, here we are.

          ADRIAN: (looking out through the door in horror)
                        I say...

148. A CAST IRON HITCHING POST IN THE SHAPE OF A SATYR
It stands glistening in the rain, a ring suspended from its
outstretched hand. A sinister smile wreathes its cast iron
lips. Behind it we see the front door of The Cloven Hoof,
with the name over it. There is a flickering light in the
windows near the door. Now a curtain is pulled back here.

149. CLOSE SHOT - THE WINDOW
An old man with a hearing aid and an old woman peek out suspiciously.

150. INTERIOR   ROLLS ROYCE - EPIFANIA AND ADRIAN
This is past the Chauffeur.

          EPIFANIA: Isn't it enchanting?

          ADRIAN: (rising and helping Epifania out) In
                        all seriousness, do you mean to tell me
                        that this...is what we've been three
                        hours getting to?

          EPIFANIA: (quietly, taking a cake box from the
                        Chauffeur) We've been a month getting
                        here, darling!

She smiles at him mysteriously and leads the way. As she
passes the cast iron satyr, she looks in her bag for money,
then turns to Adrian.

          EPIFANIA: Give me a penny, will you?

          ADRIAN: Certainly.

          EPIFANIA: (taking it) Thank you.

She puts the penny into a slot in the satyr's hand. Instantly the creature's eyes light up, a bell goes off and he
nods his head in gratitude.

          ADRIAN: Good God!

He steps back accurately into a stream of rainwater that
goes down the back of his neck.
                                        DISSOLVE

151. CLOSE SHOT - A BRASS FERN DISH ON THE FLOOR
This is catching a leak from above. The drops, at half-
second intervals, are striking D.

152. A COPPER COOKING POT
The water hitting this sounds a G.

153. A PEWTER SOMETHING OR OTHER
The water dripping this sounds a B.

154. AN IRON CONTAINER
It does not complete the   tonic chord, but is a half-tone
off.

155. EPIFANIA'S HANDS AT THE SIDEBOARD
More or less neatly they are stacking together the tawdry
remains of a vile dinner. To one side we see the cake box,
the Chauffeur gave her downstairs. By pulling back and
panning the CAMERA now finds itself on her. She looks very
pretty and very cheerful.

316

EPIFANIA: Isn't this jolly?

156. ADRIAN - AT THE END OF A TABLE SEATING TWENTY-FIVE
His feet are on a footstool. He wears his hat, his coat,
and over his lap a fur automobile robe, possibly chinchilla.

ADRIAN: (thickly) Frightfully! I...I...

He sneezes resoundingly, then straightens his hat dislodged
by the concussion, then pulls the heater closer to himself
and the blanket tighter around him.

157. EPIFANIA - AT THE SIDEBOARD
Shielding what she is doing from Adrian, she is placing a
hundred and fifty pound check under the top layer of a
piece of the cake she got from the chauffeur.

EPIFANIA: (cheerfully over her shoulder) You're
not catching cold, are you?

158. CLOSE SHOT - ADRIAN

ADRIAN: I've already caught it, thank you...Not
to mention, in all probability, trichy-
nosis...dyspepsia...gastroenteritis...

159. EPIFANIA - AT THE SIDEBOARD
She is now cementing the piece of cake back together. She
now returns the plate in the box, sticks a candle in it,
then closes the box and gets ready to leave.

ADRIAN'S VOICE: ...Pyrosis...pellagra...and colester-
itis...

Epifania picks up the tray and departs.

160. CLOSE SHOT ADRIAN

ADRIAN: ...to say nothing of permanent flatulence
....as a result of one of the most stupe-
fying dinners it has ever been my mis-
fortune...

EPIFANIA: (laughing) Oh, come on! Just because
the soup wasn't up to your standards...

ADRIAN: (in mock surprise) Soup! Was that
soup? I thought it was...

EPIFANIA: (as to a child) Don't be vulgar, darling.

ADRIAN: (relishing his words) It is impossible
to mention what I have just eaten with-
out being vulgar...The gruesome remains
of last Sunday's joint...those sprouts...
those potatoes...that rhubarb tart...and
finally, that stale, sour, synthetic,
American, axle grease...purporting to be
cheese....(then after a look at Epifania)...Why is it that the people who
know how to enjoy themselves never have
any money, and the people who have money
never know how to enjoy themselves?

EPIFANIA: Oh, you're just in a tizzy because...
(she leans on his shoulder, reaches past
him, and kills a fly on the table, then
flicks it off delicately)...Pardon me.

ADRIAN: There's one, at least, that wasn't in
the soup!   I am never in a tizzy...I
trust.

EPIFANIA: Don't you ever think about anything except food? Don't you ever think about love...romance..nightingales singing in the moonlight?

ADRIAN: On a night like this?

EPIFANIA: Use your imagination.

ADRIAN: (answering the penultimate question) Of course I do...but you promised me "a very special treat"; a delicious cottage meal in an atmosphere of primitive happiness ...and old-world charm...(then glaring around the room) If this is a special treat...

EPIFANIA: (tolerantly) Close your eyes.

ADRIAN: (looking around in stupefaction) Huh?

EPIFANIA: Close your eyes and get a surprise...Shut them tight...

ADRIAN: (his eyes closed) What are you going to do now, finish me off? Wasn't that dinner enough?

EPIFANIA: (taking the cake out of the box and arranging it) You're not peeking?

ADRIAN: A gentleman never peeks.

EPIFANIA: (after lighting the candle) There! You can look now. (and placing a piece in front of him) The piece with your initials is for you...the one with mine is for me...Isn't that nice?

ADRIAN: I'm really quite sincerely touched...I can almost guess what we are celebrating.

EPIFANIA: Can you?

ADRIAN: (tenderly) Yes. And you know how happy it makes me...My initials, however, are "A.L.B." My middle name is Llewellyn.

EPIFANIA: I didn't know...but I will learn. Now, make a wish and blow.

ADRIAN: (gallantly) To a very lovely lady.

He purses his mouth to blow, then is seized by a wild desire to sneeze. After fighting it for a moment, he turns his head and sneezes.

EPIFANIA: Oh, you missed it! That's supposed to be bad luck...Never mind, I'll do it for you. (she blows out the candle and a little wax into Adrian's eye at the same time. As he winces and puts a handkerchief to the eye)...I'm so sorry.

ADRIAN: (putting the handkerchief away) Don't mention it. What do I do now?

EPIFANIA: (happily) Eat it.

ADRIAN: (after putting the pointed end in his mouth and chewing it suspiciously) Excellent...It cannot have been made here.

He finishes it greedily.

318

EPIFANIA: (eagerly, her eyes twinkling) I brought
    it with us...go on!

ADRIAN: (cheering up) Would that you had brought
    the whole dinner! (he shoves the re-
    mainder of the cake into his mouth and
    starts chewing)

He chews and chews, slowly comes to a stop, looks at Epifania
suspiciously, then chews some more. Epifania looks at the
solemn Adrian and begins to laugh. The more she looks at
him, the more he glares at her and the more he glares at her
the harder she laughs. Finally he stops chewing, looks at
her for a moment, tries unsuccessfully to swallow, then makes
a grab for a glass of water.

EPIFANIA: (seizing his wrist) Don't do that...
    (a small tug-of-war begins, but is quick-
    ly won by Adrian, who lifts the glass to
    his lips) But you mustn't. Don't you
    understand that? (Adrian finishes the
    water and puts the glass down) Oh, no!

ADRIAN: (breathing hard) Oh no, what?

EPIFANIA: You swallowed it.

ADRIAN: I swallowed what?

EPIFANIA: The money.

ADRIAN: (coldly) What money?

EPIFANIA: The hundred and fifty pounds...you were
    supposed to find it...then you'd know...
    what everything was about...(then philo-
    sophically) It doesn't matter...I can
    stop payment on it...It was just a funny
    joke.

ADRIAN: Excruciating...especially if I had fallen
    dead at your feet!

EPIFANIA: I was only trying to be subtle. (now the
    father light begins to shine in yer eyes)
    My father used to give me surprises all
    the time that way...He was so reticent
    about giving money...He'd hide it in
    crumpets...in hot cross buns...in ham
    sandwiches...how we laughed!

ADRIAN: (removing a small piece of paper from
    his teeth) I adore practical jokes.

EPIFANIA: (enthusiastically) So did he! You should
    have known my father!

ADRIAN: I am very glad that I did not.

EPIFANIA: (stunned) What is that? (now coldly
    dangerous) What's that you say?

ADRIAN: (restraining himself) My dear Epifania:
    if we are to remain friends, I may as
    well be quite frank with you. Everything
    you have told me about your father con-
    vinces me that, though he was no doubt
    an affectionate parent and amiable enough
    to explain your rather tiresome father
    fixation, he must have been quite the
    most appalling bore that ever devastated
    even a Rotary Club.

EPIFANIA: (stunned by this blasphemy) My father!
You infinite nothing! My father made a
hundred and fifty millions! You never
even made half a million!

ADRIAN: My good girl, your father never made
anything. I have not the slightest no-
tion of how he contrived to get a legal
claim on so much of what other people
made; but I doknow that he lost four-
fifths of it by being far enough behind
thetimes to buy up the properties of
the Russian nobility in the belief that
they would squash the Soviet Revolution
in three weeks or so. Could anyone have
made a stupider mistake? Not I.

EPIFANIA: (springing up) You rotten thing! (she
grabs him by the cuffs of the pants and
tips him and the chair over backwards.
Now she leans over and taunts him) Take
that for calling my father a bore!

ADRIAN: (picking himself up clumsily and dust-
ing himself off) Epifania! For Heaven's
sake! Stop these pranks! You might have
hurt me very seriously.

EPIFANIA: Hurt you! I'll hurt you until you'll
wish you were dead! (she throws him
heavily) Scum! Filth! Take that for
sayng he never made anything!

ADRIAN: (picking himself up again) Stop it! Epifania! Stop it at once! Don't anger me
and force me to defend myself!

EPIFANIA: (approaching him menacingly) Defend
yourself, you vermin! (she throws him
backward, so that he goes over a table
and crashes heavily) And see how much
good it will do you.

ADRIAN: (after picking himself up, limping toward
the door) This is no longer funny. I've
warned you...(then seing her coming
toward him, he forgets his manhood and
takes off) Help! Murder! Police!

EPIFANIA: (running to intercept him) Dirt!
Carrion!

Just missing him, she takes a flying leap and lands on his
back. They disappear, going donw the stairs like an avalanch

161. BOTTOM OF THE STAIRS
To the accompaniment of yells from Adrian to loud thumps, the
avalanche appears, rolls across the floor and winds up against
something or other so long as it is noisy.

162. CLOSE SHOT - EPIFANIA AND ADRIAN ON THE FLOOR
As Epifania rises wobbily, his knees bend and she kneels on
Adrian's stomach. With a terrible "Ugh", he sits up a lit-
tle, then collapses heavily again.

EPIFANIA: (looking down at him) You brute! You've
killed me. (now she staggers away from
us and the CAMERA follows her as she
weaves toward the kitchen, muttering)
Help! Murder! Police! I have been at-
tacked...

320

163. THE OLD-FASHIONED KITCHEN OF THE INN
The old husband is smoking in the dim background, his legs
up on a footstool. The old wife is scrubbing the tile floor
with a hand brush and a cake of soap, the latter m uch in
evidence. Now at the sound, she looks up fearfully, past
the CAMERA, then cringes away a little, leaving her soap
where it is.

164. EPIFANIA - THROUGH THE KITCHEN DOORWAY
She staggers toward us, muttering to herself

          EPIFANIA: Help! Murder! Get me a doctor!

165. CLOSE SHOT   THE SOAP ON THE KITCHEN FLOOR
Epifania's foot steps on it, then skids forward.

EPIFANIA - DOING A SUPERB 108
She lands heavily on her back, then bounces to a floor-pound-
ing position.

166. CLOSE SHOT EPIFANIA
Pounding the floor in a rage, she hollers

          EPIFANIA: (weeping) I am dying...get me a doctor
                        and call the police.

          THE OLD MAN: What did she say?

          THE OLD WOMAN: She says she wants the doctor and the
                        police!

167. THE OLD MAN

          THE OLD MAN   (turning up the voltage on his hearing
                        aid) Says she's been what?

168. EPIFANIA - ON THE FLOOR

          EPIFANIA: (sittin g up) Oh, shut up and do as
                        you're told: Can't you see I'm dying?

                                              DISSOLVE

169. TWO POLICEMEN BEARING THEUNCONSCIOUS ADRIAN ON A
      STRETCHER
A sergeant walks beside them.

170. BIG HEAD: ADRIAN
He is sleeping mcre or less happily with the rain beating
down on his face.

          A POLICEMAN'S VOICE: 'ardly 'ave the 'andcuff him, do
                        you think, Sergeant?

          SERGEANT'S VOICE: (very base) 'ardly.

171. ADRIAN SMILES SLIGHTLY IN HIS SLEEP

      THE TOP OF THE STAIRS IN THE INN
Low CAMERA FOLLOWING Shot, the old woman leading a man in a
frock coat. The CAMERA is angled to miss his head. He carries a bag.

          THE DOCTOR'S VOICE: (as they reach the top of the
                        stairs - cultured and foreign) The
                        victim is in here?

          THE OLD WOMAN: (readily) Yes, Doctor...the poor
                        thing...she is all unstrung...that's
                        what she is...that drunken beast!

          THE DOCTOR'S VOICE: (impatiently) Yes..Yes...We shal
                        see about all that.

                              321

THE OLD WOMAN: (knocking on the door) It's the doc-
                tor, Ma'am.

172. EPIFANIA - IN AN OLD INN BEDROOM
The play tells us this Inn dates from the time of William the
Conqueror. Therefore, this room has been redone many times.
It is small and in disrepair but reasonably quaint. It has a
four-poster bed with tester. A linen chest at the foot. A
wash basin, pitcher and jar outfit against a wall, with
mirror over it; possibly a dresser with a mirror over it, and
a large mirrored wardrobe. All these mirrors are not being
asked for by mistake. Epifania, nude except for a diamond
choker, panties, stockings and shoes, sits, modestly covered
by a colorful eiderdown quilt. She sits on the edge of the
bed, her bag in her lap, checking her lip rouge.

            EPIFANIA: Just a minute. (She puts her bag away
                         hastily and stretches herself in bed, lik
                         the dying swan. From this position, she
                         croaks feebly   She closes her eyes)
                         Come in.

173. THE BEDROOM DOOR OPENING
The old woman pulls slightly to one side, revealing the doctor, plus his head for the first time. On his head he wears
a tarboosh.

            THE DOCTOR: What's the matter   What is going on here
                         Why is she pretending to be dead?

            THE OLD WOMAN: Oh, she's not pretending, Sir. What
                         she went through was orfel.

174. EPIFANIA - IN BED
Opening first one eye, then both, she lifts her head and reacts quite unpleasantly to the appearance of her visitor.

            EPIFANIA: Who the...Who the devil are you?

175. THE DOCTOR IN THE DOORWAY

            THE DOCTOR: I am an Egyptian doctor. I hear you have
                         had a great disturbance. I hasten to
                         ascertain the cause. I find you here in
                         catalepsy. Can I help?

176. EPIFANIA - IN BED

            EPIFANIA: I am dying.

177. THE DOCTOR - IN THE DOORWAY

            THE DOCTOR: You are lying! You can swear...you have
                         just rouged your lips...your catalepsy
                         is entirely fictitious. (now turning to
                         go) You can sit up now, you are quite
                         well. Good evening.

178. EPIFANIA - IN BED

            EPIFANIA: (sitting up violently and starting to
                         get on her knees) Stop! I am not quite
                         well. (She spreads the quilt modestly
                         in front of her, which removes it from
                         her back) I am on the point of death...

179. THE DOCTOR - IN THE DOORWAY
He reacts with some surprise at what he sees past Epifania.

            EPIFANIA'S VOICE: I need a doctor.

180. POINT OF VIEW SHOT - WHAT THE DOCTOR SEES
Over Epifania's shoulder, tipped in in the foreground, we see
her reflection in the wardrobe mirror behind her. Her back
is bare. The Doctor's face is also in the mirror.

EPIFANIA'S VOICE: I am a rich woman...Doctors' fees mean nothing to me.

THE DOCTOR: In that case...

181. THE DOCTOR IN THE DOORWAY PAST EPIFANIA

THE DOCTOR: ...you will have no difficulty in finding an English doctor...entirely capable of healing ailments like yours...NOW I must see the gentleman they took to gaol who fell down the stairs. He may have something broken.

He turns to go.

182. EPIFANIA - KNEELING ON THE BED
She hops off the bed and the CAMERA takes her into the shot with the Doctor.

EPIFANIA: (seizing the Doctor by the lapel) Never mind that scoundrel! If he has broken every bone in his body, it is no more than he deserves! I fell down the stairs too...he pushed me.

THE OLD WOMAN: (blocking the Doctor's exit) Twenty years 'ell get.

THE DOCTOR: (after lifting his right arm to look back at the old woman) But he was unconscious.

EPIFANIA: Faking.

THE DOCTORL   (trying to leave but still finding himself blocked by the old woman) I don't think so...when they laid him in that enormous motor car...

EPIFANIA: (indignantly) In my Rolls Royce! I will not permit it. (then to the old woman) Have them take him out of it at once.

THE DOCTOR: It has already gone...and you should be very glad to have it serve a useful purpose.

EPIFANIA: It is your business to doctor me...not to lecture me.

THE DOCTOR: (with surprising fire) It is not my business at all! Primo: I am not your doctor! Segundo; I am not in general practice! Tertio: I keep a clinic for penniless Mahometan refugees! Quarto: I work in a hospital! Quinto: I will not attend to you!

EPIFANIA: (sinking to the floor hysterically) You must attend to me, do you hear I am a sick woman...You cannot abandon me to die in this sretched place.

THE DOCTOR: I see no symptoms of any sickness about you! Get up.

EPIFANIA: (straightening up with surprising health and speaking hypnotically) Well, you WILL attend to me..because you MUST attend to me! You are not going to leave me here to die! Come IN and close the DOOR.

THE DOCTOR: (after shaking his head to free him-self from the spell) What are you try-ing to do, hypnotize me? (then after another shake of the head) I reserve myself for poor and useful people.

EPIFANIA: Then you are either a fool or a Com-munist.

THE DOCTOR: (with quiet dignity) I am nothing but a servant of Allah.

EPIFANIA: (changing tactics and becoming extremely feminine) You are abominably rude... and terribly cruel...but you inspire confidence as a doctor. (she closes the door gently behind him then groans)

THE DOCTOR: (after noticing the door closing) You are in pain?

EPIFANIA: (going to the bed and lowering herself to it with difficulty) Yes...horrible pain.

She stretches out.

THE DOCTOR: (doubtfully, putting his bag on the edge of the bed) Where?

EPIFANIA: (at a loss) Don't cross-examine me as if you didn't believe me...I must have sprained my wrist, throwing that beast all over the place.

THE DOCTOR: Which hand?

EPIFANIA: (extending first one hand and then the other) This one.

THE DOCTOR: (taking her hand in a business-like way and pulling and turning the fingers and wrist to groans from Epifania) Nothing whatever the matter.

EPIFANIA: How do you know? It's my hand, not yours

THE DOCTOR: You would scream the house down if your wrist were sprained.

EPIFANIA: (looking at him resentfully, then winc-ing) Oh! My back...

She stretches out on her side.

THE DOCTOR: (coldly) Roll over. (in a totally un-interested way, he pulls down a corner of the quilt and looks at her back) Where does it hurt?

EPIFANIA: Everywhere.

THE DOCTOR: (taking from his pocket a metal thermom-eter case and poking her shoulder blade) Here? (Epifania groans and the Doctor pokes her other shoulder blade) Here? (Epifania groans again, and the Doctor pokes her spinal column) Here? (Epifania yowls again and starts to get up)

THE DOCTOR: (poking her down again with the metal case) Be quiet. (Now he traces her lef dorsal muscle with the metal case, then puts on his spectacles and examines it more closely) Where did you get this latissiumus dorsi...weight-lifting?

324

EPIFANIA: (starting to sit up) No, you see my father felt that women should be...

THE DOCTOR: (putting his thermometer case away and taking out his watch) This back could not be injured by anything.

EPIFANIA: (starting to sit up again) Oh, but when this man overpowered me...

THE DOCTOR: (interrupting drily) He would have to have been a gorilla...Give me your wrist and be quiet. (he feels for her pulse, takes out his watch and looks at it stonily. Suddenly, an expression of unbelief comes over his face, and he speaks in a strange voice) This I have never felt anything like in my life....Remarkable.

EPIFANIA: (starting to sit up) What is?

THE DOCTOR: (pushing her down) It is like a slow sledge hammer.

EPIFANIA: (apprehensively) Too slow?

THE DOCTOR: Be quiet. (he pulls his stethoscope out of his bag, fits it into his ears, then listens to a place roughly opposite her heart)

EPIFANIA: Do you think...

THE DOCTOR: (irritably) Quiet, please...(as he listens, a beatific smile comes over his face and the background music swells as the tympani sound out the beat of life. The CAMERA pushes close) Fantastic! It is like being in the engine roomof the Queen Elizabeth. (He looks at Epifania, shakes his head, then removes his stethoscope, covers her with the quilt and gets up) Marvelous!

EPIFANIA: (sitting up tremulously) I will live?

THE DOCTOR: (drily, picking up his bag) Probably forever...like a toad! (then shaking his head) But why Allah, in His infinite wisdom...should pour a vital fluid like this...into a vessel like you...must always remain a mystery.

EPIFANIA: (resentfully) What's the matter with my vessel?

THE DOCTOR: (with great emphasis) Absolutely nothing...from stem to stern. You are shamming. Lying! Why? Is it to make yourself interesting?

EPIFANIA: (raising herself on her elbow) Make myself interesting! Man: I am interesting.

THE DOCTOR: Structurally, beyond question...Not in the least medically.

EPIFANIA: I am the most interesting woman in England.

EPIFANIA: I am Epifania Ognisanti di Parerga.

THE DOCTOR: Ah!

EPIFANIA: I am also the richest woman in England.

THE DOCTOR: Well, that is a disease for which I do not prescribe...I can do nothing for you. I must go back to my work. Good evening.

He picks up his bag and starts to go.

EPIFANIA: (outraged) You are nothing but a pig... and a beast...and a communist!

THE DOCTOR: (bowing as he exits) Madam.

183. FAST TRUCKING SHOT DOWN THE CORRIDOR AHEAD OF THE DOC-TOR AND EPIFANIA
The Doctor appears hurriedly instantly followed by Epifania clutching her quilt. The dialogue, of course, is continuous from the bedroom to the corridor.

EPIFANIA: (astonished and indignant) Well, what do you think you're doing? Where do you think you're going? How dare you walk out on me! You haven't even taken my temperature. You're just an Egyptian quack...quack! quack! quack! (the Doctor looks over his shoulder, increases his speed imperceptibly, then disappears around the corner.)

EPIFANIA: (speeding up also) What are you so high and might...

At this exact instant her quilt catches on the loose baseboard at the corner. We hear a loud tearing sound and the CAMERA follows Epifania around the corner. She yanks the attached quilt to free it, we hear another tearing sound and she departs in a cloud of feathers, leaving part of the quilt on the floor.

184. THE TOP OF THE STAIRS
The Doctor swings into the shot and Epifania, exploding with feathers runs in a second later and starts downstairs after him.

EPIFANA: What are you angry about...because I called you a pig? All right, I take it back. You're not a pig...that isn't any reason to leave a woman alone in her distresss...ill...wretched...helpless... hardly able to walk. My car is gone. I have no money. I never carry money anyway. (by now she has practically caught up with him)

THE DOCTOR: And I have none to carry. Your car will return presently. You can borrow money from your chauffeur. (he puts his hand on the doorknob)

EPIFANIA: (blocking his way) You're an unmitigated ...B...b...ashibazouk...you have the feelings of a hippopotamus. I might have known it from that ridiculous fez.. which you should have taken off in my presence! (she snatches it from his head and holds it behind her back) You have the manners of a street Arab.

326

THE DOCTOR: (suddenly getting to the other side of
the door) ...and the lightness of foot
...I used to be one. (sarcastically he
does the salutation of the Orient which
begins by touching his forehead...and
mutters the proper words)
....
(or whatever the word is)

He disappears into the rain.

185. EXTERIOR OF THE INN.
Epifania hurries through the door after him and stands in
the rain, clutching the remains of the quilt about her.

EPIFANIA: (emotionally) Please...

The CAMERA pushes close to a big head. We do not know
whether there are raindrops or tears on her cheeks. The
heartbeat music reprises and swells as we

FADE OUT

FADE IN

186. A SIGN IN ARABIC

By a fortunate happenstance this has the same proportions as
a motion picture screen. Probably it has a crescent at the
top but maybe it hasn't. In any case, it concerns itself
with the visiting hours and days of this free clinic... men-
tioning, in passing, the fact that money is acceptable if
available. Under this we hear a torrent of Arabic...mostly
women's and children's voices...a few bass male voices...
some children crying...and the yapping of some pet puppy
dogs. The CAMERA pulls back and we see the corner of a very
poor waiting room in a shabby building...barrack...warehouse
or whatever is most easily put together or available. Back-
less wooden benches parallel the walls and on these crouch,
lie, play and bark the beings we have just heard gabbling.
Research will inform us how Mohametan refugees would dress
in the year 1953, in a poor suburb forty miles out of London.
I hope it will be possible to show some fezzes and some
yashmaks. If the yashmak is not conceivably possible, might
some of the women have their faces slightly veiled? If this
is asking too much, might at least one grandmother wear some
form of yashmak? In my mind's eye, I see a small ragamuffin
wearing a fez on the back of his head. He is barefooted and
his leg is swathed in a dirty bandage. Together with his
brother and sister he is playing with a puppy. The CAMERA
pulls back revealing, along the wall, more patients...
brown...black...yellow..all poor...many with families. Suddenly we hear the shout of children from outside and a soft
automobile horn. The CAMERA stops on the open door and the
small children rush out toward an open Rolls Royce coming to
a stop at the kerb.

187. EPIFANIA'S OPEN ROLLS

It is entirely surrounded by poor residents of the neighborhood, passing bicyclists and barking dogs. You would think
a movie star had arrived. The CAMERA threads its way through
the throng and comes to rest on Epifania, the lower part of
her face veiled, in a magnificent Paris outfit, heavily
Oriental in derivation. In her hands she clasps the doctor's
fez, wrapped in tissue paper and tied with a ribbon. She
gets out of her car, the CAMERA pans her toward the clinic,
as she wends her way with a full escort of jabbering children.

188. INTERIOR CLINIC WAITING ROOM

Epifania comes in with her escort, crosses to a bench. At
the top of their lungs the children want to know who she is,
why she is wearing a yashmak, why she doesn't speak Arabic,
whether her jewels are real, etc. The mothers and fathers
shout to the children to shut up, the dogs start barking...
a clouted child starts to yell...it turns out that a mother
hit the wrong child and the child's mother starts insulting
the clouter...the din gets louder.

189. THE DOORWAY OF THE INNER OFFICE

The door opens and the Egyptian Doctor appears with his arm
around a freshly bandaged child. He wears a long off-white
laboratory coat, a stethoscope around his neck, and around
his head the band with circular concave mirror attached. He
reacts instantly to the noise, waves his arms, and speaks
severely.

> THE DOCTOR: (in Arabic) Will you shut up? What is
> going on here? How do you expect me to be
> able even to think with this... (during
> his speech we have intercut about three
> shots of the scolded Arabs, showing the
> light from the doctor's mirror, moving
> over them. Suddenly the doctor stops and
> looks past the CAMERA. All he says is)
> Oh.

190. EPIFANIA - IN THE BEAM OF REFLECTED LIGHT

The circle of light moves slightly as the doctor examines her.

    EPIFANIA: Good morning...I mean, Good Afternoon.
                          Could I talk to you for a moment?

191. THE DOCTOR - IN THE DOORWAY

    THE DOCTOR: As you see...there are many ahead of you...

He pats the freshly bandaged child on the head and looks around
for his next patient.

192. EPIFANIA
The beam of light is not on her.

    EPIFANIA: I can wait...a little while...

The beam of light comes on her again.

193. THE DOCTOR - IN THE DOORWAY
He is looking at Epifania.

    THE DOCTOR: It might not be so little...(then turning
                          to an old man)...I believe you were next,
                          Mustapha.

Mustapha hobbles to the Doctor's side, explaining in whining
Arabic about all the places where he hurts.

    THE DOCTOR: (in Arabic) It is the will of Allah.

He puts his arm around the old man and leads him into the of-
fice. Just before closing the door he takes one last look at
Epifania. The door closes and the CAMERA moves up to a clock.
The hands say 1:30.
                                          DISSOLVE

194. EPIFANIA - SEATED ON THE BENCH
She is not enjoying the waiting. Suddenly she looks toward
the office door. The Doctor comes out with a patient (not
Mustapha) and takes another one in. The CAMERA goes to the
clock. The hands say 3:30.
                                          DISSOLVE

195. EPIFANIA
She is in the very corner of the room where the benches join.
Her feet are on the bench, her back against the wall. She
turns at a sound.

196. OFFICE DOOR
The doctor comes out with another patient and goes back in with
a new one. CAMERA goes to the clock. The hands say 5:00.

                                          DISSOLVE

197. EPIFANIA - IN THE CORNER OF THE ROOM
Her back is against the wall. Her legs stretched out straight.
The waiting room is darker. Now a shaft of light falls on her
as the office door is opened...she does not see it, however...
she is sound asleep.

198. THE DOCTOR IN THE DOORWAY OF HIS OFFICE
Which is bright behind him...much brighter than the waiting
room. He looks toward Epifania, shakes his head, then speaks.
(He has removed his forehead mirror)

    THE DOCTOR: Do you want to come in now?

199. EPIFANIA
She sleeps on.

200. THE DOCTOR
He comes forward and stands looking at Epifania for a long
moment, then raises his voice and speaks with great distinctnes

THE DOCTOR: Do you wish to come...or do you not?

201. EPIFANIA
Startled into wakefulness, she comes to violently, nearly
falls between the bench and the wall, drops her bag and package to the floor, picks them up, and stands up sleepily.

      EPIFANIA: (squinting toward the light) Were you talk-
                        ing to me...or did I dream it?

202. THE DOCTOR:

      THE DOCTOR: (shrugging) Since there is no one else
                        here...(he points to the room behind him)
                        ...if you still wish to come in.

203. EPIFANIA.

      EPIFANIA: Thank you. (she starts forward, then re-
                        membering something, returns to the bench,
                        sits down, takes her shoes out from under
                        it, puts them on, and stamps her feet.
                        While doing this she looks up.) My feet
                        went to sleep too...

She rises and the CAMERA pans her past the doctor who indicates his office, then follows her into it and starts to close
the door.

204. THE DOCTOR IN HIS OFFICE.
He finishes closing the door, then goes, with the CAMERA, to
Epifania and indicates a chair. This pan shows us a little
more of the room which is part office, part surgery, and, if
the Turkish coffee pot visible is any clue, part kitchen.
For all we know the Doctor may reside in a room or alcove in
the back.

      THE DOCTOR: (purposely not sitting down) Now what did
      you want to talk to me about?

      EPIFANIA: (handing him her package) I have brought
                        you back your hat.

      THE DOCTOR: (nodding gravely and taking the package
                        and starting to open it) Thank you.

      EPIFANIA: I am sorry I took it.

      THE DOCTOR: That is quite all right.

      EPIFANIA: (then as everything seems to have come to
                        a standstill) Don't you want to know why
                        I took it?

      THE DOCTOR: I am not curious.

      EPIFANIA: I wanted to see what you looked like with-
                        out it...It is always better to see a man
                        once without his hat.

      THE DOCTOR: (completing the unwrapping and finding a
                        carnation in the hat) It is called a...
                        thank you. (this last as he picks up the
                        carnation and puts it in a carafe of
                        water. Now putting the hat on his head)
                        It is called a tarboosh.

      EPIFANIA: (her eyes twinkling) I beg your pardon...
                        I mean it's always better to see a man at
                        least once...without his tarboosh.

She reaches up and changes the tarboosh's angle.

```
          THE DOCTOR:    (putting it back the way it was) You have
                         seen me...your curiosity is satisfied.

          EPIFANIA:      My curiosity is not in the least satisfied.

          THE DOCTOR:    (ignoring this)  I work at night in the
                         hospital...You will forgive me if I go
                         now to have my supper.
```

He picks up his bag and moves to the light switch.

```
          EPIFANIA:      (trying to stall for time)  Where do you
                         eat?

          THE DOCTOR:    (switching out the light)  At the Inn.

          EPIFANIA:      Where we met?  How delightful...Do let me
                         drop you off there.

          THE DOCTOR:    Be careful of the chairs.
```

205.   EXTERIOR OF THE CLINIC - EPIFANIA AND THE DOCTOR COME
       OUT.

```
          THE DOCTOR:    (locking the door and bowing) Good night.

          EPIFANIA:      Aren't you going to let me drop you off?

          THE DOCTOR:    As a former street Arab, I doubt that a
                         short walk will hurt me.  (then starting
                         away)  Good night.
```

Epifania watches him walk out of the shot, then the CAMERA
pans to her open Rolls Royce. The Chauffeur comes to with
a start and gets his motor going. Epifania gets in beside
him.

206.   TRUCKING SHOT BEHIND THE DOCTOR...POINT OF VIEW FROM
       THE ROAD.
We get nearer and nearer to him. Now he looks around.

207.   AUTOMOBILE SHOT AHEAD OF EPIFANIA'S ROLLS ROYCE.
It is moving toward the kerb. As it includes the Doctor in
the shot,

```
          EPIFANIA:      I am sorry that I said that...You know,
                         about the street Arab?

          THE DOCTOR:    The incident is entirely forgotten.

          EPIFANIA:      Thank you.
```

The car pulls out of the shot and the CAMERA stays on the
Doctor, who does a slight double take as the car comes back
into the shot.

```
          EPIFANIA:      I am sorry I called you a pig, too.

          THE DOCTOR:    The entire incident...is entirely
                         forgotten.

          EPIFANIA:      And a Communist.

          THE DOCTOR:    ENTIRELY.

          EPIFANIA:      Oh.
```

The Doctor strides around the corner. The Rolls Royce follows. The CAMERA pans him down the street.
                                              DISSOLVE

208.   THE DOCTOR - AT ONE END OF A LONG TABLE IN THE CLOVEN
       HOOF
He wears his tarboosh and his spectacles to read an Arabic
newspaper propped up in front of him against a polished wood-
en box ten inches square and six inches high. He has just

209. EPIFANIA - AT THE OTHER END OF THE LONG TABLE
She has just finished her main dish also.

    EPIFANIA: (apparently to her plate) Well, it is a
                        public place, you know.

210. THE DOCTOR - AT THE OTHER END OF THE TABLE

    THE DOCTOR: (after looking all around) Excuse me,
                        were you speaking to me?

211. EPIFANIA - AT THE OTHER END OF THE TABLE

    EPIFANIA: (looking at him balefully) No, no, I was
                        talking to myself...a strange habit I
                        have...

212. THE DOCTOR - AT HIS END OF THE TABLE

    THE DOCTOR: I beg your pardon?

213. EPIFANIA - AT HER END OF THE TABLE

    EPIFANIA: (fast becoming hysterical) Oh, you don't
                        have to...you don't have to do anything...
                        just sit there and...

Suddenly she takes a deep breath, rises and screams. At the
climax she shakes her head and stamps her feet. At the end
she leans breathlessly against the table.

214. THE DOCTOR - AT HIS END OF THE TABLE
Without looking up, he moistens his finger, turns the page of
his newspaper and speaks placidly.

    THE DOCTOR: Feeling better?

215. EPIFANIA   AT HER END OF THE TABLE

    EPIFANIA: Oh, you...you...you...

Now she bursts into tears, throws herself into her chair,
buries her face in her arms and sobs.

216. THE DOCTOR - AT HIS END OF THE TABLE
He wets his finger again, he turns the page without looking
up, then reads with interest a small paragraph before remarking

    THE DOCTOR: Tears are good for the complexion.

217. EPIFANIA - AT HER END OF THE TABLE

    EPIFANIA: (lifting her face out of her arms) Oh,
                        you...you...you...I don't know what to
                        call you...(she gets to her feet and the
                        CAMERA takes her to his end of the table,
                        where she looks at him for a moment be-
                        fore starting humbly and ending in tears
                        again) Listen to me: You're having an
                        adventure! Don't you know what that
                        means? (she snuffles loudly) Have you
                        no romance in you? No music in your
                        soul? Don't you want to know why I threw
                        that beast downstairs? Haven't you even
                        common...curiosity?

    THE DOCTOR: (looking up gravely) You said your name
                        was Epifania, I believe! Is this any way
                        for a lady to behave...with the wonderful
                        first name of Epifania? What means
                        "Epifania"? The appearance of some divine
                        or superhman being...from the Greek
                        "Epifania"...

                              (now he points to her scornfully) Is this
                              divine? Is this superhuman?

He hands her his handkerchief.

        EPIFANIA: (taking it and using it instantly) No!
                              It's just...it's just plain human, thats
                              all...something you don't know anything
                              about. (then after another snuffle) Why
                              don't you throw away that...that...ter-
                              rible looking newspaper...and at least
                              have a cup of coffee...just for once...
                              with an interesting and attractive woman?

        THE DOCTOR: Women are neither interesting nor attrac-
                              tiveto me except when they are ill. I
                              know too much about them, inside and out.
                              You know,..and I know...that you know that
                              I know...that you are perfectly well.

        EPIFANIA: Liar! No woman is ever perfectly well...
                              nor ever has been...nor ever will be.

        THE DOCTOR: Fortunately for my profession. You must
                              have brains of a sort.

        EPIFANIA: (snuffling through her tears) Then you
                              are going to have a cup of coffee with me.

        THE DOCTOR: (after a pause) And a pipe...of peace.

He opens the square box in front of him as Epifania rises and
goes in and out of the shot while removing the dirty dishes,
taking the crumbs off the table and making everything neat in
a most feminine manner. During this time the Doctor removes
a hookah from the box, cleans out its bowl, blows through the
hose, inserts the mouthpiece, checks the amount of rose water
in the bowl and starts loading it from a tobacco container inside the box.

        EPIFANIA: (at some point of the proceedings, bring-
                              ing her coffee cup from the other end of
                              the table) That is your pipe?

        THE DOCTOR: Naturally...what else?

        EPIFANIA: (sitting down and starting to pour the
                              coffee) I used to fill my father's pipe.

        THE DOCTOR: (looking up in surprise) He smoked the
                              hookah?

        EPIFANIA: Oh, no, the Meerschaum.

        THE DOCTOR: This is the most practical pipe...The
                              smoke pulled through the rose water is
                              cooled, and freed of tars...It does not
                              scatter sparks...and being difficult to
                              carry in the pocket...it encourages mod-
                              eration...and never sets fire to your suit.

        EPIFANIA: (laughing for the first time and picking
                              up the coffee pot) How do you like your
                              coffee?

        THE DOCTOR: (working on his pipe) Any way at all...
                              nothing can help English coffee.

        EPIFANIA: I will give you two lumps of sugar to
                              sweeten your disposition...When do you

THE DOCTOR:	Now.
EPIFANIA:	(all woman) May I do it for you?
THE DOCTOR:	(as if writing in his notebook) Dangerously seductive at will...no conscience.
EPIFANIA:	(vaguely, busy with the hookah) What did you say?
THE DOCTOR:	Forgive me...I was writing out loud...(then exhaling a delicious cloud of smoke) You do all these things very well...are you married?
EPIFANIA:	Yes. But you need not be afraid. My husband is openly unfaithful to me and cannot take you into court if you make love to me ...I can divorce him if necessary.
THE DOCTOR:	(after a long exhalation) Then the beast you defended yourself against so valiantly ...the gentleman I had to wire back together again...this is not your husband?
EPIFANIA:	Certainly not....Just a fool who insulted my father's memory because his dinner was a bit off. When I think of my father, all ordinary men seem to me the merest trash. You are not an ordinary man...I should like to see more of you. Now that you have asked me confidential questions about my family, and I have answered them, you can no longer pretend that you are not my family doctor. So that is settled.
THE DOCTOR:	I see...Father fixation...reckless audacity...insane egotism...apparently sexless.
EPIFANIA:	Sexless? What completely idiotic series of false impressions could possibly lead you to the totally erroneous deduction... that I am sexless?
THE DOCTOR:	You talk to me as if you were a man... There is no mystery, no separateness, no sacredness about men to you. A man to you is only the male of your species.
EPIFANIA:	(gently) There are males and males! Five minutes with my husband would convince you that he and I do not belong to the same species. But there are some great men... like my father...and some great doctors... like you.
THE DOCTOR:	(amused) I do not know how you have arrived at this delightful...and flattering ...conclusion...but I thank you. What does your regular doctor say about you?
EPIFANIA:	I have no regular doctor. If I had, I should have had an operation a week until there was nothing left of me...or my bank balance. I shall not expect you to maul me about with a stethoscope, if that is what you are afraid of. I have the lungs of a whale and the digestion of an ostrich. I have a clockwork inside. I sleep eight hours like a log. (then

leaning a little closer and speaking
softly) Whenever I want anything I lose
my head so completely about it...I always
get it.

THE DOCTOR: (recoiling slightly) I see...What things
do you want mostly?

EPIFANIA: (moving her chair a little closer) Everything...anything...like a lightning flash!
Then there is no stopping me!

THE DOCTOR: (slightly hypnotized) Everything and anything...is nothing.

EPIFANIA: (purring) Five minutes ago I wanted you
...Now I have got you.

THE DOCTOR: (shaking his head imperceptibly) Come.
You cannot bluff your doctor. You may
want the sun and the moon,..and the stars
...but you cannot get them.

EPIFANIA: (nose to nose with him) That is why I take
good care not to want them. I want only
what I can get.

THE DOCTOR: (not moving but after a long pause)
Intellect: practical...Determination:
dynamic...Morality: zero...Vulgarity: one
hundred...plus. (Epifania turns away
slowly and the Doctor starts packing up
his hookah) What a pity this elemental
force should be wasted on nothingness.

EPIFANIA: There seems to be nothing I can get...
except more money.

THE DOCTOR: And I can never get any...However, I do
not care for it...I care only for
knowledge.

EPIFANIA: (hopefully) Knowledge is no use without
money.

THE DOCTOR: (gently) You may be right...(then
directly to Epifania) What about more
men? You can always get more men.

EPIFANIA: (wearily) More Alastairs? More Adrians?
These are not deep wants. (then turning
slowly and speaking with complete honesty)
Are you married?

THE DOCTOR: (dropping the bowl of the hookah and
catching it just in time) I am married
to science...One wife is enough for me...
though by my religion I am allowed four.

EPIFANIA: (startled) Just for you?

THE DOCTOR: I am a Mahometan, Madam.

EPIFANIA: (momentarily taken aback) Oh...Well...
You will have to be content with two if
you marry me.

THE DOCTOR: (glued to his seat) Is there any question
of that between us?

335

EPIFANIA: (quietly) Yes, I am going to marry you.

THE DOCTOR: (leaping to his feet and picking up his hookah box) Nothing doing, Lady. Science is my bride .

EPIFANIA: (getting to her feet also and crossing to him) You can have her as well... There is only one condition: I made a solemn promise to my father on his deathbed...

THE DOCTOR: (interrupting hastily) Stop! I had better tell you that I made a solemn promise to my mother on her deathbed...

EPIFANIA: (thunderstruck) You what!

THE DOCTOR: (talking fast) My mother was a very wise woman. She made me swear that if any woman wanted to marry me... I would hand that woman two hundred piastres and tell her that unless she would go out into the world with . . nothing but that...and the clothes she stood in...and earn her living alone and unaided for six months...I would never speak to her again.

EPIFANIA: (her eyes narrowed) And if she stood the test?

THE DOCTOR: (looking to the sky) Then, God help me, I must marry her if whe were the ugliest female that ever poisoned a harem!

EPIFANIA: (indignantly) And you dare ask me... to submit myself to a test...

THE DOCTOR: (retreating gently) I have not asked you anything, Madam! The idea was yours...I swore to my mother...and Allah has willed that I have a mother fixation...I cannot help myself.

EPIFANIA: (scornfully) And where die she acquire her wisdom...this great mother of yours?

THE DOCTOR: (simply) On the banks of the Nile... she was a washerwoman...a widow! She brought up eleven children. I was the youngest, the Benjamin. The other ten are honest working folk. With their help, she made me a man of learning... It was her ambition to have a son who could read and write. She prayed to Allah...and he endowed me with the necessary talent.

He smiles placidly like a man who has just won a game of chess.

EPIFANIA: You think I will allow myself to be beaten by an old washerwoman?

THE DOCTOR: (beaming) I am afraid so.

EPIFANIA: (sneering) In...deed! Any my father's test...for a husband worthy of me?

THE DOCTOR: Oh...the husband is to be tested too! As an Oriental this had not occurred to me.

EPIFANIA: Nor to your mother either, it seems!... Well, it occurred to my father: I am to give you a hundred and fifty pounds. In six months you are to increase it to fifty thousand. How is that for a test?

THE DOCTOR: I would say: conclusive...In six months I would not have a penny of it left... praise be to Allah.

EPIFANIA: You confess yourself beaten?

THE DOCTOR: Absolutely and completely.

EPIFANIA: And you think I am beaten too.

THE DOCTOR: Hopelessly...and beyond question! You do not know what homeless poverty is... and Allah the Compassionate will take care that you never learn.

EPIFANIA: (with the excitement of one going into battle) You are very much mistaken! I will take the poorest room in this Inn tonight... and starting in these clothes...which I may exchange for something more practical...live solely on what I can earn for six months! Now, how much is two hundred piastres?

THE DOCTOR: (depressed) At the rate of exchange contemplated by my mother...about thirty-five shillings.

EPIFANIA: (putting out her hand) Hand it over.

THE DOCTOR: Unfortunately, my mother forgot to provide for this contingency...I have not got thirty-five shillings...

EPIFANIA: Neither have I! We will borrow from my Chauffeur...He will give you a hundred and fifty pounds...and me, thirty-five shillings! (She extends a manly hand) Good-bye for six months!

THE DOCTOR: (making a final plea for good sense) Surely we are not accepting seriously... conditions laid down in extremis by two moribund juveniles...the one, a dear ignorant washerwoman, the other, apparently, a superannuated adolescent....

EPIFANIA: (furiously) What's that you say?

At this instant, we hear a yell and the pounding of bare feet, preceding the arrival of an Arab boy of eleven who bounds into the room and screams at the Doctor in a voice even higher than normal. With screechings and yammerings and oriental explosions of grief and horror the boy details, in Arabic, the predicament of his baby brother. Also, in Arabic, the Doctor interpolates a few questions, then rises and picks up his bag.

THE DOCTOR: (quietly to Epifania) His baby brother has swallowed a pin...they have taken him to the hospital...I will have to go immediately.

EPIFANIA: How far is it?

THE DOCTOR: About two miles.

EPIFANIA: My car would get you there in two minutes...automobiles are sometimes useful.

THE DOCTOR: The logic of Allah is all on your side.
Thank you.

He says something to the child in Arabic and they hurry
out. Epifania watches them go and crosses slowly to the
window and looks down.

218. HIGH CAMERA SHOT
Epifania's Rolls Royce. The Chauffeur, the Doctor, the Arab
child hurry into it.

219. THE BACK SEAT
The Doctor and the Arab child complete the action of sitting down. We hear the Chauffeur starting the motor and
gunning it a couple of times.

THE DOCTOR: (after feeling the upholstery, semi-
consciously to Heaven) There is no
might and no majesty save in Thee, O
Allah; but O! Most Great and Glorious,
is this another of Thy terrible jokes?

The car starts roughly. As it moves away, CAMERA appears
to pan up in one continuous shot from the Doctor to the
second floor exterior of the Inn. Here, looking down past
us and smiling the smile of the Mona Lisa, we see Epifania.

FADE OUT

FADE IN

220. A SIGN OF SCREEN DIMENSIONS
It is attached to the outside of a dilapidated building and
reads - "Girls wanted...No Previous Experience Necessary".
The N's are all printed backwards.

221. EPIFANIA IN HER FOLLS ROYCE.
She is wearing an ancient waterproof, a beaten-up man's hat
and heavy soled shoes. She has a humble handbag.

EPIFANIA: This one will do as well as any...drive
down the street a little.

THE CHAUFFEUR: Very good, Madam.

The CAMERA pans with the car. As it comes to a stop

CLOSE SHOT - EPIFANIA'S ROLLS ROYCE
She gets out, removes a handkerchief and lipstick from her
bag and turns it upside down and shakes it for the benefit
of her Chauffeur.

EPIFANIA: You see? Nothing!

THE CHAUFFEUR: (dismally) Yes, Madam...but if I might
be permitted a word of....

EPIFANIA: (not unkindly) You may not. Now give me
the thirty-five shillings.

THE CHAUFFEUR: (grumpily) Very good, Madam. (from a
side pocket, he takes an envelope with
the proper amount arranged in advance.
She holds out her bag and he pours the
money, all in silver, into it) I broke
it up small.

EPIFANIA: Good. (now she extends her hand) Goodbye, Charles. I'll see you in six
months.

THE CHAUFFEUR: (dismally) I hope so, Madam..I do hope
so. (then as Epifania walks out of the
shot) Blast!

222. A BASEMENT IN COMMERCIAL ROAD

The street and including the stairs leading down to it
is partitioned off from the workroom by a seven foot
partition which allows some air to get to the back. The
front with which we are concerned at the moment, contains a
stove, a boiler, a steam press, an old fashioned letter press
a long table for the reception of merchandise, a high
bookkeepers desk and stool, a bench, a railing, and a
partitioned office where new employees are interviewed.
The walls are sad with gas and electric meters, fuse boxes,
faded regulations and some chromos of long dead monarchs.
The ceiling is a maze of pipes connected with the workshops
above. There is a good deal of noise from the sewing
machines in the back room, the escapting steam from the
press and the thump as it comes together. An old woman is
pressing coats. An old man working on the books. There
are piles of coats on the long table. Waiting to get
in to the little office, there is a queue of nine females.
They are wretchedly dressed cockney girls. Some of them
turn and look up as Epifania comes down the stairs. Their
expressions harden as she walks innocently toward the head
of the queue. They give tongue as she reaches her
objective.

          OMNES   'ere 'ere Duchess... would you mind
                           stepping back to the tail end, your
                           majesty? Just like everybody else...
                           or would that be too much to arsk...
                           your 'ighness.

          EPIFANIA: Oh.

Considerably put out, she goes to the end of the line and
looks around fretfully.

223. THE DOOR TO THE PRIVATE OFFICE

It opens and a thin mean man of sixty sticks his head out.

          THE MAN WITH THE DEAD EYES: Next...(then to the
                           Queue as the first girl goes past him)
                           Alls we need 'll be two more... so it's
                           no good to the rest of you cluttering
                           up the shop to 'ole blinin day.
                           (he bangs his door shut and there is
                           an instantaneous groan from the queue
                           followed by disappointed remarks made
                           sotto-voice).

224. CLOSE SHOT - EPIFANIA

She thinks hard for a second, then plunges her hand into
her bag and starts removing the larger coins from her pile
of silver.

225. THE QUEUE, JUST MISSING EPIFANIA

We hear a bag fall and the tinkle of silver on the stone
floor. The whole queue turns greedily.

          EPIFANIA: (looking around in distress). Oh I
                           sy .. I dropped me bag... me cash is
                           everywhere... wot a clumsy!

She picks up her bag. The members of the queue dart between
her and the CAMERA as they descend upon sixpences. While
they are doing this Epifania moves slowly along the railing
to a position just outside the owner's door. Just as she
arrives the door is opened, the owner appears and says:

          THE OWNER: Next.

Epifania steps inside and the door starts to close.

339

226. THE MEMBERS OF THE QUEUE IN VARIOUS ATTITUDES REQUIRED
FOR THE PICKING UP OF COINS

OMNES: 'ere...I say... of all the bloody
              brass... 'old on.

We hear the door bang.

DISSOLVE

227. EPIFANIA AND THE MAN WITH THE DEAD EYES
They are in the partitioned-off office which is an
unattractive as one would expect it to be. We find
Epifania in the middle of a "selling campaign", done in
her very best Cockney.

EPIFANIA: ...and I'm positive I could be of the
              greatest 'c p to you...I knows all about
              barter...and buying and selling...and
              the laws of supply and demand...and
              prevailing trends...and economics...
              and besides that...

THE MAN: (interrupting coldly) Stow it! Wot's
              yer name?

EPIFANIA: Oh...uh...Smith...Mary Smith

THE MAN: You sew?

EPIFANIA: (archly) Wot I sy is: A woman that
              don't sew...'ardly deserves the nime
              of woman.

THE MAN: (unimpressed) Wot machine?

EPIFANIA: What? Oh! The sewing machine.

THE MAN: Well, what did you think I was talkin'
              about...a sausage machine? (then
              consulting a paper in front of him)
              A record?

EPIFANIA: (brightly) Oh, yes! Certainly.

THE MAN: (coldly) Intemperance? Boosting...
              Soliciting?

EPIFANIA: (eagerly) Oh, certainly...all three..
              I can do anything...I put my mind to.

THE MAN: Well...we're a bit fussy 'oo we 'ire...
              a shilling an hour...take it or leave
              it.

EPIFANIA: (stupefied) A shilling an hour...

THE MAN: (viciously) You 'eard me.

EPIFANIA: (hastily) Oh I wasn't complaining...
              I thought maybe you were paying too
              much...

THE MAN: (savagely) You keep a civil tongue
              in your 'ead, Miss... or you'll be
              back on the street finding out wot
              some people pays the likes of them
              without no character.

340

EPIFANIA: (rising and soaping her hands) Oh yes, Sir...thank you, Sir.

THE MAN: (pointing to the door behind him) Right through there. (He watches her go and opens the other door and calls out) Next... and last!

DISSOLVE

228. EPIFANIA AT AN OLD POWER SEWING MACHINE
She has two halves of a coat on the table. She watches the girl to her left to see how she handles them, copies her, then raises her eyebrows inquiringly.

229. THE GIRL TO EPIFANIA'S LEFT
She nods "yes" then sews a seam at full speed. Now she looks at Epifania. She lowers the foot over the two thicknesses of cloth, grits her teeth, sets her jaw, then with a terrible expression on her face tries to find the pedal on the floor. Nothing happens.

230. EPIFANIA'S FOOT UNDER THE MACHINE
The foot switch has been knocked over on its side, so that although Epifania's foot finds it, and presses on it, nothing happens.

231. EPIFANIA AT THE MACHINE
She looks rather desparate.

232. THE GIRL AT EPIFANIA'S RIGHT
She laughs and crosses to Epifania's machine, reaches under it, puts the switch upright, then motions to Epifania to go ahead. Gritting her teeth, Epifania jams the switch down to the floor (possible out of this), and the two halves of the coat shoot out from under her hands and hang over the edge of the machine, firmly sewn on the diagonal. The girl who was on Epifania's right claps her hand over her mouth, restores the pieces of goods to the top of the machine and shows Epifania how to pick the stitches out.

DISSOLVE.

233. VERY SHORT MUSICAL MONTAGE
To a piece constructed like the Anvil Chorus we cut to the girl to Epifania's left. She zips through a seam and looks to her right.

234. THE GIRL TO EPIFANIA'S RIGHT
She zips through a seam and looks to her left!

235. EPIFANIA
To a tremendous retard in the music she now slowly and wobbily sews the seam. At least having sewn it, she smiles faintly at the end.

236. THE GIRL ON EPIFANIA'S LEFT
To the accompaniment of fast music she zips through a seam.

237. THE GIRL ON EPIFANIA'S RIGHT
To fast accompaniment of fast music she zips through a seam.

238. EPIFANIA:
Taking a deep breath and to slow music that speeds up a little she wobbles through the seam.

239. THE GIRL ON EPIFANIA'S LEFT
Ditto...ditto...ditto...

240. EPIFANIA
With an excited smile she ploughs through a little
faster than before.

241. THE GIRL ON EPIFANIA'S LEFT
Ditto...ditto...ditto...

242. THE GIRL ON EPIFANIA'S RIGHT
Ditto...ditto...ditto.

243. EPIFANIA
With an excited smile she ploughs through a little
faster than before.

244. THE GIRL ON EPIFANIA'S LEFT
Ditto...ditto...ditto...

245. EPIFANIA
She does it almost in tempo.

246. THE GIRL ON EPIFANIA'S LEFT
Ditto...ditto...ditto...

247. EPIFANIA
Breathlessly she does it.   She beams to the girl on
her left.

248. THE GIRL ON EPIFANIA'S LEFT
Ditto...ditto...ditto...

249. THE GIRL ON EPIFANIA'S RIGHT
Ditto...ditto...ditto.

250. EPIFANIA
Still excitedly she does it again.   Then beams to the
girl on her right.

251. GIRL ON EPIFANIA'S RIGHT
Ditto...ditto...ditto

252. EPIFANIA
Ditto...ditto...ditto.

253. THE DOOR OF THE WORKROOM
The Man With The Dead Eyes who hired Epifania comes
through quietly, closes the door after him and starts
down the aisle between the machines. His beady little
eyes are darting from side to side.

254. TRUCKING SHOT DOWN THE WHOLE LENGTH OF MACHIND
To the rhythmic music of the girls fly through the
sewing. By the time we come to Epifania she is
whistling a little tune with a very superior expression
on her face...and apparently doing exactly as well as
the others.

255. LOW CAMERA SHOT - THE MAN WITH THE DEAD EYES
He has just come to a stop in front of Epifania.
Suddenly he does a slight double-take.

It has about two inches of thread left on it. These
are instantly exhausted.

256. LOW CAMERA SHOT - THE MAN WITH THE DEAD EYES
He stares down at Epifania with a warmth of a
basilisk.

257. HIGH CAMERA SHOT ON EPIFANIA
Unconscious of the fact that her thread is done she
continues to sew proudly. She smiles with extra satis-
faction after the third seam.

258. LOW CAMERA SHOT - THE MAN
He imitates her smile with all the sweetness of a crock
of vinegar.

259. EPIFANIA
She sews another seam in a very business-like manner.
Then, apparently at a word from the Man looks up
inquiringly, her eyebrows arched prettily.

260. THE MAN PAST EPIFANIA
He picks up her last six efforts, one after another,
and peels them apart. After the first three

261. EPIFANIA
Her face is full of horror as the last three are peeled
in the lower foreground of the picture. Now she dives
into her machine in a desparate effort to thread it,
but as she had never done this before and she is trying
to do it in a very expert manner, the results are
disastrous. She puts a new spool of thread on the top
and threads it through every visible hole so that the
machine ends up looking like a cat's cradle.

262. THE GIRL TO EPIFANIA'S LEFT
She steals a look at Epifania, then shields her eyes in
pain.

263. LOW CAMERA SHOT - THE MAN
He watches Epifania impassively.

264. EPIFANIA
Scooping the sweat off her brow, she now has a go at the
bobbin under the machine. Getting this to jump out
with great difficulty she finds a place on the right
that will hold it. Then desparately she sneaks a look
at the girl on her left.

265. THE GIRL ON EPIFANIA'S LEFT FROM EPIFANIA'S POINT OF VIEW
In fear and trembling of the boss she pantomimes that you
unscrew the disk in the center of the flywheel.

266. EPIFANIA
Full of confidence again she unscrews the disk in the
center of her flywheel until the flywheel comes off.
She now puts the bobbin where the flywheel has been
(this may require a special shaft) then taking a
desparate chance, puts her foot on the starting switch.
Something visually terrible happens to the machine: I
hope it breaks in two but this might be too much to
ask.

267. LOW CAMERA SHOT - THE MAN
He looks almost pleased at her misery. With the
tiniest movement of the foreginger he motions to her
to come with him and with the small jerk of his thumb
he indicates that her objective will be outside.

268. EPIFANIA
In pantomime she indicates: "You mean, me?" Then
slowly rises and reaches for her hat and bag on a hook
behind her.

                                                  DISSOLVE

269. THE STAIRS LEADING DOWN TO THE BASEMENT SHOP
Epifania, wearing her hat and coat, climbs up to us,
somewhat disconsolately. Reaching the sidewalk she leans
against the building and looks around dully, dejected
at her failure. Suddenly her eye catches something
and her expression hardens and becomes more alert.

270. A DILAPIDATED MOTOR VAN
From the back of this, a middle-aged character,
moustachioed and obviously not a tee-totaller, is
lifting a tied bundle of the component parts of the
coats that are manufactured in the shop below. The
CAMERA goes with him as he staggers across the sidewalk, and it stays on Epifania as he plunges down the
stairs. He reappears an instant later with two huge
bundles of finished coats, and the CAMERA goes with
him as he crosses to the van and throws them inside,
then scoops the sweat off his forehead.

271. EPIFANIA - LEANING AGAINST THE BUILDING

        EPIFANIA: 'ey...'andsome!...

272. TIM - BEHIND THE MOTOR VAN

        TIM: (pointing to himself with a
                      huge thumb)   'oo, me?

He gives his moustachos a twirl.

273. EPIFANIA - LEANING AGAINST THE BUILDING

        EPIFANIA: (seductively) Come 'ere.

Preceded by his shadow, Tim lumbers into the shot.

        TIM: Wot's on yer mind, Ducky?

        EPIFANIA: (in her best Cockney) You
                      wouldn't know of another shop
                      like this one, would you...where
                      a gel could find work?

        TIM: There's 'undreds of 'em Ducky...
                      and glad to get girls...for what
                      they py... What's the matter, you
                      get the sack?

        EPIFANIA: Us.

        TIM: 'op in...I'll take you to my next
                      one...and if you don't 'ave no
                      luck there...why we'll go on to the
                      next one...and if you don't have no
                      luck there neither...there's still
                      plenty more...

        EPIFANIA: (stunned) You mean this is a
                      regular...organized business?.. I
                      thought it was just this one...

        TIM: (interrupting her) Sweating is a
                      big business, Luv...'ighly organized..
                      come on. (then as they cross to the
                      van) What'd you sy your nime was?

        EPIFANIA: I didn't, but it's smith...just
                      plain Mary Smith

        TIM: (pushing her up in to the van)
                      Not so plain, Ducky...
                      (he gives her a little double
                      pat on the seat) Not so plain.

                                          DISSOLVE

274. TIM AND EPIFANIA - IN THE FRONT SEAT OF THE MOVING VAN

EPIFANIA:	(frowning) 'ow many coats did you sy there was in each bundle?
TIM:	(sourly) 'undred and forty-four
EPIFANIA:	And 'ow many pick-ups?
TIM:	an 'undred.
EPIFANIA:	(instantly) Why, that's fourteen thousand four hundred coats a dy.
TIM:	(blankly) Is it? No wonder I sleep so good.
EPIFANIA:	Even at a penny profit, that's sixty pounds a dy! At sixpence it's three hundred and sixty... and at a shilling, which is probably the least, they're miking... it's seven twenty... and mind you... Working five days...
TIM:	They works six.
EPIFANIA:	...that's four thousand, three hundred and twenty pounds a week! Scmebody's mikin' a bloody fcrtune out of these lousy coats.
TIM:	(grinding the van to a stop) And ain't sharin' it with nobody neither! 'ere we are, Luv,... go in and try for your job while I mikes me pick-up.
EPIFANIA:	(shaking her head) I've got a better idea.
TIM:	Wot?
EPIFANIA:	Let's go 'ave a drink instead... on me.
TIM:	(delighted) Well bless yer blinkin' little 'eart! Let us do that.

He puts the car in gear and off they go.

DISSOLV

275. TIM AND EPIFANIA - AT A TABLE IN A PUB
By his appearance, Tim must have had several already.
Epifania leans foward, eagerly, her beer untouched.

EPIFANIA:	(eagerly) But where do you take them, now they're finished...and where do you get the parts you deliver in the first place?
TIM:	(cunningly) Nah, nah, nah, that's tellin' Luv... Besides, I don't know myself...All I does is put out...pick up...put out...pick up... all the blinkin' dy... then turn it all over to 'im...like a ruddy bird dog!
EPIFANIA:	To 'oom? Wot's 'is nime?

345

TIM: (laying a finger beside his
         nose) In the first place...I
         don't know it...and in the second
         'e gimme strict hinstructions
         never even to breathe it...to a
         soul.

EPIFANIA: (leaning closer) 'oo did?

TIM: (very confidentially) Mr.
         Superflew.

EPIFANIA: (without pause) Well 'e's
         right.- after all...suppose
         some stringer was to get a 'old
         of all them nimes and street
         numbers...then found out where
         all this junk went to...and
         come in the first plice...then
         what?

TIM: Blimey!

EPIFANIA: (waving to the barmaid and
         pointing to Tim) You never
         tried to follow 'im did you, this
         Mr. Whatever 'is name is?

TIM: (in horror) 'oo me? And bump
         into 'im? And lose me ruddy job?
         Alls I know is 'e brings me the
         van in the morning...and I brings
         it back to 'im...at night!

EPIFANIA: Where?

TIM: (tossing off his last beer and
         rising unsteadily) Nah, nah,
         nah, And speaking' of jobs...

He bumps into another table.

EPIFANIA: (rising hurriedly and tossing
         some coins on the table) 'ere,
         I'll 'elp you.

As they start out of the pub.

               DISSOLVE

276. SIDEWALK OUTSIDE THE PUB
   Epifania and Tim come out and pause.

EPIFANIA: (propping him up) Now where's yer
         next stop?

TIM: (mysteriously removing a worn
         paper from his pocket and
         consulting it through broken
         glasses) Not supposed to show
         this to nobody...very serious...
         Now would this be 642 Poultry in
         the back...or 552 Putney... in
         the front... I'll feel all right
         in a minute...its me eyes.

EPIFANIA: (taking the list from him and
         steering him toward the van)
         Come on, now... upsy daisy...
         in we go.

After some refined acrobatics concerned with getting Tim's
rubber legs in the van and keeping them there, Epifania goes
around it.

277. FRONT SEAT OF THE VAN - TIM IS ALREADY ASLEEP
Epifania climbs in beside him, takes a brief look at him,
one of the list, and starts the motor and drives off in a
business-like way.

                                                    DISSOLVE

278. SHOT FOLLOWING THE VAN DOWN THE STREET
It comes to a stop and Epifaria comes around from the front,
whistling gaily. She checks the list she has just stolen
from Tim, picks out a big package of coat parts and walks
out of the shot with him. She returns in a moment with finished goods, chucks them inside, then goes around the van.
The van pulls away from us and disappears down the street.

279. THE VAN GOING DOWN THE STREET LEFT TO RIGHT

280. THE VAN GOING DOWN THE STREET RIGHT TO LEFT

281. THE VAN COMING TOWARD US AND GOING PAST US

282. THE VAN PULLING AWAY FROM US AND GOING AROUND THE
     CORNER
                                                    DISSOLVE

283. THE VAN COMING TOWARD US - NIGHT
It comes to a stop.

284. EPIFANIA AND TIM GOODENOUGH IN THE FRONT SEAT - NIGHT
They are lit by the reflected lights of the vehicles grinding past. Tim is snoring melodiously. Epifania looks at
him, then consults two lists: Tim's old one and a new one
she has made. She makes one correction on this with pencil, then folds it carefully and puts it in an inside
pocket, then holding the other one, nudges Tim awake.

TIM: (coming to) Huh? What? Oh...Just a
                pline gin, thank you, with a little
                beer on the side.

EPIFANIA: Wake up.

TIM: Huh? What? Who are you? Oh!...
                'ello, Mary, beg your pardon.

EPIFANIA: (pointing to the list) I just finished
                the last one...what do we do now?

TIM: (snatching his list away and putting it
                carefully in his pocket) 'ere! Where'd
                you get that?

EPIFANIA: How could I help you without it...it's
                all done...Where shall I drive you now?

TIM: (alarmed) Nah, nah, nah...No place,
                Ducky...This is where you get off: the
                big deal...where I meet the big wheel.

EPIFANIA: (innocently) Oh, and where is that?

TIM: (leaning over and opening the door for
                her) Nah, nah, nah...goodbye, Mary
                Smith...I 'ope I run into you again some
                time.

EPIFANIA: (getting to the ground) Maybe sooner
                than you think...goodbye...drive
                carefully.

TIM: Never a fear...with beer...my dear...
                       it clears the head instead.

He clears his throat prodigiously, grinds his gears murder-
ously, and the van leaps ahead. As the rear of the van
passes us, Epifania swings gracefully aboard. The van disappears down the street.

                                              DISSOLVE

285. THE VAN APPROACHING US IN A DARK STREET
As it squeaks to a stop a man in a black coat steps into the
foreground of the shot, his back to us.

286. EPIFANIA SITTING BETWEEN PILES OF FINISHED COATS

        MR. SUPERFLEW'S VOICE: (also cockney) Everything ac-
                       cording to 'oyle, Tim?

        TIM'S VOICE: (changing in sound as he moves from the
                       van to the street) Never better,
                       Guv'nor.

        SUPERFLEW'S VOICE: (as the van shakes with his weight
                       and his voice changes location) 'aven't
                       been drinkin' 'ave you? I mean more
                       than usual?

        TIM'S VOICE: 'oo me? Far from it, Guv'nor...far
                       from it.

        SUPERFLEW'S VOICE: (as the gears grind) Well, watch
                       it, Tim...watch it... I should 'ate to
                       'ave to replace you... See you in the
                       mornin'.

Epifania leans back as the van pulls away and the CAMERA
pans to Tim waving in the street.

        TIM: (indignantly) 'aven't been drinkin',
                       'ave you?...who the bloody 'ell does
                       he think 'e is?

                                              DISSOLVE

287. LOW CAMERA SHOT - EXTERIOR OF THE B.B. & B. WHOLESALE
      CLOTHING CO. LTD.
This is flanked by three Golden B's on each side. Under-
neath they read "Bigger & Better Bargains". We have seen
this sign partly in the reflected light of the van and to
the music of its ancient four cylinder engines.

288. HIGH CAMERA SHOT DOWN ON THE VAN
There is a high fencing or wall at the rear of the B.B.B.
Clothing Company, near its loading platform. Our van has
just come through the gate. A dark figure closes the gates,
then pulls the van near the loading platform.

289. THE VAN COMING TO A STOP
This shot is from three-quarters rear so that we see the
driver, a large heavy man in an overcoat, get down and come
to the rear of the van. Here he stops in astonishment, his
jaw hanging. We cut to what he sees.

290. EPIFANIA ON THE TAIL GATE OF THE VAN
A cigarette descends from her lips, she is smiling and
swinging her legs happily. She looks at the big man and
then removes her cigarette and speaks.

        EPIFANIA: Mr. Superflew, I hold up?

                                 348

MR. SUPERFLEW: (in horror) Who are you?

EPIFANIA: (after inhaling and exhaling some smoke
that she blows rather rudely in his
direction) I'm your partner! (she puts
the cigarette back in her mouth and
smiles)

                              FADEOUT

FADE IN

292. A POOR DOOR WITH A GROUND GLASS PANEL
On this is painted "Superflew & Smith". Under this the
word "Enterprises". To the sound of some irritated music
Mr. Superflew comes to the door, reacts unpleasantly to the
firm name and goes down the stairs.

293. TWO VANS IN THE STREET
One of them we saw driven by Tim Goodenough. The other one
is new to us. Epifania, minus her waterproof, is loading
one van from an overload in the other. As Superflew joins
her, she scoops the sweat off her forehead, hands him one
of the two lists she takes from a pocket, puts on her coat,
hops into the first van and drives away. Superflew looks
after her sourly and climbs into the second van.

                              DISSOLVE

294. A SLIGHTLY BETTER DOOR WITH MUCH FANCIER LETTERS
It bears the name of "Superflew and Smith...Distributors".
The door opens and Mr. Superflew comes out in a better hat
and suit than we saw him in the last time. As he starts
down the stairs:

295. EPIFANIA SUPERVISING THE LOADING OF FIVE VANS
These are being loaded by employees pushing those two-wheel
plus two-caster trucks that ride on no more than three
points at once. Seeing something wrong, Epifania hurries
over, straightens the matter out with large gestures.

296. MR. SUPERFLEW AT THE ENTRANCE OF THE BUILDING
He looks almost frightened.
                              DISSOLVE

297. A VERY ELEGANT OAK DOOR
On it a bronze plaque announces "Smith & Superflew - Brokers"

298. THE DOOR OF THE LIFT
It opens and Epifania steps out, still in very business-like
clothes, but in an outfit obviously more expensive and probably a different color. The CAMERA pans her over to the
beautiful office door. As she goes in,

299. INTERIOR OF THE OFFICE OF SMITH & SUPERFLEW
It is furnished as a modern London office for a business doing half a million pounds a year. A pretty secretary greets
her.

THE SECRETARY: B.B. & B. called, Miss Smith...They're
                 sorry their check is late.

EPIFANIA: (without pausing) I'll talk to them
                 later.

She goes through a door marked "Private".

300. MR. SUPERFLEW - IN HIS MAGNIFICENT NEW OFFICE
He is talking into the telephone.

SUPERFLEW: (just before hanging up) All right,
                 Barney...I'll do what I can...Oh, hello,
                 Mary...

EPIFANIA: (entering and seating herself on the edge of the desk) B.B. & B. are late with their check again.

SUPERFLEW: I know...I was just talking to Barney.. they've had bad luck...He's been ill and...

EPIFANIA: What do we need wholesalers for, anyway? Let's cut them out...or take them over.

SUPERFLEW: (horrified) What do we need them for! I've done business with them for twenty-five years, Mary! They gave us the credit to enlarge...They...they... Barney's been very ill...

EPIFANIA: Poor old Barney...But illness...accidents...wars and other disasters...are all part of the game, Morris! Called business!...March on! When you see something you want, you've got to grab it! You're too sentimental.

SUPERFLEW: (stupefied) Sentimental! Me? That's certainly the first time anyone ever called me...

EPIFANIA: (exciting) Send him some flowers.

He picks up a glass and a water pitcher...pours but misses the glass.

301. EXTERIOR OF A BUILDING
Some workmen are hoisting up a sign forty feet long, reading "Smith & Superflew...Jobbers and Wholesalers...Always a Better Buy", to replace the old sign reading "B.B. & B... Bigger and Better Bargains".

                                        DISSOLVE

302. EPIFANIA AND SUPERFLEW - IN A LONG LOFT
The shelves of merchandise converge in distant perspective lines. A few stockroom employees work in the background.

SUPERFLEW: What do you mean: Why just London?

EPIFANIA: (mildly) Well...England is small... living is cheaper in other cities. and in the country...we can get the same work for less...a lot less.

SUPERFLEW: But...but...

EPIFANIA: But what?...We'll bring it in from all over...Besides, the light is better... it's better for their eyes!

                                        DISSOLVE

303. INTERIOR OF THE NEW OFFICE - EPIFANIA AND SUPERFLEW

SUPERFLEW: (his forehead crisped) ...this Smith and Superflew...the Superflew coming after the Smith...

EPIFANIA: It bothers you?

SUPERFLEW: It just don't sound right, Mary...it. it...it..

EPIFANIA:	You're right...it doesn't sound right.. it's too long. What we need is something...pungent...easy to remember... some short one word title like...Oh, I don't know...then just think what freedom it would give you...to be the sleeping partner: you could go anywhere...do anything...overhear things.. catch people napping...and nobody would even notice you...or pay any attention to you...like a ghost!
SUPERFLEW:	(wishing he had let sleeping dogs lie) Huh?

To a great crash of music we

DISSOLVE

304. A HUGE ELECTRIC SIGN ON TOP OF A BUILDING - NIGHT
Inside a traveling border of blinking lights, it says
simply, in tasteful letters twenty feet high, that drain in
and out, and change color: "SMITH"

305. EPIFANIA AND SUPERFLEW - IN EPIFANIA'S NEW OFFICE
Radiantly happy, Epifania is talking into the telephone..
A calendar with 5½ months crossed off it is visible behind
her. Superflew stands appalled in the middle of the floor.

EPIFANIA:	I will not decide until tomorrow...I have six other offers...All I can advise you is: offer as much as possible or you'll never get it. Good day.
SUPERFLEW:	(with a terrible suspicion) What are you doing?
EPIFANIA:	(cheerfully, as she starts assembling something in a box) Well what do you think I am doing? I'm selling out! I'm through! I started out to prove something...it's proved!
SUPERFLEW:	But...but...How can you...I mean to say with everything so...so...how can you walk away from a success like this? I mean, if we can do this in six months! Why, in a year or so...
EPIFANIA:	(cutting him off quietly) I'm selling out, Morris. If you want to put a bid in with the others, I will naturally favor you a little for old times' sake, but...
SUPERFLEW:	I don't know what to say, Mary...I had a nice little sweat route...I mean gouge...I mean business...I could handle all right by myself till you... come into my life...but now...it's all growed so big...
EPIFANIA:	(amiably) Just make up your mind, Morris...If you want it...and can raise the money somehow...I'd like to see you get it. If you don't...or can't...
SUPERFLEW:	But I'd be in debt for years! I'd have to put every bloody thing I own up the spout! I'd be worse off than...than I ever been in the last...in the last...

351

EPIFANIA:	(gently) I wouldn't be too hard on you, Morris...But don't worry about it if you don't want it...I've had seven other offers so far...
SUPERFLEW:	(miserably) Oh, you have?
EPIFANIA:	Naturally...(then holding up the jewelled hookah) There! Isn't that pretty? 　　　　　　　　　　　　　　FADE OUT

FADE IN

306. ALASTAIR AND PATRICIA IN A PUNT - DAY - WATER
He wears correct boating flannels. She, her prettiest summer dress. She knits as he poles.

ALASTAIR:	I say, Seedy, isn't his jolly?
PATRICIA:	Yes, Darling, lovely.
ALASTAIR:	(turning his punt toward the float) Nothing beats a fine weekend on the river. A pole on the water in the morning to give one a good stretch...

307. A FLOAT OR DOCK WITH PROPER WATER CRAFT ATTACHED
On it we see another example of the cast iron satyr hitching post we saw in front of the old Inn. This time it holds a placard labelled: "The Devil's Disciple...Lunch...Dinner...Breakfast...Rooms".

ALASTAIR'S VOICE:	...and a good appetite...a well-made cocktail...a rattling good lunch...

308. ALASTAIR AND PATRICIA IN THE PUNT

ALASTAIR:	...and then a good laze. What more could any man desire on earth?
PATRICIA:	(without dropping a stitch) You punt so beautifully, Ally. I love to see you doing it. You look so well standing up in the stern.
ALASTAIR:	It's the quiet of it, the blessed quiet, you are so quiet; I'm never afraid of your kicking up a row about nothing. The river is so smooth. I don't know which is more comforting, you or the river, when I think of myself shooting Niagara, three or four times a day at home.

The punt scrapes alongside the dock and Alastair helps Patricia out with her knitting.

PATRICIA:	Don't think of it, darling. It isn't home: this is home.
ALASTAIR:	(making the punt fast) Yes, dear: you're right: this is what home ought to be, though it's only a hotel.
PATRICIA:	(as they walk up toward the Inn) Well, what more could anyone ask but a nice hotel? All the housekeeping done for us: no trouble with the servants; no rates nor taxes. I have never had any peace except in a hotel. But, perhaps a man doesn't feel that way.

309. INTERIOR THE LOUNGE OF THE DEVIL'S DISCIPLE - DAY
This is the former coffee room of The Cloven Hoof. That is
to say it has the same shape and possibly the wise will
identify one or two identifying features, but it has been
tastefully transmogrified into an attractive riverside hotel.
The Manager, young, blond, and very good-looking, carrying
the hotel register and a fountain pen, hurries to open the
door for his guests.

THE MANAGER: Good afternoon, Sir...I hope you've enjoyed the river...and find everything
here to your liking...Would you mind
signing the register...which I neg-
lected to have you do this morning?

ALASTAIR: (busy signing) Not at all...but what
wonders you have done to the old place!
When I was here a year ago, it was a
common pub called The Cloven Hoof.

THE MANAGER: It was so until quite lately, Sir. My
father kept The Cloven Hoof. So did his
forefathers right back to the reign of
William the Conqueror. It was on its
last legs when you saw it, Sir. I was
ashamed of it.

ALASTAIR: (as Patricia hands him a skein) Well,
you have made a first rate job of it,
now.

THE MANAGER: Oh, it was not my doing, Sir: I am
only the Manager. You would hardly believe it if I were to tell you the
story of it. But I mustn't disturb
you talking.

PATRICIA: (starting to wind a ball) I should
like to know about the old Hoof.

ALASTAIR: Fire ahead, Old Man!

THE MANAGER: Well, Madam, if you insist...It started
about six months ago...A lady had an
unfortunate adventure here with some
ruffian who tried to throw her down
the stairs..,We were most upset...but
instead of leaving us forever...she
came back next day...took the poorest
room in the house and became a permanent guest...with meals...(at this
point, we dissolve to shots of the
events being related. We are seeing
Epifania in her hat and waterproof
coming into the old Cloven Hoof)...
When she came home the first night and
found her supper wasn't ready...because
my poor old mother was a bit slow about
things...and the scullery maid was very
old...(we get a look at the old crack-
pot)...she went straight into the kitchen to get it herself. She had more
good will than experience, apparently..
because...quite unintentionally, she
broke almost all my mother's favorite
dishes at one swoop. My poor old
mother was furious: she thought the
world of her dishes. She had no suspicion, poor soul, that they were ugly
and common,cheap and altogether unattractive. She said that as the guest
had broken them, she should pay for
them, and the amount would be added to
her rent... (interior and exterior of

an antique shop in the suburbs) ...Off
went the lady to Reading and came back
with a load of crockery that made my
mother cry: she said she would be
disgraced forever, if we served a meal
on such old-fashioned things... (the
dock and riverside of the Inn. Action
to match narration)...But the very
next day, an American lady with a
boating party bought them right off
the table for three times what they
cost; and my poor mother never dared
say another word...(The antique shop
again, in the corner devoted to furniture. Epifania is apparently saying:
"I'll take this, and that, and those
three, and that one over there.")...
The lady took things into her own hands
in a way we never could have done...
but everything she touched turned to
gold...and the guests began buying
chairs right out from under themselves
and taking them home with them...and
the tables too (this is, of course,
shown in the action followed by a scene
of the father, the mother and some hungry guests in the empty dining room.
In the middle of their dismay, they
hear an automobile horn and hurry to
the window. In front of the Inn we see
a van labelled "Superflew and Smith".
The Manager of the Inn is starting to
unload more chairs and tables.
Epifania hops out of the driver's seat
and helps him. As they start toward
the Inn, we dissolve back to the modern
lounge of the Devil's Disciple containing the Manager, Alastair and
Patricia) It was cruel for us; but
we couldn't deny she was always right.

PATRICIA: Cruel! What was there cruel in getting
                 you nice crockery and pretty furniture,
                 and getting your business going?

THE MANAGER: Oh, it wasn't only that, Madam: that
                 part of it was easy and pleasant
                 enough. You see, all she had to do
                 with the old crockery and furniture was
                 to break it and throw the bits into the
                 dust bin...

We now start a dissolve back to the described action, in
which we see the old servants being dismissed, etc.

THE MANAGER'S VOICE: But what was the matter with the
                 old Cloven Hoof was not the old, thick
                 plates that took away your appetite.
                 It was the old people it had gathered
                 about itself that were past their worth
                 and had never been up to much accord-
                 ing to modern ideas. They had to be
                 thrown into the street to wander about
                 for a few days...and then go into the
                 workhouse. (the old bar in the Inn)
                 There was the bar that was served by
                 Father and Mother: she, dressed up to
                 the nines, as she thought, poor old
                 dear, never dreaming that the world
                 was a day older than when she was mar-
                 ried. Our lady told them the truth

about themselves; and it just cut
them to pieces... (Epifania takes over
the bartending for some new arrivals
as the old people walk away)...for it
was the truth...and I couldn't deny it.
The old man had to give in, because he
had raised money on his freehold and
was at his wits' end to pay the mortgage interest... (interior, suburban
bank, Epifania and bank manager)...
The next thing we knew the lady had
paid off the mortgage and got the whip
hand of us completely.

During the last words, we have dissolved back to the modern
lounge of the Devil's Disciple...The Manager, Alastair and
Patricia.

THE MANAGER: (mimicking Epifania's voice) "It's
time for you two to sell your freehold
and retire: you are doing no good
here", she said.

PATRICIA: But that was dreadful, to root those
two old people up like that.

                                          DISSOLVE

310. THE FINAL RETROSPECT SCENE OF THE TWO OLD PEOPLE
STANDING HAND IN HAND, LIKE CHILDREN, BEFORE
EPIFANIA, SEATED AT A DESK WITH HER BACK TO US. THE
SON STANDS TO ONE SIDE.

THE MANAGER'S VOICE: It was hard; but it was the
truth. We should have had the brokers
in sooner or later if we had gone on.
Business is business; and there's no
room for sentiment in it... (the two
old people turn and, hand in hand,
walk out through the door. Epifania
lights a cigarette, then starts writing
a check, which the son watches eagerly)
...And then, think of the good she
did...My parents would never have got
the price for the freehold that she
gave them. Here was I...ashamed of the
old place, but tied to it...by my feeling for my parents, with no prospects..
no hopes... (during the last two sen-
tences, we have dissolved back to The
Devil's Disciple, the Manager, Alastair
and Patricia)

THE MANAGER: Now the house is a credit to the
neighborhood and gives more employment
than the poor old "Hoof" did in its
best days; and I am the Manager of it
with a salary and percentage beyond
anything I could have dreamt of.

ALASTAIR: Then she didn't chuck you, Old Man?

THE MANAGER: No, Sir. You see, though I could never
have made the change myself, I was intelligent enough to see that she was
right...
                                          DISSOLVE

355

THE MANAGER'S VOICE: ...I backed her up all through...
I have such faith in that woman, Sir,
that if she told me to burn down the
hotel tonight, I'd do it without a
moment's hesitation. When she puts
her finger on a thing it turns into
gold every time... (We dissolve into
the suburban bank once more, with
Epifania and the bank manager)...The
bank would remind my father if he over-
drew by five pounds; but the manager
keeps pressing overdrafts on her...it
makes him miserable when she has a
penny to her credit... (we start dis-
solving back to The Devil's Disciple;
the Manager, Alastair and Patricia)

THE MANAGER: A wonderful woman, Sir: one day living
in the garret of a broken down Inn...
the next the proprietress of a first-
class hotel! More than that, for our
protection, she has bought up all the
adjoining property...and though she had
to raise the rents a bit...her tenants
all worship her...and wish to run her
for mayor! A wonderful woman, Sir.

PATRICIA: (finishing her ball of wool) She must
be! And are the old people, your father
and mother, satisfied and happy?

THE MANAGER: Well...you know how old people are...
the change was a bit of a shock to them
...my father had a slight stroke and
won't last long...and my mother has gone
a bit silly. Still...it was best for
them; and they have all the comforts...
they can...appreciate.

ALASTAIR: Well that's a very moving tale, Old
Boy...More so than you think, because I
happen to know a...uh...woman of that...
uh...stamp. Which reminds me that my
friend, Sagamore, who asked us to meet
him here, will be expecting dinner. You
can manage, I trust.

THE MANAGER: Certainly, Sir, there is always room for
Mr. Sagamore.

ALASTAIR: Oh, you know him.

THE MANAGER: Naturally, Mr....uh...uh... (he opens
the register, reads, then looks up in
astonishment) Mr. and Mrs. Fitzfassenden!

ALASTAIR: (nervously) Anything wrong?

THE MANAGER: (bowing) Quite the contrary, Sir, we are
honored!

ALASTAIR: What?...Oh!...Yes, I am the tennis...and
boxing...and so forth champion; but I
am...uh...harumph...for a holiday...and
I'd rather not hear any more about it.

THE MANAGER: (confidentially) I quite understand...
(then pointing to the register)...and I
should never have uttered a word were it
not for the unusual fact that the proprietress of this hotel...the lady I just
told you of...rejoices in the same
cognomen.

ALASTAIR: (amiably) Is that so.

He looks at Patricia to see whether she got it by any
chance, then pulls his sweater over his head and disappears
inside it.

THE MANAGER: (beaming) Oh, yes...she is Mrs. E.
Fitzfassenden.

ALASTAIR: (yelling inside the sweater) What!
(now, with both hands, he clutches the
front of the neck and with a mighty
effort, rips it in two) Let me out of
here! Quick, Seedy, pack up! (then
trying to find some money) My bill at
once!...(then pressing some money into
the Manager's hand) Here! Never mind
the bill!

THE MANAGER: (rattled) Certainly, Sir...whatever
you say, Sir...

PATRICIA: (soothingly to Alastair, removing the
remains of his sweater) But we have a
perfect right to be in her hotel,
Darling, if we pay our way just like
anybody else.

ALASTAIR: (pointing desperately to the register)
Not as Mr. and Mrs. Fitzfassenden, we
haven't.

PATRICIA: But we have to wait for Mr. Sagamore,
Dearest! That's what we...

THE MANAGER: (soothingly) Depend on it, she won't
come, Sir. She told me she was otherwise engaged this week-end.

Alastair groans and clutches his head.

DISSOLVE

312. A SIGN IN ARABIC
Under this we hear the usual Arabic abadaba.

313. THE WAITING ROOM OF THE ARAB CLINIC
The door opens and the Doctor comes out in his white coat
looking for his next charity patient.

314. EPIFANIA.
Sitting on a bench. She rises slowly, an eager expression
on her face, the hookah box in her hands.

315. THE EGYPTIAN DOCTOR.
He smiles slightly at seeing this pretty woman again, then
his smile freezes into some embarras ent.

THE DOCTOR: Oh.

316. EPIFANIA - COMING FORWARD
Her smile gets brighter and brighter as the CAMERA takes her
into the shot with the Doctor.

EPIFANIA :   I'm sorry to bother you...when you're
so busy...except that you're always so
busy...I came to bring you a present...
(she puts the hookah box in his hands)
...and to remind you that the six months
are just about up. We probably have a
lot to tell each other...

357

THE DOCTOR: (after slowly lowering his eyes and
                considering the closed hookah box
                longer than necessary) Come in.

As she goes by him, he directs one quick, anxious look to
Allah, then follows her and softly closes the door. The
CAMERA stays on it for a moment.

317. A GROUP OF ARABS
They are chattering confidentially, but in a state of high
excitement, wondering what this beautiful and obviously
wealthy woman wants with their healer.

318. THE DOCTOR - PAST EPIFANIA - IN HIS OFFICE - DAY
He sits considering the open hookah box, listening to her
talk. He does not look at her.

    EPIFANIA: (exultantly)...Then I merged them all
                into one big business, just called
                "Smith"...and sold the whole thing to
                Superflew for a whopping big price.

    THE DOCTOR: (lifting his eyes slowly) I see...You
                must have made a great deal more money.

319. EPIFANIA - PAST THE DOCTOR

    EPIFANIA: Tons of it! I'm sure your mother would
                be delighted!

320. THE DOCTOR - PAST EPIFANIA
He fingers the beautiful hookah a little sadly before and
after speaking.

    THE DOCTOR: Beyond question...she would be as
                stupefied as I am...and undoubtedly
                would not notice...that from all this
                success...the workers themselves...re-
                ceived no additional benefits...no ad-
                ditional happiness...no additional...

321. EPIFANIA
Chilled and slightly uneasily

    EPIFANIA: I don't remember that there was any
                talk about that...I was running a
                business.

    THE DOCTOR: Of course...In any case all this is
                academic as, most regrettably, I have
                totally and miserably failed to uphold
                ...my side of the bargain.

322. EPIFANIA - PAST THE DOCTOR
She looks at him miserably for a long moment before speaking.

    EPIFANIA: Oh...Did you...I mean...you did try...

323. CLOSE SHOT - THE DOCTOR

    THE DOCTOR: (getting up in the middle of the speech
                and starting to walk around) Certainly
                I tried...and at the same time...from
                certain angles one might be able to
                say that I didn't...Your money was well
                spent. Of this you can rest assured.

As the Doctor walks past Epifania, the CAMERA now finds itself upon her.

    EPIFANIA: (looking down at her hands) You
                didn't even care enough to...try...

To be put on back of p. 75.

ALTERNATE LINES TO BE USED IF,
PERADVENTURE, THE DOCTOR'S
MONTAGE IS OMITTED.

326. THE DOCTOR

THE DOCTOR: ...Unfortunately, there are no funds
as yet, to make it good...but Allah
will undoubtedly provide since it was
He who borrowed the money. With this
vast fortune sitting in the teapot just
there...

327. EPIFANIA
She starts slowly toward the door.

THE DOCTOR'S VOICE: ...and the hungry and the defenseless...standing just there...I was
commanded to introduce them....
Momentarily I must have forgotten our
pact...time is so important in matters
of emergency...I felt sure you would
want me to do as I did...I did not know
where to find you...

359

76.

324. THE DOCTOR:
He now starts marching up and down, becoming less gentle,
more male, and considerably more. oriental as he gesticu-
lates in self-justification.

THE DOCTOR: I am a very busy man...My patients are
not only numerous...like all free patients...but vociferous...like all free
patients...They are very impatient.
Their aches...their fevers...their broken bones...they do not care to forget...
while their healer amuses himself with
a tale out of the Thousand and One
Nights...no matter how delicious the
prize might be that awaited him at the
end of it.

325. EPIFANIA
She looks up at him once and starts putting her things
together preparatory to leaving.

THE DOCTOR'S VOICE: Your money will be returned to
you...I have already written out the
check...

Epifania shrugs and gets up.

326. THE DOCTOR

THE DOCTOR: Unfortunately, there are no funds yet to
make it good...but Allah will provide,
You see, I found out about this miserable
woman...totally defenseless and without
funds...

327. EPIFANIA
She starts slowly toward the door.

THE DOCTOR'S VOICE: ...I felt sure you would want me
to do what I did...merely as a form of
temporary loan... (Epifania makes a
small gesture waving all this aside as
unimportant) Time is so important in
matters of emergency...I didn't know
where to find you...

By now Epifania reaches the door, her back to it. She opens
it slowly without looking around, then sobs suddenly, puts
her handkerchief to her mouth and hurries out, slamming the
door after her.

328. THE EGYPTIAN DOCTOR
He watches her go furiously, takes a step after her, stops,
then hurries to the desk, picks up the hookah in its box,
lifts it high, then smashes it to the floor. He looks at
it, then bares his teeth and hurls imprecations at it in
low street Arabic.

FADE OUT

FADE IN

329. HIGH CAMERA SHOT - AN AUTOMOBILE COMING TO A STOP
This is in front of The Devil's Disciple. As the Chauffeur
goes around to open the door,

330. CLOSE SHOT - THE AUTOMOBILE
The Chauffeur appears, opens the door, and Mr. Sagamore gets
out.

SAGAMORE: (somewhat inside the car) Now slowly...
easy does it...

An enormous foot, bandaged as if for gout, appears out of the automobile.

331. EXTERIOR - A WINDOW OF THE DEVIL'S DISCIPLE - THE MANAGER
He is looking down past us. Now he turns and speaks to some-one inside the room. Alastair and Patricia, both in a change of costume, appear in the window and look down past us in astonishment. They disappear quickly.

332. FAIRLY HIGH CAMERA SHOT. CLOSE. SAGAMORE AND ADRIAN
We see now what the bandaged foot was, as Adrian is con-siderably bandaged, hobbling on two sticks.

ADRIAN:	(glaring around at the exterior of the Inn as he hobbles up the last step) What in Heaven's name have you brought me here for...to remind me of my injuries?
SAGAMORE:	It's all been done over...
ADRIAN:	So have I!
SAGAMORE:	I thought it might interest you.
ADRIAN:	It does not in the slightest...I can think of no place...in the entire universe...that interests me less... (then seeing something past the CAMERA)...Oh, hello there, Alastair...

333. ALASTAIR, PATRICIA AND THE MANAGER - IN THE OPEN DOORWAY
The Manager is peeking over their shoulders

ADRIAN'S VOICE:	...and you, Miss Smith.
PATRICIA:	(dismayed) But what's happened to you, Mr. Blenderbland?
ALASTAIR:	What on earth have you done to your-self, old chap?

334. ADRIAN AND SAGAMORE - OUTSIDE THE INN

ADRIAN:	(fulminating) Everyone asks me what I've done to myself! I haven't done anything to myself. I suppose you mean this...and this...and this...not to mention this! Well, they are what your wife has done to me.

He continues to hobble up and the CAMERA brings him and Mr. Sagamore into the shot with the others.

SAGAMORE:	How are you?
ALASTAIR:	I say, I'm frightfully sorry, old chap.
PATRICIA:	Do come in and sit down, Mr. Blenderbland...

335. INTERIOR - THE INN
Here we see the bottom of the famous flight of stairs which served Adrian so well on a previous occasion. The Group is coming through the door and aiming for the stairs.

PATRICIA:	Dear...dear...be careful...

361

ADRIAN: (pointing to the stairs with his stick)
These blasted stairs again! I feel
them in every bone...(he starts up)...
and so shall she...when I get through
with her. Two thousand five hundred
AND costs...not a penny less.

SAGEMORE: But hang it all, a man accusing a woman
of assault...and suing her for damages.

ADRIAN: (step by step) Assault! I shall accuse
her of felony, misdemeanor, mayhem,
disorderly conduct, and atrocious assault with intent to kill.

SAGAMORE: Ridiculous! If she had done something
really womanly like throwing vitriol...

ADRIAN: (interrupting) She pitched me down a
whole flight of stairs and left me unconscious at the bottom. Wasn't that
womanly enough? My ankle was sprained
...my knee was twisted...the small bone
of my leg was broken...I ricked my
spine...I had to give them a subscrip-
tion at the Cottage Hospital...I had
to go from there to a nursing home:
twelve guineas a week...I had to call
in three Harley Street surgeons; none
of them knew anything about dislocated
knee: they wanted to cut it open to
see what the matter was...I had to take
it to a bonesetter who charged me
fifty guineas...and buy six tickets to
the Policeman's Ball...It was an unprovoked, brutal, cowardly assault!

SAGAMORE: Was it quite unprovoked...after all,
you were unconscious...you don't know
what happened...Suppose she pleads
self-defense against a criminal attack?

ADRIAN: She dare not swear to such a lie!

PATRICIA: You might wake up in the choky.

SAGAMORE: You might, at that.

ADRIAN: Look here...are you my solicitor or
hers?

SAGAMORE: Fate seems to have made me the solicitor of everybody in this case. If I
am forced to make a choice...

Then turning toward the stairs at the sound of some pounding
footsteps.

336. THE TOP OF THE STAIRS

THE MANAGER: (leaping into the shot, tripping and
talking in a completely disorganized
manner) I'm extremely sorry, Gentlemen
...but Mrs. Fatzfissenden...(he points
down the stairs with a shaking finger)
...I mean Mrs. Fatzfassenden...has just
arrived...and...and...

337. THE GROUP

ALASTAIR: Blast!

362

The Manager walks into the shot and they all wait, quaking, as for an apparition.

338. THE TOP OF THE STAIRS
Epifania, carrying the register under her arm, her left index finger pinched in it, appears quietly and tragically... her eyes glazed with tears. She looks dully from one to another, not seeing Adrian who, being seated, is concealed behind the others.

EPIFANIA: (bitterly) Mr. and Mrs. Fitzfassenden indeed! (she pitches the register onto a table, then points a finger at the Manager) You are fired! Allowing my husband to bring a woman to my hotel... and register her in my name.

339. THE MANAGER

THE MANAGER: (between sobs) I am shattered, Madam! I had no idea of course...that this gentleman was so fortunate as...ever to have been...connected with you...in any way! You are right, of course...you are always right! Do you wish me to leave at once...or shall I carry on... (he completely sobs the last words) ...until you have...replaced me?

340. EPIFANIA

EPIFANIA: (with mild irritation) Oh, stop quivering! (then warningly and severely)...Just be more discreet in the future: this is not a motel.

341. THE MANAGER

THE MANAGER: (weeping with relief) Oh, thank you, Madam...thank you...thank you...

342. THE GROUP

SAGAMORE: I think you are a bit severe, Mrs. Fitz...

EPIFANIA: (coming into the shot) Hello, Sagamore ...what are you...(now she trips over Adrian's foot and is rewarded by a bellow)...Adrian! (then recoiling in astonishment at his condition) But what has happened to your head? What are those sticks for? Whatever have you done to yourself?

ADRIAN: (furiously) Done to myself!

EPIFANIA: (looking around in innocence) Has he been run over? Quick: send for a doctor!

THE MANAGER: (dashing out) At once, Madam.

ADRIAN: (recapturing his breath and pointing an indignant finger at Epifania) This woman has half-killed me...and she asks what I have done to myself? May I remind you, Madam, of a certain occasion on which I went down those stairs on the back of my neck!

363

EPIFANIA: (all surprised innocence) Well, why
didn't you go down properly? Were you
drunk?

ADRIAN: (strangling) Drunk! I...I... (now he
turns sputtering to Sagamore) I'll have
five hundred more for that, Sagamore.
Make a note of it.

EPIFANIA: (looking around mystified) Five hundred more what?

ADRIAN: You'll find...

SAGAMORE: (raising a hand) Just a moment. Mr.
Blenderbland declares that his injuries were inflicted by you when you
last met, Mrs. Fitzfassenden.

EPIFANIA: (thunderstruck) By me? Am I a prize-
fighter? Am I a coal heaver?

ADRIAN: (vehemently) Both! And if you...

SAGAMORE: (raising a pacifying hand) He is taking an action against you.

EPIFANIA: (all hurt innocence) Against me?
(then tragically) Very well...Since I
am forced into this repulsive role...
(she turns to Sagamore and issues her
instructions coldly and clearly) You
will file an immediate writ of attach-
ment and distraint against this individual...tie up all his assets...file
a writ of certiorari, rebutter and sur-
rejoinder, confuting and disclaiming,
by latitat, and by mandamus, all his
allegations. Counter claim ten times
the amount he asks...for his fake
injuries...We shall see whose purse
holds out the longest.

ADRIAN: (boiling) And another two hundred for:
"fake injuries"! You think your idiotic
father's money places you above the
law!

EPIFANIA: (moving toward him menacingly) Again?

ALASTAIR: (getting between them hastily) Now,
now, my girl...none of that! Remember
the last time.

EPIFANIA: (moving behind Sagamore's back) You
are my witness, Mr. Sagamore, how I
cringe before my husband's brutal violence. It is the last argument of the
lower nature against the higher...
(then coming half around Sagamore and
confronting Alastair) Go on...hit me.

ALASTAIR: (defeated again) Blast!

EPIFANIA: (turning to the others) Go on, all of
you. Batter me...threaten me...
blackmail me.

SAGAMORE: (gently and sincerely) Don't take it
that way, Mrs. Fitzfassenden. There is
no question of blackmailing you or insulting you.

364

EPIFANIA:	(brokenly) What does it matter? I'm finished anyway.
SAGAMORE:	(still more gently) Of course you're not...But quite seriously, Mrs. Fitzfassenden, Mr. Blenderbland is entitled to some compensation. You can afford it.
EPIFANIA:	Mr. Sagamore: a woman as rich as I am cannot afford anything. I have to fight to keep every penny I possess. Every beggar, every blackmailer, every swindler, every charity, every testimonial, every league and brotherhood and sisterhood, every church and chapel, every institution of every kind on earth is busy from morning till night trying to bleed me to death. If I weaken for a moment, if I let a farthing go, I shall be destitute by the end of the month. I subscribe a guinea a year to the Income Tax Payers' Defense League; and that is all: absolutely all. This is the only way in which I can write across the sky, "Hands Off My Money!"
SAGAMORE:	Nevertheless: I make an appeal to you on his behalf ad Miserecordiam.
EPIFANIA:	(impatiently) Oh, we are wasting time. Give the old buzzard a ten-pound note and have done with it.
ADRIAN:	(nearly unintelligibly) Ten pounds! I...I...
SAGAMORE:	But he wants two thousand five hundred.
EPIFANIA:	(stupefied) Pounds?
ADRIAN:	(yelling) And three fifty more for the "old buzzard"! Not forgetting the five hundred for the "drunk" and the two hundred for the "fake injuries"! Plus, of course the two thousand five hundred - plus...
EPIFANIA:	(full of loving admiration) Adrian, my child, I have underrated you. Your cheek, your gluttony, your obstinacy, impose respect upon me. I threw a half-baked gentleman down the stairs... and the police picked up a magnificently complete skunk.
ADRIAN:	(triumphantly) Five thousand for that, Sagamore, do you hear?
SAGAMORE:	Please, please, let us try to keep our tempers.
ADRIAN:	(yelling) Keep your own temper! Has she lamed you for life? Has she raised a bump on your head the size of a goose egg? Has she called you a skunk?
SAGAMORE:	(amiably) No...but she may at any moment. (then in dead seriousness) Believe me, Blenderbland: it is a

mistake to go into court in the character of a man who has been called a skunk. It puts you in bad odour with the jury...from the start.

EPIFANIA: (laughing boisterously and throwing her arms around Mr. Sagamore's neck) Ha, ha! My Sagamore! My treasure!

SAGAMORE: (extricating himself from the embrace) You see, old chap, it is difficult to get sympathy in the character of a man who has been thrashed by a woman! (then pleasantly enumerating the alternatives) If Mrs. Fitzfassenden had stabbed you, or shot you, or poisoned you, or done something really feminine like feeding you ground glass...that would have been quite compromised. But Mrs. Fitzfassenden knows better.

ADRIAN: I will not be talked out of my case.

SAGAMORE: (drily) You have no case: the law is equal before all of us...but we are not all equal before the law! On the day of the trial Mrs. Fitzfassenden will come into court...simply but beautifully dressed...probably in black.

EPIFANIA: (nods gently) ...No woman can be more ladylike...more feminine... (Epifania looks down and shrugs modestly)...when it is her cue to play the perfect lady... (Epifania looks up at him coldly) Long before the case comes up, the bump on your head will have subsided, your broken bone will have set, and the color will have come back into your cheeks... unless you can provoke Mrs. Fitzfassenden to assault you again... the day before the trial... The chances are a million to one against you.

ADRIAN: (giving up) Is there no justice for a man against a woman?

ALASTAIR: (bitterly) Not against that one.

EPIFANIA: (turning on him) And what justice is there for me, I should like to know? I cannot keep a husband...I cannot keep a lover...I cannot even keep a cook! (then down at Alastair and Patricia who are very close together) And there you two sit...before my very eyes...giggling and snuggling... like a pair of half-baked titmice... and you are happy ... and she is happy while I...

PATRICIA: (mildly) That's all very fine, dearie: but the truth is that no one can live with you!

366

EPIFANIA: (with a very surprising remnant of violence) And anyone can live with you...and apparently you can live with anybody.

ALASTAIR: What Seedy says is God's truth, Eppy... nobody could live with you.

EPIFANIA: But why, why, why?

SAGAMORE: (gently) Do be reasonable Mrs. Fitzfassenden. Can one live with a tornado? With an earthquake? With an avalanche?

EPIFANIA: (violently) Well, thousands of people do, don't they? On the smoking slopes of Vesuvius...and how about the Pompeiians...how about the West Indians? They are brought up on tornadoes! Look at the Swiss! They build their houses on avalanches! But with a woman who can live life to the full, who can wield the power she was born with, and rise to her destiny, no! (then bitterly) Well, be it so. I shall sit in my lonely house... and be myself...and pile up millions until...until...

She breaks lightly.

PATRICIA: (sympathetically) Dear wise old Father used to say that solitude...

EPIFANIA: (violently) Damn your dear wise old father! (then breaking again) Oh, I can bear no more of this. I will not have my life dragged down to planes of vulgarity on which I cannot breathe. (she turns to Patricia) Take your Alastair! I throw him to you! Let him punch you to his heart's content. Arrange the divorce, Mr. Sagamore! I will live in utter loneliness and keep myself sacred until I find the right man,..the man with brains enough to use me...

343   THE DOORWAY OF THE LOUNGE
The Egyptian Doctor, his frock coat buttoned askew, his stethoscope dangling from his pocket, his unlatched doctor's bag in his hand, enters hurriedly. He stops just inside the door.

EPIFANIA'S VOICE: The man who can stand with me on the utmost heights and not lose his head...the mate created for me in Heaven...

344   EPIFANIA AND THE GROUP

EPIFANIA: (concluding tragically) ...He must be somewhere.

PATRICIA: (in a small voice) Well, I hope you won't have to wait too long dearie.

EPIFANIA: (snapping out of her tragic mood) Why, you...

THE DOCTOR'S VOICE: The Manager says I am wanted
          here...

Epifania turns rigidly at the sound of his voice.

345 THE EGYPTIAN DOCTOR - INSIDE DOOR

THE DOCTOR: Who wants me?

346 EPIFANIA AND THE GROUP
Epifania looks at him a long moment and walks slowly toward
him, the CAMERA going with her until the Doctor is included
in the shot.

EPIFANIA: I want you... but I did not send for
                  you...I mean I think I asked for a
                  doctor because of...(she vaguely
                  indicates Adrian) ...but I did not
                  know it would be you.

THE DOCTOR: (quietly) I believe you.

347 SAGAMORE, ADRIAN, ALASTAIR AND PATRICIA
They are watching Epifania and this strange-looking man.

ALASTAIR: (reacting to the Doctor's fez)
                  Who's that bloke?

ADRIAN: By Jove, it's the Johnny who took care
                  of me the night I took the cropper...
                  bloody good too...for an Arab.

PATRICIA: Hasn't he beautiful eyes?

SAGAMORE: (plucking his lower lip) I was
                  looking at his hat.

348 EPIFANIA AND THE DOCTOR

THE DOCTOR: (sincerely and quietly) I am very
                  glad to see you again...but if no
                  one needs me...I am due back at the
                  hospital...

EPIFANIA: (urgently, stalling for time) Not
                  yet...I mean...uh...come and meet...
                  this is my Egyptian Doctor...my
                  husband...my ex-fiance...my
                  solicitor...and the lady who is to be
                  his next wife...I mean my husband's...

THE DOCTOR: (blankly) I beg your pardon?

SAGAMORE, ADRIAN, ALASTAIR AND PATRICIA

EPIFANIA: (coming into the shot with the
                  Doctor) This is the man I want to
                  marry...I mean I would like to marry...
                  Unfortunately, he won't have me.

THE DOCTOR: (raising a polite hand) That is not
                  exactly...

SAGAMORE: (stupefied) He won't have you!
                  Good Heavens! (then to the Doctor)
                  You don't know who she is!

EPIFANIA: (as the Doctor opens his mouth)
                  Oh, yes he does.

THE DOCTOR: (embarrassed) The lady has not given
                you an accurate statement. The project
                is not possible. We are bound by
                our vows.

SAGAMORE: (after looking from one to the other)
                Cannot vows be...uh...modified?

THE DOCTOR: (with quiet dignity) A vow is a vow.

ALASTAIR: (joining in uninvited) But I say,
                old chap, are you sure you have
                considered this from every angle?
                Viewed from certain aspects...

EPIFANIA: Don't help me.

SAGAMORE: (with legal unction) Would not a
                quiet reconsideration of all the
                facts...

THE DOCTOR: There is nothing to reconsider: I
                made a pact with the lady...she was
                to do a certain thing... I was to do
                anothe , but...

EPIFANIA: (desperately) Well, have I not
                passed your mother's test? Do you
                want an accountant's certificate?
                I made enough in the first week to
                support me for a hundred years.

THE DOCTOR: Admitted...and beyond question. But
                all this talk is idle for I most
                certainly have not fulfilled the
                lady's fathers condition.

SAGAMORE: (brightly) Are you quite certain of
                your facts? Sometimes one thinks
                one has not succeeded in something,
                but on reanalysis...

THE DOCTOR: (angrily) What do you mean, am I
                "quite certain of my facts?" Do
                you think I am a boy--- in a frock
                coat? The very next morning after
                making this...(he searches for the
                word with a helpless gesture)...
                adolescent agreement, I picked up
                my paper...

We now start a montage of the events described by the
Doctor.

                                      DISSOLVE

350   THE DOCTOR READING HIS NEWSPAPER IN THE INN

      THE DOCTOR'S VOICE: ...And there under the heading,
                "Wills and Bequests"...

351   INSERT - A NEWSPAPER IN ARABIC
For the benefit of spectors familiar with Arabic, the
facts must be stated correctly.

      THE DOCTOR'S VOICE: ...I read a name that I cannot
                remember: Mrs. Somebody or other of
                Clapham Park...one hundred and twenty-
                two thousand pounds...She had never
                done anything but live in Clapham
                Park...

369

352   THE DOCTOR AT BREAKFAST

       THE DOCTOR'S VOICE: ...and she left one hundred
                and twenty-two thousand pounds.
                (the Doctor shakes his head in sad
                comment, then lifts his coffee cup
                to his lips) But what was the
                next name? (he lowers his untouched
                cup in astonishment)...it was that
                of a teacher who changed my whole
                life...and gave me a new soul...by
                opening the world of science to me.

353   THE DOCTOR AND HIS TEACHER IN A CHEMICAL LABORATORY

       THE DOCTOR'S VOICE: I was his assistant for four
                years. He used to make his own
                apparatus for his experiments....

354   CLOSE-UP OF HANDS AND APPARATUS

       THE DOCTOR'S VOICE: One day he needed a filament
                of metal that would resist at a
                temperature that melted platinum
                like sealing wax...

355   THE DOCTOR AND HIS TEACHER IN THE LABORATORY

       THE DOCTOR'S VOICE: He never took out a patient.
                He believed that knowledge is no
                man's property. And he had neither
                time nor money to waste in patent
                offices...

356   RANDOM SHOTS OF MANUFACTURING PROCESSES IN SOME
GREAT FACTORY

       THE DOCTOR'S VOICE: ...the good woman who had been
                a second mother to me...(during the
                next speech the widow hears the
                doorbell, goes to the door and
                ushers in the Egyptian Doctor)...
                a shilling a day for her at most...
                not even one piaster an hour. But
                have no fear. The Merciful, the
                Compassionate, heard the prayer of
                the widow. Listen...I once cured a
                prime minister...

357   EXTERIOR OF NO. 10 DOWNING STREET
The Doctor arrives and rings the bell.

       THE DOCTOR'S VOICE: ...when he imagined himself to
                be ill. I went to him and told him
                that it was...

358   INTERIOR OF PRIME MINISTER'S OFFICE
We see the Doctor pass a gentleman's shoulder; he is
talking passionately.

       THE DOCTOR'S VOICE: ...the will of Allah, that the
                widow should have a civil list
                pension. She received it. (the
                Doctor beams as the Prime Minister
                picks up a phone) ...a hundred
                pounds a year.

359   A BOARD OF DIRECTOR'S ROOM
A number of important-looking businessmen are being
harangued by the Egyptian Doctor.

THE DOCTOR'S OFFICE: I went to the great Metallurgical Trust which exploits his discovery, and told them that her poverty was a scandal in the face of Allah! (it goes without saying that the Doctor's forefinger is always pointing to Heaven on the word of Allah) They were rich and generous...

360   A GENTLEMAN'S HANDS SIGNING SOME STOCK CERTIFICATES

THE DOCTOR'S VOICE:... They made a special issue of founders'shares for her...worth three hundred a year to her. They called it 'letting her in on the ground floor"...

361   THE WIDOW IN HER FLAT RECEIVING THE NEWS FROM THE EGYPTIAN DOCTOR

THE DOCTOR'S VOICE: May her prayers win them favor from Him save in whom there is no Might and no Majesty! But all this took time. The illness, the nurse, the funeral, the disposal of the laboratory, the change to a cheaper lodging had left her without a penny.

362   THE DOCTOR, EPIFANIA, SAGAMORE, ADRIAN, ALASTAIR AND PATRICIA.

THE DOCTOR: (concluding) Between the death and the pension, there was a gap exactly one hundred and fifty pounds wide. He Who is Just and Exact supplied that sum... (he bows to Epifania) ...by your Chauffeur's hands... and by mine. It rejoiced my heart as money had never rejoiced it before But instead of coming to you with fifty thousand pounds...I am in arrear with my rent and am expecting at any moment to have my clinic thrown out into the street. (he pauses and frowns, then finishes) It would be difficult to interpret this as my having fulfilled the lady's father's condition.

SAGAMORE: I am not at all certain of that! One might say that retroactively...

EPIFANIA: (suddenly and startlingly) Damn the lady's father's condition! (then as all look at her gaping) He is dead! Let him sleep! We are alive...and there is no question about my having fulfilled your mother's condition.

ALASTAIR: Let's see you get out of that one, Doc.

THE DOCTOR: (furiously) Then damn my mother's condition! You may have passed it technically...But it was not the way of Allah, the Merciful, the Compassionate. Had you added a

farthing an hour to the wages of
those sweated women, that wicked
business would have crashed on your
head. You sold it to the man Superflew
for the last penny of his savings...
and the women still slaved for him at
a shilling an hour.

EPIFANIA: You cannot change the market price of
labor: not Allah Himself can do that..
(then pointing to the beautiful sur-
rounding)...and look at this hotel:
I lived in its poorest room...and without spending anything at all I made it
what it is and own it. There is no
shilling an hour here. Think what I
could do for your clinic, or anything
you wanted...possibly a hospital, or
even...or even...

THE DOCTOR: (looking around coldly) ...it undoubtedly looks well in photographs... but
what of the old people whose natural
home this place had become? The old
man with his paralytic stroke...the
old woman gone mad? The castout crea-
tures in the workhouse? You see, I
know more about you than you think.
Was this not preying on the poverty
of the poor? Shall I, the servant
of Allah, live on such gains? (now
he concludes with full fire) Shall
I, the healer, the helper, the guardian of life and the counsellor of health,
unite with the exploiter of misery?

EPIFANIA: (at a loss) I...I have to take the
world...as I find it.

THE DOCTOR: (frighteningly) The wrath of Allah
shall overtake those who leave the
world no better than they found it!

ALASTAIR: Look here, you know, Doc...that
won't go down in this country. We
don't believe in Allah.

THE DOCTOR: That does not disconcert Allah in
the least, my friend. There is
only Allah...by whatever name one
worships Him.

EPIFANIA: I think Allah loves those that make
money.

SAGAMORE: (loyally) All the evidence is that
way, certainly.

THE DOCTOR: I do not see it so! I see that
riches are a curse...poverty is a
curse...Only in the service of
Allah, can one find justice, happiness
and fulfillment. His voice is all
about us...if one would but listen.

ADRIAN: (sourly) Well don't listen to her...
Doctor, or you'll wind up on crutches.
She is a terrible woman! She was un-
faithful to her husband in wanting me!
She is unfaithful to me in wanting
you...

SAGAMORE: (moving menacingly toward Adrian) One
more remark of that nature, Blenderbland
....

EPIFANIA: (holding up a hand) Please...(then
turning to the Doctor) You must learn
to take chances in this world. This
disappointed philanderer tries to
frighten you with my unfaithfulness. He
has never been married: I have. And
I tell you that in the very happiest
marriages not a day passes without
a thousand moments of unfaithfulness.
You begin by thinking you have only
one husband: you find you have a
dozen. There is a creature you
hate and despise and are tied to
for life; and before breakfast is
over the fool says something nice
and becomes a man whom you admire
and love; and between these extremes
there are a thousand degrees with a
different man and woman at each of
them. A wife is all woman to one
man: she is everything devilish: the
thorn in his flesh, the jealous
termagant,the detective dogging all
his movements, the nagger, the
scolder, the worrier. He has only
to tell her an affectionate lie and
she is his comfort, his helper, at
best his greatest treasure, at
worst his troublesome but beloved
child. All wives are all of these
women in one, all husbands all these
men in one. What do the unmarried
know of this infinitely dangerous
heart-tearing, ever-changing life of
adventure that we call marriage?
Face it as you would face a dangerous
operation: have you not performed
hundreds of them?

```
THE DOCTOR:      Of a surety, there is no wit and no
                 wisdom like that of a woman ensnar-
                 ing the mate she has decided to
                 make her own...(as the Doctor talks,
                 Epifania, realizing at last that
                 she is totally defeated, turns away
                 and lowers herself weakly into a
                 chair)...But I am a busy man...I
                 have no time for parasites, whilst
                 poverty, dirt, disease, misery and
                 slavery surround me like a black
                 sea.  If you will excuse me, I have
                 much work waiting me...Good day.
                 (he picks up his bag, then addresses
                  Epifania before departing)
                 May Allah in His infinite Compassion
                 guide your footsteps in the paths
                 of human sympathy.

EPIFANIA:        (weakly from her chair)  But I love
                 you...I don't believe I have ever
                 loved before...I am sure I will
                 never love...again.

SAGAMORE:        (the tears rolling down his cheeks)
                 Please.

EPIFANIA:        (in a dead voice)  Do you want to
                 be alone always..without a home...
                 without a wife...without children...

THE DOCTOR:      (crossly)  There is plenty of time
                 for all that...My father was a
                 hundred and seven...

EPIFANIA:        (dully and without interest)
                 When he died?

THE DOCTOR:      (impatiently)  No, when he had me...
                 I was his last.
```

He turns to go, then, from the corner of his eye, sees
Epfania slump in the chair. He stops.

```
SAGAMORE:        (alarmed)  I believe she has
                 fainted.
```

He hurries to her and starts slapping her hand. The
Doctor looks at this scene suspiciously, then crosses
to Epifania, throws his bag to the floor, takes out his
watch, pushes Sagamore out of his way, then kneels,
lowers Epifania's head a little, then reaches for her
wrist.

```
PATRICIA:        Shall I get some water?

ADRIAN:          Ammonia is better.

ALASTAIR:        She'll come out of it.

THE DOCTOR:      (sternly)  Quiet.
```

Now, very faintly at first, the distant war drums of
Epifania's heartbeat steal onto the sound track. The
CAMERA starts pushing in, and as it does so, the music
swells in volume and the Doctor looks slowly up toward
the ceiling. As the CAMERA reaches its final close-up of
the two heads, the music culminates in a deafening
piatti, then ceases altogether. Epifania's eyes flutter,
she looks around, then smiles gently at the Doctor. Now,
into the startling silence, the Doctor speaks excitedly:
in a low voice at first, triumphantly, and with full

underscoring at the end.

THE DOCTOR: I hear Thee..I hear Thee, O Mighty
One...I hear Thy clear command!
(the beautiful underscoring starts
here)   At last I perceive...in the
degree Thou deemest wise...the path
Thou hast outlined for me...
through the convolutions of Thy
Infinite Arabesque. I, the healer...
the helper...the guardian of life...
must unite with this force of Nature.
this vital urge for either good or
evil...incomplete in itself as I
am incomplete...two halves of the
apple of Eden! For only through
love...

363 STILL BIGGER HEAD EPIFANIA PAST THE DOCTOR
She is listening half drowsily to the Doctor's voice...
She doesn't know what he is saying...she doesn't care.

THE DOCTOR'S VOICE: ...and through love alone can
the torrent of energy...raging
through these magnificent arteries..

364 TWO BIG HEADS AS BEFORE

THE DOCTOR: ...be tamed...and guided into
humane and useful channels...
(he looks tenderly down at
Epifania)...I thank Thee, O Wise
and Merciful One...in Whom all
Majesty resideth...I am thy
servant!

He bends over and kisses Epifania. As her arms tighten
around his neck, the music swells again, the great
African war drums beat out the song of passion.

365 SAGAMORE, ADRIAN, ALASTAIR AND PATRICIA
They watch in astonishment, then relax as the drums
diminish in volume. Now they are electrified again
as the drums burst out in one last passionate flare. Now
the sound diminishes again...They sigh.

366 EPIFANIA AND THE DOCTOR
He has already started to pick her up in his arms. He
straightens up and turns to them.

THE DOCTOR: I will take her to bed.

366 SAGAMORE, ADRIAN, ALASTAIR AND PATRICIA

ALASTAIR: I say, don't you need some help?

367 EPIFANIA AND THE DOCTOR

THE DOCTOR: (quietly) Not at all, thank you.

He turns and starts for the stairs. The CAMERA follows
him. Now he starts muttering something in Arabic.

368 CLOSE TRUCKING SHOT AHEAD OF EPIFANIA AND THE
DOCTOR.
Vaguely we see the four others following in the background
as the Doctor walks carrying her (consult Director about
this shot), he finishes his muttering in Arabic.

EPIFANIA: (sleepily) What were you saying?

THE DOCTOR: (quietly) I was praying that our
                   union be blessed...with seventeen
                   sons to carry on my work...and one
                   daughter to help you around the
                   house...

Epifania looks at him for a second, then closes her eyes
and sinks back comfortably in his arms. The Doctor now
takes a turn to the right and the CAMERA lets him go.
As he approaches the stairs.

369   ADRIAN, SAGAMORE, ALASTAIR AND PATRICIA FOLLOWING

SAGAMORE: (stepping forward alarmed)
                   I say...I think she's fainted
                   again.

370   LONG SHOT EPIFANIA - IN THE DOCTOR'S ARMS
She waves a hand...either to say "goodbye" or "Don't
worry about me". We shall never know.

                         FADE OUT

As the screen becomes dark, the shadowy figure of the
clovenhoofed satyr we saw under the Forward appears on
the screen, then the words:

          AND SO THEY LIVED HAPPILY EV ER AFTERWARD
          ...ALLAH, IN HIS INFINITE WISDOM, MAKING
          ONLY ONE SMALL CHANGE IN THE PATTERN OF THEIR
          BLISS: THEY HAD ONE SON AND SEVENTEEN
          DAUGHTERS.

               T H E   E N D

January 8, 1954

www.ingramcontent.com/pod-product-compliance
Lightning Source LLC
Chambersburg PA
CBHW060124130626
46556CB00006B/2224